Social Dynamics
of the
Prehistoric Central Mediterranean

Social Dynamics
of the
Prehistoric Central Mediterranean

edited by

Robert H. Tykot

Jonathan Morter

John E. Robb

1999

VOLUME 3

ACCORDIA SPECIALIST STUDIES ON THE MEDITERRANEAN

(Series Editors: Edward Herring, Ruth D. Whitehouse, John B. Wilkins)

ACCORDIA RESEARCH INSTITUTE, UNIVERSITY OF LONDON

Published by

Accordia Research Institute
University of London

British Library Cataloguing in Publication Data
A catalogue record of this book is available from the British Library

Computer typeset by the Accordia Research Institute

ISBN 1 873415 19 2

Contents

Preface   *vii*

Abstracts   *1*

Introduction
  Albert J. Ammerman   9

Unveiling Inequality: Social Life and Social Change in the Mesolithic
and Early Neolithic of East-Central Italy
  Robin Skeates   *15*

Coasts and Uplands in Liguria and Northern Tuscany from the Mesolithic
to the Bronze Age
  Roberto Maggi   *47*

Islands in the Stream: Stone Age Cultural Dynamics in Sardinia and Corsica
  Robert H. Tykot   *67*

A 'Social' Structure and 'Social Structure': Recent Architectural Finds
from the Middle Neolithic Site at Capo Alfiere, Calabria
  Jonathan Morter   *83*

An Examination of Architectural Stability and Change: Contributions
from Southern Italy
  Gary D. Shaffer   *97*

Great Persons and Big Men in the Italian Neolithic
  John E. Robb   *111*

Farmers or Pastoralists in Sardinian Prehistory? Settlement and Environment
  Paula Kay Lazrus   *123*

Long-term Dynamics of an Island Community: Malta 5500 BC – 2000 AD
  Simon Stoddart   *137*

Short-term Cultural Dynamics within the Mediterranean Cultural Landscape
  Sebastiano Tusa   *149*

The Sicilian Bronze Age Pottery Service
  Laura Maniscalco   *185*

Spatial Analysis of a Castelluccian Settlement in Early Bronze Age Sicily
  Brian E. McConnell and Bruce W. Bevan   *195*

The Walled Bronze Age Settlement of Coppa Nevigata, Manfredonia
and the Development of Craft Specialisation in Southeastern Italy
  Alberto Cazzella and Maurizio Moscoloni   *205*

Human Skeletons from the Greek Emporium of Pithekoussai on Ischia (NA): Culture
Contact and Biological Change in Italy after the 8th Century BC
  Marshall Joseph Becker   *217*

Addresses of Contributors   *231*

Preface

Social Dynamics of the Prehistoric Central Mediterranean is intended to present original research on pre- and proto-historic sites and materials from the Central Mediterranean, including Italy and the adjacent islands of Sicily, Sardinia, Corsica, and Malta. The Central Mediterranean offers one of the richest archaeological records of the Old World. Yet, because of differing theoretical traditions and political and linguistic boundaries, it has received much less attention from anthropologically-oriented archaeologists than either the "primary" centres of neolithisation and urbanisation found in the Near East or other, contemporary phenomena such as the megalithic architecture of Atlantic Europe. Nevertheless, many theoretically active prehistorians have worked in the region over the last two decades, and it is their theoretical and methodological approach – complementary to that of archaeologists who focus on the literary and architectural/artistic evidence – that unifies this volume.

Until recently archaeological interest in the Central Mediterranean was limited to subsistence, chronology, and culture history, often viewing the area in relation to earlier, Eastern Mediterranean developments. After several decades of environmental and socially oriented research, the data exist from which social information may be derived. Furthermore, the dynamic, rather than static, nature of human society is seen here as central to understanding the development of behavioural sub-systems including environmental exploitation, resource manipulation, gender, ideological and kin relations, and evolving social asymmetries. The papers in this volume approach this goal through the study of ecology, resource exploitation and exchange (Maggi; Tykot; Lazrus; Maniscalco); architecture and settlement (Stoddart; Morter; Shaffer; McConnell & Bevan; Cazzella & Moscoloni); and gender and social relations (Skeates; Robb; Tusa; Becker). In so doing they provide a dynamic, chronological perspective for understanding Central Mediterranean prehistory in particular, and prehistoric societies in general. It should be noted that, while all contributions are specifically interested in the social aspects of prehistoric life, they represent diverse theoretical approaches originating both in Anglo-American and Italian traditions of study rather than a single, programmatic agenda.

This volume has its origins in two symposia held at Annual Meetings of the Society for American Archaeology, the first in 1992 in Pittsburgh and the second in 1995 in Minneapolis; selected papers from these symposia have been updated and supplemented by additional works. We appreciate the patience of the original symposia participants and invited contributors and note that although the papers have been up-dated, they were first written in 1992 or 1995. We also thank Ruth Whitehouse and anonymous reviewers for their insightful comments and suggestions. We are also grateful to the Dr M. Aylwin Cotton Foundation for a publication subvention grant.

The final stages of preparing this volume have been overshadowed by a tragic event, the sudden death of our co-editor, friend and colleague, Jon Morter, who was killed in a car accident in Virginia in May 1997. As many of the contributors to this volume know well, Jon's life was marked by a great steadiness and seriousness of purpose combined with quick understanding, gentle irony, and a great skill at relating to people. His biography was a long archaeological odyssey. Born in 1956, he grew up in the British Midlands and began digging on Romano-British sites before entering his local university, the University of Birmingham, where he completed a BA in 1977. Years of excavation-hopping in Europe and the Near East followed, before he emigrated to the US and worked in contract archaeology in the high plains of Montana. Re-entering academic life at the University of Texas, he completed an MA on Hittite archaeology in 1986 and a PhD on the Southern Italian Neolithic in 1992. In the process, he became a valued member of the Institute for Classical Archaeology at Texas, and carried out fieldwork on their behalf at Metaponto, Crotone, and in the Crimea. In the process, Jon published a number of papers and reports, including several relating to the excavations at Metaponto and Crotone in southern Italy, headed by Joseph C. Carter. His dissertation, *Capo Alfiere and the Middle Neolithic Period in Eastern Calabria, Southern Italy*, is an important contribution on early agricultural settlements and increasing social complexity in the central Mediterranean, with portions published in the *Journal of Mediterranean Archaeology* (1994, 7: 115–23), and in *The Chora of Croton, 1983-1989* (J.C. Carter ed., University of Texas, 1990).

Several years of academic job-hunting followed. Both of us were in the same cohort of job-seekers as Jon, and will remember the unruffled calm with which Jon endured this stressful period. At the time of his death, Jon had just completed his first year teaching in the Department of Sociology and Anthropology at the College of Charleston, South Carolina. One of us visited him there a month before his death. He and his family had settled in happily, and it was clear that both Jon's students and his colleagues were delighted to have him there.

In presenting this volume, we would like to remember Jon Morter, and to offer our condolences to his wife Hilary, their daughters Kate and Clare, his parents, Ron and Margaret Morter, and his friends and other family. We dedicate this volume in Jon's memory.

Robert H. Tykot & John E. Robb
February 1998

Abstracts

Unveiling Inequality: Social Life and Social Change in the Mesolithic and Early Neolithic of East-Central Italy

Robin Skeates

This paper is broadly concerned with the structures and dynamics of past societies, and in particular with the nature and development of institutionalised social inequality and social differentiation. It focusses upon the Mesolithic and Early Neolithic in east-central Italy. Throughout the Mesolithic, social relations within and between gatherer-hunter groups seem to have remained basically egalitarian, although a slight degree of social differentiation may have developed within the context of occasional rituals and long-distance exchanges performed by increasingly permanent, non-storing, sedentary groups in the Fucino lake basin. The northward spread of the 'Neolithic package' from south-east to east-central Italy was delayed for almost a millennium, perhaps not only as a result of ecological and economic factors, but also as a result of a deliberate strategy of mutual avoidance followed by the culturally and structurally incompatible agriculturalists of south-east Italy and gatherer-hunters of east-central Italy. The eventual transition to the Neolithic occurred along at least three different geographical axes. In the coastal lowlands of south-east Abruzzo, small kin-based groups of immigrants established agricultural colonies at well-chosen sites. In the inner lowlands of southern Abruzzo and in the lowlands to the north, indigenous groups now rapidly adopted the 'Neolithic package' of conceptually linked agricultural resources and social relations, as a result of symbiotic exchanges with the colonists and growing socio-economic demands and pressures within their own societies. This led to their rapid cultural disintegration and to their regeneration as satellite agricultural communities along the borders of the newly established coastal colonies. The process of transition also led to the development of inequalities, dependencies, and differentiation in the lowlands on a variety of scales: between south-east Italy and Abruzzo, between the colonists and the locals, and within each agricultural community. In the inlands of Abruzzo and Marche, indigenous groups of gatherer-hunters adopted the 'Neolithic package' in a more gradual and adaptive process of transition, and retained more of their traditional culture due to their lack of direct contact with the colonists and the more densely forested and less agriculturally productive nature of their environment.

Coasts and Uplands in Liguria and Northern Tuscany from the Mesolithic to the Bronze Age

Roberto Maggi

In the area of Liguria and northern Tuscany the Apennine mountain chain lies very close to the sea, leaving very little room for coastal plains; where they do exist they are almost entirely of post-Roman alluvial formation.

The availability of both coastal/maritime and mountain resources within a short distance of one another was a potentially positive factor for the Mesolithic economy. Nonetheless it seems that the Mesolithic did not develop in a homogeneous manner throughout the territory under consideration.

In the 'Alpine' area of western Liguria Mesolithic industries are virtually unknown. None of the many cave sites has produced a single artefact attributable to the Mesolithic, not even any of those which have stratigraphic sequences showing occupation in the Final Epigravettian and the Early Neolithic. The only two known open sites are also of doubtful interpretation. Contrary to what has been stated in earlier works, in the light of new evidence it seems possible that the 'late' dates, in the 9th millennium BP, for the Final Epigravettian of L'Arma dello Stefanin might indicate that this area is atypical in comparison to neighbouring regions, in terms of the form and chronology of the adoption of Mesolithic forms. However, even if we accept the late dates for the local Final Epigravettian, the caves in this area still seem to demonstrate a period of abandonment of more than one thousand years.

In eastern Liguria Sauveterrian and Castelnovian settlements occur on high ground both close to the coast and on the main range. The Mesolithic of this area is very different from that of the eastern Alps. The lithic industries are dominated by the substratum. Specialised hunting camps seem to be absent. Workshops with many cores are found everywhere, even at middle and high altitudes. At the higher altitudes there are notably more sites of the Castelnovian than the Sauveterrian.

One might ask whether the well known precocity of the Neolithic in western Liguria might be connected in some way with the complementary 'scarcity' of Mesolithic remains in this area. Perhaps this zone was chosen first precisely because it was of less interest to the Mesolithic communities. This is supported by the fact that the slight indications we have for eastern Liguria and northern Tuscany suggest that the Neolithic in this zone was not as early as in the area of Finale Liguria.

The spatial distribution of sites and sporadic finds indicates clearly that for a long time the Neolithic groups, provided with domesticated animals and the technology of agriculture, had little interest in mountain resources. Such interests emerged only during the Late Neolithic, around 5000 BP, through the adoption of upland pastoralism. Exploitation of the mountains developed further during the succeeding Copper Age, when there is evidence for the deforestation of the upper margin of the forest, presumably with the aim of increasing the area available for pasture. The development of upland pastoralism seems to have occurred at the same time throughout the area under consideration. While in the eastern area we have evidence of deforestation, in the west we find that small caves along the routes leading to the high pastures were used as stalls for the transhumant animals.

The physical anthropology of the human remains from the burial caves situated not far from potential areas of upland pasture suggests that pastoralism was practised by whole family groups and not by specialist shepherds.

From the Middle Bronze Age, watershed routes and strategic high places for a pastoralist economy were controlled by permanent settlements, provided with terraced structures built of dry stone. The organisation of the watershed routes suggests more systematic territorial control and this seems to be confirmed by evidence for deforestation and agro-pastoral use of the areas immediately outside the settlement sites.

Islands in the Stream: Stone Age Cultural Dynamics in Sardinia and Corsica

Robert H. Tykot

Recent research on Sardinia and Corsica demonstrates the antiquity of human occupation on these islands, the extent and continuity of extra-insular contacts, and the overwhelming evidence for indigenous development of complex societies. Sufficient data are available to describe these Stone Age cultures in some detail, and to illustrate the dynamic nature of insular developments and inter-regional interactions.

Pre-neolithic settlements on both Sardinia and Corsica demonstrate the maritime capabilities of local populations, and their ability to subsist on these islands without the benefit of domesticated plants or animals. In the Early Neolithic, the appearance of ceramics and domesticates is paralleled by long-distance exchange in obsidian and probably other prestige materials, perhaps as a way of maintaining ethnic or kin connections in increasingly sedentary societies.

During the Middle Neolithic, expanding village settlements are accompanied by evidence for social differentiation in burial treatment and access to material resources. By the Late Neolithic, a fully agricultural economy was in place, and the elaboration of burial monuments and megaliths illustrates the participation of Sardinia and Corsica in a wider western Mediterranean phenomenon. The precocious use of metal, locally produced, is further evidence of developing social competition.

From the earliest settlement of Sardinia and Corsica, Stone Age societies there were neither isolated from surrounding cultural entities, nor unitary in their spatio-temporal characteristics. Important relationships with the mainland, although dynamic and variable, were maintained throughout the Neolithic. Just as Sardinia is now recognised as having been an important part of Bronze Age Mediterranean cultural networks, it should be recognised that Sardinia and Corsica belonged to the main stream of Stone Age prehistory as well.

A 'Social' Structure and 'Social Structure': Recent Architectural Finds from the Middle Neolithic Site at Capo Alfiere, Calabria

Jonathan Morter

Excavations at the site of Capo Alfiere, near Crotone, Calabria, have revealed an unusual structural complex dating to the second half of the fifth millennium cal.BC. The features recovered include two stretches of large stone walling and a large portion of a cobbled hut floor. Based on known features in Sicily and Malta, a reconstruction of a walled enclosure around a hut is proposed, presumably within the larger confines of the site. The size and peculiar construction technique of the walls suggest a communal construction with an architectural focus on the interior, rather than a purely defensive rationale.

Given that the ceramics may represent something transitional between the Stentinello tradition and the Diana style, which broadly agrees with the radiocarbon dates obtained, the suggestion is made that these walled enclosures may have had a communal function, possibly as a shrine. This might have been something to do with a response to a shift in settlement patterns at the beginning of the Late Neolithic period, such as maintenance of social cohesion during site agglomeration.

An Examination of Architectural Stability and Change: Contributions from Southern Italy

Gary D. Shaffer

Neolithic wattle and daub buildings in Calabria, Italy, display constructional variability in the preparation of wattles, materials used for cordage or lashing, kinds of tempers and fillers incorporated into daubing soil, and thicknesses of daub plasters. Despite this prehistoric architectural dynamism and later introductions of alternative building materials and technologies, wattle and daub structures persisted and remained largely similar in the study area into the 20th century. Explanations for this stability of both general architectural form and specific constructional details focus on economic, natural environmental, and social factors. One of the most noteworthy observations is that certain distinctive constructional components (the uses of bracken ferns for temper and of willow shoots for cordage) apparently became enmeshed in cycles of more generalised agricultural work and persisted for 7000 years. The wider application of these architectural elements in rural labour may have helped to reinforce the utility of the constructional system. This phenomenon of the multiple utility of a tradition deserves more attention in the study of sociocultural stability and change.

Great Persons and Big Men in the Italian Neolithic

John E. Robb

Italian prehistory has never fit comfortably within social evolutionary schemes such as Service's sequence of 'bands', 'tribes', 'chiefdoms' and 'states'. One of the principal reasons for this is that these schemes don't take into account the great variation possible within a single 'stage'. For example, recent ethnographic work shows that 'tribal' societies vary a great deal in terms of how prestige is constituted and how leadership responsibilities are distributed among positions of authority.

This paper proposes a re-interpretation of the end of Neolithic in terms of models known from tribal ethnography. It is argued that Neolithic societies were generally similar to 'Great Man' societies as defined by Godelier. They do not appear to have had leadership roles which allowed authority over multiple aspects of life to have been concentrated in a single figure of a generalised leader, and sources of prestige were multiple and not easily convertible into one another. In contrast, Final Neolithic and Copper Age societies may have been more like 'Big Man' societies, particularly in the importance of exchange as a means of converting success in varied endeavours, personal contacts, and economic production into personal prominence. The transition thus would have involved the concentration of prestige sources and leadership roles into new, generalised forms. Furthermore, the symbolic content of a generalised Copper Age ideology of leadership may have been based on a culturally invented male capacity for violence; this would explain the flourishing of weapon iconography in artefacts, burials, and art which accompanied the rise of exchange and the abandonment of the Neolithic village landscape.

Farmers or Pastoralists in Sardinian Prehistory? Settlement and Environment

Paula Kay Lazrus

This paper examines the idea, recurrent in the archaeological literature, that Neolithic Sardinians were farmers and post-Neolithic Sardinians were pastoralists. After evaluating the current data, it reaches the conclusion that there is no firm basis for identifying any major change in economic strategy, not only between the Neolithic and the Bronze Age, but in fact at any point up to the late nineteenth century. The notion of a warrior-pastoralist society has been imposed on the archaeological record, which actually reveals a prehistory of vital, stable, thriving communities based on farming and small-scale animal husbandry with a limited amount of hunting, fishing and gathering. From the Neolithic onward, an increasing number of environments and landscapes were exploited, but economic diversification rather than specialisation was the rule until very recently. A broad-based economy which utilised all of the food and material resources available would have made Late Neolithic and Bronze Age societies very stable. The gradual increase in the complexity of monuments that are distributed in the landscape indicates the richness and sophistication of religious and daily activities, most of which appear to have been communal rather than individual in nature.

Long-term Dynamics of an Island Community: Malta 5500 BC – 2000 AD

Simon Stoddart

Small islands exhibit highly distinctive trajectories of social and political development and interaction with their neighbours. This article reviews the prehistory and history of the Maltese islands within the context of their unique position in the Central Mediterranean. The Maltese islands were first colonised around 5500 BC by Neolithic people from Sicily, and their societies were similar to Italian societies until the fourth millennium BC. At this point, they developed their unique material cultures and began the process of building monumental temples, a process which culminated in the third millennium temple-based cultures. Re-incorporation within the Mediterranean came midway through the third millennium, and Bronze Age settlement was based on defended domestic sites linked to Sicily by ceramic styles. With the Phoenician colonisation in the first millennium, Malta began a history of domination by foreign states, each of which left its mark in the settlement, material culture, and economy of the islands. The Phoenicians were followed by the Romans, the Arabs and Normans, the order of the Knights of Malta, and ultimately the British.

Short-term Cultural Dynamics in Sicily within the Mediterranean Cultural Landscape

Sebastiano Tusa

There is a period of about 7–8 centuries in Sicilian prehistory during which important socio-economic, as well as ethnic and cultural, stresses played an important role in the development of the insular culture, as well as in the economic and cultural ties in the framework of the entire Mediterranean scene. This period starts around the last two centuries of the third millennium BC. In terms of cultural chronology, we are dealing with what has been traditionally defined as the Early and Middle Bronze Age.

In this period, in terms of social anthropology, Sicilian society showed great changes. During the Early Bronze Age there was a typical village economic system which developed into a well-defined proto-urban system, as can be seen in the case of Thapsos. An important role in this change was played by the incoming Mediterranean trade that connected Sicily with the Aegean and Near East on the one side and with peninsular Italy, Sardinia, Spain and Malta on the other, in the first half of the second millennium BC. Within this framework, Mycenaean trade was essential in strengthening local trends towards a more dynamic society.

But we cannot forget that another phenomenon of profound cultural exchange took place in western Sicily some centuries before the rise of Aegean trade. The strong presence of many Bell Beaker complexes scattered mainly along the Belice Valley in the southwest of the island shows a close connection with Sardinia and through this region with mainland Europe.

The diachronic comparison between the 'European' and 'Eastern' connections provides a stimulus for studying in detail the cultural connections between Sicily and adjacent areas, as well as the change in economic and trade systems.

The Sicilian Bronze Age Pottery Service

Laura Maniscalco

From the Early Bronze Age to the Iron Age in Sicily, there was in use in both domestic and funerary contexts, a pottery service which remained fundamentally unchanged for a period of more than one thousand years and which comprised as fixed elements a vessel on a high pedestal and a dipper. This group of pottery vessels appears in the Early Bronze Age (2000–1400 BC) both in huts and in burial contexts, but only as goods placed outside the tomb. Subsequently, in the Middle (1400–1270 BC) and Late (1270–800 BC) Bronze Age, it occurs also inside the tombs, only to disappear completely with the advent of the Iron Age. The presence of this service in tombs, especially in the earlier phases as collective rather than individual goods, is an expression of the strong family links which drove the Bronze Age people to reproduce in the tomb the domestic equipment of the home. The survival of this service for such a long period of time can probably be linked to the great stability and continuity of indigenous Sicilian societies.

Spatial Analysis of a Castelluccian Settlement in Early Bronze Age Sicily

Brian E. McConnell and Bruce W. Bevan

The site of La Muculufa is distributed along a rocky crest along the Salso river valley in southern Sicily. It includes a village, a necropolis, and what is probably an open-air sanctuary. The site is dated to the middle and later third millennium BC. The village consisted of round and oblong hut-structures with stone foundations and superstructures of wattle-and-daub set on a wooden frame. The buildings used terraces based on natural outcrops of bedrock, and at least three building phases can be identified. Geophysical survey and excavation brought to light a small terrace wall or fence and a number of hut foundations, along with some later remains including Greek ceramics and two Arab burials. The necropolis of La Muculufa includes over 250 tombs which are located above the settlement. These Castelluccian chamber tombs were used for multiple burials, and crevices as well as chamber tombs were used for burial. The open-air sanctuary is located on a natural terrace at the eastern end of the ridge, and includes a large number of high-quality Castelluccian ceramics jumbled within a crevice along with many bones of sheep or goat and large amounts of charcoal. The rites, though poorly understood, seem to have involved feasting within a panoramic landscape.

The Walled Bronze Age Settlement of Coppa Nevigata, Manfredonia and the Development of Craft Specialisation in Southeastern Italy

Alberto Cazzella and Maurizio Moscoloni

This paper describes the walled Bronze Age site of Coppa Nevigata. Coppa Nevigata is located on a rise just above a former lagoon off the Gulf of Manfredonia. Bronze Age occupation at the site includes repeated architectural remodellings. The Early Bronze Age site was walled defensively. After 1500 BC this wall fell into disuse, and a series of furnaces or ovens was built, probably for craft purposes rather than domestic baking. After an episode in which the site was used as a burial ground, a new boundary wall was built in the Late Apennine phase (14th century BC); this wall involved complex masonry and had two defensive towers. A series of circular non-domestic structures was built inside it, and evidence for the production of purple dye from *Murex* shells was found here. In the late Bronze Age (Subapennine), metal production took place at the site, and fine pottery was also made here. The overall impression is of a process of social transformation. Coppa Nevigata arose as a stable trading centre specialising in the exchange of goods and some craft activities. At the peak of the Bronze Age, some areas within the site were allocated for specialised craft production, perhaps controlled by an elite. In the Late Bronze Age, a road structure and a two-room dwelling structure with much Aegean pottery attest some increasingly centralised control, association with the importation of an increasing amount of non-local material and craft production based on local materials.

Human Skeletons from the Greek Emporium of Pithekoussai on Ischia (NA): Culture Contact and Biological Change in Italy after the 8th Century BC

Marshall Joseph Becker

By 775 BC Greek traders from Euboea had established a trading post on a promontory on the island of Ischia in the Bay of Naples, Italy. From this location, on the southern fringe of the Etruscan cultural sphere, these enterprising merchants brought spices, silks and many other goods from the Orient to exchange for metals and various other products of central Italy. Excavations at Pithekoussai have identified over 700 tombs. Some bones or teeth have been recovered from more than 100 of the nearly 200 cremation burials, but much less material has been gathered from over 500 inhumations. Problems with ground water and the intense heat generated by thermal springs have reduced the bones in most of the inhumations to powder, but were less destructive of the tooth roots and bones of the cremations. High temperature alteration of human remains through the cremation process allowed these bones to withstand harsh soil conditions, leaving material by which age and sex can be evaluated.

A double blind system of analysis confirmed an extremely high reliability in the determination of the sex of the cremations when at least 200 grams of bone could be recovered. These results both verify the accuracy of sex evaluation based on associated artefacts as well as providing sex evaluations for the majority of tombs which have no associated offerings by which gender might be inferred. Age and sex evaluations provide clear insights into mortuary patterning during this period.

Studies of the skeletal biology of the residents of the Greek outpost of Pithekoussai provide hints regarding the social dynamics taking place between the Euboean settlers and their native hosts as the settlement developed into a major Greek colony. Evidence of Phoenicians also appears among the skeletal remains. Evidence of Canaanite mortuary rituals as recorded in the Bible is here presented for the first time, in addition to further examples of the Roman custom of burying an *os resectum* with the dead.

Introduction

Albert J. Ammerman

"This was the order of human institutions: first the forests, after that the huts, then the villages, next the cities, and finally the academies." The words are those of Giambattista Vico as he wrote them in the third edition of *Scienza nuova*, the New Science, which appeared in 1744 (Bergin & Fisch 1968: 78). At a time long before anthropology was recognised as a field of study in its own right, Vico drew this brief sketch of the dynamics of human development in an attempt to go beyond the chronological table (with its seven columns each listing the great figures and major events for one of the old civilisations in the Mediterranean world; Bergin & Fisch 1968: 28) then at the centre of discourse. His purpose – like that of many of the contributors to the present volume – was to search for a deeper social pattern behind the ragbag of detail in the chronological table. Today Vico's statement of the problem has an innocent charm to it. Indeed, it serves to remind us that the expression of a good idea will itself age with time. If his formulation strikes us as all too obvious, this was not always the case. As a new departure, Vico's treatment of the question preceded by more than a century the pioneering effort of Lewis H. Morgan (1877) in *Ancient Society* and by more than two centuries the well-known works by Service (1962) on *Primitive Social Organization* and by Sahlins (1972) on the social dimensions of economics in the Stone Age. The archaeologist today is encouraged to appropriate such categories as the band, the tribe, the chiefdom and the state as proposed by Service and Sahlins and refined by other anthropologists often of a younger generation and to apply them to the remote past. In the case of Italian prehistory, while some early forays into social archaeology were occasionally made, it is only in the last decade or so that attempts to explain patterns of continuity and change in social terms have become more common in the literature. The chapters of this book confirm that there is an active interest in this new approach among the younger scholars now working on the prehistory of the central Mediterranean. What we have before us then are trial explorations that are being done across a broad front: ones in which there is often an attempt to recast an old problem in a new language. It is, of course, far from clear at this stage how many of the contributions to the present volume will actually pass the test of time (as many scholars in the human sciences now believe that Vico did). What can be said at this point is that we have many signs of a sincere wish to turn in a new direction and even the desire on the part of some to make a completely fresh start.

Or perhaps it might be more appropriate to say the second chance at such a start. This is indeed not the first time that Italian prehistory, in terms of its own history, has placed social life high on its agenda. And again this happens to bring us back to a theme dear to Vico: that of cycles or *ricorsi* in human affairs. It will be recalled that an interest in palaeoethnology was at the heart of the study of prehistory in Italy, a field under the influence of Pigorini, during its formative years (e.g. Maggi 1997: 12–17). This was, however, an orientation that went into total eclipse in the period from the First World War through the 1960s. While the label *paletnologia* remained officially on the books, there was no real interest in social issues. Given the political climate of these years (Fascism and the Cold War), this development is, in part, understandable; primary emphasis was placed instead on the classification of finds, the construction of typologies and the refinement of chronological tables. In other words, chronology often became an end in itself. The eventual return to a wider set of interests in the 1970s – subsistence strategies, settlement patterns, burial practices, the exchange of materials and so forth – would coincide with the growing use of new dating methods such as radiocarbon (and still more recently dendrochronology and the refitting of artefacts as a control on the integrity of the stratigraphy recovered at a site; in addition, some of the typologies themselves had begun to reach maturity by this time). Thus, as chronology became in effect a more technical matter, it lost its dominant grip over much of the discipline. It was time once again to look behind the columns in the chronological table (still the simplest form in which to summarise the systematics of time and space in prehistory) and to allow artefacts and sites to tell stories of another kind. In short, it was now time to turn (or return, as Vico would have it) to social questions in the study of prehistory in Italy – hopefully with more success this time around.

In looking over the titles of the chapters, we find that the contributions to the book are quite diverse in character. They deal with different regions and cover different time periods. There are, in addition, differences in the approaches taken by the authors and in the motivations for their studies. And yet notwithstanding this great variety, the chapters seem to fall into several groups and they share a number of common threads. For example, the chapters by Tykot, Lazrus, Stoddart, Maggi and Tusa all involve a regional survey of one kind or another; they try to update and rechart the situation in a given region over a time span of some duration. Tykot reviews what is currently known about the large, adjacent islands of Sardinia and Corsica from the late Palaeolithic through the late Neolithic period, where much new evidence has come to light over the last ten years and yet many basic questions still remain open. The fundamental problem for Neolithic studies on both islands is the bias toward the excavation of caves and rock shelters (and the limitations of much of the earlier fieldwork at such sites) and the need for more work at open air settlements, which may yield a different picture of Neolithic development. Lazrus also deals with Sardinia comparing the Neolithic and Bronze Age in terms of their economic strategies and social organisation. She challenges the traditional interpretation (a shift from an egalitarian society with a farming economy to 'warrior-pastoralists' living in a stratified society) and argues for basic continuity between the two periods. It will be of interest to follow how this debate unfolds. There is, of course, the possibility that both the old interpretation and the new one by Lazrus have the defect of offering what amounts to a "totalizing" view of culture (Barth 1993); social organisation in different areas of Sardinia may have been more of "a luminous mosaic" in *both* the Neolithic period and the Bronze Ages.

Stoddart takes a broad look at the situation on the island of Malta over the long time span from the Neolithic through the present day. His main interest here (a new book on Malta is in progress) is to explore how we conceptualise patterns of continuity and change over the long haul. Maggi reports on the region of peninsular Italy that runs from the French border to northern Tuscany (Liguria and the Tusco-Emilian Apennine) giving the results of the latest work on the Mesolithic and Neolithic. One of the findings of particular interest is the complete lack of the late Mesolithic in western Liguria. Mention should be made in passing of the important volume on Arene Candide that Maggi (1997) edited recently; it presents the new results of the comprehensive re-analysis by a team of specialists of the 1940–50 excavations by Bernabò Brea and Cardini at the site. In his chapter, Tusa provides a review of the different cultures found on the island of Sicily from the end of the third millennium BC (with the arrival of bell beakers) through the Bronze Age (with active Mycenaean traffic). In all three of the island surveys (Tykot, Stoddart and Tusa), a common thread is the tension between the good evidence for external contact and exchange and the indigenist impulse to assert local, autonomous development (I find it somewhat surprising that no one makes reference to Sahlins 1985). While each of the regional surveys makes a useful contribution to the literature, none of them attempts to delve into social issues in any real depth. What we have instead are the tentative first steps toward rewriting regional prehistories in terms of social dynamics.

"And in no nation, however savage and crude, are any human actions performed with more elaborate ceremonies and more sacred solemnity than the rites of religion, marriage and burial." Again the words are those of Vico in *The New Science* (Bergin & Fisch 1968: 97). Vico is trying here to put his finger on some of the key events in social life; he was one of the first modern writers to recognise the importance of ritual practice. For the prehistorian, burial is obviously the strong suit. In sharp contrast, we still know very little about marriage rites and practices in most areas of the world and, for the most part, we can only speculate about acts of religious practice. With regard to the latter, we may be able to recognise religious symbols in the general sense but it is extremely difficult in the absence of language to work out their more specific fields of meaning for those who actually lived in a given prehistoric society (it is instructive to recall the case of the Baktaman of New Guinea where the symbol of a flying fox does not have a single, fixed meaning but varies with age and gender: Barth 1975; the prehistorian usually starts by assuming that a specific symbol has only one valence to decode). The student of prehistory probably stands a better chance when it comes to burial practice. This is certainly the case in Italy where the excavation of prehistoric cemeteries has a long tradition. Indeed, the recent work by Bietti Sestieri (1992a; 1992b) at the cemetery of Osteria dell'Osa represents the leading case study in social archaeology in the country to date. Two of the chapters in the book involve this domain. Maniscalco identifies a basic pottery service in Sicily which seems to have lasted from the Early Bronze Age down to the Early Iron Age (while the ceramics changed in style over time, a vase on pedestal and a dipper persisted at the core of the service). She also shows that the service moved from a position on the exterior of a tomb in the Early Bronze Age to one inside the tomb in the Middle Bronze Age as part of a re-orientation of burial practice and that it seems to have been appropriated by an emergent group in the Late Bronze Age. Becker presents the results of his study of the human skeletal remains recovered in the excavations by Buchner and Ridgway (1993) at the cemetery on Pithecusae. Bones and teeth are not well preserved at the site (due to problems of ground water and high soil temperatures) and yet Becker is able to obtain valuable information on the sex, age and health of individuals buried at this early Greek *emporium* by means of his patient analysis of skeletal biology. His study provides some of the building blocks needed for the wider interpretation of burial practices at the site, where some family plots have been identified so far. It is perhaps worth adding that the cemeteries at Osteria dell'Osa and Pithecusae belong to the very twilight of prehistory (or protohistory); the two cemeteries offer, in fact, the earliest evidence for writing in Italy.

The four chapters by Morter, Shaffer, McConnell and Bevan, and Cazzella and Moscoloni form another cluster where the focus is on architecture or the layout of a settlement. Settlement archaeology has long stood as one of the underdeveloped arenas of Italian prehistory. For example, prior to the 1980s there were almost no well-known huts or houses for the Neolithic period in most regions of the country. And there was no settlement where one could examine the spatial distribution of such structures (as one could do in other parts of Europe). The study of the household, as a fundamental unit of social and economic organisation (Hendon 1996), was still in its infancy in Italy (Ammerman 1988–89; Ammerman *et al.* 1988). Due to the work of several contributors to this volume, this situation has begun to change. Morter describes the excavations at the site of Capo Alfiere in Calabria which revealed two stretches of large stone walling. Dated by radiocarbon to the Middle Neolithic, he carefully develops an interpretation of them as part of an enclosure around a hut and then tries to place the structure in the wider context of other architectural remains that are known in southern Italy. Shaffer provides a review of the important work that he did on wattle and daub huts of Stentinello age in the Acconia area of Calabria and adds his current thinking on the long persistence of this tradition of vernacular architecture which lasted down to the current century. The methods that Shaffer developed for the study of daub fragments – a class of material not analysed systematically before – now form the starting point for all work on such huts. Finally, one can reconstruct the huts that Vico had in mind so long ago and that somehow eluded the prehistorian in Italy for decades. McConnell and Bevan present the architectural remains uncovered at La Muculufa, an Early Bronze Age settlement in Sicily. These consist of several round or oblong hut-like structures (again with walls of wattle and daub supported by a wooden framework). The results of a geophysical survey help to fill out the general layout of the site. Cazzella and Moscoloni return to Coppa Nevigata, the walled settlement near Manfredonia in Puglia which dates to the Bronze Age, and update their interpretation of this important coastal site. This includes the evidence for craft specialisation and the role that it played in different phases of the site's history.

The two chapters that show the most originality are those by Skeates and Robb. They are the most theoretical and ambitious contributions to the volume as well. Skeates is interested in the transition to the Neolithic in the region on the Adriatic side of peninsular Italy that runs from the Tavoliere to the Marche. He develops a wide-ranging discussion of the Late Mesolithic and the Early Neolithic which tries to take more cognisance than the previous literature of the social dimensions of the two ways of life and the role of inequality in their interaction with one another. One obvious limitation is the thinness of the evidence on the Late Mesolithic (again largely cave bound) in this part of Italy. In my own view, we want to avoid taking a "totalizing" view of early attempts at food production (as something akin to an ideology) as some have done in the recent literature.

Robb would like to explain some of the paradoxes that he sees in the late Neolithic of central and southern Italy. Why, for example, does domestic architecture become rare exactly when mortuary architecture begins to flourish? He turns to the anthropological literature for an answer and borrows off the shelf the concept of 'Big Man' societies. They involve a form of tribal society (first recognised in New Guinea) in which adult males vie with one another for the leadership of a community by mobilising economic resources on the basis of kinship for ceremonial feasts. This is an idea of major interest. Robb also considers another possibility: what Godelier (1986) has called 'Great Man' societies. There is no need to think in monolithic terms, however. Again with the notion of a luminous mosaic of social forms in mind, both 'Big Man' societies and 'Great Man' societies (and even other forms of social organisation) may well have existed side by side in the Italian Late Neolithic (just as they are observed in New Guinea in this century). The real challenge, as always, is that of moving down from the general proposal to the individual community in prehistory.

In closing, I would like to commend the editors for the breadth of the volume that they have put together. There are two suggestions that I have to offer in the hope that future studies of social life and social dynamics in the prehistoric central Mediterranean will continue to grow. First, in order to capture more fully the richness of social life in small-scale, face-to-face, traditional societies – something that most of us, unless we have had the good fortune to visit a place like New Guinea, have no firsthand experience with – it may be useful to follow the advice of Geertz (1973; 1995) and to try our hand at "thick" description more often. Social life as it is lived on a day-to-day basis is not some sort of general scheme or an abstraction. The style of writing in most of the contributions to this volume, as is common in prehistory, tends to run on the 'thin' side. Second, we should try as best we can to avoid falling into what Vico has called the conceit of scholars – the great temptation to believe that what we know today was also known by the people in the remote past that we wish to study. In all likelihood, very few of those who ever lived in a prehistoric society had the slightest idea of where social dynamics were headed over the long run. It is all too easy for us to lose sight of the *unlikeness* of the past (Lowenthal 1985: 102). The prehistoric past is indeed a foreign country – one with a great variety of cultures each with its own (not our own) way of looking at social life.

BIBLIOGRAPHY

Ammerman, A.J. 1988–89. Towards the study of Neolithic households. *Origini*, 14: 73–82.

Ammerman, A.J., Shaffer, G.D. & Hartmann, N. 1988. A Neolithic household at Piana di Curinga, Italy. *Journal of Field Archaeology*, 15: 121–40.

Barth, F. 1975. *Ritual and Knowledge among the Baktaman of New Guinea*. Yale University Press, New Haven.

Barth, F. 1993. *Balinese Worlds*. University of Chicago Press, Chicago.

Bergin, T.G. & Fisch, M.H. 1968. *The New Science of Giambatista Vico. Revised Translation of the Third Edition (1744)*. Cornell University Press, Ithaca.

Bietti Sestieri, A.M. 1992a. *La necropoli Laziale di Osteria dell'Osa*. Quasar, Rome.

Bietti Sestieri, A.M. 1992b. *The Iron Age Community of Osteria dell'Osa. A Study of Socio-Political Development in central Tyrrhenian Italy*. Cambridge University Press, Cambridge.

Buchner, G. & Ridgway, D. 1993. *Pithekoussai I*. Monumenta Antichi dei Lincei Vol. 4, Rome.

Geertz, C. 1973. Thick description: Towards an interpretive theory of culture. In *The Interpretation of Cultures*. Basic Books, New York.

Geertz, C. 1995. *After the Fact*. Harvard University Press, Cambridge, Mass.

Godelier, M. 1986. *The Making of Great Men. Male Domination and Power among the New Guinea Baruya*. Cambridge University Press, Cambridge.

Hendon, J.A. 1996. Archaeological approaches to the organization of domestic labor: Household practice and domestic relations. *Annual Review of Anthropology*, 25: 45–61.

Lowenthal, D. 1985. *The Past is a Foreign Country*. Cambridge University Press, Cambridge.

Maggi, R. (ed.) 1997. *Arene Candide: A Functional and Environmental Assessment of the Holocene Sequence*. Memorie dell'Istituto Italiano di Paleontologia Umana No. 5, Rome.

Morgan, L.H. 1877. *Ancient Society*. Kerr, Chicago.

Sahlins, M.D. 1972. *Stone Age Economics*. Aldine, Chicago.

Sahlins, M.D. 1985. *Islands in History*. University of Chicago Press, Chicago.

Service, E.R. 1962. *Primitive Social Organization: An Evolutionary Perspective*. Random House, New York.

Unveiling Inequality

Social Life and Social Change in the Mesolithic and Early Neolithic of East-Central Italy

Robin Skeates

INTRODUCTION

Previous discussions of the transition to the Neolithic in the central Mediterranean region have generally taken place within a palaeo-economic framework or orthodoxy, in which the 'Neolithic' is regarded, above all, as an agricultural economy (e.g. Barker 1975; 1981; Lewthwaite 1986; Barker & Malone 1992). In this view the 'neolithic package' is basically defined according to its material and archaeologically-visible elements, including Impressed Ware, ground-stone axes, ditched settlements, and domesticated plants and animals (e.g. Whitehouse 1987). Recent 'post-processual' theoretical developments in archaeology, on the other hand, emphasise the need to go beyond the data in order to make statements about the dynamics of past societies and about social structures which are not themselves directly observable (Hodder 1985; 1992). According to this perspective, the definition of terms such as the 'Neolithic' and the 'neolithic package' needs to be modified. To begin with, the social dimensions of agriculture, such as the relations and rules of agricultural production and of social reproduction, need to be added to the equation. But above all, these terms should be defined as a set of ideas or social knowledge (which might be described either as an ideology, an oral tradition, or a religion) which structured these material things, practices, and social relationships (Thomas 1988; Hodder 1990). The Neolithic appears to be characterised, for example, by the emergence of new ideas concerning the production and consumption of food, involving new types of food, new types of food-preparation and food-serving vessels, and new performative contexts for its consumption, including ritual feasts, through which new reciprocal social relationships and obligations could have been established between participants (Chapman 1988).

Novelty can, however, easily be overemphasised by archaeologists, particularly in relation to the 'New Stone Age', and so, despite a traditional reluctance amongst specialists of the Mesolithic to consider the question of social dynamics and social structures, it is precisely this task that we must begin with if we are to redefine the Neolithic.

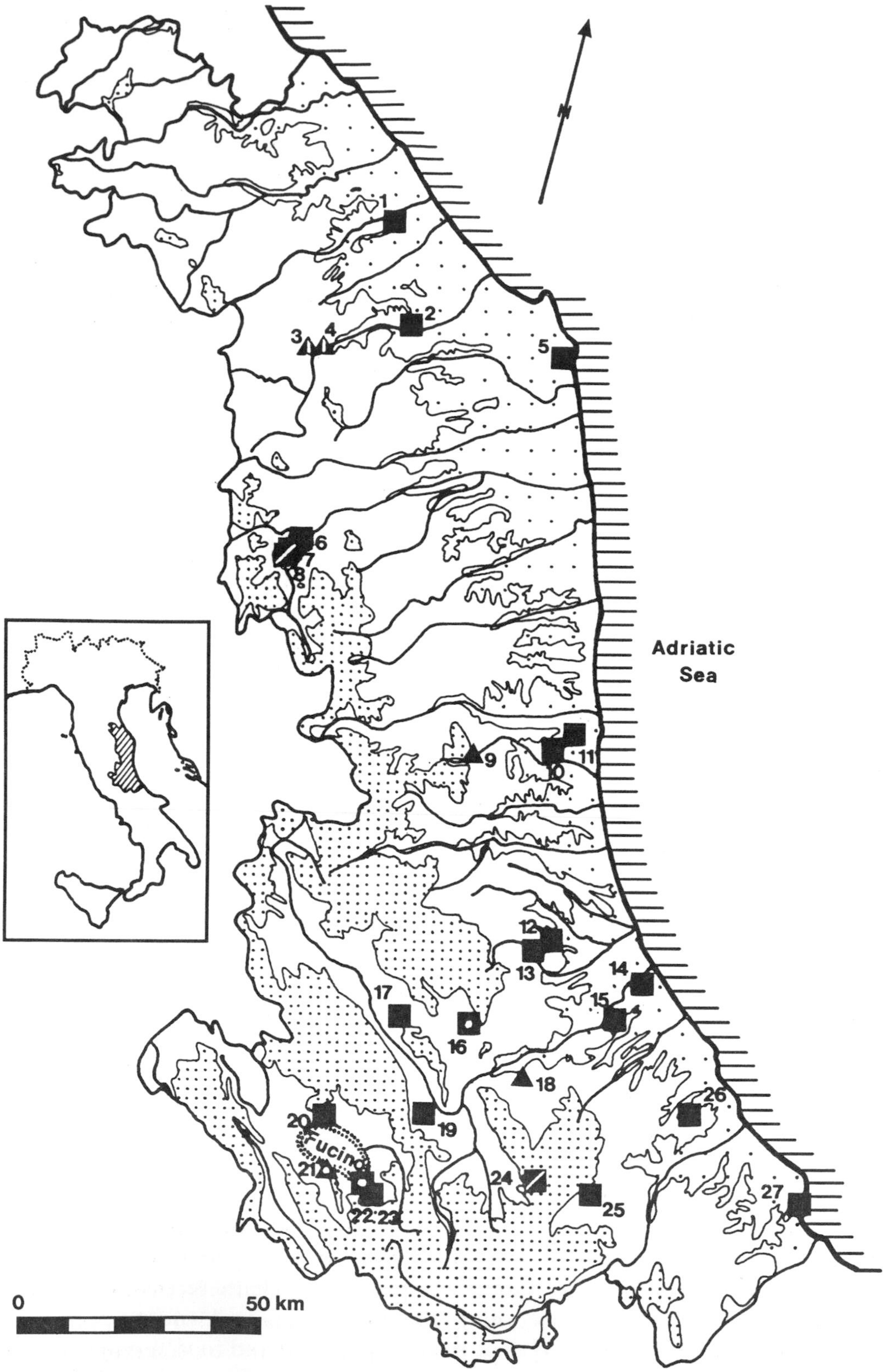

Fig. 1   Map of Mesolithic and Early Neolithic sites in Abruzzo and Marche
1. Ripabianca 2. Monte Cappone 3. Grotta del Prete 4. Cava Romita 5. Monte Colombo 6. La Maddalena 7.
Campo Sportivo 8. Lucciano 9. Grotta S. Angelo 10. Colle S. Savino 11. Ripoli 12. Colle Maggio 13. Villaggio
Leopardi 14. Fontanelle 15. Crocefisso 16. Capo d'Acqua 17. La Valle 18. Grotta dei Piccioni 19. Madonna del
Soccorso 20. Cellitto 21. Grotta Continenza 22. Ortucchio 23. Santo Stefano 24. Campo di Giove 25.
Fonterossi 26. Villaggio Rossi 27. Colle Sinello
Key to symbols: square – open site; triangle – cave site; symbol with line – Mesolithic; symbol with dot –
Mesolithic and Neolithic; filled symbol – Neolithic; lightly dotted zone – coastal lowlands at 0–200m above sea
level; undotted zone – inner lowlands and intermontane areas at 200–1000m; densely dotted zone –
mountains over 1000m; bold lines – rivers

Working within this theoretical framework, this paper focusses upon the issues of social inequality and social differentiation, which are central to the discussion of social structures, and which are marked by unacceptable extremes in our own (western) society. Institutionalised social inequality can be defined as the differential access to material and social resources, such as relative wealth, power, and prestige, within a society. Differentiation in social structure can be defined as the distribution of people among different social groups, such as those defined by sex, age, kinship, ethnicity, religion, occupation, and class (McGuire 1983). It is assumed that potential social inequalities, differences, and conflicts exist in *all* societies, even in the most egalitarian groups, and that it is social mechanisms which either hold them in check or loosen their grip upon them. Furthermore, equality and inequality, as with war and peace, are seen as two sides of the same coin, with the existence of potential inequalities and conflicts necessitating the existence of social mechanisms which seek to restrain them within socially acceptable limits (Sahlins 1968: 4–13; Woodburn 1982).

Spatially, this paper is concerned with the modern political regions of Abruzzo and Marche, which lie within a major geographical unit bounded to the east by the Adriatic Sea, to the west by the watershed of the Apennine mountains, to the northwest by the southern edge of the Po plain, and to the south by the northern edge of the Tavoliere plain (fig. 1). A certain degree of cultural homogeneity appears to have been established across this area during the Early Neolithic, with, for example, the widespread production and use of the Adriatic-style of impressed and incised ware within it (e.g. Bagolini 1980: fig. 41), but this point should not be overemphasised, for intra-regional variations in material culture are increasingly being identified.

The area can be sub-divided into four main geographical zones with reference to major landscape features, a model of climate and vegetation during the warm and humid 'Atlantic phase' (derived from palaeo-environmental studies in west-central Italy – e.g. Bonatti 1966; 1970; Frank 1969; Eisner *et al.* 1984; Hunt *et al.* 1990), and known patterns of settlement during the Mesolithic and Early Neolithic. The Adriatic coastal lowlands extend up to 200m above sea level and as far as 25km inland from the present-day coastline. Pliocene, Pleistocene, and Holocene geological deposits predominate here, and they were probably covered by a relatively open woodland dominated by *Quercus ilex*, the evergreen or holm oak. The inner lowlands, which lie over 25km inland from the Adriatic coast, mainly comprise Miocene deposits, and would have been covered by a dense, mixed deciduous, climax forest dominated by the deciduous oaks *Quercus pubescens* and *Quercus petraea*. They extend as far inland as the edge of the Apennine mountains, which is generally well defined locally by a change to a limestone-based geology and much steeper hill slopes. The mountains lie over about 1000m above sea level, and would probably have been covered by a more open woodland with tree species especially including fir (*Abies*), beach (*Fagus sylvatica*), and spruce (*Picea*). The inland intermontane basins, valleys, and depressions, which comprise the fourth zone, are characterised by locally variable microclimates, which in some cases may have influenced the development of less densely wooded conditions.

Chronologically, this paper deals with the Mesolithic and Early Neolithic, which fall within a time-span of about 7500–4850 cal.BC (table 1). This period follows on from the late Upper Palaeolithic or Final Epigravettian (c.13,500–7500 cal.BC) and precedes the Middle Neolithic (c.4850–4700 cal.BC in Abruzzo). The Mesolithic, or late Final Epigravettian, which is characterised by microlithic industries in Abruzzo and Marche, can be assigned to a period of about 7500–5500 cal.BC with reference to radiocarbon dates from late Mesolithic sites in the neighbouring regions of Tuscany (see Skeates 1994a for full details). The Early Neolithic, which is especially characterised by the presence of impressed and incised pottery, can be assigned to a period of about 5500–4850 cal.BC according to a relatively good sample of nine reliable radiocarbon dates from sites in Abruzzo and Marche (see Skeates 1994b for full details and discussion). This phase can be subdivided into an earlier and a later part, again according to radiocarbon dates, but also with regard to the range and complexity of decorative motifs present in ceramic assemblages. The earlier part, which is characterised by the presence of simple Abruzzo-Marche and Guadone-style impressed and incised ware, can be assigned to a time-span of about 5500–5350 cal.BC; and the more recent part, which is characterised by the addition of early painted decoration and more complex Guadone-style impressed and incised motifs to the repertoire, can be assigned to a time-span of about 5350–4850 cal.BC.

The quality and representativeness of the data used in this study, which are mainly drawn from published reports, are far from ideal. For example, no palaeo-environmental work has been carried out in the region, plant remains have been overlooked at all of the sites, radiocarbon dates have not been produced for any of the Mesolithic sites, publication details regarding the precise spatial and stratigraphic contexts of artefacts and features within excavated sites are generally limited, and a greater intensity of archaeological fieldwork and discovery has occurred in Abruzzo compared with Marche (at least in relation to the Mesolithic and Neolithic). Problems such as these are due to the work of archaeologists, and will hopefully be overcome in the future through the adoption of more scientifically rigorous techniques of archaeological investigation. However, rises in the level of the Adriatic Sea since the Neolithic period may also mean that a significant number of coastal sites are missing from the sample of existing data (Delano Smith 1979; Shackleton *et al.* 1984), which is a more difficult (but not impossible) problem to resolve. Despite these problems, I am still optimistic that we can see patterns in the existing body of data, and that they are not simply 'academic constructs' imposed onto the past (cf. Hodder 1992). For instance, many of the patterns of settlement and subsistence first identified by Graeme Barker (1973; 1975; 1976; 1981) over 20 years ago remain intact today, despite a number of new discoveries during the 1980s.

cal.BC	Phase	Typical Artefacts	Key Chronological Sites
4700–4850	M Neo	Catignano Painted	Catignano & Grotta dei Piccioni 20–18
4850–5350	EN2	Early Painted with Abruzzo-Marche and Guadone Impressed and Incised Ware	Grotta dei Piccioni spits 26–21 and Ripabianca
5350–5500	EN1	Abruzzo-Marche and Guadone Impressed and Incised Ware	Villaggio Leopardi, Villaggio Rossi & La Maddalena
5500–7500	Meso	Microlithic industries	Grotta Continenza spits 29–25
7500–13500	Late UP	Final Epigravettian industries	Grotta Ortucchio & Grotta Maritza

Table 1 General and simplified chronological framework for the Mesolithic and Early Neolithic in Abruzzo and Marche

POTENTIAL SOCIAL DIFFERENTIATION IN MESOLITHIC SOCIETIES
(c.8000–5500 cal.BC)

Patterns in the Data

The eight known Mesolithic sites from the Abruzzo-Marche region, which are characterised by the presence of microlithic industries, can, for the purposes of this analysis, be placed along a continuum according to three main archaeological criteria for which data are generally available (i.e. the locations of the sites, and the compositions of their lithic and faunal assemblages).

The site at Campo di Giove in the Maiella mountains of Abruzzo can be placed at one end of this continuum. The site comprises a small surface-scatter of lithics found on the edge of the tiny lake Tescino, which lies on the 'altopiano' of Campo di Giove at an altitude of 1065m above sea level. The lithic assemblage comprised a very restricted range of tool-types. These features suggest that this may have been a small, specialist, high altitude, hunting camp which was frequented during the summer (although no animal bones were recovered). It can be compared to the Grotta di Peschio Ranaro, an upland cave site, located at an altitude of 800m in the pre-Apennines of Lazio, which appears to have served as a seasonal camp for specialist ibex and red deer hunting during the Upper Palaeolithic, to judge from the faunal remains (Cardini 1969; Alessio *et al.* 1976: 332; Barker 1981: 117).

The site at Capo d'Acqua which lies in the Ofena intermontane basin in Abruzzo, and the sites at Lucciano, Grotta del Prete, and Cava Romita which lie in inland valleys situated along the edge of the Marche Apennines, can be placed along the central part of the continuum. The former lies close to some perennial springs and a medium-sized lake, in the inland intermontane Ofena basin. Excavations produced a lithic assemblage with a relatively high proportion of tools (41.5%), and a faunal assemblage including 50% red deer and 41% aurochs. Excavations at the site at Lucciano, which lies close to the River Chienti in the bottom of its narrow valley which leads down from the Apennines, produced a lithic assemblage comprising backed points, endscrapers, burins, and geometrics, including semi-lunates, triangles, and trapezes. Excavations in the upper stratum of Grotta del Prete, which lies close to the western mouth of the Sentino gorge, produced a similar lithic assemblage and a faunal assemblage comprising unspecified quantities of red deer, wild pig, and ibex bones. No details are available concerning the Mesolithic remains found in Cava Romita, but considering that this cave lies just 6km away from Grotta del Prete, in a similar gorge-side location by the River Esino, the two sites can probably be linked. Compared to the site at Campo di Giove, these four sites might be interpreted as slightly more intensively occupied camps, situated at lower altitudes (461–228m above sea level), along waterways. They would have been seasonally occupied by gatherer-hunter groups, whose activities may have been slightly less specialised, but whose hunting strategies also focussed on a few, local, forest-dwelling, species of large game.

The sites at Ortucchio and Grotta Continenza which lie in the inland intermontane Fucino basin, and probably also the site at Ripoli which lies in the coastal lowlands of northern Abruzzo, can be placed at the other end of the continuum. The Ortucchio site probably lay close to the point where the Lecce stream would have met the edge of the freshwater lake Fucino. Grotta Continenza lies on the lower slope of Monte Albo, at a height of about 40m above the southern edge of the floor of the lake basin, and Mesolithic deposits were found here in the entrance to the cave. They contained traces of hearths, and an assemblage of lithic, bone and shell tools, bone and shell ornaments, and a wide range of faunal remains, including large quantities of fish bones, edible *Helix* shells, and bones of marsh and water fowl. Fourteen pieces of a red mineral, probably red ochre, were also found. A disturbed human burial was discovered further inside the cave, by the entrance to the second chamber, and, in addition to some of the ornamental objects found towards the front of the cave, would seem to suggest that this site served not only an 'economic' or residential function, but also a ritual one. The site at Ripoli lies on the end of a fluvial terrace in the middle of the Vibrata river valley, about 4km inland from the present-day Adriatic coastline.

In contrast to the other Mesolithic sites, subsistence strategies pursued at these three sites appear to have combined broader-spectrum gathering and hunting of a wide range of species (plant and faunal) with an intensive focus upon the rich aquatic resources of lacustrine and riverine areas. Their occupation may have been sedentary, according to Rafferty's (1985: 115) definition of the term, which specifies that only part of the population need remain at the same location throughout the entire year, allowing for the absence of some members of the group for varying periods (on seasonal hunting parties and trading expeditions, for example) and their establishment of temporary sites elsewhere. Studies of the available archaeological data are insufficient to be conclusive about this. But what can be stated, on the basis of the relatively mild winter climate which characterised the Fucino basin before its drainage (Letta 1884: 20), the apparently seasonally overlapping range of faunal species remains found in the Mesolithic levels at Grotta Continenza, and a consideration of the range of other food resources which might have been available both in and around the Fucino basin at that time (Skeates 1987), is that there was certainly a potential for Mesolithic year-round settlement in the Fucino basin, even if at least part of the population actually dispersed seasonally to sites located in other areas, such as Campo di Giove in the Apennine mountains, where particular food resources could have been more abundant, especially during the summer.

Discussion

Traditionally, gatherer-hunters have been labelled as 'band' or 'egalitarian' societies in which groups are small, mobile, and unstratified, and in which differences of wealth and power are minimally developed. However, the fairly recent recognition of ambiguities in this definition has led to a distinction being drawn between 'generalised' or 'egalitarian' groups with 'immediate-return systems' and more socially differentiated 'complex' groups with 'delayed-return systems' (e.g. Woodburn 1980, 1982; Price & Brown 1985; Testart 1988; Lee 1992). These new classifications are difficult to sustain as opposed dichotomies, but, when seen as falling along a continuum, they do seem to provide a useful basis for discussion of the archaeological data (Tilley 1989: 247–8). Below, they will be used as a starting point for a dialectical discussion of the social implications of four main subjects: ceremonial and ritual practices, exchange, settlement (especially residential permanence and territorial rights), and subsistence (particularly storage and economic specialisation).

Ceremonial and ritual practices in most foraging societies remain few and relatively unelaborated (Tilley 1989), but in more complex gatherer-hunter societies they can become more frequent and elaborate, sometimes serving to reinforce group membership (Woodburn 1982), but also permitting the control rather than the dissemination of social and religious knowledge by individuals seeking authority or prestige (Bender 1990). Some sort of ritual performance probably surrounded the burial of the individual in Grotta Continenza and might also have accompanied the use and deposition of the shell and bone ornaments and the pieces of red mineral towards the front of the shelter, but, by comparison with the great painted caves of the Upper Palaeolithic in southwest France and northern Spain (Bender 1990), or the cemeteries of Mesolithic Europe (Whittle 1985: 33; Zvelebil 1986a: 172), this example would seem to fall at the less elaborate end of the scale. In fact it shows continuity with, but perhaps even less elaboration than, the mortuary deposits and special artefacts of the Upper Palaeolithic found in this and other caves in the Fucino basin (summarised in Radmilli 1981). Relatively speaking, then, the fairly simple and conservative nature of the 'special deposits' found in the Mesolithic levels of Grotta Continenza perhaps suggests that any associated ceremonies and rituals were not used (at least not to any significantly greater extent than before) to enhance the authority and prestige of particular individuals or to strengthen group identity and territoriality.

However, a slight degree of social differentiation, at the level of the individual (as opposed to the family unit or kinship group) is still perhaps suggested by the singling out of a particular individual for burial treatment (Whittle 1985: 33; Bender 1985a).

The social implications of exchange vary likewise between 'complex' and 'egalitarian' gatherer-hunter societies. The former are, like agricultural societies, characterised by developing systems of marital alliance and reciprocal gift-exchange, which generate an extended network and hierarchy of long-term and binding kin relations and dependencies (Bender 1981; Cohen 1985). Egalitarian societies also engage in trade and exchange, which may likewise be formalised as exchange partnerships, but, due to social mechanisms such as an emphasis upon sharing and mutuality, sanctions on the accumulation of personal possessions, and the existence of chance-based gambling, individuals are able to obtain goods from people of their choosing without entering into dependent relations with them. The circulation of breeding partners and of scarce and local goods through a region is ensured by the frequent, voluntary, and positively valued movement of individuals of both sexes between groups (Tilley 1989; Woodburn 1982). The evidence from Grotta Continenza, comprising the perforated sea shells of *Columbella rustica*, one of which was coloured red, which must have been transported over a distance of at least 80km overland from the Mediterranean Sea, could easily fit in with either of these models (assuming that they were obtained by long-distance exchange rather than directly procured from the coast by inland groups). However, the balance shifts slightly towards the first, when similar evidence of the special use and long-distance exchange of *Columbella rustica* shells during the Mesolithic in the Alpine region is taken into account (e.g. Rähle 1980; Barfield 1981), for these shells then appear not simply as unusual ornaments, but as widely valued tokens of exchange and display. The social implications of this might have involved the control of access to exchange networks carrying socially valued and exotic objects and marriage partners, and the accumulation of some debts.

Gatherer-hunter settlement strategies which involve prolonged aggregation often bring with them an increased likelihood of intra-group social tensions and conflicts (due to factors such as the greater degree social interaction, crowding, and feelings of lack of personal control). In the case of sedentary groups this may lead to the development of more complex social institutions designed to regulate or resolve such problems. Some characteristic features and functions of such institutions include: the co-ordination and social differentiation of sub-groups within communities in order to guarantee access to scarce or concentrated resources; the erection of physical and social barriers which organise social interactions in such a way as to minimise congestion and provide control and privacy for individuals; the stereotyping of peoples' behaviour and the announcement of group membership and ownership through visual cues in order to reduce the total perceptual information load upon individuals in their social interactions; and, the establishment of more permanent institutionalised leadership and the performance of elaborated rituals which serve to reinforce group membership, participation, and solidarity (Cohen 1985). In relatively large but less sedentary groups, on the other hand, seasonal mobility and social fluidity may be maintained, not only in order to cope with seasonality and variable resource distribution, but also as mechanisms which serve to relieve social stresses by allowing people to segregate themselves easily from those with whom they are in conflict. In such cases there may still be continuities in the composition of local groupings, but none which seriously limit an individual's freedom of movement, which is seen positively as something healthy and desirable in itself. Such mobility also has the effect of keeping simpler egalitarian structures intact, by subverting the development of authority, restricting claims of ownership or property, and limiting the development of local variations in wealth or standards of living (Bender 1981: 152; Woodburn 1982).

The existing pattern of Mesolithic sites in the Abruzzo-Marche region (see above), which seems to reveal some sort of a continuum ranging from longer-term settlements located in the Fucino basin and possibly also on the coastal lowlands to temporary camps situated in the mountains and in certain intermontane valleys and basins, would seem to suit both sides of the coin. The situation remains best described by Graeme Barker's (1981) two models of gatherer-hunter settlement and subsistence in Mesolithic central Italy: on the one hand, "the diversity of resources in a few areas such as the coast and inland lake basins was sufficiently rich to enable all-year-round subsistence", and on the other hand, "the annual territory of an epipalaeolithic band in central Italy would normally have encompassed both lowlands and highlands, with an annual subsistence round methodically using a series of sites to exploit a series of resources at the time of their seasonal abundance, in the manner of many hunter-gatherer bands today. Such a system might involve winter hunting and fishing on the coast, spring and summer hunting and fishing in the Fucine basin, ibex hunting in the early fall as the bad weather began to force them down to lower elevations, deer and cattle hunting in the middle valleys in the late autumn and early spring" (Barker 1981: 141–2). Barker added (and I would emphasise that these two models do not have to be regarded as mutually exclusive, indeed a combination of the two might be more accurate), that such groups may have combined development of residential permanence in certain 'central places' with the maintenance of a fair degree of mobility throughout the region. The social implications of this are, then, that there was some potential for the development of more complex social institutions among groups occupying the more permanent residential sites in the region, particularly in the Fucino basin where increased ceremonial and residential permanence can be traced back to the Upper Palaeolithic (see Radmilli 1981), but that the emergence of social inequalities in such groups may have been held in check through the continued seasonal mobility and social fluidity of at least some of their members.

A second set of settlement-related contrasts can be derived, this time on an inter-group level, from a consideration of gatherer-hunter territories, which may generally be described as specific places or sites and paths or tracks (which afford movement from one place to another) within a landscape whose definition varies according to the place from which it is viewed (Ingold 1986). Among more 'complex' groups the valued assets of a territory, including its wild food resources, water, raw materials, geographical sites, paths, and sacred knowledge, may be socially appropriated and controlled by corporate groups within a community claiming exclusive rights of access and ownership over them. This may also lead to more pronounced territorial behaviour, such as the signalling of group identity and the definition and defence of boundaries. Among 'egalitarian' gatherer-hunters, on the other hand, the notion of ownership is a broad one, which tends to mean long-term association with, involvement in, and identification with, a territory rather than the narrow possession of it. In such cases territorial rights are sometimes asserted over the natural resources of an area by a core group of people most closely associated with that area, but it does not become a matter of tightly defined groups monopolising the resources of their areas and excluding outsiders, for the supposed 'owners' of a territory cannot refuse outsiders access to its resources, and in every case individuals maintain full rights of access to resources in several other areas with which they have kinship or affinial ties. Territorial boundaries are therefore conceived of as open, and function in particular as part of a system of practical communication (rather than of social control) serving to indicate the presence of people and resources within a territory (Woodburn 1982).

In northern Europe, studies of artefactual diversity suggest that 'social territories' diminished in size and became better defined between the Upper Palaeolithic and Mesolithic (e.g. Price 1983: 770; Whittle 1985: 31–2; Rowley Conwy 1986: 21–2), but it is difficult to make the same claim for the existing evidence from east-central Italy. Admittedly this evidence is limited, and it may not have been studied in sufficient detail, but there are few visible signs of increased attempts to define boundaries or to signal group identities, and there is no clear evidence of a growing separation of more sedentary groups situated in the Fucino basin from those based in the coastal lowlands. This again implies the maintenance of economic and social mobility, and of open territorial boundaries, during the Mesolithic in the Abruzzo-Marche region.

Technological, economic, and social investment in the storage of food surpluses and in specialised forms of gathering and hunting are not simply characteristic features of gatherer-hunters found in areas where food resources are prone to seasonal peaks and fluctuations in availability and abundance (Zvelebil 1986a). They are as well, perhaps more importantly, typical features of those groups which are described as having either 'complex' societies or socio-economic systems of 'delayed-return' (Woodburn 1980; Testart 1988), and, more specifically, as having social relations of production similar to those of agricultural societies. Specialist economic activities in such groups, for example, are sometimes associated with the extension of divisions of labour beyond simple distinctions of age and gender. The direction and control of the production, storage, and redistribution of food surpluses can lead to an elaboration of decision hierarchies, and in particular to the enhancement of the temporary authority or leadership of household heads (Cohen 1985). Access to stored food resources, representing a form of delayed return or yield on previous labour, or to specialist gathering and hunting skills and equipment, may become controlled as property by corporate groups within the community, which can lead to the development of binding and long-term kinship and age-based commitments, dependencies, and institutionalised inequalities in social relations (Woodburn 1982). Strategies of storage and of specialisation (and sedentism – see above) have been identified among certain Mesolithic groups in temperate Europe (Zvelebil 1986a). They are thought to have emerged, from an economic point of view, as a means of coping with the seasonal scarcities and unpredictable fluctuations of food resources which escalated with the establishment of post-glacial climatic and environmental conditions (Zvelebil 1986a), and, from a social perspective, as a means of coping with the greater demands made upon local subsistence strategies caused by increased ceremonial (and sometimes residential) permanence in certain places (Bender 1985b: 26).

However, in east-central Italy, and indeed in the central Mediterranean as a whole, the relevant evidence remains conspicuously absent. In the Abruzzo-Marche region, for example, the excavated deposits at Mesolithic sites, which generally comprise fairly shallow, dark, soil layers and occasional hearths, do not (despite the small areas investigated) seem to reflect the massive harvesting, processing, and intensive storage of one or two seasonal resources (usually in fixed dwellings) seen in ethnographic examples of 'complex' gatherer-hunter groups with systems of 'delayed-return' (e.g. Testart 1982; Woodburn 1982). In fact they compare most closely with the deposits of the Upper Palaeolithic found in the Fucino caves and at the open site at Campo delle Piane (Radmilli 1981; 1983). Similarly, on a broader scale, Donahue (1992) points out that, "Although plant foods are demonstrably important during the Mesolithic in Mediterranean Europe, there is still no evidence for intensive collecting, processing, or storing of plant foods." Instead he argues in favour of "frequent foraging for plant foods, rather than intensive long-term storage strategies" (Donahue 1992: 77). Neither is there evidence of a significant elaboration of specialist subsistence-related artefacts at Mesolithic sites in the east-central Italy, such as bone harpoons or fish-hooks, which might have been expected at the Fucino basin sites, with their partial emphasis upon the food resources of the lake.

The social implications of this are that Mesolithic groups in east-central Italy may have retained an economic system primarily based upon immediate-returns, which is characteristic of 'egalitarian' gatherer-hunter societies. In such systems, individuals have freedom of access to food and other resources, food is shared and consumed immediately after its production, there is little investment of food surpluses or other products of labour, and the composition of work groups remains short-lived due to the instability of social relations and the fluidity of group membership. Socio-economic features such as these contribute to the maintenance of egalitarian social relations, by restricting claims of ownership, and by constraining the development of authority, dependencies, and extended family organisation (Meillassoux 1972; Woodburn 1982; Tilley 1989).

My overall impression, then, of social relations within and between gatherer-hunter groups in Mesolithic east-central Italy is that they continued to be basically egalitarian. Socio-economic features, including continued residential mobility and social fluidity, and the apparent dominance of a system of immediate-returns in subsistence practices, would have continued to act as social 'levelling mechanisms' which suppressed and ironed out potential social inequalities. However, there are also hints of a slight development of social differentiation during the post-glacial period, particularly in the ceremonial system of ritual and long-distance exchange practiced by the old-established, 'non-storing sedentary' (Testart 1981), gatherer-hunters of the Fucino lake-basin, with its abundant natural food resources. Social and ceremonial gatherings here, involving occasional mortuary rituals and the exchange and display of socially valued and exotic goods and people such as sea shell ornaments and marriage partners, might not only have provided an initial arena for greater social control and leadership, but might also have enabled the establishment of more permanent institutionalised leadership in associated, and increasingly permanent, residential contexts (cf. Bender 1978; 1985b; 1990). But, as in their economic practices (Lewthwaite 1986: 64), there is no evidence to suggest that such groups were on the verge of developing the social institutions and inequalities characteristic of agricultural societies.

A STATIC FRONTIER (c.6500–5500 cal.BC)

During the seventh millennium cal.BC, east-central Italy, as well as the northern part of the Adriatic zone, appear to have been by-passed by an initial wave of neolithic innovations which spread from the east via northwest Greece to coastal parts of southeast Italy, Sicily, Corsica, west-central Italy, and southern France. The pattern of existing radiocarbon dates for the earliest Neolithic in the different regions of Italy flanking the Adriatic sea indicates that there was a chronological 'break' of about 900 calendar years between the first appearance of the 'neolithic package' in the southeastern region of Puglia at around 6400 cal.BC, and its earliest appearance in the east-central Italian regions of Abruzzo, Marche and Emilia-Romagna at around 5500 cal.BC (Sargent 1985; Skeates 1994b). Cassano (1985: 736–7) has plausibly suggested that this break reflects the establishment and maintenance of a stable frontier between the earliest neolithic agricultural groups in Puglia and mesolithic gatherer-hunters to the north. This suggestion assumes that the gap will not be filled by future radiocarbon dates, but this seems acceptable considering the strong consistency of the earliest radiocarbon dates for the Neolithic in east-central Italy. The northwestern edge of the flat, fertile, and extensive Tavoliere plain may have formed the southern edge of such a frontier, but it may also have extended, as a frontier zone, into the modern neighbouring region of Molise.

Accepting this interpretation, then, the discussion of two related questions becomes relevant: why was a stable frontier established, and why was the 'neolithic package' of conceptually linked material things and social relations delayed in its northward transmission? Traditionally, such questions have been answered according to a point of view dominated by the ecological and economic concerns of the agriculturalists. Alexander (1977; 1978), for example, argues that a static frontier is established, particularly along an ecological boundary, either when all of the currently usable (in terms of the existing technology) land is taken up, or when the limits of the ecological tolerance of plants and animals currently domesticated are reached (see also Lewthwaite 1982: 315). According to such a view, the northern edge of the Tavoliere plain might have formed an ecological barrier to the northward spread of the earliest Neolithic wheat-dominated crop-complex from southeast Italy. This barrier would have been overcome only by the re-adaptation of that complex to the different (and, in particular, wetter) environmental conditions of central and northern Italy, to which barley was better suited (Skeates 1992: 195; Barker & Malone 1992: 63). Early Neolithic crop remains from Italy provide some support for this suggestion, for in the south wheat predominates strongly over barley, whereas in the north the more limited botanical evidence seems to indicate a predominance of barley, which can generally tolerate a wider range of soils than emmer wheat and which has wide climatic adaptability due to its shorter vegetational cycle (Spurr 1986: 14–15). More recent discussions of the rate of transition to farming have also taken into account the role of the indigenous gatherer-hunters, as in central Italy, where the "success and stability" of Mesolithic subsistence strategies are now thought to have contributed to the delayed adoption of early Neolithic crops and domesticated animals (Barker 1981; Lewthwaite 1986). However, the existence of a frontier cannot simply be understood in terms of ecological or economic factors (and cannot therefore be described simply as an 'agricultural frontier'): it must also be considered from a socio-cultural perspective.

The available evidence, which provides little or no indication of contacts between the earliest agriculturalists on the Tavoliere plain and the most recent gatherer-hunters in the Abruzzo-Marche region to the north, suggests that a 'static closed frontier' (Dennell 1983) might have been established between them, comprising a broad zone of mutual avoidance. Moreover, such a 'frontier' could have been maintained as a deliberate social and economic strategy, particularly in order to maintain peace (as opposed to relations of negative reciprocity) between these two somewhat culturally and structurally incompatible groups. As Sahlins (1968) says, "good relations may be maintained by preventing direct relations". The strength of this suggestion should be tested against potentially available evidence from known, but as yet only superficially investigated, sites in the geographically intermediate regions of Molise and southeast Abruzzo (including Mesolithic sites along the lower Biferno valley and an Early Neolithic site at Colle Sinello near Vasto – Barker 1976: 68; D'Ercole 1987–88: 406). The presence of six chert blades at the coastal Mesolithic site at Ripoli in northern Abruzzo, which measure up to six centimetres long (Radmilli & Cremonesi 1963) and appear to stand out as possible 'Neolithic' traits in contrast to the predominantly microlithic industry at this site, provide a hint that the situation might not be as simple as it seems. Furthermore, we need to consider the possibility that groups in east-central and southeast Italy began to diverge from their earlier forms quite significantly, both economically and socially, before the transition to the Neolithic in either area (cf. Bender 1981: 152), even with the acceptance of an immigrant hypothesis for the origins of the Tavoliere Neolithic, and the signs of a gradual transition to the Neolithic among gatherer-hunters to the south (Whitehouse 1971). In Puglia (and other parts of southern Italy), for example, there is growing evidence that the late Upper Palaeolithic (i.e. the Final Epigravettian and 'Romanellian') saw the development of a degree of social and economic complexity not found in central Italy. Notable differences in scale can be seen, for instance, in the degree of: ceremonial and ritual investment (e.g. in decorated cave sites and stone artefacts – Graziosi 1973); maritime exchange (e.g. of Lipari obsidian – Phillips 1992); settlement density and economic intensification along the coast (e.g. around the Alimini coastal lagoons – Milliken & Skeates 1989); and early post-glacial coastal land-loss with rising sea levels (Shackleton et al. 1984).

TRANSITIONS TO THE NEOLITHIC (c.5500–4850 cal.BC)

The processes involved in the transition from gatherer-hunter societies to early farming communities in the Abruzzo-Marche region were complex and varied, and require detailed discussion. Many alternative models have been proposed over the last 10 years in relation to these processes in the Mediterranean region, ranging from those which emphasis the role of large-scale maritime colonisation by immigrant agriculturalists bringing a 'neolithic package' of agricultural techniques, resources, and knowledge (e.g. Ammerman & Cavalli Sforza 1984) to those which favour an almost entirely local process of change amongst indigenous gatherer-hunters using locally available wild and domesticated resources (e.g. Dennell 1983; Barker 1985). (For a summary of these models see Donahue

1992). Jim Lewthwaite has made a number of important advances in this area, particularly in his application of Zvelebil and Rowley Conwy's (1984) 'availability model' to the Mediterranean region, and through his development of an 'active filter model' for the Tyrrhenian region (Lewthwaite 1985; 1986; 1987). In the former, he argues that the transition took place gradually in a number of stages which spanned two or more millennia, and that a distinction should be drawn between the availability of knowledge of the techniques of food production and the actual commitment to agriculture as a dominant economic strategy. In the latter, he assigns the role of active filter to the islands of Corsica and Sardinia, which selectively transmitted certain economic innovations from a donor region (southern Italy and Sicily), to a recipient zone in the south of France. Above all, he emphasises the point that different processes operated on various geographical and chronological scales. Both of these models can be usefully applied to parts of central Italy (e.g. Lewthwaite 1987; Skeates 1992: 200–3; Barker & Malone 1992: 62–3). However, despite a few brief mentions of the reciprocal exchange of 'prestige goods' circulating within a context of incipient social stratification and social competition (e.g. Lewthwaite 1982; 1986), a detailed social dimension is generally lacking in these models. It is this aspect, then, that I wish to pay greater attention to below, both in relation to general models of gatherer-hunter and agricultural societies, and, more specifically, in terms of differing degrees of social and geographical access to important long-distance networks of communication, gift-exchange, and kinship by immigrant and indigenous populations.

The Lowlands

In the coastal lowlands of southeast Abruzzo, two Early Neolithic settlement sites found at Crocefisso near Chieti and Fontanelle near Pescara were recently excavated. Both lie on the slopes of Pleistocene hills flanking the wide lower section of the Pescara river valley, and, more specifically, both were found to be lying on the remains of Neothermal 'brown soils' (Agostini 1986–87a), which would originally have comprised well-drained, easily worked, and highly productive agricultural soils. No plant remains were recovered from these sites, but scarce faunal remains were identified which belonged exclusively to domesticated species, and in particular to sheep/goat (Sorrentino 1986–87). Crops might have been grown in small, intensively cultivated, fixed plots situated close to these sites; and soil fertility could have been maintained by a combination of the initially high and durable edaphic potential of the soils selected for use, the cultivation of nitrogen-fixing pulses alongside cereal crops, the dumping of domestic refuse on these plots, and the seasonal penning of sheep on the plots in order to manure them (Halstead 1980; Sherratt 1980). Local pottery production is suggested by thin-section analyses of the ceramic fabrics which appear to have been made from raw materials found at Crocefisso (Agostini 1986–87b). Pottery at this site comprised a range of simple forms, including flasks, short-necked oval vessels with handles, large troncoconical vessels, and a variety of bowls, decorated with small impressions and incised slashes and lines (fig. 2.1–2.2).

These two Early Neolithic sites, along with a possible third found at Colle Sinello, which lie within 10km of the present-day Adriatic sea shore in the coastal lowlands of southeast Abruzzo, have a strong claim to be regarded as settlements founded by small groups of immigrant agriculturalists from southeast Italy. Their more complex techniques and motifs of pottery decoration exhibit close typological similarities to the Guadone style of pottery decoration, which was produced at sites in southeast Italy from c.6000 cal.BC onwards (Tinè & Bernabò Brea 1980; Cremonesi & Tozzi 1987). (Similarities between decorated pottery found at Early Neolithic sites in east-central Italy and in Dalmatia seem to be indirect and mediated through shared contacts with southeast Italy.) Furthermore, the particular positioning of these sites, in ecotonal locations and on brown soils found within what was probably a not too densely wooded zone lying below an altitude of 200m in the coastal lowlands, can be closely compared with Early Neolithic settlement locations identified in parts of southeast Italy (including the Tavoliere plain and the lower and middle sections of the Ofanto river valley), which also clustered on light, well-drained, and fertile soils (e.g. Sargent 1983; Cipolloni Sampò 1977–82: 192). This suggests that a previously established southeast Italian system of agricultural settlement and subsistence was simply transferred, with limited adaptation to the system or modification of the local environment, to suitable parts of southeast Abruzzo. In addition, the limited lithic and faunal assemblages found at these sites certainly do not contradict the suggestion that a fairly well-established agricultural way of life was followed at them.

Assuming that this immigration hypothesis is correct, the process of colonisation deserves greater attention, particularly from a socio-cultural point of view. To begin with, the northern half of the Tavoliere plain can be identified as a possible place of origin, not only because the type-site for the Guadone-style of pottery is found in this area, but also because aerial surveys have revealed a high density of small-sized settlements here during the Early Neolithic (Jones 1987). This high density of settlement suggests that significant 'push' factors could have existed, particularly in the form of growing socio-economic pressures upon restricted resources, and a continuing process of settlement fissioning. Migrations of farming populations across ecological and cultural boundaries are generally planned, with known destinations chosen as attractive targets for specific goals, particularly since such groups depend upon a relatively narrow range of highly productive but relatively inelastic and localised food resources which can only be produced in restricted favorable locations (Anthony 1990). This could have been the case in southeast Abruzzo where specific site locations appear to have been selected along the Pescara river valley which were similar to those favoured in southeast Italy, and which would have required limited adaptation of either the local environment or the pre-existing agricultural system. A migration and communications route appears to have been established northwards along the Adriatic coast after about 5500 cal.BC (or 5750 cal.BC at the earliest), extending over a distance of about 100km between Lésina and Pescara. The friction of this distance may have been reduced in part by the use of simple boats following typical Mediterranean coast-hugging routes (cf. Braudel 1972: 103–48; Camps 1976), and also by its division into stages, as is suggested by the establishment of a possible Early Neolithic coastal colony at Colle Sinello near Vasto (half way between Lésina and Pescara). This migration process was probably restricted in scale, involving relatively small kin-based groups of people. However, it appears to have been sustained by the maintenance and strengthening of communication and exchange with relatives in the homeland (Chapman 1988: 18; Donahue 1992) (suggested by the steady flow of Lipari obsidian and new techniques and styles of pottery decoration from southeast Italy to lowland groups in Abruzzo throughout the Neolithic – Skeates 1993). It was also sustained by a continued stream of migration extending northwards along the coast of Abruzzo during the later Neolithic, to new coastal colonies such as Fossacesia and Ripoli (Cremonesi 1965; 1973). This seems to have led to the development of a degree of long-term economic and cultural dependency, throughout the Neolithic, of relatively marginal communities in lowland Abruzzo upon groups in the core region of southeast Italy.

In the inner lowlands of southern Abruzzo, on hills flanking tributary rivers and streams in a more densely forested zone (situated at a distance of more than 10km inland from the Adriatic coast and at an altitude of more than 275m above sea level), and in the lowlands of northern Abruzzo and Marche, along major river valleys, another collection of Early Neolithic open settlement sites exhibits both similarities and contrasts to those found on the coastal lowlands. Examples include: Villaggio Rossi near Lanciano, Fonterossi near Lama dei Peligni, Villaggio Leopardi and Colle Maggio near Penne, Colle S. Savino near Nereto, Monte Colombo near Ancona, and Ripabianca near Monterado. Related Early Neolithic deposits have also been found in two large caves in this area, Grotta dei Piccioni and Grotta S. Angelo, which appear to have served as non-crop-growing residential sites and as places for the performance of rituals. Material remains found at the open sites indicate that a full

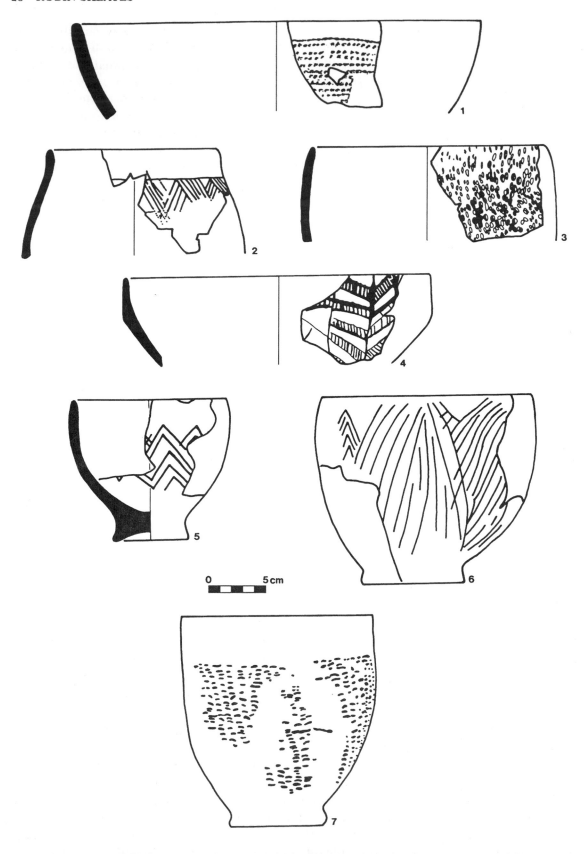

Fig. 2   Examples of Early Neolithic impressed and incised pottery vessels from Abruzzo and Marche
1. Impressed bowl from Tricalle (after Ducci *et al*. 1986–87). 2. Incised jar from Tricalle (after Ducci *et al*. 1986–87). 3. Impressed beaker from level II, area IA, Villaggio Rossi (after Geniola 1982b). 4. Incised carinated bowl from level I, area IA, Villaggio Rossi (after Geniola 1982b). 5. Incised pedestalled beaker from spit 25, Grotta dei Piccioni (after Cremonesi 1976). 6. Incised pedestalled beaker from La Maddalena (after Lollini 1965). 7. Impressed pedestalled beaker from Ripabianca (after Lollini 1965)

agricultural way of life was led at them, which was comparable to that followed in the coastal lowlands. At Villaggio Leopardi, for example, impressions of barley and emmer wheat (*Triticum dicoccum*), along with bones of the three main domesticated animal species, were identified (Evett & Renfrew 1971). However, the artefacts found at these sites exhibit far fewer links with southeast Italy. Decorated pottery, for example, was characterised by the use of finger and fingernail impressions, and incised slashes and lines, arranged in simple motifs, in the common Abruzzo-Marche style of Impressed Ware (fig. 2.3, 2.5 & 2.7); more exclusively southeast Italian features, such as the more complex incised and shell-impressed motifs of the Guadone-style, and red-filled and red painted decoration, were generally absent. Some examples of the latter have, however, been found in the upper parts of the stratified Early Neolithic deposits at Villaggio Rossi (fig. 2.4) and in Grotta dei Piccioni, and might be regarded as imports from the coastal lowlands (or even from southeast Italy) (cf. Barnett 1990), which suggests a slight strengthening of contacts during the second part of the early Neolithic, towards the end of the six millennium cal.BC.

This collection of sites might be regarded as having been established by indigenous groups who adopted a full and integrated 'neolithic package', including the basic elements of the Adriatic-style of impressed and incised ware, quite rapidly via contacts with the immigrant agriculturalists who settled in the neighbouring coastal lowlands of southeast Abruzzo. (I favour this idea over alternatives which might see these sites as having been established either directly by sea-borne colonists, or by secondary colonial groups which fissioned off from early coastal colonies – mainly because the decorated pottery found at them exhibits, on the one hand, too few distinctive southeast Italian elements, and, on the other hand, close connections with that found on inland sites which have a strong claim to be regarded as the settlements of indigenous groups – see below.). Continuity of indigenous groups is indirectly hinted at by the proximity of a few Upper Palaeolithic and Mesolithic sites to some of the Early Neolithic sites in these areas. A few Upper Palaeolithic (Epigravettian) tools were found at San Martino, for example, which lies near to the Early Neolithic site of Villaggio Rossi at Lanciano (Radmilli 1981: 152); likewise, the Upper Palaeolithic open site at Montebello di Bertona lies close to the two Early Neolithic sites found in the area of Penne (Radmilli 1983); and, the Mesolithic site at Ripoli lies 6km downstream along the Vibrata valley from the Early Neolithic site at Colle S. Savino.

If this argument is accepted, then a series of developing interactions between the immigrants and the indigenous population need to be considered. (The following discussion is based partly upon models proposed by Sahlins (1968), Friedman and Rowlands (1977), Tilley (1989), and Chapman (1989: 504)). The settlement of small groups of immigrant agriculturalists in the coastal lowlands of southeast Abruzzo could have been achieved either by negotiation or by conquest. This process may have led to the displacement of some local gatherer-hunters from the coastal portions of their lowland territories. No evidence has yet been found of Mesolithic sites in this area, but two Upper Palaeolithic (Epigravettian) sites are known from along the lower section of the Pescara valley, at Cavatticchio inferiore and between the S.S. n. 5 road and the Fosso Valvone (Radmilli 1981: 152), in the same general area as the Early Neolithic sites at Crocefisso and Fontanelle. More certainly, the settlement of the farmers in this area would have brought the two different cultural groups into much closer proximity with each other than before. Both populations were probably relatively small and dispersed (compared, for example, with the dense populations suggested by settlement patterns in parts of southern Italy during the Mesolithic and early Neolithic – e.g. Milliken & Skeates 1989; Whitehouse 1981), and so direct competition and conflict over local resources may have been avoided. Indeed, peaceful and increasingly close cross-cultural relations, based upon symbiotic and reciprocal exchanges, may have been established across a new and closer 'porous frontier'. The newcomers, who, like most agricultural communities, would not have been wholly self-sufficient (Sahlins 1968), might have been particularly dependent on their indigenous neighbours for information concerning local resources, for supplies of things such as 'bush meat' to supplement an essentially vegetarian diet, and for agricultural labour during certain phases in the seasonal cycle when it would have been in short supply.

The indigenous gatherer-hunters, for their part, who already appear to have circulated socially valued objects such as sea-shell ornaments between coastal sources and inland ceremonial sites (see above), might have been willing to accept novel domestic goods in return, such as crops and pottery, not only for use within the domestic sphere, but also to supply their developing systems of exchange and ceremonial. Within the course of a few generations interactions between the two cultural groups might have been stabilised and strengthened by the establishment of more formal exchange relations, such as trade-partnerships or marriages. The likelihood of this would have been increased if, as might have been the case, the coastal gatherer-hunters of east-central Italy (and at Ripoli in particular) had previously developed a degree of social complexity and sedentism. The development of such relations would increasingly have led the lowland gatherer-hunters to be exposed to and drawn into the agricultural way of life of their immigrant neighbours, which they had previously succeeded in avoiding at a distance. Segments of gatherer-hunter society, especially the young, might even have been drawn to emulate the farming way of life. At the same time, socio-economic demands and pressures upon wild resources and upon traditional social structures may have continued to grow within the slightly more sedentary and complex gatherer-hunter communities of the coastal lowlands (cf. Bender 1978), particularly now with interferences in their social and economic life caused by the immigrant agriculturalists. The combined effect, then, of an increased exposure to and involvement in a foreign agricultural economy and society, and of continued local demands for the intensification of food production, may have led to the rapid cultural disintegration of lowland gatherer-hunter societies in east-central Italy and to their regeneration as satellite agricultural communities situated along the edge of the coastal territories acquired by the immigrants.

The social relations between the members of these two cultural groups may initially have been established according to the principles of mutuality and balanced reciprocity. But social differentiation, inequalities, and dependencies may have developed following the adoption of an agricultural way of life by the indigenous groups and the establishment of closer social relations between them, particularly during the second phase of the Early Neolithic. The fall-off in quantities of south Italian inspired pottery, including more complex incised and shell-impressed 'Guadone-style' pottery and red-filled and red painted pottery, at sites located inland and to the north of the coastal lowlands of southeast Abruzzo might reflect this. It might indicate, for example, that the coastal communities of southeast Abruzzo controlled, or at least had greater geographical and social access to, networks of communication, exchange, and kinship which linked east-central Italy to the donor region of southeast Italy. If so, they may have only selectively passed on limited quantities of socially-valued goods, marriage partners, and cultural knowledge to their less well-connected and somewhat dependent neighbours (cf. Lewthwaite's 1985 'filter model'). Differences in economic wealth might also have developed due to the location of the coastal communities on some of the most productive arable land in the region (see Phillips 1987: fig. 2). This early and relatively weak pattern of social, stylistic, and economic dependency and inequality between lowland and inland groups gradually increased during the Neolithic in east-central Italy, within a context of growing social competition between communities. This can be seen most clearly during the late and final stages of the Neolithic (c.4700–3250 cal.BC) with the emergence of outstanding regional centres of settlement, agricultural and pottery production, exchange, and ceremonial in the coastal lowlands of Abruzzo, such as at Ripoli (Skeates 1993).

At an intra-group level, the evidence of mortuary practices performed at five of these sites provides some indication of social relations and strategies within these early Neolithic lowland communities. It is difficult to order these data neatly, for a significant degree of variation is exhibited by the mortuary deposits found at each site. However, for the purposes of this analysis, they can be divided according to two basic types of burial rite (primary and delayed), and into two types of site (open and cave). Relatively simple primary burial rites were performed at three of the sites: Fonterossi, Ripabianca, and the Grotta dei Piccioni (Rellini 1914; 1932; Manzi & Macchiarelli 1989; Corrain & Capitanio 1968; Radmilli *et al.* 1978). At the two open sites, the fairly complete and articulated skeletons of a few adults (one at Fonterossi and four at Ripabianca) were buried in pits, at least sometimes in a flexed position, with few or no associated artefacts. In the cave site, Grotta dei Piccioni, the fairly complete, articulated, and crouched skeleton of a child was placed on the floor of the chamber, apparently without any directly associated deposits of artefacts or animal remains, although a piece of red ochre and a grindstone stained with this mineral were found in the same stratigraphic level. Longer and more elaborate rites of delayed burial and cremation were performed at the other two sites: Villaggio Rossi and Grotta S. Angelo (Geniola & Mallegni 1975; Geniola 1982b; Radmilli 1975). The repeated performance of mortuary rites at these sites is indicated by the existence of numerous, superimposed, stratigraphic units and layers containing human remains in the cavities at Villaggio Rossi, and the digging of one of the group of nine pits into the fill of another in Grotta S. Angelo. A general analogy might be drawn here with the seasonal or 'calendrical' rites repeatedly performed at well-delineated points in the annual productive cycle of certain agricultural societies (Turner 1969). At both sites, groups of disarticulated and mixed human bones, which were frequently broken and sometimes cremated, were deposited in or around these pits or shallow ditches. In the Grotta S. Angelo, the human remains belonged to numerous individuals (at least 12), but although a wide range of body parts was represented only a few bones per individual were deposited in the pits. Feasting may have been associated with the mortuary rites performed at both sites, for hearths and ash lenses were found around the pits, and the pits also contained deposits of ashes, animal bones (belonging predominantly to meat parts of the body at Grotta S. Angelo), plant remains, sherds, and lithic and bone artefacts. Furthermore, those pits in Grotta S. Angelo *with* human remains contained a greater range of artefacts, animal bones, and plant remains than those without. The main difference between the mortuary deposits found at these open and cave sites was, as with the group of sites with primary burials, one of age, with the skull of an old adult aged between 50 and 55 years receiving special treatment at the open site, in contrast to the cave site where the remains of children and juveniles (over 6 individuals aged between 3 and 16 years) and young adults (at least 4 individuals aged between 18 and 20 years) were found predominantly, if not exclusively.

It is now widely accepted that social divisions are not necessarily reflected, directly and unambiguously, in mortuary data, and that mortuary practices often serve to idealise, distort, or invert the reality of social roles and relations (Chapman & Randsborg 1981: 14; Hodder 1982; Bloch 1986). Above all, mortuary data provide evidence of a particular type of social practice in which the living respond to and cope with the death of members of society (Barrett 1988). However, such situations often bring to the fore more fundamental social and cosmological concerns, such as the definition of social positions, cultural categories, and religious beliefs, which may be expressed and discussed through the material symbolism of the mortuary rituals, and with reference to the ancestors and gods. Any explicit interpretations must, of course, be limited, for the 'meaning' of ritual symbolism can be ambiguous, multiple, and variable (Turner 1967; Lewis 1980; Gerholm 1988), but an attempt at interpretation might still be made at a more general, structural, level (e.g. Hodder 1982; Shanks & Tilley 1982; Thomas 1985). Ritual is, for example, concerned with the demarcation of boundaries between elements of the social world, and so the spatial organisation and patterning of people, places, and things in ritual contexts may be used indirectly to draw attention to certain structural classifications and divisions in society, such as divisions based upon age and gender, or between the living and the dead (Turner 1969). Secondary burial rites, in particular, are thought to increase the room for manoeuvre in those aspects of funerary rituals which are concerned with the renewing, re-legitimising, or re-organising of relations between the living (Humphreys 1981a: 268).

To begin with, the intentional deposition of human remains within (rather than away from) settlements in the lowlands (which included not only open sites but also the large lowland cave sites), might suggest that the distinction between the dead and the living (and between the sacred and the profane) was not as great as in our own society, and that, following their death, certain members of society were publicly re-incorporated or resituated, both physically and conceptually, as ancestors within the ongoing daily life of the community. More specifically, at Villaggio Rossi and in Grotta S. Angelo, the living may have expressed a message of group unity and continuity through their recurrent delayed mortuary rites, in reaction to the loss of members of their societies, and with the associated threats of death, infertility, economic misfortune, and social division. The disarticulation, breakage, cremation, and mixing of bones belonging to different people might, for example, be interpreted as an attempt to obliterate all traces of the deceased person as an individual and to emphasise the solidarity of the kinship group, including both the living and the dead – i.e. a collective ancestry (cf. Bloch 1971; Shanks & Tilley 1982: 150–1; Thomas 1985: 553). The association of food remains and feasting with these rites might likewise be interpreted as an attempt to promote and practise co-operation and sharing between members of the group – particularly through the ritualised production, preparation, serving, and sharing of food. Again, the significance of this clearly cuts across our own society's distinction of the economic and the ritual. On another level, these rites, and those performed at the other three sites, may also have referred to certain structural divisions within lowland societies. A distinction appears to have been drawn, for example, between elders and juniors (cf. Ucko 1969: 270–1), through the primary burial rites at open sites which were mainly restricted to adults, and the delayed burial rites in the cave sites which were restricted to children, juveniles, and young adults. Further distinctions could have been drawn between particular adults or elders by according special burial rites to only certain of them, who, perhaps significantly, included older women at Fonterossi and Villaggio Rossi in the Chieti province of Abruzzo.

More speculatively, the transitional or 'liminal' locations of the two cave sites (Grotta dei Piccioni and Grotta S. Angelo), which lie in hidden places on the edge of the mountains and along a number of geographical boundaries, including the edge of the Early Neolithic lowland settlement zone, could have been exploited symbolically in relation to the ritual demarcation of social and cultural boundaries. They appear to have been used, for example, for 'rites of passage or transition', which might not only have included funerary rites, but also the liminal stage of initiation ceremonies involving elders and young initiates, considering their secret locations and the emphasis upon the remains of young people within them (Van Gennep 1909; Turner 1967; 1969; 1977; Whitehouse 1990; 1992; Skeates 1991). The ritual use of these special places might also have contributed to the cultural mapping and organisation of the lowland landscape, particularly with the transition there to agricultural-based patterns of settlement and subsistence – reinforcing the symbolic properties of the geographical boundaries between the mountains and the lowlands, and emphasising the transition from one area to another.

Using these suggestions as a guide-line, it seems worth attempting to paint a brief, but more complete, outline of social relations within Early Neolithic communities in the lowlands of east-central Italy with reference to models of simple agricultural societies developed by social anthropologists. In agricultural societies, which characteristically involve much investment of labour, a systematic division and co-ordination of labour around a calendrical year, and the accumulation of the products of labour, a premium is placed upon the establishment and maintenance of long-lasting, co-operative, relatively fixed, and hierarchical social relations, commitments, and dependencies between individuals, households, groups, and lineages (Tilley 1989). Relations of kinship, which can form extended networks, are an important example, and are closely related to the reproduction of the social group, which involves the reproduction of a definite and restricted set of social relations both within and between relatively bounded and closed social groups, especially through a regulated system of marriage exchanges or alliances. Institutionalised social control and power tend to be held by the elders who emphasise and exploit a principle of anteriority in social relations, which encourages the dependency of 'those who come after' upon 'those who come before'. This can be seen, in particular, in the delayed system of agricultural production, where a hierarchy of dependencies can be built up by the continually renewed sequence of advance and restitution of resources (especially food and seeds) and knowledge between the producers of each successive season (Meillassoux 1972). Similarly, in a mature migrant community some of the earliest migrant kin groups typically emerge as 'apex families' due to their provision of housing and advice to newly arrived kin or friends (Anthony 1990). Social control based upon the principle of anteriority may also be legitimated and extended by its religious and ritual incorporation within a cosmos that is anthropomorphised as an extension of the world of the living, with the wealth and prosperity of the living conceptualised as being controlled by the supernatural spirits which are linked directly through the ancestors to the elders, who act as ritual mediators (Tilley 1989). Through these means, the elders can gain some control in practice over, for example, the supervision and co-ordination of agricultural production, and the organisation of rituals, including initiation ceremonies, funerary feasts, and marriage exchanges, which can in turn enhance their authority over labour and reproduction (Bender 1985b: 24–5). Women may, in particular, be subject to organised aggression and exploitation by men, both for their agricultural and domestic labour (as wives), and for their capacity to reproduce (which is repressed and revered at the same time). It may only be with the loss of their physiological capacity of reproduction, and especially as grandmothers, that they can gain an authority that was denied them as wives or mothers (Meillassoux 1981). (I would not like to assume, however, that local lineages were patrilineal and patrilocal, and therefore that it was groups of men who exchanged women – *contra* Friedman & Rowlands 1977: 207). Juniors are also exploited by the elders for their labour, the immediate product of which they cannot accumulate on their own account; however, age is only a transitional moment in the life of an individual, and so juniors eventually become elders (Meillassoux 1981).

The Inlands

Turning to the interior of the region, which in terms of Neolithic settlement patterns comprised the intermontane valleys, depressions, and basins of Abruzzo and Marche, nine Early Neolithic sites have so far been discovered. They are: Capo d'Acqua, La Valle near Tussio, Madonna del Soccorso, Cellitto near Paterno, Ortucchio, Santo Stefano near Ortucchio, Grotta Continenza near Trasacco, La Maddalena near Muccia, and Campo Sportivo near Pieve Torina.

Continuity of indigenous populations in this part of the region is suggested by the proximity of many of these Early Neolithic sites to Mesolithic ones, by the relatively high proportions of wild animal bones found in their faunal assemblages, and by the composition of some of their lithic assemblages. The strongest evidence of spatial continuity is found at two of the Fucino sites, Ortucchio and Grotta Continenza, where Early Neolithic deposits actually overly those of the Mesolithic, although in Grotta Continenza the two sets of deposits were apparently separated by a sterile, 0.6m deep, layer of clay (Barra *et al.* 1989–90: fig. 1). Elsewhere, slight shifts in site locations seem to have occurred. In the Ofena basin, for example, the Mesolithic and Early Neolithic sites at Capo d'Acqua are separated by just a few hundred metres, and in the Chienti valley the Early Neolithic sites at La Maddalena and Campo Sportivo are located at distances of just 1.4km and 2.75km from the Mesolithic site at Lucciano. Similarly, the Early Neolithic site at Santo Stefano lies just 2km along the Rio di Lecce stream from the Mesolithic site at

Ortucchio. These site patterns could reflect a process of settlement fissioning, and, in the case of La Maddalena and Santo Stefano, a shift on to more cultivable soils with the transition to agriculture. Faunal assemblages likewise show continuity, with relatively high proportions of bones of wild animal species being recorded at Capo d'Acqua (over 50%), Santo Stefano (45%), and La Maddalena (at least 25% – more if some of the 50% pig were wild) (Bonuccelli & Faedo 1968; Radi & Wilkens 1989; Barker 1975: 133; B. Wilkens pers. comm. 1990), compared with Early Neolithic sites in the lowlands which have much lower proportions, as at Villaggio Leopardi (0.5%) and Ripabianca (about 7%) (Cremonesi 1967; Barker 1975: 134; B. Wilkens pers. comm. 1990). Continuity has also been noted between the lithic industries of the two sites at Capo d'Acqua, where both assemblages included small round scrapers, backed blades and points, truncated blades, denticulated pieces, and microburins, as well as retouched flakes and blades (Barker 1981: 54). The lowest Neolithic levels in the Grotta Continenza sequence (spits 24–22) likewise exhibit Mesolithic elements, including relatively high proportions of trapezes and a tendency towards microliths, particularly compared with the overlying Neolithic levels.

The transition to farming in the inner part of the region can be described as a more adaptive process than that which took place in the lowlands. The herding and breeding of domestic stock, for example, was added to (rather than replacing) the existing range of faunal-based subsistence strategies which included hunting, fowling, and fishing. This can be seen, in particular, at the relatively well-studied sites of Santo Stefano and Grotta Continenza where the remains of a wide range of faunal species were found, including wild species obtained from in and around the Fucino lake basin (Radi & Wilkens 1989: 112–15; Wilkens 1989–90: 93–4). Furthermore, the proportions of the bones of the three main domesticates found on inland sites appear to reflect adaptations to local environmental conditions. The high proportion of sheep/goat bones at Santo Stefano (71% of all domestic animal bones), for example, probably suited relatively open woodland conditions in the Fucino basin (as in the lowlands, where relatively high proportions of sheep/goat bones were also found); whereas the high proportion of pig bones found at La Maddalena (up to 68% of all domestic animal bones) probably suited a more densely forested environment along the upper Chienti valley.

However, the transition to the Neolithic in this part of the region does not appear to have been a particularly selective process, for the available evidence suggests that, as in the lowlands, neolithic innovations were still adopted here as an integrated package. There is no evidence to suggest, for example, that pottery and caprines were adopted here (or in the lowlands) in advance of cereals (*contra* Lewthwaite 1986; cf. Chapman & Müller 1990: 132). The question of cereals is tricky, because, on the one hand, they have not yet been found on any of the inland sites in the Abruzzo-Marche region (a point emphasised by Barker 1976: 69), but on the other hand they have not been seriously looked for (except at La Maddalena where traces of somewhat ambiguous 'straw' were identified in plaster fragments – Evett & Renfrew 1971). My own opinion is that cereals were cultivated at most early Neolithic inland sites in the region (Skeates 1992: 206), and particularly at Cellitto and Santo Stefano which are located on potentially cultivable soils on the raised sides of the Fucino lake basin. This view now seems to be confirmed by the excavations at the Early Neolithic site at San Marco in the Gubbio basin, which lies even further inland in the region of Umbria, where a large sample of plant remains was intentionally recovered (in addition to Abruzzo-Marche style impressed and incised ware). The results show that a wide range of cereals and legumes were cultivated around the settlement, which lay on the lower part of an alluvial fan, on soils prone to flooding; and that edible fruits and nuts were collected as a supplement from the surrounding marshes and forests (Hunt *et al.* 1990; Malone & Stoddart 1992). This ties in with the pattern identified in northern Italy, where crops appear to have been initially cultivated on water-retentive soils surrounding the earliest Neolithic settlements, which were located on alluvial fans, fluvial terraces, and the shores of intermorainic lakes (Biagi *et al.* 1985; also see Sherratt's (1980) 'ground-water model' of European Neolithic horticulture).

Material elements of the Neolithic agricultural package, including domesticated animals and crops, the locally produced Abruzzo-Marche style of incised and impressed ware (fig. 2.6), and a few imports such as vessels of Guadone-style impressed ware and simple red painted ware (in inland Abruzzo), imported sea shells, small greenstone axes, and pieces of obsidian, were initially obtained by these indigenous inland groups from Early Neolithic communities settled in the lowlands of Abruzzo and Marche, and, to a lesser extent, from Early Neolithic groups in west-central Italy. More specifically, however, they could have been obtained from indigenous groups situated in the inner lowlands of southeast Abruzzo and in the lowlands of northern Abruzzo and Marche (who can be distinguished by their use of the simple Abruzzo-Marche style of impressed and incised ware – see above). They may, therefore, have spread inland via previously established networks of communication, gift-exchange, and kinship which linked lowland and inland groups of gatherer-hunters. Slight confirmation of this suggestion is provided by the sourcing of obsidian found at Villaggio Rossi, which might be regarded as the site of an indigenous lowland group (see above), to the island of Palmarola, which is situated off the west coast of central Italy (Bigazzi *et al.* 1992). This obsidian is likely to have been transported overland, across the Apennines from west-central Italy, via a network of indigenous obsidian-using Early Neolithic groups, which in Abruzzo included those based at sites in the Fucino basin (i.e. Ortucchio, Grotta Continenza, Cellitto, and especially at Santo Stefano where obsidian comprised 7.6% of the total quantity of lithic artefacts), in the Castelnuovo-Navelli depression (La Valle), and in the inner lowlands (Grotta S. Angelo and Grotta dei Piccioni).

The 'Neolithic package' appears to have spread quite rapidly to a few of these sites from the lowlands. The site at La Maddalena, for example, which lies some 60km inland from the Adriatic coast, has a radiocarbon date of c.5640–5340 (1 sigma) cal.BC (Alessio *et al.* 1970) that ties in closely with the earliest radiocarbon measurements for the Early Neolithic in the lowlands of Abruzzo which cluster around a date of about 5500 cal.BC (Skeates 1994b). However, the majority of these sites can probably be assigned to a second phase of the Early Neolithic, according to typological criteria (e.g. the presence of red painted sherds at Capo d'Acqua and Cellitto, which only appear in the upper strata of the Early Neolithic stratigraphic sequence in the Grotta dei Piccioni). This suggests that, in general, the transition to an agricultural way of life by indigenous groups based in interior parts of the region was a relatively slow and gradual process.

As an integrated package, the Neolithic set of conceptually linked material resources, techniques, and social relations appears to have been accepted, adopted, and incorporated by inland groups of gatherer-hunters, such as those in the Fucino basin, both as a significant addition to their increasingly broad-based and specialised subsistence strategies and increasingly sedentary settlement patterns, and in the form of socially valued, novel, and exotic goods and knowledge. Both as goods and knowledge it could have been used, both practically and symbolically, to service more numerous and elaborate ceremonial occasions and ritual performances, which served a growing, increasingly sedentary, and more socially complex indigenous population. As in the lowlands, an intermingling of the sacred and secular can be seen through the use of some generally plain, domestic, pottery storage vessels as cremation urns and the use of domestic sheep as ritual sacrifices in the mortuary rites in Grotta Continenza.

In Grotta Continenza, human remains have been found throughout the Early Neolithic levels (spits 24–4) in the inner part of the first chamber, and in the second, inner, chamber (Grifoni Cremonesi & Mallegni 1978; Grifoni Cremonesi 1984; 1985; Barra *et al.* 1989–90). These mortuary deposits exhibit a number of general similarities to those found at Early Neolithic sites in the lowlands, and particularly in Grotta S. Angelo. These include: the repeated performance of mortuary rites; the performance of secondary burial rites involving the disarticulation, fragmentation, and cremation of human remains; the deposition of human remains towards the back of the cave; the presence of the remains of infants, children, and juveniles; the construction of pits, shallow ditches, and stone features as part of the ritual deposits; the deposition of broken pottery vessels and animal remains; and the ritual use of red ochre. However, a number of significant differences also exist, particularly in relation to the lowland ritual cave sites. The remains of more individuals were found in Grotta Continenza (36), and these included the bones of adults as well as young people, in fairly equal numbers. The remains of individuals were generally kept relatively separate from each other, even when cremated, except perhaps in the pile of stones and in the lowest level (spit 24) where numerous fragmented human bones may have been mixed together. Relatively few artefacts and faunal remains were deposited there; and the latter are distinguished by belonging exclusively to domestic species and by their articulation, which is more suggestive of sacrifice than feasting. In general, Grotta Continenza seems to have served a local population as a relatively straight-forward burial cave and monument to the dead and to the continuing group, in contrast to the lowland caves which appear to have been used for the performance of a greater variety of more elaborate rituals and also as residential sites.

On one level, these distinctions seem to reflect differences between the types of caves being used and their locations in relation to contemporary settlement zones. Grotta Continenza is significantly smaller than either Grotta dei Piccioni or Grotta S. Angelo, both in terms of its surface area (Grotta Continenza covers an area of about 162m², whereas Grotta dei Piccioni extends over an area of 260m²) and, in particular, its height (Grotta Continenza has a maximum height of about 8m, whereas Grotta dei Piccioni has a minimum height of about 13m), in addition to which numerous stalactites hang down from its ceiling, which must have seriously restricted the degree of group size, personal movement, and ritual elaboration within it. The Continenza cave also appears to have been located slightly closer to, and in a slightly less hidden and more easily accessible position in relation to, its associated Neolithic settlement zone, which comprised the floor of the Fucino basin, above which it lies by about 50m.

The distinctions seen in the ritual use of this inland cave site and the lowland ones might also reflect differences between Early Neolithic groups living in the Fucino basin and in the lowlands of east-central Italy, in terms of their history, culture, and social structure, and above all in the way in which they perceived and acted upon the set of concepts surrounding the 'Neolithic package'. Local continuity in ritual tradition is suggested, for example, by the repeated use of Grotta Continenza as a burial place during the Upper Palaeolithic, Mesolithic, and Early Neolithic, particularly when contrasted with the lowland Grotta dei Piccioni, which was newly established as a residential and burial site during the Early Neolithic. A slight cultural difference is also indicated by the presence of an incised pottery flask with horizontal strap handles in Grotta Continenza, for which the closest parallels are found in contemporary deposits in Grotta dell'Orso in Tuscany (Grifoni Cremonesi & Mallegni 1978: figs. 2.2 and 3.3; Grifoni 1967: fig. 10.7), although the majority of pottery found in Grotta Continenza conforms to the Abruzzo-Marche style of impressed and incised ware. More specifically, relatively simple and traditional religious and social messages may have been expressed through the mortuary rites performed in Grotta Continenza, in contrast to rites performed in the lowlands, which seem to hint at a concern with structural divisions in society. Appeals to 'the Other World' are indicated not only by the use of a cave (whose natural properties, including its stalactites, might have been incorporated into the symbolism of the rituals – Skeates 1991: 127), but more specifically by the deposition of whole animals, which, as sacrificial offerings, might have been left in the hope of receiving reciprocal benefits (Leach 1976). An attempt to overcome the death of children, particularly within a context of high infant and child mortality and health stresses (Robb 1994), might have been made through the transformation of their decaying remains into stable ashes via cremation, and their permanent storage in solid pottery vessels (Humphreys 1981b). A general message of group unity, continuity, and identity may also have been expressed through the deposition of the remains of a relatively large and representative sample of the whole society, and through the disarticulation and breakage of their bones. However, the continued acceptance and maintenance of traditional, gatherer-hunter, individuality is perhaps indicated by the separate deposition of the remains of individuals and by their less intentional mixing and rearrangement. A relatively low degree of social inequality may therefore have been maintained within and between such inland communities, through the continued functioning of traditional belief systems and wealth levelling mechanisms, and due to the existence of indigenous groups in the lowlands which acted as a filter and buffer between these inland communities and the socially complex Neolithic societies of the coastal lowlands, and due to the relatively low returns obtained from limited, small-scale, farming on less productive agricultural soils in this area (cf. McGuire & Netting 1982).

SUMMARY AND CONCLUSIONS

For the Mesolithic (c.7500–5500 cal.BC), social relations within and between gatherer-hunter groups seem to have remained basically egalitarian. Potential social inequalities would generally have been ironed out by factors including the continued residential mobility and social fluidity of individuals and groups, and the dominance of a system of immediate-returns in subsistence practices, which acted as social levelling mechanisms. A slight degree of social differentiation, involving in particular the emergence of more permanent institutionalised leadership, may, however, have developed within the ceremonial context of occasional rituals and long-distance exchanges performed by increasingly permanent, non-storing, sedentary groups in the Fucino lake basin, where abundant wild food resources could be relied upon throughout most of the year.

For the second half of the Mesolithic (c.6500–5500 cal.BC), the northward spread, along the western coast of the Adriatic Sea, of the 'neolithic package' was held up along the northern edge of the Tavoliere plain. The establishment of this static closed frontier cannot only be understood in terms of ecological boundaries, agricultural frontiers, and the 'success and stability' of gatherer-hunter subsistence strategies, but might also be regarded as part of a deliberate social and economic strategy of mutual avoidance followed by gatherer-hunters and agriculturalists in order to maintain peaceful relations between these two (as yet) culturally and structurally incompatible groups.

The eventual transition to the Early Neolithic (c.5500–4850 cal.BC) took place gradually on at least three different geographical levels.

In the coastal lowlands of southeast Abruzzo, small, kin-based, groups of immigrant agriculturalists from the densely populated northern half of the Tavoliere plain seem to have established colonies at sites well-chosen to suit to their pre-existing southeast Italian system of agriculture. This migration process led to the development of an important communications route along the Adriatic coast, which connected the colonists to their relatives in the homeland, and along which new goods, personnel, and information continued to flow northwards throughout the Neolithic. This appears to have led to establishment of a long-term economic and cultural dependency of groups in Abruzzo upon those in southeast Italy.

In the inner lowlands of southern Abruzzo, indigenous groups now rapidly adopted the 'Neolithic package' of conceptually linked agricultural resources and social relations. The combined effect of symbiotic exchanges with the agriculturalists, with whom they were now brought into much closer contact (both spatially by the arrival of the farmers in their coastal territories, and socially by the reciprocal nature of their exchanges which established increasingly binding relations between members of the two groups), and of growing socio-economic demands and pressures upon wild resources and upon traditional social structures, contributed to the rapid cultural disintegration of indigenous groups in the lowlands, and to their regeneration as satellite agricultural communities along the borders of the newly established colonies.

Social inequalities and dependencies may have developed between these two groups of agriculturalists in the lowlands, particularly with the establishment of closer social relations between them, with the immigrant coastal communities maintaining greater geographical and social access to socially-valued novel goods and information supplied by their southeast Italian homeland, and enjoying territorial rights over some of the most productive arable land in the region. Within these lowland communities, mortuary practices seem to have referred to, and indeed may actively have attempted to promote beliefs in: the influential role of the Other World, and of the ancestors in particular, in the ongoing daily life of the agricultural community; the need for co-operation and solidarity within the kinship group in order to ensure its continuity and survival; and the legitimacy of social distinctions between members of the group, especially between elders and juniors.

In the inlands of Abruzzo and Marche, indigenous groups of gather-hunters would have obtained the integrated 'Neolithic package' from the newly converted indigenous groups of the inner lowlands via pre-existing long-distance lines of communication and kinship. The process of transition to the Neolithic was, in general, a more gradual and adaptive one, compared with that which occurred in the lowlands, in which Neolithic goods, practices, and concepts were incorporated within: an increasingly broad-based and specialised range of substinance strategies; an increasingly sedentary pattern of settlement; an increasingly frequent and elaborate ceremonial system; and an increasingly complex social structure. Mortuary rites performed at Grotta Continenza exhibit a number of general similarities to those seen at Early Neolithic sites in the lowlands, but the differences suggest that indigenous groups in the Fucino basin retained more of their traditional culture and identity, including a more egalitarian social formation, due to their lack of direct contact with the immigrant agriculturalists, and due to the more densely forested and less productive nature of the vegetation and arable soils in their territories.

It is in the light of these developments that we must view the significant expansion in social competition, inequality, and differentiation which took place during the later stages of the Neolithic (c.5350–4200 cal.BC).

APPENDIX: MESOLITHIC AND EARLY NEOLITHIC SITES IN THE ABRUZZO-MARCHE REGION

CHIETI province

1. Colle Sinello, Vasto – surface finds from Early Neolithic open site (Ducci et al. 1986–87: 107; D'Ercole 1987–8: 406).
2. Crocefisso, Tricalle, Chieti – Early Neolithic open site (Agostini 1986–87a; 1986–87b; Ducci et al. 1986–87; Ducci & Perazzi 1987).
3. Fonterossi, Lama dei Peligni – Early Neolithic open site (Pigorini 1896; Dall'Osso 1910: 394–5; 1915: 17–18; Rellini 1914; 1932; Barker 1975: 160; Radmilli 1981: 273–4, 284–5, 380; Manzi & Macchiarelli 1989; Geniola 1989–90; Hedges et al. 1990: 212).
4. Villaggio Rossi, Marcianese, Lanciano – Early Neolithic open site (Geniola 1975; Geniola & Mallegni 1975; Geniola 1982a; 1982b; Ronchitelli & Sarti 1982; Radmilli 1981: 337, 381; Ambers et al. 1987; Bowman et al. 1990).

PESCARA province

5. Colle Maggio, Penne – surface finds from Early Neolithic open site (M. Costantini pers. comm. 1988).
6. Fontanelle, Pescara – Early Neolithic open site (Giove Ruggeri 1978: 438; Agostini 1986–87a; Ducci et al. 1986–87; Ducci & Perazzi 1987).
7. Grotta dei Piccioni, Bolognano – Early Neolithic cave site (Ferrara et al. 1961; Barker 1975; Cremonesi 1976; Radmilli et al. 1978).
8. Villaggio Leopardi, Pluviano, Penne – Early Neolithic open site (Radmilli 1959: 888; Ferrara et al. 1961; Cremonesi 1967; Evett & Renfrew 1971; Barker 1975; Radmilli 1981: 277–80).

L'AQUILA province

9. <u>Campo di Giove</u> – surface finds from Mesolithic open site (Radmilli 1981: 244).
10. <u>Capo d'Acqua, Capestrano</u> – Mesolithic and Early Neolithic open sites (Tozzi 1966; Bonuccelli & Faedo 1968; Barker 1975; Radmilli 1981).
11. <u>Cellitto, Paterno</u> – Early Neolithic open site (Di Fraia 1971; Barker 1975; Cremonesi 1985; Grifoni Cremonesi 1985: 721–2; 1988: 23).
12. <u>Grotta Continenza, Trasacco</u> – Mesolithic-Early Neolithic cave site (Grifoni Cremonesi & Mallegni 1978; Grifoni Cremonesi 1984; 1985; 1987–88: 377, 1988; Barra *et al.* 1989–90).
13. <u>La Valle, Tussio</u> – Early Neolithic open site (Mattiocco 1986: 31–7).
14. <u>Madonna del Soccorso, Castel d'Ieri</u> – Early Neolithic open site (D'Ercole 1987–88: 406).
15. <u>Ortucchio</u> – Mesolithic-Early Neolithic open site (Cremonesi 1962; Radmilli 1981: 237–40; Cremonesi 1985).
16. <u>Santo Stefano, Ortucchio</u> – Early Neolithic open site (Radi 1987–8: 407–8; Radi & Wilkens 1989).

TERAMO province

17. <u>Colle S. Savino, Nereto</u> – ? Early Neolithic open site (D'Ercole 1988: 2).
18. <u>Grotta S. Angelo, Le Ripe</u> – Early Neolithic cave site (Cremonesi *et al.* 1965; Radmilli 1965: 375; Grifoni 1966: 160–1; Radmilli 1967a: 446; Radmilli 1968: 416; Barker 1975; Radmilli 1975; Sorrentino 1978; Radmilli 1981: 276, 287, 303, 383).
19. <u>Ripoli, Tortoreto</u> – Mesolithic open site (Radmilli & Cremonesi 1963; Barker 1975).

MACERATA province

20. <u>Campo Sportivo, Pieve Torina</u> – Early Neolithic open site (Lollini 1979: 67; Barker 1975).
21. <u>La Maddalena, Muccia</u> – Early Neolithic open site (Lollini 1965; Corrain & Capitanio 1968; Alessio *et al.* 1970; Evett & Renfrew 1971; Evett 1973; Barker 1975; 1981; Lollini 1979; Wilkens 1989: 4).
22. <u>Lucciano, Pieve Torina</u> – Mesolithic open site (Lollini 1970: 422; Barker 1975; Lollini 1979: 47–8).

ANCONA province

23. <u>Cava Romita, Falcioni</u> – Mesolithic cave site (Broglio & Lollini 1981: 27).
24. <u>Grotta del Prete, Frasassi</u> – Mesolithic cave site (Lollini 1964; 1970; Broglio & Lollini 1981; Bisi *et al.* 1983).
25. <u>Monte Cappone, Jesi</u> – Early Neolithic open site (Lollini 1977).
26. <u>Monte Colombo, Numana</u> – Early Neolithic open site (Dall'Osso 1915: 15–17; Rellini 1931).
27. <u>Ripabianca, Monterado</u> – Early Neolithic open site (De Sanctis 1961; Broglio & Lollini 1963; Lollini 1964: 307; 1965; Corrain & Capitanio 1968; Alessio *et al.* 1970; Evett & Renfrew 1971; Evett 1973; Barker 1975).

BIBLIOGRAPHY

Agostini, S. 1986–87a.   Considerazioni geomorphologiche sui siti di Tricalle (CH) e di Fontanelle (PE). In Ducci, C., Perazzi, P. & Ronchitelli, A. (eds), Gli insediamenti neolitici Abruzzesi con Ceramica Impressa di Tricalle (CH) e Fontanelle (PE). *Rassegna di Archeologia*, 6: 116–22.

Agostini, S. 1986–87b.   Osservazioni petrografiche sulle ceramiche di Tricalle (CH). In Ducci, C., Perazzi, P. & Ronchitelli, A. (eds), Gli insediamenti neolitici Abruzzesi con Ceramica Impressa di Tricalle (CH) e Fontanelle (PE). *Rassegna di Archeologia*, 6: 123–5.

Alessio, M., Bella, F., Improta, S., Belluomini, G., Cortesi, C. & Turi, B. 1970.   University of Rome carbon-14 dates VIII. *Radiocarbon*, 12: 599–616.

Alessio, M., Bella, F., Improta, S., Belluomini, G., Calderoni, G., Cortesi, C. & Turi, B. 1976.   University of Rome carbon-14 dates XIV. *Radiocarbon*, 18: 321–49.

Alexander, J. 1977.   The 'frontier' concept in prehistory: the end of the moving frontier. In Megaw, J.V.S. (ed.), *Hunters, Gatherers and the First Farmers Beyond Europe. An Archaeological Survey*: 25–40. Leicester University Press, Leicester.

Alexander, J. 1978.   Frontier studies and the earliest farmers in Europe. In Green, D., Haselgrove, C. & Spriggs, M. (eds), *Social Organisation and Settlement: Contributions from Anthropology, Archaeology and Geography*: 13–30. BAR International Series 47 (i). British Archaeological Reports, Oxford.

Ambers, J., Burleigh, R. & Matthews, K. 1987.   British Museum natural radiocarbon measurements XIX. *Radiocarbon*, 29: 61–77.

Ammerman, A.J. & Cavalli Sforza, L.L. 1984.   *The Neolithic Transition and the Genetics of Population in Europe*. Princeton University Press, Princeton.

Anthony, D.W. 1990.   Migration and archeology: the baby and the bathwater. *American Anthropologist*, 92: 895–914.

Bagolini, B. 1980. *Introduzione al Neolitico dell'Italia Settentrionale*. Società Naturalisti "Silvia Zenari", Pordenone.

Barfield, L.H. 1981. Patterns of north Italian trade 5000–2000 B.C. In Barker, G. & Hodges, R. (eds), *Archaeology and Italian Society. Prehistoric, Roman and Medieval Studies*: 215–23. BAR International Series 102. British Archaeological Reports, Oxford.

Barker, G. 1973. *Prehistoric economies and cultures in central Italy*. Unpublished Ph. D. thesis, St John's College, Cambridge.

Barker, G. 1975. Prehistoric territories and economies in central Italy. In Higgs, E.S. (ed.), *Palaeoeconomy*: 111–75. Cambridge University Press, Cambridge.

Barker, G. 1976. Economic archaeology, neolithic studies and the early history of agriculture: central Italy east of the Apennines. *Bollettino del Centro Camuno di Studi Preistorici*, 13–14: 65–76.

Barker, G. 1981. *Landscape and Society. Prehistoric Central Italy*. Academic Press, London.

Barker, G. 1985. *Prehistoric Farming in Europe*. Cambridge University Press, Cambridge.

Barker, G. & Malone, C. 1992. Conclusions: the Neolithic of central Italy. In Malone, C. & Stoddart, S. (eds), The Neolithic site of San Marco, Gubbio (Perugia), Umbria: survey and excavation 1985–7. *Papers of the British School at Rome*, 60: 59–63.

Barnett, W.K. 1990. Small-scale transport of early Neolithic pottery in the west Mediterranean. *Antiquity*, 64: 859–65.

Barra, A., Grifoni Cremonesi, R., Mallegni, F., Piancastelli, M., Vitiello, A. & Wilkens, B. 1989–90. La Grotta Continenza di Trasacco. I livelli a ceramiche. *Rivista di Scienze Preistoriche*, 42: 32–100.

Barrett, J.C. 1988. The living, the dead and the ancestors: Neolithic and Early Bronze Age mortuary practices. In Barrett, J.C. & Kinnes, I.A. (eds), *The Archaeology of Context in the Neolithic and Bronze Age. Recent Trends*: 30–41. Department of Archaeology and Prehistory, University of Sheffield, Sheffield.

Bender, B. 1978. Gatherer-hunter to farmer: a social perspective. *World Archaeology*, 10: 204–22.

Bender, B. 1981. Gatherer-hunter intensification. In Sheridan, A. & Bailey, G. (eds), *Economic Archaeology. Towards an Integration of Ecological and Social Approaches*: 149–57. BAR International Series 96. British Archaeological Reports, Oxford.

Bender, B. 1985a. Emergent tribal formations in the American midcontinent. *American Antiquity*, 50: 52–62.

Bender, B. 1985b. The fallacy of "Hot" and "Cold" societies: a comparison of prehistoric developments in the American Midcontinent and Brittany, northwest France. In Price, D. & Brown, J. (eds), *Complexity Among Hunter-Gatherers*: 21–57. Academic Press, London.

Bender, B. 1990. The dynamics of nonhierarchical societies. In Upham, S. (ed.), *The evolution of political systems: sociopolitics in small-scale sedentary societies*: 247–65. Cambridge University Press, Cambridge.

Biagi, P., Cremaschi, M. & Nisbet, R. 1985. Palaeoecological implications for the later prehistory of northern Italy. In Malone, C. & Stoddart, S. (eds), *Papers in Italian Archaeology IV. The Cambridge Conference. Part ii. Prehistory*: 243–72. BAR International Series 244. British Archaeological Reports, Oxford.

Bigazzi, G., Meloni, S., Oddone, M. & Radi, G. 1992. Nuovi dati sulla diffusione dell'ossidiana negli insediamenti preistorici italiani. In Herring, E., Whitehouse, R. & Wilkins, J. (eds), *Papers of the Fourth Conference of Italian Archaeology 3. New developments in Italian Archaeology, part 1*: 9–18. Accordia Research Centre, London.

Bisi, F., Broglio, A., Guerreschi, A. & Radmilli, A.M. 1983. L'Épigravettien évolué et final dans la zone haute et moyenne Adriatique. *Rivista di Scienze Preistoriche*, 38: 244–65.

Bloch, M. 1971. *Placing the Dead*. Seminar Press, London.

Bloch, M. 1986. *From Blessing to Violence. History and Ideology in the Circumcision Ritual of the Merina of Madagascar*. Cambridge University Press, Cambridge.

Bonatti, E. 1966. North Mediterranean climate during the last Würm glaciation. *Nature*, 209: 984–5.

Bonatti, E. 1970. Pollen sequence in the sediments. In Hutchinson, G.E. (ed.), Ianula: an account of the history and development of the Lago di Monterosi, Latium, Italy. *Transactions of the American Philosophical Society*, 60, part 4: 26–31.

Bonuccelli, G. & Faedo, L. 1968. Il villaggio a Ceramica Impressa di Capo d'Acqua. *Atti della Società Toscana di Scienze Naturali*, 75: 87–101.

Bowman, S.G.E., Ambers, J.C. & Leese, M.N. 1990. Re-evaluation of British Museum radiocarbon dates issued between 1980 and 1984. *Radiocarbon*, 32: 59–79.

Braudel, F. 1972. *The Mediterranean and the Mediterranean in the Age of Philip II. Volume I*. Fontana Press, London.

Broglio, A. & Lollini, D.G. 1963. Nuova varietà di bulino su ritocco a stacco laterale nella industria del neolitico medio di Ripabianca di Monterado (Ancona). *Annali dell'Università di Ferrara*, 1: 143–55.

Broglio, A. & Lollini, D.G. 1981. I ritrovamenti Marchigiani del Paleolitico Superiore e del Mesolitico. In *Atti del I convegno sui beni culturali ed ambientali delle Marche. Numana. 8–10 maggio 1981*: 27–59. Paleani, Roma.

Camps, G. 1976. Navigations et relations interméditerranées préhistoriques. *Colloque II. Prétirage*: 168–78.

Cardini, L. 1969. Lo scavo del Peschio Ranaro a Colleparto (Frosinone). *Quaternaria*, 11: 284.

Cassano, S.M. 1985. Considerazioni sugli inizi dell'economia produttiva sulle sponde dell'Adriatico. In Liverani, M., Palmieri, A. & Peroni, R. (eds), *Studi di paletnologia in onore di Salvatore M. Puglisi*: 731–43. Dipartimento di Scienze Storiche, Archeologiche e Antropologiche dell'Antichità, Università di Roma "La Sapienza", Roma.

Chapman, J.C. 1988. Ceramic production and social differentiation: the Dalmatian Neolithic and the western Mediterranean. *Journal of Mediterranean Archaeology*, 1: 3–25.

Chapman, J.C. 1989. Demographic trends in neothermal southeast Europe. In Bonsall, C. (ed.), *The Mesolithic in Europe. Papers presented at the Third International Symposium. Edinburgh, 1985*: 500–15. Donald, Edinburgh.

Chapman, J.C. & Müller, J. 1990. Early farmers in the Mediterranean basin: the Dalmatian evidence. *Antiquity*, 64: 127–34.

Chapman, R. & Randsborg, K. 1981. Approaches to the archaeology of death. In Chapman, R., Kinnes I. & Randsborg, K. (eds), *The Archaeology of Death*: 1–24. Cambridge University Press, Cambridge.

Cipolloni Sampò, M. 1977–82. Scavi nel villaggio neolitico di Rendina (1970–1976). Relazione preliminare. *Origini*, 11: 183–323.

Cohen, M.N. 1985. Prehistoric hunter-gatherers: the meaning of social complexity. In Price, T.D. & Brown, J.A. (eds), *Prehistoric Hunter-Gatherers. The Emergence of Cultural Complexity*: 99–119. Academic Press, London.

Corrain, C. & Capitanio, M. 1968. I resti scheletrici umani di Maddalena di Muccia e di Ripabianca di Monterado, nelle Marche. *Rivista di Scienze Preistoriche*, 23: 223–44.

Cremonesi, G. 1962. I resti degli ultimi mesolitici del Fucino. *Atti della Società Toscana di Scienze Naturali*, 69: 1–10.

Cremonesi, G. 1965. Il villaggio di Ripoli alla luce dei recenti scavi. *Rivista di Scienze Preistoriche*, 20: 85–155.

Cremonesi, G. 1967. Il villaggio Leopardi presso Penne in Abruzzo. *Bullettino di Paletnologia Italiana*, 18: 27–49.

Cremonesi, G. 1973. Il villaggio neolitico di Fossacesia (Chieti). Nota preliminare. *Bollettino del Centro Camuno di Studi Preistorici*, 10: 79–88.

Cremonesi, G. 1976. *La Grotta dei Piccioni di Bolognano nel quadro delle culture dal Neolitico all'Età del Bronzo in Abruzzo*. Giardini, Pisa.

Cremonesi, G. 1985. Note su nuovi insediamenti dell'Età dei Metalli nella piana del Fucino. In Liverani, M., Palmieri, A. & Peroni, R. (eds), *Studi di paletnologia in onore di Salvatore M. Puglisi*: 791–804. Dipartimento di Scienze Storiche, Archeologiche e Antropologiche dell'Antichità, Università di Roma "La Sapienza", Roma.

Cremonesi, G. & Tozzi, C. 1987. Il Neolitico dell'Abruzzo. In *Atti della XXVI riunione scientifica dell'Istituto Italiano di Preistoria e Protostoria. Il Neolitico in Italia*: 239–51. Istituto Italiano di Preistoria e Protostoria, Firenze.

Cremonesi, G., Occhiolini, C. & Bertolucci, P. 1965. Ricerche preistoriche in Abruzzo – anno 1964. *Atti della Società Toscana di Scienze Naturali*, 72: 508–14.

Dall'Osso, I. 1910. Alla scoperta dell'Abruzzo preistorico. *Rivista Abruzzese*, 1910: 369–404.

Dall'Osso, I. 1915. *Guida illustrata del Museo Nazionale di Ancona*. Museo Nazionale di Ancona, Ancona.

Delano Smith, C. 1979. *Western Mediterranean Europe. A Historical Geography of Italy, Spain and Southern France Since the Neolithic*. Academic Press, London.

Dennell, R. 1983. *European Economic Prehistory*. Academic Press, London.

D'Ercole, V. 1987–88. Notiziario. Abruzzo. *Rivista di Scienze Preistoriche*, 41: 405–7.

D'Ercole, V. 1988. L'Abruzzo dalle comunità di villaggio alle società urbane. Unpublished paper.

De Sanctis, L. 1961. Il Neolitico a Ceramica Impressa nella valle del fiume Cesano. *Rivista di Scienze Preistoriche*, 16: 243–6.

Di Fraia, T. 1971. Tracce di uno stanziamento neolitico all'aperto presso Paterno (L'Aquila). *Atti della Società Toscana di Scienze Naturali*, 77: 289–307.

Donahue, R.E. 1992. Desperately seeking ceres: a critical examination of current models for the transition to agriculture in Mediterranean Europe. In Gebauer, A.B. & Price, T.D. (eds), *Transitions to Agriculture in Prehistory*: 73–80. Prehistory Press, Madison.

Ducci, S., Perazzi, P. & Ronchitelli, A. 1986–87. Gli insediamenti neolitici Abruzzesi con Ceramica Impressa di Tricalle (CH) e Fontanelle (PE). *Rassegna di Archeologia*, 1986–87: 65–128.

Ducci, S. & Perazzi, P. 1987. Tricalle (CH), Fontanelle (PE): nuovi aspetti del Neolitico Abruzzese a Ceramica Impressa. *Atti della XXVI riunione scientifica dell'Istituto Italiano di Preistoria e Protostoria. Il Neolitico in Italia*: 645–54. Istituto Italiano di Preistoria e Protostoria, Firenze.

Eisner, W., Kamermans, H. & Wymstra, A.T. 1984. The Agro Pontino survey: results from a first pollen core. *Dialoghi di Archeologia*, 4: 145–53.

Evett, D. 1973. A preliminary note on the typology, functional variability, and trade of Italian neolithic ground stone axes. *Origini*, 7: 35–54.

Evett, D. & Renfrew, J.M. 1971. L'agricultura neolitica italiana: una nota sui cereali. *Rivista di Scienze Preistoriche*, 26: 403–9.

Ferrara, G., Fornaca-Rinaldi, G. & Tongiorgi, E. 1961. Carbon-14 dating in Pisa-II. *Radiocarbon*, 3: 99–104.

Frank, A.H.E. 1969. Pollen stratigraphy of the lake of Vico (central Italy). *Palaeogeography, Palaeoclimatology, Palaeoecology*, 6: 67–85.

Friedman, J. & Rowlands, M.J. 1977. Notes towards an epigenetic model of the evolution of 'civilisation'. In Friedman, J. & Rowlands, M.J. (eds), *The Evolution of Social Systems*: 201–76. Duckworth, London.

Geniola, A. 1975. Il villaggio neolitico di Marcianese presso Lanciano (Chieti). *Civiltà preistorica e protostorica della Daunia. Atti del colloquio internazionale di preistoria e protostoria della Daunia, Foggia, 24–29 aprile, 1973*: 143–4.

Geniola, A. 1982a. Considerazioni conclusive sullo scavo archeologico dell'insediamento neolitico di Marcianese. *Atti 2 convegno sulla preistoria-protostoria-storia della Daunia. San Severo, 28–29–30 novembre, 1980*: 59–67.

Geniola, A. 1982b. *Marcianese. Il villaggio Rossi. Entità del neolitico medio arcaico Abruzzese*. Itinerari, Lanciano.

Geniola, A. 1989–90. Fonterossi (Lama dei Peligni, Prov. di Chieti). *Rivista di Scienze Preistoriche*, 42: 380–1.

Geniola, A. & Mallegni, F. 1975.   Il calvario neolitico di Lanciano (Chieti): note paletnologiche e studio antropologico. *Atti della Società Toscana di Scienze Naturali,* 82: 237–54.

Gerholm, T. 1988.   On ritual: a postmodernist view. *Ethnos,* 53: 190–203.

Giove Ruggeri, M. 1978.   Notiziario. Abruzzo. *Rivista di Scienze Preistoriche,* 33: 438.

Graziosi, P. 1973.   *L'arte preistorica in Italia.* Sansoni, Firenze.

Grifoni, R. 1966.   Esplorazione paletnologiche in Abruzzo – anno 1965. *Atti della Società Toscana di Scienze Preistoriche,* 73: 157–61.

Grifoni, R. 1967.   La Grotta dell'Orso di Sarteano. *Origini,* 1: 53–116.

Grifoni Cremonesi, R. 1984.   Alcuni dati relativi a fenomeni funerari con implicazioni cultuali nella preistoria e problemi di interpretazione. *Dialoghi di Archeologia,* 4: 265–9.

Grifoni Cremonesi, R. 1985.   Nuovi dati sul Mesolitico e sul Neolitico nella piana del Fucino. In Liverani, M., Palmieri, A. & Peroni, R. (eds), *Studi di paletnologia in onore di Salvatore M. Puglisi*: 717–28. Dipartimento di Scienze Storiche, Archeologiche e Antropologiche dell'Antichità, Università di Roma "La Sapienza", Roma.

Grifoni Cremonesi, R. 1987–88.   Notiziario. Abruzzo. *Rivista di Scienze Preistoriche,* 41: 377.

Grifoni Cremonesi, R. 1988.   L'area del parco nazionale d'Abruzzo a del pre-parco dal Paleolitico all'Età del Bronzo. *Atti del 1 convegno nazionale di archeologia. Villetta Barrea, 1/2/3 Maggio 1987*: 19–26.

Grifoni Cremonesi, R. & Mallegni, F. 1978.   Testimonianze di un culto ad incinerazione nel livello a Ceramica Impressa della Grotta Riparo Continenza di Trasacco (L'Aquila) e studio dei resti umani cremati. *Atti della Società Toscana di Scienze Naturali,* 85: 253–79.

Halstead, P. 1980.   Counting sheep in Neolithic and Bronze Age Greece. In Hodder, I.R., Isaac, G. & Hammond, N. (eds), *Pattern of the Past: Studies in Honour of David Clarke*: 307–39. Cambridge University Press, Cambridge.

Hedges, R.E.M., Housely, R.A., Bronk, C.R. & Van Klinken, G.J. 1990.   Radiocarbon dates from the Oxford AMS system: *Archaeometry* datelist 11. *Archaeometry,* 32: 211–37.

Hodder, I. 1982.   *The Present Past. An Introduction to Anthropology for Archaeologists.* Batsford, London.

Hodder, I. 1985.   Postprocessual archaeology. *Advances in Archaeological Method and Theory,* 8: 1–26.

Hodder, I. 1990.   *The Domestication of Europe. Structure and Contingency in Neolithic Societies.* Blackwell, Oxford.

Hodder, I. 1992.   *Theory and Practice in Archaeology.* Routledge, London.

Humphreys, S.C. 1981a.   Death and time. In Humphreys, S.C. & King, H. (eds), *Mortality and Immortality. The Anthropology and Archaeology of Death*: 261–83. Academic Press, London.

Humphreys, S.C. 1981b.   Introduction: comparative perspectives on death. In Humphreys, S.C. & King, H. (eds), *Mortality and Immortality. The Anthropology and Archaeology of Death*: 1–13. Academic Press, London.

Hunt, C.O., Malone, C., Sevink, J. & Stoddart, S. 1990.   Environment, soils and early agriculture in Apennine central Italy. *World Archaeology,* 22: 34–44.

Ingold, T. 1986.   Chapter 6. Territoriality and tenure: the appropriation of space in hunting and gathering societies. In Ingold, T. (ed.), *The Appropriation of Nature. Essays on Human Ecology and Social Relations*: 130–64. Manchester University Press, Manchester.

Jones, G.D.B. (ed.) 1987.   *Apulia I: the Neolithic Settlement in the Tavoliere.* Society of Antiquaries of London, Reports of the Research Committee 44, London.

Leach, E.R. 1976.   *Culture and Communication. The Logic by Which Symbols are Connected. An Introduction to the Use of Structuralist Analysis in Social Anthropology.* Cambridge University Press, Cambridge.

Lee, R.B. 1992.   Art, science, or politics? The crisis in hunter-gatherer studies. *American Anthropologist,* 94: 31–54.

Letta, C. 1884.   *Le condizioni economiche dei contadini della Marsica alla fine dell'Ottocento. (Inchiesta agraria).* Adelmo Polla, Avezzano.

Lewis, G. 1980.   *Day of Shining Red. An Essay on Understanding Ritual.* Cambridge University Press, Cambridge.

Lewthwaite, J. 1982.   Cardial disorder: ethnographic and archaeological comparisons for problems in the early prehistory of the west Mediterranean. *Le Néolithique ancien Méditerranéen. Actes du colloque international de préhistoire. Montpellier 1981*: 311–18. Archéologie en Languedoc, no. special.

Lewthwaite, J. 1985.   From precocity to involution: the Neolithic of Corsica in its west Mediterranean and French contexts. *Oxford Journal of Archaeology,* 4: 47–68.

Lewthwaite, J. 1986.   The transition to food production: a Mediterranean perspective. In Zvelebil, M. (ed.), *Hunters in Transition. Mesolithic Societies of Temperate Eurasia and their Transition to Farming*: 53–66. Cambridge University Press, Cambridge.

Lewthwaite, J. 1987.   Three steps to leaven: applicazione del modello di disponibilità al Neolitico Italiano. *Atti della XXVI riunione scientifica dell'Istituto Italiano di Preistoria e Protostoria. Il Neolitico in Italia*: 89–102. Istituto Italiano di Preistoria e Protostoria, Firenze.

Lollini, D.G. 1964.   Notiziario. Marche. *Rivista di Scienze Preistoriche,* 19: 297–9, 307–8.

Lollini, D.G. 1965.   Il Neolitico nelle Marche alla luce delle recenti scoperte. *Atti del VI congresso internazionale delle scienze preistoriche e protostoriche, 1962, volume II*: 309–15. Union Internationale des Scienzes Préhistoriques et Protohistoriques, Firenze.

Lollini, D.G. 1970.   Notiziario. Marche. *Rivista di Scienze Preistoriche,* 25: 422.

Lollini, D.G. 1977.   Notiziario. Marche. *Rivista di Scienze Preistoriche,* 32: 335–6.

Lollini, D.G. 1979.   Pieve Torina nella pre-protostoria. In *Pieve Torina*: 47–69. Micheloni, Recanati.

Malone, C. & Stoddart, S. (eds) 1992.   The Neolithic site of San Marco, Gubbio (Perugia), Umbria: survey and excavation 1985–7. *Papers of the British School at Rome,* 60: 1–69.

Manzi, G. & Macchiarelli, R. 1989. "Pre-Neolithic Man" from La Maiella (Lama dei Peligni, Abruzzo) II – the radiometric date of the skeleton. *Rivista di Antropologia*, 67: 249–69.

Mattiocco, E. 1986. *Centri fortificati Vestini*. Soprintendenza Archeologica dell'Abruzzo, Museo Civico di Sulmona, Sulmona.

McGuire, R.H. 1983. Breaking down cultural complexity: inequality and heterogeneity. *Advances in Archaeological Method and Theory*, 6: 91–142.

McGuire, R.H. & Netting, R.McC. 1982. Levelling peasants? The maintenance of equality in a Swiss alpine community. *American Ethnologist*, 9: 269–90.

Meillassoux, C. 1972. From reproduction to production. A Marxist approach to economic anthropology. *Economy and Society*, 1: 93–105.

Meillassoux, C. 1981. *Maidens, Meal and Money. Capitalism and the Domestic Community*. Cambridge University Press, Cambridge.

Milliken, S. & Skeates, R. 1989. The Alimini survey: the Mesolithic-Neolithic transition in the Salento peninsula, south-east Italy. *University of London Institute of Archaeology Bulletin*, 26: 77–98.

Phillips, P. 1987. The development of agriculture and peasant societies in the west Mediterranean. In Guilaine, J., Courtin, J., Roudil, J-L. & Vernet, J-L. (eds), *Premières communautés paysannes en Méditerranée occidentale. Actes du Colloque International du C.N.R.S., Montpellier, 26–29 avril 1983*: 275–80. Centre National de la Recherche Scientifique, Paris.

Phillips, P. 1992. Western Mediterranean obsidian distribution and the European Neolithic. In Tykot, R.H. & Andrews, T.K. (eds.), *Sardinia in the Mediterranean: a Footprint in the Sea. Studies in Sardinian Archaeology Presented to Miriam S. Balmuth*: 71–82. Sheffield Academic Press, Sheffield.

Pigorini, L. 1896. Antichità primitive degli Abruzzi. *Bullettino di Paletnologia Italiana*, 22: 301–4.

Price, T.D. 1983. The European Mesolithic. *American Antiquity*, 48: 761–78.

Price, T.D. & Brown, J.A. (eds) 1985. *Prehistoric Hunter-Gatherers. The Emergence of Cultural Complexity*. Academic Press, London.

Radi, G. 1987–88. Notiziario. Abruzzo. Santo Stefano. *Rivista di Scienze Preistoriche*, 41: 407–8.

Radi, G. & Wilkens, B. 1989. Il sito a Ceramica Impressa di Santo Stefano (Ortucchio, L'Aquila). Notizia preliminare. *Rassegna di Archeologia*, 8: 97–117.

Radmilli, A.M. 1959. Gli insediamenti preistorici in Abruzzo. *Universo*, 39: 861–98.

Radmilli, A.M. 1965. Notiziario. Abruzzo. *Rivista di Scienze Preistoriche*, 20: 374–5.

Radmilli, A.M. 1967a. Notiziario. Abruzzo. *Rivista di Scienze Preistoriche*, 22: 444–6.

Radmilli, A.M. 1967b. I villaggi a capanne del Neolitico Italiano. *Archivio per l'Antropologia e l'Etnologia*, 47: 53–62.

Radmilli, A.M. 1968. Notiziario. Abruzzo. *Rivista di Scienze Preistoriche*, 23: 416.

Radmilli, A.M. 1975. Culti di fertilità della terra testimoniati in alcuni giacimenti neolitici Italiani. *Valcamonica Symposium '72. Actes du symposium international sur les religions de la Préhistoire, Capo di Ponte*: 175–84. Centro Camuno di Studi Preistorici, Capo di Ponte.

Radmilli, A.M. 1981. *Storia dell'Abruzzo dalle origini all'Età del Bronzo*. 2nd edition. Giardini, Pisa.

Radmilli, A.M. 1983. Ricerche sul Bertoniano cultura dell'Epigravettiano Italiano. Località Campo delle Piane. *Quaderno (Archeoclub di Pescara)*, 1: 7–46.

Radmilli, A.M. & Cremonesi, G. 1963. Note di preistoria Abruzzese. *Atti della VII riunione scientifica dell'Istituto Italiano di Preistoria e Protostoria. Firenze, 2–3 febbraio, 1963*: 127–53. Istituto Italiano di Preistoria e Protostoria, Firenze.

Radmilli, A.M., Mallegni, F. & Fornaciari, G. 1978. Recenti scavi nella Grotta dei Piccioni di Bolognano (Pescara) e riesame dei resti scheletrici umani provenienti dai circoli. *Atti della Società Toscana di Scienze Naturali*, 85: 175–98.

Rafferty, J.E. 1985. The archaeological record on sedentariness: recognition, development, and implications. *Advances in Archaeological Method and Theory*, 8: 113–56.

Rähle, W. 1980. Schmuckschnecken aus mesolithischen Kulturschichten Süddeutschlands und ihre Herkunft. In Taute W., (ed.), *Das Mesolithikum in Süddeutschland. Teil 2: Naturwissenschaftliche Untersuchungen*: 163–8. Institut für Urgeschichte der Universität Tübingen, Tübingen.

Rellini, U. 1914. L'Età della Pietra sulla Maiella. *Bullettino di Paletnologia Italiana*, 40: 30–42.

Rellini, U. 1931. Le stazioni enee delle Marche di fase seriore e la civiltà Italica. *Monumenti Antichi*, 34: 129–280.

Rellini, U. 1932. L'uomo fossile della Maiella e i primi Mediterranei. *Atti del convegno storico Abruzzese-Molisano. 1931. Casalbordino*: 3–20.

Robb, J. 1994. The Neolithic of peninsular Italy: anthropological synthesis and critique. *Bullettino di Paletnologia Italiana*. In press.

Ronchitelli, A.& Sarti, L. 1982. L'industria litica del villaggio neolitico di Marcianese (CH): nota preliminare. In *Atti 2 convegno sulla preistoria-protostoria-storia della Daunia. San Severo, 28–29–30 novembre, 1980*: 69–70.

Rowley Conwy, P. 1986. Between cave painters and crop planters: aspects of the temperate European Mesolithic. In Zvelebil, M. (ed.), *Hunters in Transition. Mesolithic Societies of Temperate Eurasia and their Transition to Farming*: 17–32. Cambridge University Press, Cambridge.

Sahlins, M.D. 1968. *Tribesmen*. Prentice-Hall, Englewood Cliffs, New Jersey.

Sargent, A. 1983. Exploitation territory and economy in the Tavoliere of Apulia. In Cassano, S.M. & Manfredini, A. (eds), *Studi sul neolitico del Tavoliere della Puglia. Indagine territoriale in un'area-campione*: 223–36. BAR International Series 160. British Archaeological Reports, Oxford.

Sargent, A. 1985. The Carbon-14 chronology of the early and middle Neolithic of southern Italy. *Proceedings of the Prehistoric Society*, 51: 31–40.

Shackleton, J.C., Van Andel, T.H. & Runnels, C.N. 1984. Coastal paleogeography of the central and western Mediterranean during the last 125,000 years and its archaeological implications. *Journal of Field Archaeology*, 11: 307–14.

Shanks, M. & Tilley, C. 1982. Ideology, symbolic power and ritual communication: a reinterpretation of neolithic mortuary practices. In Hodder, I. (ed.), *Symbolic and Structural Archaeology*: 129–54. Cambridge University Press, Cambridge.

Sherratt, A. 1980. Water, soil and seasonality in early cereal cultivation. *World Archaeology,* 11: 313–30.

Skeates, R. 1987. *Sedentism and Mobility in the Settlement of the Fucino Basin in Central Italy During the Neothermal Period.* Unpublished B.A. dissertation, University of London.

Skeates, R. 1991. Caves, cult and children in Neolithic Abruzzo, central Italy. In Garwood, P., Jennings, D., Skeates, R. & Toms, J. (eds), *Sacred and Profane. Proceedings of a Conference on Archaeology, Ritual and Religion*: 122–34. Oxford University Committee for Archaeology, Oxford.

Skeates, R. 1992. *The Neolithic and Copper Age of the Abruzzo-Marche Region, Central Italy.* Unpublished D. Phil. thesis, The Queen's College, Oxford.

Skeates, R. 1993. Neolithic exchange in central and southern Italy. In Healy, F. & Scarre, C. (eds), *Trade and Exchange in Prehistoric Europe. Proceedings of a Conference held at the University of Bristol, April 1992*: 109–14. The Prehistoric Society, London.

Skeates, R. 1994a. A radiocarbon date-list for prehistoric Italy (c.46,400 BP – 2450 BP/400 cal.BC). In Skeates, R. & Whitehouse, R. (eds), *Radiocarbon Dating and Italian Prehistory*: 147–288. Accordia Research Centre and The British School at Rome, London.

Skeates, R. 1994b. Towards an absolute chronology for the Neolithic in central Italy. In Skeates, R. & Whitehouse, R. (eds), *Radiocarbon Dating and Italian Prehistory*: 62–72. Accordia Research Centre and The British School at Rome, London.

Sorrentino, C. 1986–87. I reperti faunistici. In Ducci, S., Perazzi, P. & Ronchitelli, A. (eds), Gli insediamenti neolitici Abruzzesi con Ceramica Impressa di Tricalle (CH) e Fontanelle (PE). *Rassegna di Archeologia* 1986–7: 86, 105–6.

Sorrentino, R. 1978. Abruzzo. In Radmilli, A.M. (ed.), *Guida della preistoria italiana*: 103–15. Sansoni, Firenze.

Spurr, M.S. 1986. *Arable Cultivation in Roman Italy c.200 B.C.– c.A.D. 100.* Society for the Promotion of Roman Studies, London.

Testart, A. 1981. Pour une typologie des chasseurs-cuilleurs. *Anthropologie et sociétés,* 9: 177– 221.

Testart, A. 1982. The significance of food storage among hunter-gatherers: residence patterns, population densities, and social inequalities. *Current Anthropology,* 23: 523– 37.

Testart, A. 1988. Some major problems in the social anthropology of hunter-gatherers. *Current Anthropology,* 29: 1–31.

Thomas, J. 1985. The social significance of Cotswold-Severn burial practices. *Man,* 23: 540–59.

Thomas, J. 1988. Neolithic explanations revisited: the Mesolithic-Neolithic transition in Britain and south Scandinavia. *Proceedings of the Prehistoric Society,* 54: 59–66.

Tilley, C. 1989. Hunter-gatherers, farmers and the social structuring of material culture. In Larsson, T.B. & Lundmark, H. (eds), *Approaches to Swedish Prehistory. A Spectrum of Problems and Perspectives in Contemporary Research*: 239–85. BAR International Series 500. British Archaeological Reports, Oxford.

Tinè, S. & Bernabò Brea, M. 1980. Il villaggio neolitico del Guadone di S. Severo (Foggia). *Rivista di Scienze Preistoriche,* 35: 45–74.

Tozzi, C. 1966. Il giacimento mesolitico di Capo d'Acqua (L'Aquila). *Bullettino di Paletnologia Italiana,* 75: 13–25.

Turner, V.W. 1967. *The Forest of Symbols. Aspects of Ndembu Ritual.* Cornell University Press, Ithaca.

Turner, V.W. 1969. *The Ritual Process. Structure and Anti-Structure.* Routledge & Kegan Paul, London.

Turner, V.W. 1977. Variations on a theme of liminality. In Moore, S.F. & Myerhoff, B.G. (eds), *Secular Ritual*: 36–52. Van Gorcum, Amsterdam.

Ucko, P. J. 1969. Ethnography and archaeological interpretation of funerary remains. *World Archaeology,* 1: 262–80.

Van Gennep, A. 1909. *Les rites de passage.* Nourry, Paris.

Whitehouse, R.D. 1971. The last hunter-gatherers in southern Italy. *World Archaeology,* 2: 239–54.

Whitehouse, R.D. 1981. Prehistoric settlement patterns in southeast Italy. In Barker, G. & Hodges, R. (eds), *Archaeology and Society. Prehistoric, Roman and Medieval Studies*: 157–65. BAR International Series 102. British Archaeological Reports, Oxford.

Whitehouse, R.D. 1987. The first farmers in the Adriatic and their position in the Neolithic of the Mediterranean. In Guilaine, J., Courtin, J., Roudil J-L. & Vernet, J-L. (eds), *Premières communautés paysannes en Méditerranée occidentale. Actes du Colloque International du C.N.R.S., Montpellier, 26–29 avril 1983*: 357–65. Centre National de la Recherche Scientifique, Paris.

Whitehouse, R.D. 1990. Caves and cult in Neolithic southern Italy. *The Accordia Research Papers,* 1: 19–38.

Whitehouse, R.D. 1992. *Underground Religion. Cult and Culture in Prehistoric Italy.* Accordia Research Centre, University of London, London.

Whittle, A. 1985. *Neolithic Europe: A Survey.* Cambridge University Press, Cambridge.

Wilkens, B. 1989. Il cervo dal Mesolitico all'età del Bronzo nell'Italia centro-meridionale. *Rassegna di Archeologia,* 8: 63–95.

Wilkens, B. 1989–90. La fauna dei livelli neolitici della Grotta Continenza. In Barra, A., Grifoni Cremonesi, R., Mallegni, F., Piancastelli, M., Vitiello, A. & Wilkens, B. (eds), La Grotta Continenza di Trasacco. I livelli a ceramiche. *Rivista di Scienze Preistoriche,* 42: 93–100.

Woodburn, J. 1980. Hunters and gatherers today and reconstruction of the past. In Gellner, E. (ed.), *Soviet and Western Anthropology*: 95–117. Duckworth, London.

Woodburn, J. 1982. Egalitarian societies. *Man,* 17: 431–51.

Zvelebil, M. 1986a. Mesolithic societies and the transition to farming: problems of time, scale and organisation. In Zvelebil, M. (ed.), *Hunters in Transition. Mesolithic Societies of Temperate Eurasia and their Transition to Farming*: 167–88. Cambridge University Press, Cambridge.

Zvelebil, M. (ed.) 1986b. *Hunters in Transition. Mesolithic Societies of Temperate Eurasia and their Transition to Farming*. Cambridge University Press, Cambridge.

Zvelebil, M. & Rowley Conwy, P.A. 1984. Transition to farming in northern Europe: a hunter-gatherer perspective. *Norwegian Archaeological Review*, 17: 104–28.

Coasts and Uplands in Liguria and Northern Tuscany from the Mesolithic to the Bronze Age

Roberto Maggi

FOREWORD

The Apennine chain runs all along the Italian peninsula, from its very southern tip, the *Stretto di Messina* in Calabria, to western Liguria, where the Alpine chain takes over without any physical interruption. While south of the Arno river, in Tuscany, the mountains lie in the middle of the peninsula, north of it the Apennines turn toward the sea, and meet it in the very northern part of Tuscany and in Liguria.

This paper takes into consideration this latter part: an arc-shaped region where the mountains form a continuous chain, lying very close to the sea (fig. 1). In eastern and central Liguria the main watershed is a very short distance from the coast (to a minimum of less than 10km), and starts to diverge in the western part, where the Maritime Alps begin. Thus, along the almost 300km of coast from Massa in the east to the French border in the west, the landscape is always very hilly; within a few kilometres from the coast the hills rise steeply to over 1000/1500m; most of the valleys are very short and steep, with streams that easily flood or dry up with the variation in rainfall. In fact the only real river is the Magra, fed by the waters of the Lunigiana basin. The other basins are generally small, sometimes of only a few tens of square kilometres, with very steep slopes. Quite often the seaward hills drop steeply into the sea, leaving almost no room for coastal plains. In fact, most of the few, small and isolated present-day coastal plains are formed by colluvium of mainly post-Roman age.

The geology of this area is definitely complicated and very diverse. As an extreme simplification, it can be subdivided into three parts. To the west lie the Maritime Alps, mainly composed of calcareous rocks. Here altitudes easily pass 2000m a.s.l. Karstic activity is present in several areas, and there are many cave sites. Shortly after Finale, the Alps finish and the Apennines take over. In central/eastern Liguria, ophiolithes and schist formations are dominant. Here the mountain height is lower, reaching a maximum of 1799m a.s.l. at Monte Maggiorasca, however, due to the proximity of the main watershed to the sea, the sea-facing slopes are even steeper and coastal plains more restricted. In this area karstic morphologies are reduced and caves are rare and very small.

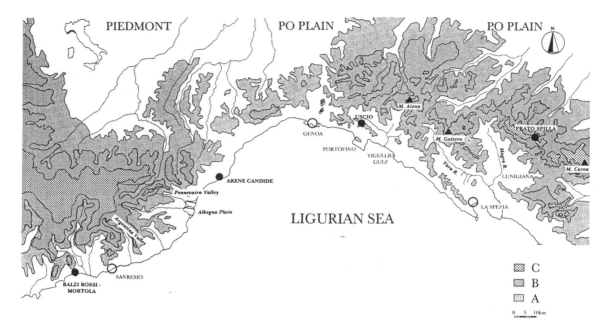

Fig. 1 The very northern part of the Apennines (to the right) and the beginning of the Maritime Alps (to the left). A: land above 500m a.s.l.; B: land above 1000m a.s.l.; C: land above 1500m a.s.l.

Around the Lunigiana basin and toward the Tusco-Emilian Apennines are arenite formations. Due to the slope of the stratified rock, in several cases the Lunigiana facing slopes of the main ridge are very steep (fig. 2), while the northern slopes may be quite gentle. In northern Tuscany, around Massa and Carrara, the so-called Apuan Alps are again of limestone, the metamorphic aspect of which provides the famous Carrara marble.

North of this barrier of mountains lies the large and fertile Po Plain. The connection between this important area and the western sea is difficult; there are only two passes just below 500m in altitude. The Passo dei Giovi (472m a.s.l.) is located at the tip of the region. It provides the western and central Po Plain with the best communication to the Mediterranean, which is reached at the point where the city of Genoa originated: this seaport city dominated the Medieval and Modern history of the region. The other connection runs from the Savona/Finale area to the surroundings of the Langhe hills and was of some importance for the neolithisation of the southern Piedmont.

THE ARCHAEOLOGY OF THE REGION

During the 19th century, Liguria was one of the first regions of Italy to be investigated with excavations of prehistoric sites. In 1825 Paolo Savi published the results of his exploration of the Cassana Cave (near La Spezia) were he discovered remains of *Ursus spelaeus* (Savi 1825; quoted by Issel 1892: 159). Prince Florestano I of Monaco began excavations at Balzi Rossi (near Grimaldi, close to the present-day French border) in the year 1846. He was followed by numerous scholars and 'treasure hunters', who also paid attention to several other sites. Among them, geologist Arturo Issel started his lengthy research at Arene Candide Cave, near Finale, in the year 1864. Several priests as well, such as Don Perrando, Don Morelli and Don Amerano, were very active in several caves, looking for evidence to counter Darwin's theories. As a result of all of these investigations, a handbook on Ligurian prehistory was published by A. Issel as early as 1892.

The 20th century saw the introduction of more scientific methods of investigation. In 1928 the Istituto Italiano di Paleontologia Umana started its research in several caves of the Balzi Rossi, where in addition to the use of a rigorous stratigraphic approach, geological, palaeo-environmental and palaeo-economic records were investigated. Top quality excavation was reached with the investigation of the Late-glacial and Holocene

Fig. 2   Aerial view of the rugged Apennine morphology

deposit of Arene Candide Cave, carried out by Luigi Bernabò Brea and Luigi Cardini from 1940 to 1950. This work produced one of the most remarkable Late Palaeolithic and Neolithic stratigraphic sequences of the northwestern Mediterranean (fig. 3). Fifty years later, the full potential of the environmental, economic and functional data, systematically and thoroughly recorded by these two scholars, has yet to be fully exploited.

By 1956, the date of publication of Bernabò Brea's second monograph on the pottery sequence of Arene Candide, the prehistory of Liguria was considered to be quite well known. However, most of the data were from cave sites, and almost nothing was known about open air settlement.

In fact, the dense woodland covering a large part of the north-facing slopes, the widespread transformation of low/middle altitude south-facing slopes by centuries (and millennia) of deforestation, erosion and terracing, and finally the thick colluvial deposits that seal pre-Roman valley sites several metres below the present-day surface, meant that the archaeology of the region was very poor outside caves. Furthermore, the Early Holocene coastal remains were submerged by the rising postglacial sea levels (Shackleton & van Andel 1985). Therefore mountain terrain is the most favourable for archaeological investigation.

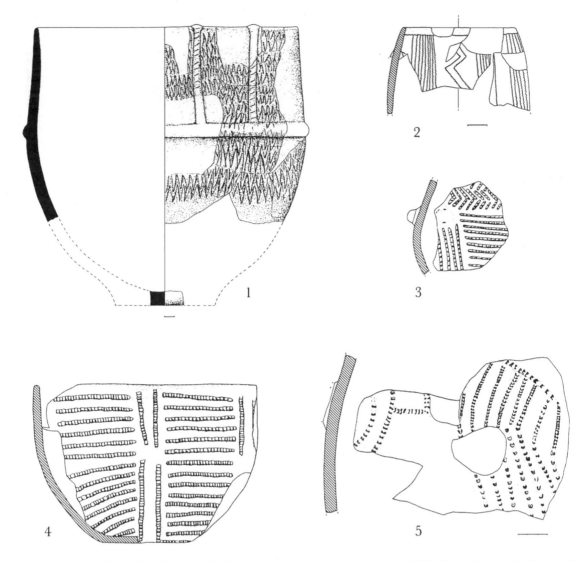

Fig. 3   Early Neolithic Cardial-style (1, 2) and stamped-impressed pottery (3-5), from Grotta del Pertusello (1) and Arene Candide (2-5)

Surveys and excavations of open air sites have mainly concentrated in four areas of eastern Liguria and of the Tusco-Emilian Apennine, where caves are scarce:

(1) In the central part of the eastern Ligurian Apennines (fig. 4), surface collections, carried out during the last twenty years, recovered about 60 Holocene sites spread over an area of about 300km (Maggi & Nisbet 1991). A few peat sites recently studied (Macphail 1988; Cruise 1992) provide useful environmental information.

(2) The mountains between the Vara and the Magra rivers (M. Gottero and M. Molinatico) yielded several Mesolithic sites at higher altitudes (Ghiretti & Guerreschi 1990), while a group of Neolithic, Copper and Bronze Age settlements was discovered towards the south, below 1000m a.s.l. Some of the latter have been excavated (Mannoni & Tizzoni 1980; Fossati *et al.* 1985; Maggi *et al.* 1987) (fig. 5).

(3) The Garfagnana region is rich in Mesolithic and Copper/Bronze Age remains (Guidi *et al.* 1985; Biagi *et al.* 1981; Cocchi Genick & Grifoni Cremonesi 1985; Castelletti *et al.* 1994) (fig. 5).

(4) The Tusco-Emilian Apennines north of the Garfagnana, including the massif of Monte Cusna, have been intensively surveyed. During the seventies three Mesolithic sites were excavated by M. Cremaschi and associates (Cremaschi & Castelletti 1975; Castelletti *et al.* 1976; Biagi *et al.* 1981; Cremaschi *et al.* 1984) (fig. 5).

On the main Apenninic dorsal, mid-way between the *Cusna* and the *Gottero-Molinatico* groups, at an altitude of 1550m, lies the peat site of Prato Spilla A. Its sediment

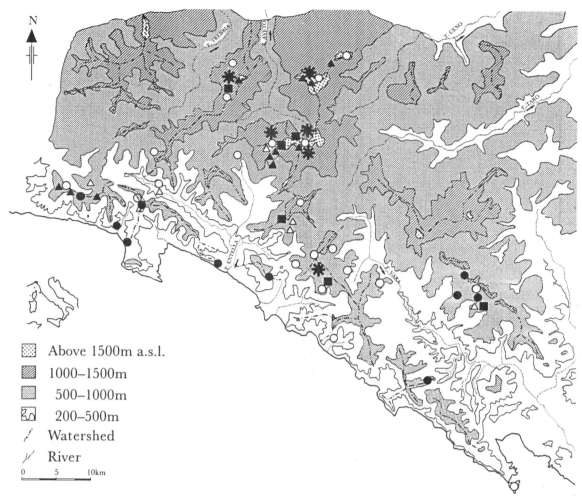

Fig. 4 Eastern Liguria: location of the main Early Mesolithic (triangles), Late Mesolithic (diamonds), Neolithic (squares), Copper/Early Bronze Age (empty circles), Late Bronze Age (black circles), and peat (asterisks) sites (modified from Maggi & Nisbet 1991)

stratigraphy presents a full Holocene data series and radiocarbon dates, the potential of which for the understanding of the pattern and intensity of land-use during the mid- to late-Holocene has been recently discussed (Lowe *et al.* 1994).

THE MESOLITHIC HIATUS IN WESTERN LIGURIA

In western Liguria, the Final Epigravettian is dated to the 11th millennium BP in the stratigraphic series of the coastal cave Arene Candide (Bietti 1987). The latest evidence of occupation is radiocarbon dated to 9980 ± 140 BP (Beta-48694: Maggi 1997). This is in good correspondence with the earliest datings of the Early Mesolithic obtained at Romagnano in the Alps (9830 ± 90 BP: R-1147; Alessio *et al.* 1983) and at Isola Santa in the Apennines (9980 ± 160 BP; Biagi *et al.* 1981).

More inland, in the Pennavaira Valley, a major excavation carried out by M. Leale Anfossi between 1952 and 1962 (Leale Anfossi 1972) and a minor one by P. Biagi and the present author between 1982 and 1986 (Biagi *et al.* 1987a) at the cave Arma dello Stefanin, produced a well defined stratigraphy. The dates of the last Final Epigravettian layer of Anfossi's excavation (R-126: 8100 ± 90 BP; R-145: 8800 ± 300 BP; R-148: 8400 ± 100 BP) have been criticised as too young for a Final Epigravettian lithic assemblage (Biagi & Maggi 1983: 166): it seemed unacceptable that in this area some groups continued to use the Final Epigravettian tool-kit, while in the neighbouring regions (northern Tuscany, Alps, southern France) the Sauveterrian tradition took over perhaps a millennium before. This assumption seemed to be confirmed by the date HAR-6915 (12700 ± 300 BP; Biagi *et al.*

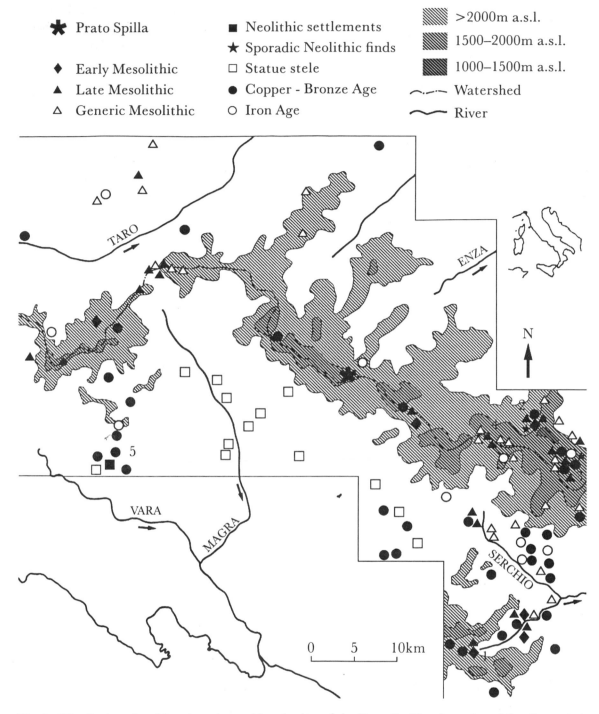

✱ Prato Spilla

◆ Early Mesolithic
▲ Late Mesolithic
△ Generic Mesolithic

■ Neolithic settlements
★ Sporadic Neolithic finds
□ Statue stele
● Copper - Bronze Age
○ Iron Age

▨ >2000m a.s.l.
▨ 1500–2000m a.s.l.
▨ 1000–1500m a.s.l.
⌇⌁ Watershed
⌁ River

Fig. 5 Distribution of prehistoric and protohistoric sites of the Tusco-Emilian Apennines (after Lowe *et al.* 1994)

1987a), obtained from a layer of a new excavation that is little deeper than those dated by M. Leale Anfossi. Typological and environmental considerations (Palma di Cesnola 1993), as well as a new radiocarbon dating (8895 ± 270 BP: GX-16959) of a layer equivalent to Anfossi's, suggest more prudence in rejecting the possibility that in western Liguria the Final Epigravettian tradition continued into the earliest part of the Holocene. The nearby Nasino Cave also presents a Final Epigravettian assemblage, 'Romanellian' aspects of which suggest it to be later than the Terminal Pleistocene industry known at Arene Candide (Martini 1995).

The question is complicated by the fact that no traces of Mesolithic activity are documented in the Ligurian caves. At Arene Candide, Stefanin and Nasino, the Final

Epigravettian occupation is followed by a period of abandonment, until the onset of the Early Neolithic at the beginning of the 7th millennium BP. Thus, even accepting the 'late' chronology of the local Final Epigravettian, the cave-system of sites was abandoned for more than a millennium between the last Palaeolithic occupations and the first Neolithic. This contrasts with both Provence and Languedoc, which are rich in rock-shelters showing evidence of continuous occupation from the Late Glacial to the Atlantic period (Escalon de Fonton 1976). Continuity between the Final Epigravettian and the Sauveterrian is also shown in northern Tuscany at the open air site of Isola Santa. Here the Final Epigravettian occupation (dated 10720 ± 140 BP: R-1524; Alessio *et al.* 1983) is followed by the Sauveterrian (9980 ± 160 BP as already quoted; and 9220 ± 90 BP: R-1529a; Alessio *et al.* 1983).

It might not be a coincidence that Sauveterrian aspects are very poorly known in our area. The only site known so far, Punta della Mortola, near Balzi Rossi, is doubtful (Baroni & Biagi 1991), and might be contemporaneous with layer A of Riparo Mochi, which is considered to represent the very end of the Palaeolithic rather than an early Sauveterrian (Onoratini 1982; F. Negrino pers. comm.). It looks as if in 'Alpine' western Liguria the stimulus to adopt the Mesolithic tool-kit did not act the same way as in the neighbouring areas.

Very little is known also about the Castelnovian Mesolithic. The only site that yielded a 'trapeze' Mesolithic industry, Pian del Re, inland from Sanremo, was disturbed by the building of a Bronze Age tumulus, and neither environmental and economic data nor radiocarbon dates are yet available.

THE MESOLITHIC IN THE EASTERN LIGURIAN APENNINES

In this area both Sauveterrian and Castelnovian assemblages are present. The postglacial rising of the Mediterranean has removed the coastal evidence, thus Mesolithic sites are known only from the inner valleys and mainly on the relief topography.

Figure 6 illustrates the location of the major Mesolithic and Neolithic finds. Rhomboids represent Early Mesolithic, triangles the Late Mesolithic and asterisks the Early Neolithic. Only two of the Mesolithic sites, both of them situated on valley floors, have been excavated so far; all of the others are known from surface collections, no radiocarbon dates are available, nor are bone remains preserved. The chipped assemblages are attributable to the Sauveterrian or to the Castelnovian lithic tradition according to the tool typology (Biagi & Maggi 1983). In fig. 6, the continuous and the dotted-and-dashed lines mark two cross-sections, whose profiles are representative of the idealised cross sections of this part of the Apennines (fig. 7).

The pericoastal submarine profile is drawn from bathimetric maps. It shows that during the early Holocene, when the sea was just beginning to rise (Shackleton & van Andel 1985), the coastal slopes were more gentle than today.

The highest mountain of the area and the main watershed are situated at short distance from the coast (25–30km). The coastal hills situated in between generally follow a direction parallel to the coast (see fig. 1). As shown by cross-section A, they can be very steep, reaching an elevation of some 7–800m a.s.l. within 5km or so.

The proximity of relatively high mountains to the sea can be regarded as a condition favourable to the Mesolithic economy, since maritime/coastal and mountain resources were available within a very short distance of each other. Only a few hours are required to walk from the coast to the top of the closest hills, and 1–2 days to the major mountains. In fact, signs of Mesolithic occupation are quite evident.

In this area, the structure of the industry and the location of sites suggest that highland exploitation differed considerably from the model established for the well studied area of the eastern Alpine chain (Maggi & Negrino 1994).

The location of finds is plotted in fig. 7 relative to height (in metres) and to the distance from the sea (in kilometres), against the profile of the two cross-sections given in fig. 6. The

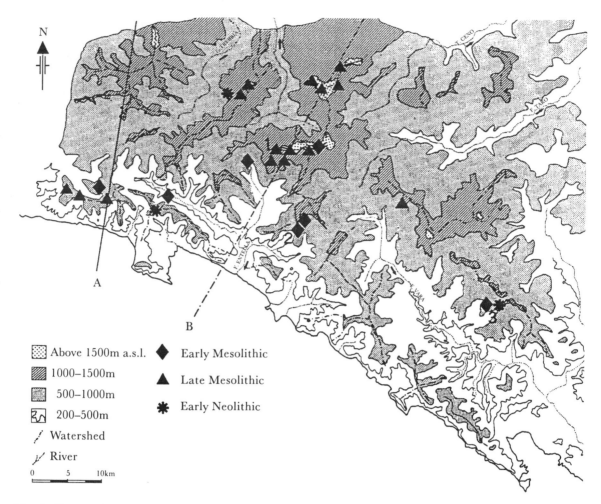

Fig. 6   Eastern Liguria: the location of Mesolithic and Early Neolithic sites. (1) Bosco delle Lame; (2) Passo della Camilla; (3) Suvero. A and B: cross sections of fig. 7

mountain Sauveterrian finds cluster in an area that does not exceed 1000m a.s.l. and is situated between 6 to 18km from the sea. Castelnovian sites are markedly more numerous. They are also present on the top of the highest coastal hills, but most of them cluster at higher altitude on the reliefs of the main Apennine watershed, between 1100 to 1650m a.s.l. and from 16 to 33km from the sea.

In Figure 7, the number of cores recovered from each site is also plotted. Most of the locations yielded 0–8 cores. A large number of such items have been found only in two localities. One is Sauveterrian: Passo della Camilla, at 720m a.s.l., with 31 cores and about 500 artefacts. The other is Bosco delle Lame, Castelnovian, located on a ridge at about 1350m a.s.l., with 240 cores out of about 1800 artefacts (Maggi & Negrino 1994). To date, that of Bosco delle Lame is the largest collection of Mesolithic cores known in Italy. The location on the mountains, within a group of possibly contemporaneous sites, is also worth noting. Similarly, Passo della Camilla is situated within a mountain area where the other nearby Sauveterrian sites are coreless. Neither of the sites lie in the proximity of a jasper outcrop. Therefore, it seems that both Early and Late Mesolithic communities, in addition to smaller sites with few or no cores, had middle-high altitude larger settlements where substantial on-site primary and differentiated chipping activity is demonstrated by the occurrence of pre-cores and several diversified categories of cores (Maggi & Negrino 1994).

The quantity of cores is probably the main differentiating element among the chipped assemblages of the mountain Mesolithic sites of Eastern Liguria. In fact the structure of the industry of all of the sites is rather homogeneous (Biagi & Maggi 1983). The substratum (*sensu* Laplace 1964: points [P] + scrapers [L,R] + undifferentiated pieces

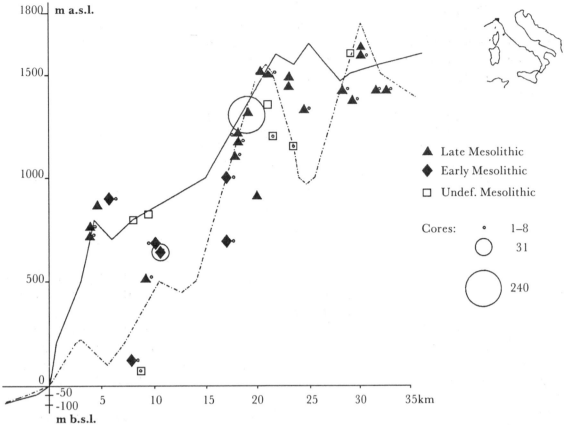

Fig. 7   The location of Mesolithic sites in relation to distance from the sea and height above sea level. A and
B: reference cross-sections of the Apennine chain

with abrupt retouch [A] + denticulated [D]) is by far dominant, with values between 60 to
79%. It is followed by the 'common' tools, such as burins [B], end-scrapers [G], truncations
[T] and borers [Bc]. Armatures [Gm] are always scarce, as well as the residuals of their
construction ('microburins') [Mb]. The maximum percentage of armatures is 12%, and
that of microburins 16%.

This is quite different from the evidence of the Dolomite mountains and the Trento
basin, the best studied area of Mesolithic Italy. Here, according to Lanzingher (1987) and
Broglio and Lanzingher (1990), high altitude (above 1900m a.s.l.) exploitation was
organised into "maintenance tasks camps" with more than 30% of "common tools" and
"hunting camps", characterised by chipped assemblages with more than 70% of armatures.
Base camps, core-rich, were located in the valley bottoms.

The situation is perhaps consistent with the ecological diversity of the two areas. At the
beginning of the Atlantic, even the highest elevations of the Ligurian Apennines (the
maximum altitude is 1799m a.s.l.) were far below the upper tree line. This suggests that
upper mountain grasslands were restricted, if there were any; consequently grazing
animals could have played a minor role in the composition of game. It can be argued that
hunting strategies did not develop the same way as in the Dolomites, where grasslands
were widespread at higher altitudes; thus specialised hunting camps could have had little
significance. The structure of the Mesolithic industries of the Ligurian Apennines may
reflect such different hunting strategies, where the 'armatures technology' played a minor
role, and where gathering activities were perhaps more important.

Mesolithic communities of Eastern Liguria exploited local jasper and flint for their
chipped stone artefacts (Maggi & Garibaldi 1986; Biagi et al. 1987b). The raw material was
relatively easy of access: jasper and flint outcrops are widespread not far from many of the
Mesolithic sites, and pebbles were available in several riverbeds and beaches. To date, no
exogenous flint has been recognised, as opposed to the Po Plain side of the Apennines, which
received Alpine flint (Cremaschi in Biagi et al. 1981; Ghiretti & Guerreschi 1990).

The emerging picture is that of fairly self-supporting communities, living in the territory encompassing the land between the coast and the nearby mountains. Base camps were probably located on the coast, however the cases of Passo della Camilla and Bosco Lame suggest the possibility of summer base camps located at middle to high altitudes.

Given the number and distribution of sites, Late Mesolithic groups apparently increased the exploitation of the highest mountains of the main watershed. This might be related either to a possible increase of the population, and/or to the changes in the distribution of the available resources (e.g., an increase of the forest covering on the mountains, rise of the upper tree line, changes in the composition of the woodland).

THE MESOLITHIC IN NORTHERN TUSCANY

The Mesolithic of this area has been intensely investigated through surveys and excavations. Here, late Epigravettian sites occur on the maritime side of the Apennines at low to medium (up to 1100m) altitudes (Biagi et al. 1981; Castelletti et al. 1994).

Several mesolithic sites have been discovered at lower altitudes along the Serchio and Turrite Secca valley in the Garfagnagna, and at higher altitudes on the massif of Monte Cusna, most of them around and above 1500m a.s.l.

As already quoted, at Isola Santa (Garfagnana) (fig. 5.1), the earliest occupation was with Final Epigravettian industry, that suddenly evolved into a Sauveterrian typology. The mesolithic occupation continued perhaps until the beginning of the Atlantic period, as suggested by the appearance of a few trapezes in the upper layer (Tozzi 1980; Biagi et al. 1981).

Three sites have been excavated on the Cusna massif: Monte Bagioletto (fig. 5.2) (Cremaschi et al. 1984), Sauveterrian up to the beginning of the Castelnovian; Lama Lite (fig. 5.3) (Castelletti et al. 1976) and Passo della Comunella (fig. 5.4) (Cremaschi & Castelletti 1975) are both Castelnovian.

In this area, there is no sharp increase of sites from Sauveterrian to Castelnovian as shown in Eastern Liguria. Furthermore the structure of the industries (percentages of retouched tools and armatures) are comparable with the eastern Alps rather then with the close sites of eastern Liguria.

The palynological sequence from Prato Spilla A shows minor fluctuations around about 7500 BP (Lowe et al. 1994). Whether this reflects anthropogenic disturbance or other environmental variables is under discussion. In fact behavioural information suggests that during the Sauveterrian the main watershed of the Tosco-Emilian Apennines was visited seasonally by a few specialised groups of hunters for short time hunting trips, during which they used only fallen branches to feed their hearths (Castelletti 1983).

As a conclusion, it can be observed that the three areas examined so far present rather different situations.

– In western Liguria, the Final Epigravettian tradition may have endured more than a millennium after the beginning of the Holocene and the first appearance of Sauveterrian industries elsewhere in northern Italy. The Mesolithic (especially the Sauveterrian) is elusive. Neither the caves with a stratigraphy including Final Epigravettian and Early Neolithic occupations, nor the many others with mainly Neolithic remains, either on the coast or inland, have yielded a single Mesolithic artefact. Among other things, this should preclude the possibility of the Sauveterrian industry having been introduced from southern France to Italy through Liguria.[1]

– In eastern Liguria, Mesolithic open air sites are quite common, even very close to the coast. The presence on the higher mountains sharply increased during the Castelnovian. The structure of the chipped industry is clearly different from what is known in northeastern Italy and Tuscany. At all sites the assemblages are dominated by the substratum, while armatures are rare. Specialised hunting camps similar to those of the Alps have not been discovered so far. Large sites, with knapping workshops, were located at medium/high altitudes, and might be interpreted as summer base camps. The raw material is exclusively local. Environmental data are scarce. All but two of the peat basins explored so far began accumulating peat during the Middle to Late Holocene, and the analysis of the only site that preserved a rather complete Holocene series is still in progress. Also in progress is the analysis of the charcoal of a firing horizon dated 8670 ± 180 BP (Beta-60703) from Lagorara Valley (Bracco *et al.* 1993), at about 750m a.s.l.

– In northern Tuscany, Sauveterrian industries appear to develop precociously from the local Final Epigravettian, as in the Eastern Alps. The structure of the industries is also similar to those of the Alps. Hunting camps, either Sauveterrian and Castelnovian, were located on the highest reliefs.

THE NEOLITHIC ONSET

Neolithic settlement appeared first in coastal and pericoastal areas. A major concentration of Early Neolithic evidence, characterised by the so-called 'Impressed Ware Culture' occurs in the area of Finale, in Western Liguria. Sites from this area also provided the oldest Neolithic dates for the area studied and for all of northern and central Italy (Bagolini & Biagi 1990). At Arene Candide, a detailed radiocarbon chronology of the Neolithic sequence, with more than fifty dates (Maggi 1997), assigns the appearance of the first Neolithic groups to the beginning of the 7th millennium BP. The Impressed Ware Culture had a fully Neolithic technology: pottery, agricultural implements, greenstone axes/adzes, domestic animals. At Arene Candide, a major part of Early Neolithic food refuse is represented by sheep. Hunting of wild boar and red deer played a minor role in the meat supply strategy (Rowley-Conwy 1997). It also seems that the flint tool-kit did not develop from a "Mesolithic substratum" of continental north-central Italy (Biagi 1991: 51, 52; Starnini & Voytek 1997). These varied data suggest close maritime relationships and that the group that first settled the Finale area could have arrived by sea.

Some Early Neolithic sites were located about 20km inland from the coast, in the very narrow Pennavaira Valley, that penetrates into a rugged topography with hills rising steeply over 1500 metres. Here two caves (Pertusello and Stefanin) and one rock shelter (Nasino) yielded occupation layers of the Impressed Ware Pottery Culture (fig. 3). At every site there is pottery decorated with cardial shells, grinding equipment and faunal remains of domesticates, suggesting relationships with coastal sites such as Arene Candide (Barker *et al.* 1990). The date 6610 ± 60 BP (Bln-3276) from Arma dello Stefanin indicates the time of the penetration inland by Neolithic groups.

The Arene Candide and Pollera caves present dates that are a few centuries older than any other Neolithic dates of northern and central continental Italy (Biagi 1991: 51; Maggi 1997). Whether this can apply to eastern Liguria and northern Tuscany is problematic, since there are no direct dates for the onset of the Neolithic in these areas. The only indirect indications available so far do not seem to support an early chronology as in the Finale area. In fact, in the peat basin of Bargone, located on seaward-facing slopes at less than 10km from the coast, pollens of cultivated cereals do not appear before around 6300/6400 BP (indirect dating by interpolation with dated levels) (G.M. Macphail pers. comm). In the stratigraphic record of Prato Spilla A, a fluctuation that might be related to the initial inland penetration of the Neolithic is also indirectly dated to around 6300 BP (Lowe *et al.* 1994).

One goal for future research will be to understand if the precocity of the Neolithic in the Finale area was related to the lack of Mesolithic occupants. At the moment this is nothing but a suggestion to be explored, however if it can be demonstrated that the local Final Epigravettian did not develop into the Mesolithic as happened in other regions, but that the area became deserted instead, this could explain why Neolithic groups could have chosen to concentrate their early settlement there first rather than in the neighbouring areas.

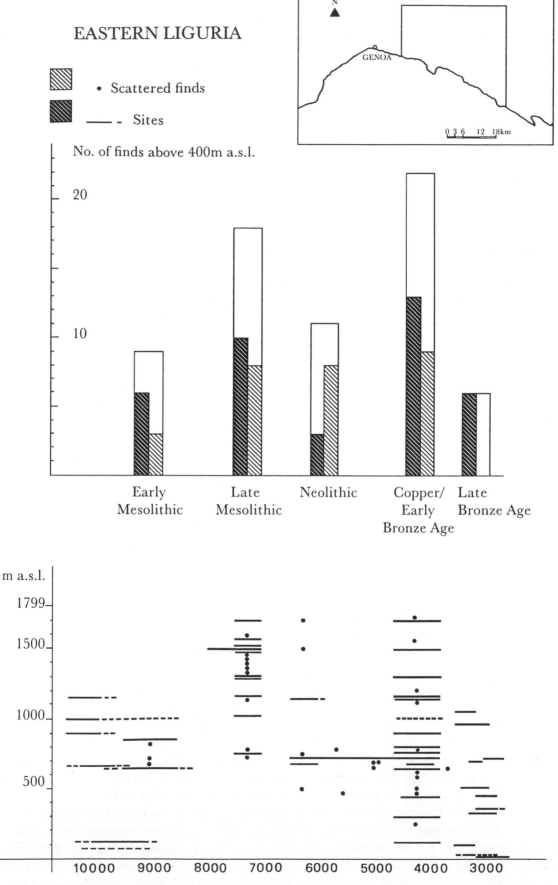

Fig. 8 Eastern Liguria: occurrence of site (lines) and scattered finds (dots) according to chronology and altitude

Fig. 9 Western Liguria: caves in the Finale Ligure (1-4), Val Pennavaira (5-7) and Toirano (8) areas. 1 = Arene Candide; 5 = Grotta del Pertusello; 6 = Arma dello Stefanin; 7 = Tana del Barletta; 8 = Grotta dell'Olivo (after Maggi & Nisbet 1991)

POST-MESOLITHIC DYNAMICS OF SETTLEMENT

The distributions of sites recorded so far in northern Tuscany, eastern Liguria and the Pennavaira Valley all suggest that during the Early and Middle Neolithic little attention was paid to the highlands.

The diagram in Figure 8 is based on the distribution of sites and scattered finds in eastern Liguria. The finds have been subdivided into two main categories:

a) contemporaneous assemblages of differentiated tools, which may suggest differentiated activities carried out by one (maybe very small) group;

b) scattered tools, or just a few artefacts, which can be considered related to sporadic (unsystematic) visits.

By plotting such finds according to chronology and to the height a.s.l., it appears that the Late Mesolithic increase in evidence for human presence on the mountains, both in numbers and in the altitudes of the finds, was followed by a sharp decrease during the Neolithic. The subsequent new sharp increase during the Copper Age, has been attributed mainly to the introduction of pastoral economies at high altitudes (Maggi & Nisbet 1991). Several pieces of information show that such a phenomenon began during the Late Neolithic. The Late Neolithic is characterised by the Chassey Culture, which originated in France and spread to Liguria around 5300 BP (Maggi 1997).

In several mountain basins of eastern Liguria, peat accumulation started during the Middle to Late Holocene (Cruise 1990b). Anthropogenic activity is considered one of the main factors that determined the onset of such accumulation. Beside Prato Mollo (about 1500m a.s.l.) – the site that first showed evidence of Copper Age clearings for pastoral purposes (Baffico *et al.* 1987; Cruise *et al.* 1988) – other sites have indicators of clearing dating to around 5000 BP, that is in the Late Neolithic (Macphail 1988; Cruise 1992; Maggi & Nisbet 1991: 274). Such clearings contributed to the reduction of the *Abies alba* forest between the end of the Atlantic and the beginning of the Subboreal. Thereafter *Abies alba*

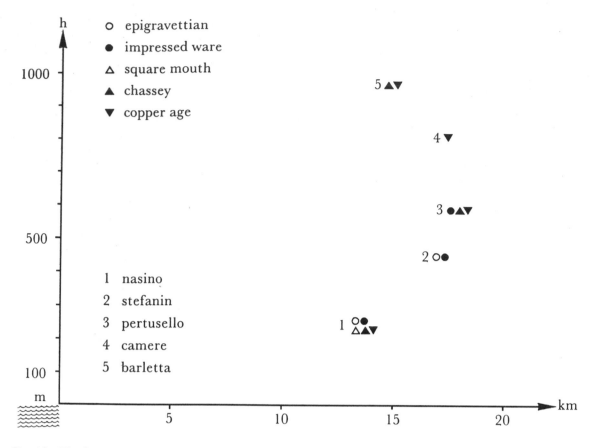

Fig. 10   The location of the Val Pennavaira caves in relation to distance from the sea and height above sea level (after Barker *et al.* 1990)

was replaced as the dominant species by *Fagus*. Some kind of management of the forest probably continued during the Bronze Age, as suggested by the minor presence of charcoal throughout the upper part of the Prato Spilla A pollen diagram (Lowe 1992a: 157).

In the Pennavaira Valley, Early and Middle Neolithic settlement does not exceed 550m altitude (figs 9 & 10). Later, a small and remote cave, the Tana del Barletta, located at about 1000m a.s.l., close to a very steep ridge that quickly takes the terrain above 1500m a.s.l. was used. Here sheep/goats, pigs and cattle were housed, as shown by the occurrence of deciduous teeth with resorbed roots (Barker *et al.* 1990: 117). Wild animals are virtually absent, showing that the cave can be interpreted as temporary shelter for flocks, herds and herders on the way between the residential sites in the lowlands and the highland pastures. The initial occupation (layer III) is of Late Neolithic age, being dated to 4980 ± 100 BP (HAR-8388). This is followed by the Copper Age occupation (layer II), dated 3880 ± 120 BP (HAR-6435) and then by a Middle Bronze Age layer (I), dated : 3270 ± 100 BP (HAR-8805).

In the Toscano-Emilian Apennines the distribution of sites (fig. 5) again shows a similar trend in highland occupation already registered in eastern Liguria: Mesolithic increase, Neolithic decrease and new increase during the Copper Age. Also similarly, pollen records show that the attempt to exploit the high pastures began during the Late Neolithic. At Prato Spilla A, a definite anthropogenic and intense episode of clearing spanned from 5035 ± 50 BP to about 3890 ± 45 BP, and continued thereafter with some fluctuations (Lowe 1992a; Lowe *et al.* 1994).

Due to the morphology of valley and slopes, in many cases watersheds and ridges must have been the best route for moving flocks, herds, goods and people. At the cross-point of two watersheds, some 5km inland from Portofino headland, is located the Castellaro di Uscio (Maggi 1990a) (fig. 11.7). The excavation showed a discontinuous occupation from

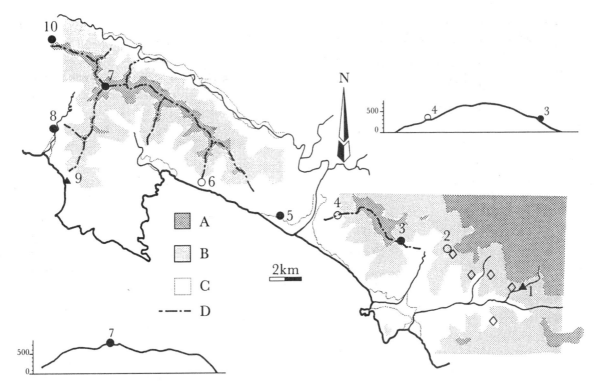

Fig. 11   The Tigullio basin: diamonds = copper ores; 2 = the Copper Age copper mine of Libiola; black circles = Late Bronze Age sites. A = land above 500m a.s.l.; B = land above 200m a.s.l.; C = post-Bronze Age coastal plains; D = watershed routes

Early Neolithic to the Roman conquest of the region (2nd century BC). During the Copper and the Early Bronze Ages, the settlement was continuous and rather intense. The dates range from 4490 ± 70 BP to 3390 ± 70 BP (that is from the beginning of the local Copper Age to the very end of the Early Bronze Age). The anthropogenic impact on the hilltop, where the settlement was located, induced an intense erosive episode of the soil, that much probably was the main cause of the abandonment of the site at the end of the Early Bronze Age. Most of the occupation soil was lost into the erosion gullies. After the abandonment and the infilling of the erosional gullies, the soil stabilised, and the site was occupied again during the Late Bronze Age.

Episodes of soil erosion related to Copper/Early Bronze Age occupation are widespread in the Apennines, even at high altitudes. Bands of mineral inwash are present in several peat sites of Eastern Liguria (Macphail 1988). Soil erosion is also attested on the Tusco-Emilian Apennines (Cremaschi 1990). At Bagioletto, located at 1550m a.s.l. on the massif of Monte Cusna, the soil that had accumulated with practically no disturbance during the Atlantic, was severely eroded with the presence of episodes of fire. One of these is dated 3790 ± 100 BP (I-12687: Cremaschi *et al*. 1984: 18).

During the Mid-Late Bronze Age, the number of sites decreased, but it has to be stressed that all the sites of this period known so far had permanent structures, such as stone-made terraces, used either for domestic or for agro-pastoral purposes. This is probably related to a change of the organisation of mountain settlement. The locations on crossing-points of watershed tracks, and/or on rocky hilltops strategic for controlling wide areas of pastures, the distribution at different altitudes, generally lower than during the Copper Age, suggest a more systematic and firm utilisation of landscape resources.

At medium altitudes, land was now cleared even at some distance from the village. This seems to be the case of the site Case Cordona, located at about 770m a.s.l., and only 4km from the coast (fig. 11.10). Here a quite large area (a few thousand square metres) was deforested and used for agro-pastoral activities, without any evidence (pottery or such) of domestic occupation in the surrounding areas (Cremaschi *et al*. 1992).

The social side of such changes can be inferred from some indicators. It has been suggested that the Copper/Early Bronze Age highland pastoralism was carried out by rather 'complete' family groups, as shown by the skeletal remains found in the contemporary collective burials in caves located in the mountains (Maggi & Nisbet 1991).

The increase in number of sites from the Neolithic to the Copper Age corresponded to a real increase in population, that was supported by the activation of new resources, such as mobile (transhumant) pastoralism and the precocious mining of the copper ores (Campana *et al.* in press). The large-scale exploitation of jasper quarries for chipping arrowheads and flat-retouched bifacial preforms also started at the very end of the Neolithic or beginning of the Copper Age (GrA-5115: 4830 ± 50 BP) (Maggi *et al.* 1996; Campana & Maggi in prep.)

The analysis of the pottery temper and of the lithic raw material from Castellaro di Uscio (Maggi 1990b; Mannoni 1990) show that the mobile Copper/Early Bronze Age local communities exploited resources located all over the central and western part of the region. For example, three kinds of pottery were used, one 'local' (made in the surroundings of the site), the others manufactured with tempering materials which are available to a minimum distance of some 30–40km east and some 40–50km west, respectively. Greenstones to make axes were carefully selected from sources located some 60–70km to the west.

The sites within this area share similar aspects of the material culture. In particular red jasper was widely used for chipped artefacts, especially barbed-and-tanged arrowheads. The westernmost part of the region also shares funerary customs (collective burial caves) and economic traits such as the increase of pastoralism and the early introduction of copper artefacts; however there are marked differences concerning some aspects of the material culture, such as the pottery style, the occurrence of *ailettes* beads and of bipointed-leaf and lozenge arrowheads, chipped out from whitish-greyish flint rather that from red jasper as in the central-eastern area. The association of *ailettes* beads with leaf and lozenge arrowheads is known in the neighbouring region of Provence in south-east France.

The emergence of such micro-regional differences during the Copper Age, is consistent with the disaggregation of the cultural uniformity of the larger Neolithic areas already observed elsewhere (Whittle 1996). In Liguria such process probably led to the formation of at lest two socially differentiated groups (tribes?), sharing 'basic' spiritual and economic traits but holding different aspects of the material culture (Del Lucchese & Maggi 1998). Other related groups are possibly to be seen in the neighbouring Lunigiana area (the basin of the Magra and Vara rivers, some 450km^2 in between the easternmost part of Liguria and the northernmost part of Tuscany), marked by the presence of anthropomorphic standing-stones (Ratti 1994), and in the remaining part of coastal Tuscany north of the Arno river (Cocchi Genick & Cremonesi 1985; Cocchi Genick 1996).

The Late Bronze Age settlement of Liguria was mainly scattered, with small sites on hill-top (sometimes fortified) and watershed strategic locations. Only a few larger sites have been found on the coast so far.

Going back again to the Castellaro di Uscio, the local community returned to the use only one kind of pottery: the 'eastern' one, manufactured with temper derived from the weathering of gabbro rocks. The 'western' variety was abandoned, as was the 'local'. Gabbro-tempered pottery is used exclusively in all of the Late Bronze Age sites of the Tigullio basin (fig. 11). This, and substantial data from other sites, such as Castellaro di Zignago (Giannichedda & Mannoni 1991), suggests that the Late Bronze Age social organisation operated at smaller territorial scale than during the Copper-Early Bronze Age. Fig. 11 illustrates a possible system of Late Bronze Age territorial organisation, with copper ores to the East (gabbro-temper sources are located a bit further to east), a coastal 'capital', and some mountain watershed routes . A few centuries later, such area will be known by Romans as the core area of the land occupied by the *Tigullia* tribe of Ligurians (Mennella 1989).

It is worth noting that the so-called *Tavola del Polcevera*, a decree of the Roman Senate of 117 BC concerning a territorial dispute between the town of Genoa and the inland tribe of the *Viturii* (Pastorino 1995), informs us that the latter group were settled in small scattered sites, without any 'capital' town but with a *castellum*, that is a fortified hill-top site. Such a description of settlement links early history with the picture emerging from the archaeology of the Late Bronze Age. The *Tavola del Polcevera* suggests that in the area studied an effective social organisation system was compatible with a small-site scattered settlement model. In fact, the rural community of the *Viturii* succeeded in defending their rights against the urbanised *Genuates* before the Senate in Rome 2116 years ago.

NOTES

1   This is in addition to the general agreement about the derivation of the 'Italian' Sauveterrian from the local Final Epigravettian background.

BIBLIOGRAPHY

Alessio, M., Allegri, L., Bella, F., Broglio, A., Calderoni, G., Cortesi, C., Improta, S., Preite Martinez, M., Petrone, V. & Turi, B. 1983. ¹⁴C datings of three mesolithic series of Trento Basin in the Adige Valley (Vatte di Zambana, Praedestel, Romagnano) and comparisons with mesolithic series of other regions. *Preistoria Alpina*, 19: 245–54.

Baffico, O., Cruise, G.M., Macphail, R.I., Maggi, R. & Nisbet, R. 1987. Monte Aiona – Prato Mollo. In Melli, P. & del Lucchese, A. (eds), *Archeologia in Liguria, III.1*: 57–66. Soprintendenza Archeologica della Liguria, Genova.

Bagolini, B. & Biagi, P. 1990. The radiocarbon chronology of the Neolithic and Copper Age of Northern Italy. *Oxford Journal of Archaeology*, 9: 1–23.

Barker, G., Biagi, P., Clark, G., Maggi, R. & Nisbet, R. 1990. From hunting to herding in the Val Pennavaira. In Biagi, P. (ed.), *The Neolithisation of the Alpine Region*: 99–121. Monografie di "Natura Bresciana" 13. Brescia.

Baroni, C. & Biagi, P. 1991. Le ricerche archeologiche alla Punta della Mortola (Giardini Hanbury, Imperia): campagne 1985 e 1987. *Rivista di Scienze Preistoriche*, 43: 257–61.

Bernabò Brea, L. 1956. *Gli scavi nella caverna delle Arene Candide (Finale Ligure), Gli strati con ceramiche, vol. 2*. Istituto Internazionale di Studi Liguri, Bordighera.

Biagi, P. 1991. The prehistory of the early Atlantic period along the Ligurian and Adriatic coasts of northern Italy in a Mediterranean perspective. *Rivista di Archeologia*, 15: 46–54.

Biagi, P., Castelletti, L., Cremaschi, M., Sala, B. & Tozzi, C. 1981. Popolazione e territorio nell'Appennino Tosco-Emiliano e nel tratto centrale del bacino del Po, tra il IX ed il V millennio. *Emilia Preromana*, 8: 13–36.

Biagi, P. & Maggi, R. 1983. Aspects of the Mesolithic Age in Liguria. *Preistoria Alpina*, 19: 159–68.

Biagi, P., Maggi, R. & Nisbet, R. 1987a. Liguria: 11,000–7,000 BP. In Bonsall, C. (ed.), *The Mesolithic in Europe*: 533–40. Edinburgh University Press, Edinburgh.

Biagi, P., Maggi, R. & Nisbet, R. 1987b. Primi dati sul Neolitico della Liguria Orientale. In *Atti della XXVI Riunione Scientifica "Il Neolitico in Italia" (Firenze 1985)*: 523–33. Istituto Italiano di Preistoria e Protostoria, Firenze.

Bietti, A. 1987. Some remarks on the new radiocarbon dates from the Arene Candide Cave (Savona-Italy). *Human Evolution*, 2: 185–90.

Bracco, R., Campana, N., Guglielmucci, M., Maggi, R., Martini, S., Negrino, F. & Vallin, P. 1993, in press. Grotticella sepolcrale "Tana del Bandito". *Rivista di Scienze Preistoriche*, notiziario 1992–93.

Broglio, A. & Lanzigher, M. 1990. Considerazioni sulla distribuzione dei siti tra la fine del Paleolitico superiore e l'inizio del Neolitico nell'Italia nord-orientale. *Monografie di "Natura Bresciana"*, 13: 53–69.

Campana, N. & Maggi, R. (eds) in preparation. *La Cava preistorica di diaspro in Valle Lagorara*. Luna Editore, La Spezia.

Campana, N., Maggi, R. & Pearce, M. in press. Libiola e Monte Loreto: due miniere di rame preistoriche nella Liguria orientale. In *Atti della 4a Giornata de "Le scienze della terra e l'archeometria"*, Napoli 20–21 febbraio 1997.

Castelletti, L. 1983. Il combustibile legnoso negli insediamenti mesolitici dell'Italia settentrionale. *Preistoria Alpina*, 13: 235–41.

Castelletti, L., Cremaschi, M. & Notini, P. 1976. L'insediamento mesolitico di Lama Lite sull'Appennino Tosco-Emiliano (Reggio Emilia). *Preistoria Alpina*, 12: 7–32.

Castelletti L., Maspero, A. & Tozzi, C. 1994. Il popolamento della Valle del Serchio (Toscana settentrionale) durante il Tardiglaciale Wurmiano e l'Olocene antico. In Biagi, P. & Nandris, J. (eds), *Highland zone exploitation in southern Europe*: 189–204. Monografie di Natura Bresciana, 20. Brescia.

Cocchi Genick, D. 1996. *Manuale di Preistoria III. L'età del Rame*. Octavo, Firenze, 2 vols.

Cocchi Genick, D. & Grifoni Cremonesi, R. 1985. *L'Età dei Metalli nella Toscana Nord-Occidentale*. Pacini Editore, Pisa.

Cremaschi, M. 1990. Pedogenesi medio olocenica ed uso dei suoli durante il Neolitico in Italia settentrionale. In Biagi, P. (ed.), *The Neolithisation of the Alpine Region*: 71–90. Monografie di Natura Bresciana, 13. Brescia.

Cremaschi, M., Biagi, P., Accorsi, C.A., Mazzanti, M.B., Rodolfi, G., Castelletti, L. & Leoni, L. 1984. Il sito mesolitico di Monte Bagioletto (Appennino Reggiano) nel quadro delle variazioni ambientali oloceniche dell'Appennino Tosco-Emiliano. *Emilia Preromana*, 9/10: 11–46.

Cremaschi, M. & Castelletti, L. 1975. Deposito mesolitico del Passo della Comunella (Reggio E.), Appennino Tosco-Emiliano. *Preistoria Alpina*, 11: 133–54.

Cremaschi M., Ferraris, M.R., Maggi, R. & Ottomano, C. 1992. Case Cordona: da bosco a campo durante l'Età del Bronzo. In Maggi, R. (ed.), *Archeologia preventiva lungo il percorso di un metanodotto*: 43–52. Quaderni della Soprintendenza Archeologica della Liguria 4, Genova.

Cruise, G.M. 1990a. Pollen stratigraphy of two Holocene peat sites in the Ligurian Apennines, northern Italy. *Review of Palaeobotany and Palynology*, 63: 299–313.

Cruise, G.M. 1990b. Holocene peat initiation in the Ligurian Apennines, northern Italy. *Review of Palaeobotany e Palynology*, 63: 173–82.

Cruise, G.M. 1992. Environmental change and human impact in the upper mountain zone of the Ligurian Apennines: the last 5,000 years. In Maggi, R., Nisbet, R. & Barker, G. (eds), *Archeologia della pastorizia nell'Europa Meridionale, II. Rivista di Studi Liguri*, 57 (1991): 169–88.

Cruise, G.M., Macphail, R.I., Maggi, R. & Nisbet, R. 1988. Prato Mollo (Genova). *Rassegna di Archeologia*, 7: 604–6.

Del Lucchese A. & Maggi, R. (eds) 1998. *Dal diaspro al bronzo (L'Età del Rame e l'Età del Bronzo in Liguria)*. Quaderni della Soprintendenza Archeologica della Liguria, 5, Luna Editore, La Spezia.

Escalon de Fonton, M. 1976. Les civilisations de l'Epipaleolithique et du Mesolithique en Provence littorale. In de Lumley, H. (ed.), *La Prehistoire Francaise, I*: 1367–78. Centre Nationale de la Recherche Scientifique, Paris.

Fossati, S., Messina, W. & Milanese, M. 1985. Il Castellaro di Vezzola (La Spezia). *Rivista di Studi Liguri*, 48(1982): 178–92.

Ghiretti, A. & Guerreschi, A. 1990. Il Mesolitico nelle Valli di Taro e Ceno (Parma). *Preistoria Alpina*, 24: 69–102.

Giannichedda, E. & Mannoni, T. 1991. Alcuni dati archeologici sulla pastorizia nell'Appennino settentrionale tra protostoria e medioevo. In Maggi, R., Nisbet, R. & Barker, G. (eds), *Archeologia della pastorizia nell'Europa Meridionale, II. Rivista di Studi Liguri*, 56: 297–314.

Guidi, O., Pioli, M. & Rossi, G. 1985. *Il Mesolitico della Garfagnana*. Gruppo Archeologico Garfagnana, Barga.

Issel, A. 1892. *Liguria Geologica e Preistorica*. Donath, Genova.

Lanzigher, M. 1987. Modificazioni dei prodotti della scheggiatura tra Mesolitico e Neolitico Antico: l'esempio del Bacino dell'Adige. *Atti della XXVI Riunione Scientifica dell'Istituto Italiano di Preistoria e Protostoria, Il Neolitico in Italia*: 157–69. Istituto Italiano di Preistoria e Protostoria, Firenze.

Laplace, G. 1964. Essai de typologie systématique. *Annali dell'Università di Ferrara*, sez. XV, vol. I.

Leale Anfossi 1972. Il giacimento dell'Arma dello Stefanin (Val Pennavaira-Albenga). Scavi 1952–1962. *Rivista di Scienze Preistoriche*, 27: 249–332.

Lowe, J.J. 1992a. The chronology and correlation of evidence for prehistoric pastoralism in southern Europe. In Maggi, R., Nisbet, R. & Barker, G. (eds), *Archeologia della pastorizia nell'Europa Meridionale, II. Rivista di Studi Liguri*, 57: 151–74.

Lowe, J.J. 1992b. Late Glacial and early Holocene lake sediments from the northern Apennines, Italy – pollen stratigraphy and radiocarbon dating. *Boreas*, 21: 193–208.

Lowe, J.J., Davite, C., Moreno, D. & Maggi, R. 1994. Holocene pollen stratigraphy and human interfernce on the woodlands of the northern Apennines, Italy. *The Holocene*, 4(2): 153–64.

Macphail, G.M. 1988. *Pollen stratigraphy of Holocene peat sites in Eastern Liguria, Northern Italy*. Unpublished PhD Thesis, City of London Polytechnic.

Maggi, R. 1977. Lo strato a ceramiche graffite delle Arene Candide. *Preistoria Alpina*, 13: 205–11.

Maggi, R. (ed.) 1990a. *Archeologia dell'Appennino Ligure. Gli scavi del Castellaro di Uscio: un insediamento di crinale occupato dal Neolitico alla conquista romana*. Istituto Internazionale di Studi Liguri, Bordighera.

Maggi, R. 1990b. Considerazioni sull'approvvigionamento di materia. In Maggi, R. (ed.), *Archeologia dell'appennino Ligure. Gli scavi del Castellaro di Uscio: un insediamento di crinale occupato dal Neolitico alla conquista romana*, Istituto Internazionale di Studi Liguri, Bordighera: 251–6.

Maggi, R. 1997. The radiocarbon chronology. In Maggi, R. (ed.), *Arene Candide: a functional and environmental assessment of the Holocene sequence (Excavations Bernabò Brea – Cardini 1940–50)*, Memorie dell'Istituto Italiano di Paleontologia Umana, N.S. 5: 31–52.

Maggi, R. & Garibaldi, P. 1986. Report on the raw material exploited for chipped stone artefacts by the mesolithic and neolithic communities of Eastern Liguria. In *Papers for the International conference on prehistoric flint mining and raw material identification in the Carpathian Basin*: 91–6. Budapest.

Maggi, R., Macphail, R.I., Nisbet, R. & Tiscornia, I. 1987. Pianaccia di Suvero. In Melli, P. & del Lucchese, A. (eds), *Archeologia in Liguria III.1*: 23–32. Soprintendenza Archeologica della Liguria, Genova.

Maggi R., Campana, N., Negrino, F. & Ottomano, C. 1996. The quarrying and workshop site of Valle Lagorara (Liguria – Italy). *Accordia Research Papers*, 5: 73–96.

Maggi, R. & Negrino, F. 1994. Upland settlement and technological aspects of the eastern Ligurian Mesolithic. *Preistoria Alpina*, 28: 373–96.

Maggi, R. & Nisbet, R. 1991. Prehistoric pastoralism in Liguria. In *Archeologia della pastorizia nell'Europa Meridionale I. Rivista di Studi Liguri*, 56: 265–96.

Mannoni, T. 1990. Considerazioni sull'uso e provenienza dell'industria litica scheggiata. In Maggi, R. (ed.), *Archeologia dell'appennino Ligure. Gli scavi del Castellaro di Uscio: un insediamento di crinale occupato dal Neolitico alla conquista romana*: 257–60. Istituto Internazionale di Studi Liguri, Bordighera.

Mannoni, T. & Tizzoni, M. 1980. Lo scavo del Castellaro di Zignago (La Spezia). *Rivista di Scienze Preistoriche*, 35 (1–2): 249–79.

Martini, F. 1995. L'Epigravettiano Finale dell'Arma di Nasino (scavi M. Leale Anfossi). *Bullettino di Paletnologia Italiana*, vol. 86, N.S. IV: 97–151.

Mennella, G. 1989. I *Tigulii* e la Liguria Orientale in nuovi documenti epigrafici. In *Serta Historica Antiqua, II*: 175–90. Giorgio Bretschneider, Roma.

Onoratini, G. 1982. *Prehistoire, sediments, climats du Wurm III a l'Holocene dans le Sud-Est de la France*. C.N.R.S., Aix-en-Provence – Marseille.

Palma di Cesnola, A. 1993. *Il Paleolitico Superiore in Italia*. Garlatti & Razzai, Firenze.

Pastorino, A.M. (ed.) 1995. *La Tavola del Polcevera*. Civico Museo di Archeologia Ligure, Genova.

Ratti, M. (ed.) 1994. *Antenati di Pietra*. Sagep, Genova.

Rowley-Conwy, P. 1997. The animal bones from Arene Candide (Holocene sequence): Final Report. In Maggi, R. (ed.), *Arene Candide: a functional and environmental assessment of the Holocene sequence*: 153–278. Memorie dell'Istituto Italiano di Paleontologia Umana, N.S., 5, Roma.

Savi, P. 1825. Quoted by Issel 1892: 159.

Shackleton, J.C. & Van Andel, T.H. 1985. Late Palaeolithic and Mesolithic coastlines of the Western Mediterranean. *Cahiers Ligures de Prehistoire et de Protohistoire*, n.s., n. 2: 8–20.

Starnini, E., & Voytek, B. 1997. The Neolithic chipped stone artefacts from the Bernabò Brea – Cardini excavations. In Maggi, R. (ed.), *Arene Candide: a functional and environmental assessment of the Holocene sequence*: 349–426. Memorie dell'Istituto Italiano di Paleontologia Umana, N.S., 5, Roma.

Tozzi, C. 1980. Il mesolitico dell'Appennino Tosco-Emiliano. In *Atti del I Congresso di Archeologia "La Toscana settentrionale dal Paleolitico all'alto medioevo"*: 43–59. Lucca.

Whittle A. 1996. *Europe in the Neolithic*. Cambridge University Press, Cambridge.

Islands in the Stream

Stone Age Cultural Dynamics in Sardinia and Corsica

Robert H. Tykot

> The persistent myth that Corsica and Sardinia are isolated by virtue of being islands may be challenged not only on the historical record but through the archaeological facts of the great antiquity of their settlement and their participation in such wide-ranging cultural phenomena as that of the Impressed Ware sphere of the Early Neolithic and of the sphere of a precocious Copper-Bronze Age *'incastellamento'*.
>
> (Lewthwaite 1988: 180)

INTRODUCTION

Recent research suggests that previous assumptions about the marginal role of Sardinia and Corsica in Mediterranean prehistory were severely biassed by the historic period status of these islands. Recent discoveries include the antiquity of human occupation on these islands, the extent and continuity of extra-insular contacts, and the overwhelming evidence for indigenous development of complex societies. It is now possible to describe these Stone Age cultures in some detail, rather than as generically 'Neolithic' or 'Pre-Nuragic' (referring to the monumental Bronze Age towers of Sardinia and southern Corsica), and to illustrate both their dynamic, distinctive individuality and their central place in the cultural and economic stream of the prehistoric Mediterranean world.

It is only in the last twenty-five years that the island of Sardinia has been recognised as having had a rich indigenous culture dating from at least the Early Neolithic period, if not earlier. Our knowledge of Sardinian prehistory has benefited in the past three decades from an explosion of archaeological research (see Lilliu 1988; Balmuth 1992; Webster 1996). Earlier, the only real evidence that the island had been inhabited early on came from the finds of obsidian, assumed to be from Sardinia, associated with Early Neolithic ceramics at sites outside of Sardinia such as Arene Candide in Liguria, and Basi in Corsica (fig. 1). Lilliu (1967) has even suggested that obsidian, a sort of 'black gold', may have played a significant role in the settlement and Neolithic economy of Sardinia. This paper establishes that long-term continuity of extra-insular communication and interaction was in fact characteristic of Sardinia and Corsica in the Stone Age, and effectively integrated

Fig. 1 Mediterranean islands and sites mentioned in the text

these islands within a prehistoric Mediterranean *koiné*. At the same time, the extent and nature of these interactions were considerably variable over the course of the Neolithic, a period of more than 2500 years.

PRE-NEOLITHIC

It is impossible to discuss the dynamics of Neolithic settlement and socio-economic systems in Sardinia and Corsica without first establishing their characteristics in the preceding period as a framework for subsequent development. The question of when these islands were first settled has been the subject of some debate in the last several years. The prevailing evidence appears to indicate that Pre-Neolithic occupation of islands is exceptional in the Mediterranean, with the limiting factors relating more to subsistence and 'attractiveness' (Cherry 1990) than the basic maritime capabilities necessary to get there. The exceptions include the large islands of Sardinia, Corsica, Cyprus and perhaps Mallorca.

The earliest evidence for island occupation anywhere in the Mediterranean comes from Corbeddu Cave (Olièna) in Sardinia, where human remains have now been found in a layer dated approximately 20,000 BP (Sondaar *et al.* 1995; Sondaar 1998). Middle Pleistocene lithic assemblages also have been reported in Sardinia (Arca *et al.* 1982) and now in Corsica (Bonifay 1994); these finds are however controversial and/or not yet fully published, and are of no immediate relevance to the Holocene focus of this paper. At Corbeddu, several stone tools have been reported from later levels of Hall 1 of the cave (Martini 1992), while Hall 2 contains a remarkable accumulation of deer bones including several mandibles seemingly used as cutting or scraping tools (Klein Hofmeijer & Sondaar 1992; 1993). The anthropogenic origins of these materials has been questioned (Cherry 1992), as has the chronological relationship between the two parts of the cave (Tykot 1994). If the bone accumulation is in fact evidence of human activity, it indicates that Corbeddu Cave was frequently occupied for the latter half of the Upper Palaeolithic, a time when Sardinia and Corsica were a single land mass due to lowered sea levels, but remained separated from the mainland as the endemic nature of the island fauna attest. These finds suggest therefore that sea travel and long-distance interactions between the mainland and Sardinia/Corsica began many millennia before obsidian from the Aegean island of Melos first found its way to Franchthi Cave in mainland Greece (Perlès 1987).

By the beginning of the Mesolithic, sea-levels had risen significantly, to about -35m by 8000 cal.BC, putting coastlines near to their present location, and separating the islands of Sardinia and Corsica (Shackleton *et al.* 1984). The anthropogenic origin of the subsequent deposits in Corbeddu Cave are undisputed, since two human bones are associated with the butchered remains of *Prolagus sardus*, a now extinct lagomorph. More importantly, contemporary settlement has been documented at several rock-shelter sites in Corsica (Lanfranchi 1998): Curacchiaghju (Lanfranchi 1967; 1974; 1987a); Araguina-Sennola (Lanfranchi *et al.* 1973; Lanfranchi & Weiss 1977); Strette II (Magdeleine 1985; Magdeleine & Ottaviani 1986); Pietracorbara (Magdeleine 1991); Longone (Lanfranchi 1987b); and Monte Leone (Lanfranchi 1991; Vigne 1992a). Except for Curacchiaghju, all of these sites are located on coastal plains within a few kilometres of the sea. Monte Leone, still under excavation, is the only site with actual domestic structures (hearths), although burials have been found at Araguina-Sennola and Pietracorbara. Associated lithic assemblages are largely idiosyncratic, and always made of local quartz and rhyolite. Typologically, they have been related to the Final Epigravettian and Sauvetterian of Tuscany (Tozzi 1977). Faunal remains suggest that subsistence was based on *Prolagus sardus*, along with other small terrestrial mammals and birds, and was supplemented by some fish and to a lesser extent shellfish (Vigne 1998).

During the Mesolithic, then, it appears that human occupation of Sardinia and Corsica may have become somewhat more common. Nevertheless, there is no evidence of regular traffic between the islands and the mainland, and the human remains from Corbeddu Cave are reported to have morphologies "outside the range of modern human variation and probably due to endemism in an isolated population" (Spoor & Sondaar 1986; Spoor & Germanà 1987). There is also no evidence for the movement of artefactual materials of any kind. No obsidian has been found at any of the pre-neolithic sites in Sardinia and Corsica, nor in Mesolithic levels at Grotta dell'Uzzo in Sicily, nor Arene Candide in Liguria. The only two examples of western Mediterranean obsidian excavated from pre-neolithic contexts come from Perriere Sottano (Ramacca, Catania) in Sicily, where a single fragment of obsidian from Lipari is associated with a flint industry radiocarbon dated to the 8th millennium cal.BC (Aranguren & Revedin 1996), and from a Final Epigravettian layer at Arma dello Stefanin in Liguria (Leale Anfossi 1972), which by all accounts was not contaminated (Williams-Thorpe *et al.* 1979; Barker *et al.* 1990). Obsidian was not found, however, during more recent excavations at Stefanin (Biagi *et al.* 1987), and at minimum cautions that the significance of the single scraper found in layer V not be over-interpreted (cf. Cherry 1990: 190–1). The geological source of this piece has not been determined (*contra* Camps 1986: 37).

EARLY NEOLITHIC

The tripartite Neolithic chronology for Italy developed by Bernabò Brea from his excavations at Arene Candide is still widely used, but it must be emphasised that a particular Neolithic phase (e.g. Late Neolithic) in one region is not necessarily contemporary with the same descriptive phase in another. Radiocarbon dating, especially with the extension of the calibration curve, is helping to address the issue of regional contemporaneity, but limited numbers of good dates from good stratigraphic sequences means that contemporaneity is still usually established on typological grounds.

Radiocarbon and obsidian hydration dates from several sites suggests that the Early Neolithic in Sardinia and Corsica (c.5700–4700 cal.BC) was largely contemporary with Early Neolithic sites in northern Italy and southern France (Tykot 1994; Skeates 1994a; Bagolini & Biagi 1990; Evin 1987); the Early Neolithic probably appeared somewhat earlier in southern Italy and Dalmatia (Sargent 1985; Chapman 1988; Chapman & Müller 1990; Skeates 1994b). In Sardinia, the Early Neolithic is subdivided into Cardial I, Cardial II, and Epicardial (Filiestru) phases (Tanda 1998a); in Corsica, a fourth Early Neolithic phase (Punched = Curasien; Lanfranchi 1992; 1993) is contemporary with the Sardinian Middle Neolithic.

The Early Neolithic in the western Mediterranean is defined by the appearance of ceramics, and domesticated animals and plants presumably with eastern Mediterranean origins, direct evidence at least of interaction between neighbouring groups on a local scale within a regional interaction sphere. There is some evidence that not all of these elements of the 'Neolithic package' appeared simultaneously in the western Mediterranean, a situation which has complicated our interpretation of this transitionary phase. Three major hypotheses exist for the appearance of the Neolithic: (1) adoption of Neolithic elements through social and economic interaction between neighbouring indigenous populations; (2) demic diffusion of a growing farming population; and (3) long-distance migration/colonisation by eastern agro-pastoralists (García 1997; Barnett 1995; Zilhão 1993; Donahue 1992; Binder 1989; Lewthwaite 1986a; 1989; Whitehouse 1987; Guilaine 1979). Since neither Sardinia nor Corsica were entirely unoccupied territories, the indigenous peoples must be considered in any acculturation or assimilation process, especially their potential motivation for a substantial change in their subsistence practices. Every known site of Pre-Neolithic type predates the Neolithic, and most have subsequent Early Neolithic occupations. Long-term continuity of the indigenous population, both originating from and continuing to have interactions with the nearby mainland, and supplemented by continuing local expansion and colonisation, is therefore more likely than two separate biological populations of indigenous hunter-gatherers and immigrant farmers from the east.

Twenty-five Early Neolithic sites have been identified in Sardinia, and an equal number in Corsica, including caves and rockshelters concentrated in the less mountainous parts of the islands or near the coasts, but including a few open-air sites as well. Some are located well in the interior of the islands, away from fluvial systems. Stratigraphic excavations at Grotta Filiestru (Trump 1983; 1985; 1986) and Sa Corona di Monte Maiore (Foschi Nieddu 1982; 1987) have provided the best sequence for Sardinia, with data from Corbeddu Cave still only preliminarily published (Sanges 1987). For Corsica, the Curacchiaghju stratigraphy is probably unreliable (Lewthwaite 1983: 151; Lanfranchi 1987a), but good sequences come from Araguina-Sennola (Lanfranchi et al. 1973; Lanfranchi & Weiss 1977), Basi (Bailloud 1969a; 1969b), Strette I and II (Magdeleine & Ottaviani 1986), and Longone (Lanfranchi 1987b; 1992; 1993).

Early Neolithic sites are characterised by Cardial Impressed Ware pottery, a style in use not only in Sardinia and Corsica, but especially common in southeastern Italy, southern France, and both Mediterranean and Atlantic coasts of the Iberian peninsula. At Grotta Filiestru in Sardinia, for example, Cardial impressed bowls, plates, and jars comprise 7% of the ceramic assemblage (Trump 1983). Guilaine (1980) has subdivided the Cardial

Impressed Wares into three regional facies: south Italian/Sicilian; Tyrrhenian; and Classic Cardial. An extremely important study of the provenance of Cardial wares, from six sites in the Aude region of southern France and one in Portugal, has demonstrated the existence of intra-regional, multi-directional interaction networks, with vessels found 50–70km from their production area (Barnett 1989; 1990a; 1990b; 1992); no other analytical studies have been done to determine whether this model holds true for other areas of the western Mediterranean, or if some of the widespread distribution of Impressed Wares is due to extra-regional exchange of pots rather than just decorative concepts. Either way, we may interpret the Cardial phenomenon as suggesting a common cultural base over much of the western Mediterranean, with broad inter-group interaction evidenced not only by the ceramics (Chapman 1988; Barnett 1995) but also by inter-regional movement of ground and chipped stone artefacts including obsidian on Sardinia and Corsica (Lilliu 1989; Contu 1990–91). In Italy, other neolithic ceramic types are generally considered to be of local origin, although this has not been explicitly tested by thin-section or chemical characterisation studies (cf. Skeates 1992).

Lithic assemblages are typically composed of geometric microliths, and larger implements including scrapers, burins, and transverse tranchet arrowheads. These tools were fashioned from flint, quartz, rhyolite, and above all obsidian which was available from three main sources (SA, SB2, SC) in the Monte Arci region of Sardinia (Tykot 1995; 1997). These sources are located in different areas in the Monte Arci volcanic complex and vary in their accessibility, as well as in the quantity and quality of the obsidian available at each locality. Obsidian artefacts can be attributed to specific sources using various methods of elemental analysis, and a recent provenance study of more than 2700 artefacts from about 50 archaeological sites in Sardinia and Corsica revealed distribution patterns which were not apparent in earlier studies of limited numbers of artefacts (Tykot 1996). At archaeological sites in Corsica, obsidian is rare (Basi, Curacchiaghju) or non-existent (Longone) in the Cardial I phase, although the flint from which most tools were made was imported from the Perfugas area in Sardinia (Lanfranchi 1980; 1993). In Sardinia, obsidian is found at all Early Neolithic sites, and accounts for 17% of the Cardial I lithic assemblage at Grotta Filiestru (Trump 1983). In Cardial II, obsidian becomes abundant at Corsican sites, although obsidian cores are small and rare, and arrowheads are infrequently made of obsidian. Lanfranchi and Weiss (1973) note that the obsidian can be opaque or translucent, and that there appears to be a drop off in obsidian frequency from south to north. Sardinian obsidian has been found in Early Neolithic contexts on Isola Pianosa between Corsica and the mainland, and at Arene Candide, Grotta Pollera, and Pianaccia di Suvero in Liguria (Tykot 1995; 1996; Ammerman & Polglase 1997; Williams-Thorpe et al. 1979). It is not possible at this time to say whether any obsidian comes from strictly Cardial I contexts at these sites. The impressed ceramics found on Isola del Giglio may be Cardial I, judging from reports of its similarity to material at Basi and Su Carroppu (Brandaglia 1991), and are associated with obsidian, some of which is probably Sardinian, despite the excavator's assumption otherwise (Brandaglia 1985). The strong similarities in relative obsidian source representation (type SB2 obsidian most common; SA and SC also important) between Early Neolithic sites in Sardinia, Corsica, the Tuscan archipelago, and mainland Italy suggest multiple down-the-line type exchanges (Tykot 1996; Renfrew 1977).

The exchange of these materials is undoubtedly related to the introduction and spread of domesticated animals and the transition to an agricultural way of life. Remains of sheep and pig are present in Cardial levels at Basi, Strette and Araguina-Sennola in Corsica (Vigne 1984; 1987; 1988), and Filiestru (Levine 1983) and Corbeddu (Sanges 1987) in Sardinia. Goat has been identified in the same levels at Basi and Strette, and perhaps is represented among the indeterminate caprine remains at Araguina-Sennola. Domestic cattle appear in the Cardial Neolithic at Filiestru, but account for less than 2% of the domestic faunal remains. In Corsica, cattle are not present in the Cardial levels at either Basi or Araguina-Sennola, but do appear by the end of the Early Neolithic at Strette.

Incipient agriculture in the Early Neolithic is suggested by the finds of carbonised domestic grains (*Triticum monococcum*, *Triticum dicoccum*) at Filiestru (Trump 1983) and the presence of grinding stones at Filiestru and Sa Corona di Monte Maiore in Sardinia (Foschi Nieddu 1982), and Basi and Strette in Corsica (Lanfranchi 1993). The evidence for subsistence in Neolithic Sardinia is discussed further by Lazrus (in this volume).

Neolithisation was based then on the adoption of ceramic technology of a widespread decorative type, the cultivation of already-domesticated plants and the raising of non-indigenous animals. This Neolithic package was most likely introduced by expanding mainland populations and/or through local experimental adoption, especially in coastal and insular environments. In all instances, this transition went hand in hand with an accelerated involvement of Sardinia and Corsica in Mediterranean interrelations (see Camps 1991), highlighted in the archaeological record by the long-distance distribution of Sardinian obsidian to Corsica, the Tuscan archipelago, and mainland Italy.

MIDDLE NEOLITHIC

The Middle Neolithic Bonu Ighinu culture, first recognised in 1971 with the excavation of the cave site Sa 'Ucca de Su Tintirriolu (Loria & Trump 1978; Trump 1984a; 1984b), has been identified now at some 38 sites in Sardinia, with additional stratigraphic sequences coming from Corbeddu, Filiestru, Sa Corona di Monte Maiore (Foschi Nieddu 1987), and Cuccuru s'Arriu (Santoni 1989; 1992). The culture appears to be largely homogeneous throughout the island, in contrast to Corsica where multiple Middle/Late Neolithic cultures have been defined (see Lewthwaite 1983 for a review). The recently identified Presian culture, with dates from the type-site (Presa-Tusiu) spanning the 5th millennium cal.BC (see Tykot 1995: table V), is apparently contemporary with both Bonu Ighinu and the Curasien cultures (Lanfranchi 1992). The Basien (Corsica) and Chasséen (southern France) cultures, dating from the mid-5th through the mid-4th millennia cal.BC, are contemporary with the latter part of the Middle Neolithic and the first half of the Late Neolithic in Sardinia, a period which also encompasses the recently defined San Ciriaco-Cuccuru s'Arriu facies (Ugas 1990; Meloni 1993).

Although most known Bonu Ighinu sites are caves and rock-shelters, many village settlements dot the fertile Campidano plain which extends northwest from Cagliari to Oristano. The Cabras lagoon open-air sites are the earliest known settlements in the Sinis area, despite a recent intensive field survey there (Lazrus 1992). In the Iglesiente region in southwest Sardinia, all known Bonu Ighinu sites are caves or rockshelters, as were their Early Neolithic predecessors (Atzeni 1987b); in the Cagliari area, open-air and cave sites are known from both periods (Atzeni 1986). Insufficient data exist to assess the longevity and potential seasonality/functional specialisation of the cave sites, but a limited number of obsidian hydration dates from several sites suggest discontinuous occupation (Michels *et al.* 1984). In northern Sardinia, however, Trump (1983; 1984a; 1986) notes a change in the intensity of occupation at Grotta Filiestru, which he interprets as a shift to permanent settlement elsewhere with continued use of the cave by shepherds. Faunal assemblages from several sites attest to the continued presence and dietary significance of cattle, pig, sheep, goat, and *Prolagus* (Vigne 1988; Levine 1983). Frequent finds of ground stone axes at Sardinian and Corsican sites, however, suggest more intensive clearing of forests for cultivation, and grinding implements may have been used for cereal processing (Lanfranchi 1990). Some structures at Scaffa Piana (Saint-Florent) in Corsica have been interpreted as having functioned in the processing of oil extracted from wild olive and mastic trees, a practice that lasted in Sardinia and Corsica well into the 20th century (Lanfranchi & Thi Mai 1998).

Bonu Ighinu ceramics exhibit a greater degree of craftsmanship in both their production and decoration than Early Neolithic pottery. A wide variety of hemispherical or carinated bowls, jars, flasks, and ladles, with distinctive necks and handles, are frequently decorated with original geometric designs, occasional human and animal figures, and characteristic borders of fine punchmarks; the incised designs were often coloured with white or red mineral pigments after firing. The forms are similar to those of the contemporary Curasien punched-ware tradition in Corsica, and the incised motifs are in some cases reminiscent of painted motifs on Ripoli and Serra d'Alto wares from southern Italy (Atzeni 1987a); no argument can be made, however, for significant extra-insular communication based on ceramic decorative similarities as is apparent with Impressed Wares during the Early Neolithic.

By the second half of the 5th millennium cal.BC, however, considerable quantities of obsidian were distributed inter-regionally, judging from finds at numerous Chasséen sites in southern France and Square Mouth Pottery (VBQ) sites in northern Italy (Williams-Thorpe *et al.* 1979; 1984; Ammerman *et al.* 1990; Randle *et al.* 1993; Crisci *et al.* 1994; Binder & Courtin 1994; Guilaine & Vaquer 1994; Ammerman & Polglase 1993; 1997; Tykot 1995; 1996). In Sardinia, the ready availability and exploitation of obsidian is evident from the surface collections of many thousands of obsidian tools from sites in the Oristano-Campidano area and including the Monte Arci zone itself (Contu 1990–91; Atzeni 1992). In this region, obsidian most likely was acquired directly from the source, while obsidian found elsewhere in Sardinia, and on Corsica and the mainland, would have been obtained indirectly through exchange. It is uncertain to what extent specialists were involved in the procurement, production or transport of obsidian from Monte Arci, as no workshop sites have been excavated, nor detailed studies done to determine lithic reduction skill and efficiency, although at Grotta Filiestru there was technological improvement and increasing standardisation of forms relative to the Early Neolithic (Hurcombe & Phillips 1998). At Filiestru, more than 75km from Monte Arci, obsidian accounts for at least 30% of the lithic assemblage (Trump 1983), and was used for a variety of tasks but primarily animal processing (Hurcombe 1992; 1993). In Sardinia, Corsica, and northern Italy the use of type SB2 obsidian decreased significantly relative to the Early Neolithic, with type SC becoming the dominant subsource represented; in southern France, however, where Lipari obsidian was more common in the earlier Neolithic, Sardinian obsidian now predominates, and is almost entirely of type SA (Tykot 1996).

Other materials in circulation in Sardinia were shell, chlorite and aragonite beads, greenstone axes, and polished stone rings or bracelets. Greenstone axes, in particular those of jadeitite and eclogite, have a wide distribution on the mainland, from their western Alpine source to sites in southern France and northern Italy (Ricq-de Bouard 1993; Ricq-de Bouard & Fedele 1993), and to southern Italy and Sicily (Leighton 1992; Leighton & Dixon 1992). The stone rings are also widely distributed in central and northern Italy (Tanda 1977). No provenance study of the Sardinian stone material has yet been undertaken, but sources of nephrite and serpentinite apparently exist in northern Sardinia. Additional hints of mainland-island cultural interactions comes from the so-called *dea madre* figurines, well-known from the Cuccuru s'Arriu necropolis and other sites in Sardinia, and from Liguria and elsewhere on the mainland (Atzeni 1978; Gimbutas 1988; Antona 1998).

LATE NEOLITHIC

The Late Neolithic in Sardinia is also characterised by a relatively homogeneous, island-wide culture, named after the type site of San Michele di Ozieri, with a regional variant in the northeast (Gallura) part of the island. Ozieri settlements, mainly open-air sites, are truly found everywhere on the island, in all ecological zones, but are concentrated in alluvial plains, lagoonal and coastal areas; more than three times as many sites are known than in the preceding Middle Neolithic period (Atzeni 1981). The dating of the Ozieri period to the 4th millennium cal.BC is based on a limited number of radiocarbon dates; a late or sub-Ozeri phase extends into the 3rd millennium cal.BC (Tykot 1994; 1995; Santoni

1992). In Corsica, Ozieri is contemporary with the latter half of the Basien culture, and the early part of the Terrinien culture. It is anticipated that full publication of the Presa-Tusiu material will clarify that island's sequence and allow direct comparison with nearby Sardinia, independent from any typological considerations.

In Corsica, faunal assemblages from Araguina-Sennola, Scaffa Piana, and Terrina IV document the importance of cattle, pig, sheep and goat, with cattle and then pig the most significant dietarily, and *Prolagus* least significant (Vigne 1984; 1987; 1988; 1992b). At Filiestru in Sardinia, in contrast, sheep/goat continue to dominate the faunal assemblage, while the frequency of pig remains continued to decline relative to earlier Neolithic phases (Levine 1983). Since Filiestru appears to be a functionally specialised site, it would be unwise to conclude that differences existed between Sardinia and Corsica in terms of animal husbandry practices. Archaeobotanical remains are scanty, and it is mainly the density and location of settlements – many of them villages with several dozen wattle and daub huts – which argues for a fully agricultural economy by this time. This interpretation is reinforced by the numerous grindstones, mortars and pestles, storage vessels and pits, and even stone tools with sickle gloss that are known. In Corsica, less dynamic growth has been attributed to topographical/ecological limitations on the adoption of cereal-ovicaprine based subsistence (Lewthwaite 1983; 1984a; 1984b; 1985).

Ozieri ceramics come in a rich variety of forms and decorations, including new types of bowls and cups with carinated rims, globular vases with tunnel handles, tripods and amphoras, with geometric and stylised figurative motifs impressed or incised in the clay and coloured red or white. The find of Ozieri ceramics under the Piazza della Signoria in Florence demonstrates, for the first time, the movement to the mainland of something other than obsidian, although flint, salt, and metal ores have been proposed as additional candidates. Sardinian obsidian continued to be widely distributed to mainland Italy and France, with the continued predominance of type SA in later Chasséen contexts extending also now to Lagozza sites in northern Italy; this situation contrasts sharply with Sardinia and Corsica where types SB2 and SC remain well represented in Late Neolithic assemblages (Tykot 1995; 1996). The selective consumption of transparent, high-quality type SA obsidian is perhaps related to the increased availability in northern Italy of pre-formed obsidian blades from Lipari (Ammerman & Polglase 1993; 1997), although very few pieces of Lipari obsidian ever made it as far as southern France.

The schematic figurines attributed to the Ozieri culture (Antona Ruju 1980; Antona 1998) are apparently earlier than the well-known Cycladic types (produced mainly in the Early Cycladic II period, c.3100–2400 BC; see Getz-Preziosi 1985), and therefore not imported or copied after Aegean models; even the open-work type, perhaps of post-Ozieri, Chalcolithic date, can then be understood as having developed from a long sequence of local prototypes. The Late Neolithic is also rich in the variety of its material culture, from new forms of flaked stone tools in obsidian, flint and other stones, to greenstone axes, to bone tools, to decorated spindle whorls, to baskets. The manufacture of textiles is evident from the spindle whorls, loom weights and bone shuttles found. Copper and silver metal first appear in Late Ozieri (Lo Schiavo 1989) and Terrinien (Camps 1988: 123–34) contexts, suggesting similar (and contemporary) social developments in terms of prestige display in both island and mainland societies.

The increase in the exchange of material goods during the later Neolithic in peninsular Italy has been linked to changes in burial practices (Robb 1994a). Presumably, prestige competition in the circulation of obsidian and other materials was manifested as well in agricultural intensification and the observed shift to formal cemeteries with simple tombs and grave goods. Gender inequalities may have resulted from changes in labour specialisation and a male focus on secondary products (Robb 1994b; Sherratt 1981; 1982; 1983). The Sardinian sample of contextual burial remains is insufficient to statistically corroborate the mainland trend towards more burial goods (Robb 1994c), but elaboration of burial architecture with a presumed emphasis on kin relations is certainly evident in the hypogean rock-cut tombs known as *domus de janas* (house of the witches) which are found all over Sardinia. These tombs, found isolated or in clusters of up to 40, often are presumably modelled after Ozieri houses, with architectural details carved in the rock including the roof beams, support columns, doorways, windows, benches, niches and even hearths. Symbolic-religious motifs are also cut in bas-relief, especially the horns or silhouettes of bulls and rams, and are commonly interpreted as having connotations of fertility (Tanda 1984; 1985; 1989; 1998b). Inhumations are primary and secondary, and accompanied by ceramics, arrowheads, small votive axes, and *dea madre* figurines; while most interments were of adults, children and even infants were sometimes entombed, and Webster (1996) suggests that a system of ascribed status may have existed in some areas of Sardinia by this time.

Late Neolithic burial structures also exhibit some variety, for example the megalithic circle graves at Li Muri in Arzachena (Puglisi 1941–42), the corridor dolmen (*allée couverte*) at Motorra in Dorgali (Lilliu 1968), and the tumulus complex at Pranu Mutteddu in Goni (Atzeni 1989) associated with large concentrations of menhirs (Atzeni 1982; 1988). The megalithic phenomenon is also well-known in Corsica, with particularly close ties with northern Sardinia (Cesari 1992; Lanfranchi 1992; Lanfranchi & Weiss 1994). The appearance and development of the Sardinian and Corsican tombs are paralleled by similar, but often later, megalithic constructions in much of the central and western Mediterranean (Whitehouse 1981; Joussaume 1985; Guilaine 1992). The 55m long 'altar' of Monte d'Accoddi, located between Sassari and Porto Torres in northwest Sardinia, is unique in the western Mediterranean (Tinè *et al.* 1989; Tinè & Traverso 1992). Constructed on top of an early Ozieri village and probably dating to the end of the classic Ozieri period (Tykot 1994: n. 2; cf. Tinè 1998), a ramp leads up to a platform reconstructed into a ziggurat-like shape with a red-painted shrine at its centre. There is not yet agreement on the ceramic sequence and the multiple construction phases of the monument, nor on its interpretation.

By the Late Neolithic, it is strongly suggested then from ritualistic and burial manifestations, from intensified agricultural production and from the diversified production and exchange of material culture, that at least an incipient level of social hierarchy had begun to appear in Sardinia, relative to the unstratified, egalitarian societies of the Early and Middle Neolithic (Lewthwaite 1984c). In the millennium to follow, increasing socio-political hierarchisation is evident, although not yet fully documented.

POST-NEOLITHIC

The Chalcolithic period in Sardinia is a still poorly understood millennium-long transition between the widespread and well-known Late Neolithic Ozieri culture and the Bronze Age Bonnanaro and Nuragic cultures (Atzeni *et al.* 1988). Currently recognised in five aspects – sub-Ozieri, Filigosa, Abealzu, Monte Claro, and Beaker – stratigraphic sequences come only from Monte d'Accoddi and La Tomba dei Vasi Tetrapodi in Santu Pedru (Contu 1966). Other than the Beaker material (Ferrarese-Ceruti 1981; 1988), there is little direct evidence of extra-insular contacts, as little obsidian has been identified in mainland Chalcolithic contexts (but see Pollmann 1993) although it remains the most common lithic material in Sardinia until at least the Iron Age. It is likely that, at least in peninsular Italy and southern France, obsidian had somewhat more than a simple functional utility, and that by the end of the Chalcolithic this role was replaced by objects in metal. As early as the Filigosa-Abealzu phase of this period, however, sites enclosed by megalithic walls are known, perhaps denoting a response to increased economic interests in prospecting and metallurgy and developing social tensions between groups. Increasing population density and subsequent competition over prime agricultural lands may have resulted in the marginalisation of some communities and the development of asymmetrical relationships based on differential access to draft animals, plough technology, and intensified agricultural production (Lewthwaite 1986b; Webster 1990; 1996).

DISCUSSION AND CONCLUSION

In this brief review, I have emphasised the dynamic nature of the Stone Age in Sardinia and Corsica. Just as it is no longer necessary to ascribe indigenous Bronze Age architectural feats to 'higher' Aegean civilisations, we need not describe the early settlement and Neolithic development of Sardinia and Corsica as the simple, generic consequence of diffusion from the eastern Mediterranean. Rather, there is now documented evidence of significant Pre-Neolithic occupation of these islands, extending back to the Upper Palaeolithic and demonstrating the maritime capabilities of local populations. Thousands of years later, the 'Neolithic package' was selectively adapted to local conditions and integrated with local cultural manifestations.

In the Early Neolithic, the widespread distribution of ceramics – a new technology – in the Impressed Ware style and the exploitation of Sardinian obsidian reflect cultural interactions on a large scale in the western Mediterranean, and suggest the movement of additional materials not evident in the archaeological record including salt, basketry, domesticated grains, animals and animal products. In contrast to the eastern Mediterranean, regional exchange here coincides with instead of preceding the Neolithic and its new subsistence base of domesticated cereals and animals. Long-distance exchange, therefore, is probably a consequence of this new way of life rather than a potential incentive for the adoption of agriculture and the production of surplus in order to acquire non-local goods (see Runnels & van Andel 1988; Tangri 1989; Runnels 1989). I have argued elsewhere that long-distance prestige exchange of obsidian and other materials was an important way of maintaining ethnic or kin connections in increasingly sedentary Neolithic societies, connections which must have extended from Sardinia and Corsica to the mainland (Tykot 1996).

In the Middle Neolithic, the expansion of village settlements was probably accompanied by changes in social relations and perhaps uneven access to material resources. This is reflected at the island level in changing representation of the multiple Monte Arci obsidian sources, by greater local and regional diversity in ceramic styles, and by variability in burial treatments. Sardinian obsidian is even more widely available on the mainland, although the generally small quantities found at large numbers of individual sites emphasises its social rather than economic importance. The selection of specifically type SA obsidian in southern France argues not only for changes there in preference, but also in the mechanism(s) by which obsidian was obtained. The presence of obsidian from Pantelleria in Malta and Sicily indicate the capability of making open-water crossings (to a tiny destination) of at least 100km; this presents the possibility then that some direct contacts may have taken place between southern France and Corsica/Sardinia.

By the Late Neolithic, further economic and socio-political developments had taken place. Much denser settlement of Sardinia and Corsica suggests the emergence of a fully agricultural economy; at the same time elaboration of burial monuments and megaliths signals both further social changes and participation in a phenomenon widespread in the western Mediterranean. The continued importance of island obsidian in northern Italy and southern France attests to ongoing inter-regional interactions, as does the contemporary appearance of metal artefacts at later Neolithic and Chalcolithic sites on both the islands and the mainland. It is probably this latter material – primarily copper – which led to the abrupt decline in obsidian use on the mainland; the absence of obsidian, however, implies only that its prestige value declined, not that interaction with the islands ceased as the search for metal resources would have been an important activity for Chalcolithic cultures in the western Mediterranean and Sardinia is rich in metalliferous deposits including copper, lead and tin.

Stone Age societies in Sardinia and Corsica were neither isolated from surrounding cultural entities, nor unitary in their spatio-temporal characteristics. From the introduction of domesticated animals and cereals, to the exploitation and distribution of obsidian and other materials, to the appearance of megalithic monuments and the development of metallurgy, these islands maintained important relationships with the mainland throughout the Neolithic. The Bronze Age cultures of the central Mediterranean are now recognised as having been an important part of Mediterranean and specifically Aegean cultural networks; it should be recognised that Sardinia and Corsica belong to the main stream of Stone Age prehistory as well.

BIBLIOGRAPHY

Ammerman, A.J., Cesana, A., Polglase, C. & Terrani, M. 1990. Neutron activation analysis of obsidian from two neolithic sites in Italy. *Journal of Archaeological Science*, 17 (2): 209–20.

Ammerman, A.J. & Polglase, C. 1993. The exchange of obsidian at Neolithic sites in Italy. In Healy, F. & Scarre, C. (eds), *Trade and Exchange in European Prehistory*: 101–7. Oxbow Monograph 33, Oxbow Books, Oxford.

Ammerman, A.J. & Polglase, C. 1997. Analyses and descriptions of the obsidian collections from Arene Candide. In Maggi, R. (ed.), *Arene Candide: A Functional and Environmental Assessment of the Holocene Sequence*: 573–92. Memorie dell'Istituto Italiano di Paleontologia Umana 5. Il Calamo, Rome.

Antona, A. 1998. Le statuette di 'dea madre' nei contesti prenuragici. Alcune considerazioni. In Balmuth, M.S. & Tykot, R.H. (eds), *Sardinian and Aegean Chronology. Studies in Sardinian Archaeology V*. Oxbow Books, Oxford.

Antona Ruju, A. 1980. Appunti per una seriazione evolutiva delle statuette femminili della Sardegna prenuragica. *Atti della XXII Riunione Scientifica dell'Istituto Italiano di Preistoria e Protostoria, "Sardegna Centro-Settentrionale", 21–27 ottobre 1978*: 115–39. Istituto Italiano di Preistoria e Protostoria, Firenze.

Aranguren, B. & Revedin, A. 1996. Problemi relativi all'insorgenza del Mesolitico in Sicilia. In Leighton, R. (ed.), *Early Societies in Sicily. New Developments in Archaeological Research*: 31–9. Accordia Specialist Studies on Italy 5, Accordia Research Centre, University of London.

Arca, M., Martini, F., Pitzalis, G., Tuveri, C. & Ulzega, A. 1982. *Il Paleolitico dell'Anglona (Sardegna settentrionale). Ricerche 1970–1980*. Quaderni della Soprintendenza ai Beni Archeologici per le Provincie di Sassari e Nuoro 12. Dessì, Sassari.

Atzeni, E. 1978. La dea-madre nelle culture prenuragiche. *Studi Sardi*, 24 (1975–77): 3–69.

Atzeni, E. 1981. Aspetti e sviluppi culturali del neolitico e della prima età dei metalli in Sardegna. In *Ichnussa: La Sardegna dalle origini all'età classica*: 19–51. Libri Scheiwiller, Milano.

Atzeni, E. 1982. Menhirs antropomorfi e statue-menhirs della Sardegna. *Annali del Museo Civico U. Formentini della Spezia* 1979–80 (II): 9–64.

Atzeni, E. 1986. Cagliari preistorica (nota preliminare). In *S. Igia, Capitale Giudicale. Contributi all'Incontro di Studio "Storia, Ambiente Fisico e Insediamenti Umani nel Territorio di S. Gilla (Cagliari)", 3–5 novembre 1983*: 21–57. ETS, Pisa.

Atzeni, E. 1987a. Il neolitico della Sardegna. *Atti della XXVI Riunione Scientifica, "Il Neolitico in Italia", novembre 1985, Firenze*, Volume I: 381–400. Istituto Italiano di Preistoria e Protostoria, Firenze.

Atzeni, E. 1987b. *La Preistoria del Sulcis-Iglesiente*. STEF, Cagliari.

Atzeni, E. 1988. Megalitismo e arte. *Rassegna di Archeologia*, 7: 449–56.

Atzeni, E. 1989. Nota sulla necropoli megalitica di Pranu Mutteddu-Goni: i monumenti. In Campus, L.D. (a cura di), *La Cultura di Ozieri. Problematiche e nuove acquisizioni. Atti del I convegno di studio (Ozieri, gennaio 1986–aprile 1987)*: 201–11. Il Torchietto, Ozieri.

Atzeni, E. 1992. Reperti neolitici dall'Oristanese. In *Sardinia Antiqua. Studi in Onore di Piero Meloni in Occasione del Suo Settantesimo Compleanno*: 35–62. Edizioni della Torre, Cagliari.

Atzeni, E., Contu, E. & Ferrarese Ceruti, M.L. 1988. L'età del Rame nell'Italia insulare: la Sardegna. *Rassegna di Archeologia*, 7: 449–67.

Bagolini, B. & Biagi, P. 1990. The radiocarbon chronology of the neolithic and copper age of northern Italy. *Oxford Journal of Archaeology*, 9 (1): 1–23.

Bailloud, G. 1969a. Fouilles de Basi (Serra-di-Ferro – Corse). Campagne 1968. *Corse Historique*, 9 (33): 49–64.

Bailloud, G. 1969b. Fouille d'un habitat néolithique et torréen à Basi (Serra-di-Ferro – Corse). Premiers résultats. *Bulletin de la Société Préhistoire Française*, 66: 367–84.

Balmuth, M. 1992. Archaeology in Sardinia. *American Journal of Archaeology*, 96 (4): 663–97.

Barker, G., Biagi, P., Clark, G., Maggi, R. & Nisbet, R. 1990. From hunting to herding in the Val Pennavaira (Liguria – northern Italy). In Biagi, P. (ed.), *The Neolithisation of the Alpine Region*: 99–121. Monografie di "Natura Bresciana" 13.

Barnett, W.K. 1989. *The Production and Distribution of Early Neolithic Pottery in the Aude Valley, France*. PhD dissertation, Boston University. University Microfilms, Ann Arbor.

Barnett, W.K. 1990a. Small-scale transport of early Neolithic pottery in the west Mediterranean. *Antiquity*, 64 (245): 859–65.

Barnett, W.K. 1990b. Production and distribution of early pottery in the west Mediterranean. In Kingery, W. (ed.), *The Changing Roles of Ceramics in Society: 26,000 B.P. to the Present*: 137–57. The American Ceramic Society, Westerville, OH.

Barnett, W.K. 1992. The physical analyses of Early Neolithic impressed pottery from Gruta do Caldeirão. In Zilhão, J., *Gruta do Caldeirão: O Neolítico Antigo*: 297–312. Trabalhos de Arqueologia 6. Instituto Português do Património Arquitectónico e Arqueológico, Lisbon.

Barnett, W.K. 1995. Putting the pot before the horse: Earliest ceramics and the Neolithic transition in the western Mediterranean. In Barnett, W.K. & Hoopes, J.W. (eds), *The Emergence of Pottery. Technology and Innovation in Ancient Societies*: 79–88. Smithsonian Institution Press, Washington, DC.

Biagi, P., Maggi, R. & Nisbet, R. 1987. Excavations at Arma dello Stefanin (Val Pennavaira-Albenga, Northern Italy) 1982–1986. *Mesolithic Miscellany*, 8 (1): 10–11.

Binder, D. 1989. Aspects de la néolithisation dans les aires padane, provençale et ligure. In Aurenche, O. & Cauvin, J. (eds), *Néolithisations*: 199–225. BAR International Series 516. British Archaeological Reports, Oxford.

Binder, D. & Courtin, J. 1994. Un point sur la circulation de l'obsidienne dans le domaine Provençal. *Gallia Préhistoire*, 36: 310–22.

Bonifay, E. 1994. Rogliano, grotte de la Coscia. *Bilan Scientifique du Service Régional de l'Archéologie*, 59. Ministère de la Culture et de la Francophonie, Paris.

Brandaglia, M. 1985. Il Neolitico a ceramica impressa dell'Isola del Giglio. L'industria litica. *Studi per l'ecologia del Quaternario*, 7: 53–76.

Brandaglia, M. 1991. Il Neolitico a ceramica impressa dell'Isola del Giglio: La ceramica. *Studi per l'ecologia del Quaternario*, 13: 43–104.

Camps, G. 1986. The young sheep and the sea: early navigation in the Mediterranean. *Diogenes*, 136: 19–45.

Camps, G. 1988. *Préhistoire d'Une Île. Les Origines de la Corse*. Paris: Errance.

Camps, G. 1991. Le peuplement prenéolithique de la Corse. *Actes du 113ᵉ Congrès National des Sociétés Savantes, "Mésolithique et Néolithisation en France et dans les Régions Limitrophes", Strasbourg, 5–9 avril 1988*: 37–51. Editions du C.T.H.S., Paris.

Cesari, J. 1992. New contributions to the study of the Megalithic in Corsica. In Tykot, R.H. & Andrews, T.K. (eds), *Sardinia in the Mediterranean: A Footprint in the Sea. Studies in Sardinian Archaeology Presented to Miriam S. Balmuth*: 105–17. Monographs in Mediterranean Archaeology 3. Sheffield Academic Press, Sheffield.

Chapman, J.C. 1988. Ceramic production and social differentiation: the Dalmatian neolithic and the western Mediterranean. *Journal of Mediterranean Archaeology*, 1 (2): 3–25.

Chapman, J.C. & Müller, J. 1990. Early farmers in the Mediterranean basin: the Dalmatian evidence. *Antiquity*, 64: 127–34.

Cherry, J. 1990. The first colonization of the Mediterranean islands: A review of recent research. *Journal of Mediterranean Archaeology*, 3 (2): 145–221.

Cherry, J. 1992. Palaeolithic Sardinians? Some questions of evidence and method. In Tykot, R.H. & Andrews, T.K. (eds), *Sardinia in the Mediterranean: A Footprint in the Sea. Studies in Sardinian Archaeology Presented to Miriam S. Balmuth*: 28–39. Monographs in Mediterranean Archaeology 3. Sheffield Academic Press, Sheffield.

Contu, E. 1966. La tomba dei vasi tetrapodi. *Monumenti Antichi*, 47: 1–196.

Contu, E. 1990–91. L'ossidiana e la selce della Sardegna e la loro diffusione. *Origini*, 15: 241–53.

Crisci, G.M., Ricq-de Bouard, M., Lanzaframe, U. & de Francesco, A.M. 1994. Nouvelle méthode d'analyse et provenance de l'ensemble des obsidiennes néolithiques du Midi de la France. *Gallia Préhistoire*, 36: 299–309.

Donahue, R.E. 1992. Desperately seeking Ceres: a critical examination of current models for the transition to agriculture in Mediterranean Europe. In Gebauer, A.B. & Price, T.D. (eds), *Transitions to Agriculture in Prehistory*: 73–80. Monographs in World Archaeology No. 4. Prehistory Press, Madison, WI.

Evin, J. 1987. Révision de la chronologie absolue des débuts du Néolithique en Provence et Languedoc. In Guilaine, J., Courtin, J., Roudil, J.-L. & Vernet, J.-L. (eds), *Premières Communautés Paysannes en Méditerranée Occidentale. Actes du Colloque International du C.N.R.S., Montpellier, 26–29 avril 1983*: 27–36. C.N.R.S., Paris.

Ferrarese Ceruti, M.L. 1981. La cultura del vaso campaniforme. In *Ichnussa: La Sardegna dalle origini all'età classica*: 55–65. Libri Scheiwiller, Milano.

Ferrarese Ceruti, M.L. 1988. Il Campaniforme in Sardegna. In E. Atzeni, E. Contu, & M.L. Ferrarese Ceruti, L'età del Rame nell'Italia insulare: la Sardegna. *Atti del Congresso Internazionale "L'Età del Rame in Europa", Viareggio, 15–18 ottobre 1987*: 456–60. Rassegna di Archeologia 7.

Foschi Nieddu, A. 1982. Il neolitico antico della Grotta Sa Korona di Monte Majore (Thiesi, Sassari): Nota preliminare. In R. Montjardin (ed.), *Le Néolithique Ancien Méditerranéen: Actes du Colloque International de Préhistoire, Montpellier 1981*: 339–47. Archéologie en Languedoc No. Special 1982. Fédération Archéologique de l'Hérault, Sète.

Foschi Nieddu, A. 1987. La Grotta di Sa Korona di Monte Majore (Thiesi, Sassari). Primi risultati dello scavo 1980. *Atti della XXVI Riunione Scientifica "Il Neolitico in Italia", Firenze, 7–10 novembre 1985*, Volume II: 859–70. Istituto Italiano di Preistoria e Protostoria, Firenze.

García, J.M.V. 1997. The island filter model revisited. In Balmuth, M.S., Gilman, A. & Prados-Torreira, L. (eds), *Encounters and Transformations: The Archaeology of Iberia in Transition*: 1–13. Monographs in Mediterranean Archaeology 7. Sheffield Academic Press, Sheffield.

Getz-Preziosi, P. 1985. *Early Cycladic Sulpture: An Introduction*. The J. Paul Getty Museum.

Gimbutas, M. 1988. Divinità femminili della Sardegna neolitica. *L'Umana Avventura. Volume Stagionale Internazionale di Scienza, Cultura ed Arte*, 3 (8): 58–64.

Guilaine, J. 1979. The earliest Neolithic in the west Mediterranean: A new appraisal. *Antiquity*, 53: 22–30.

Guilaine, J. 1980. Problemes actuelles de la néolithisation et du Néolithique Ancien en Méditeranée occidentale. In Best, J.G.P. & de Vries, N.M.W. (eds), *Interaction and Acculturation in the Mediterranean. Proceedings of the Second International Congress of Mediterranean Pre- and Protohistory, Amsterdam, 19–23 November 1980*: 3–22. Gruner, Amsterdam.

Guilaine, J. 1992. The Megalithic in Sardinia, southern France and Catalonia. In Tykot, R.H. & Andrews, T.K. (eds), *Sardinia in the Mediterranean: A Footprint in the Sea. Studies in Sardinian Archaeology Presented to Miriam S. Balmuth*: 128–36. Monographs in Mediterranean Archaeology 3. Sheffield Academic Press, Sheffield.

Guilaine, J. & Vaquer, J. 1994. Les obsidiennes à l'ouest du Rhône. *Gallia Préhistoire*, 36: 323–7.

Hurcombe, L. 1992. The function of Sardinian obsidian artefacts. In Tykot, R.H. & Andrews, T.K. (eds), *Sardinia in the Mediterranean: A Footprint in the Sea. Studies in Sardinian Archaeology Presented to Miriam S. Balmuth*: 83–97. Monographs in Mediterranean Archaeology 3. Sheffield Academic Press, Sheffield.

Hurcombe, L. 1993. The restricted function of Neolithic obsidian tools at grotta Filiestru, Sardinia. In Anderson, P., Beyries, S., Otte, M. & Plisson, H. (eds), *Traces et Fonction: Les Gestes Retrouvés*: 87–96. Colloque International de Liège. Edition ERAUL 50. Centre de Recherches Archéologiques du CNRS, Études et Recherches Archéologique de L'Université de Liège.

Hurcombe, L. & Phillips, P. 1998. Obsidian usage at the Filiestru Cave, Sardinia: choices and functions in the Early and Middle Neolithic periods. In Balmuth, M.S. & Tykot, R.H. (eds), *Sardinian and Aegean Chronology. Studies in Sardinian Archaeology V*: 93-102. Oxbow Books, Oxford.

Joussaume, R. 1985. *Les Dolmens pour les Morts. Les mégalithismes à travers le monde*. Hachette, Paris.

Klein Hofmeijer, G. & Sondaar, P.Y. 1992. Pleistocene humans in the island environment of Sardinia. In Tykot, R.H. & Andrews, T.K. (eds), *Sardinia in the Mediterranean: A Footprint in the Sea. Studies in Sardinian Archaeology Presented to Miriam S. Balmuth*: 49–56. Monographs in Mediterranean Archaeology 3. Sheffield Academic Press, Sheffield.

Klein Hofmeijer, G. & Sondaar, P.Y. 1993. The Upper Paleolithic taphonomy in Corbeddu cage (Oliena, Sardinia). Post-mortem damage of the lower dentition of Megaloceros cazioti. *Atti della XXX Riunione Scientifica, "Paleosuperfici del Pleistocene e del Primo Olicene in Italia, Processi di Formazione e Interpretazione", Venosa ed Isernia, 26–29 ottobre 1991*: 277–88. Istituto Italiano di Preistoria e Protostoria, Firenze.

Lanfranchi, F. de 1967. La grotte sépulcrale de Curacchiaghiu (Levie, Corse). *Bulletin de la Société Préhistorique Française*, 64: 587–612.

Lanfranchi, F. de 1974. Le Néolithique Ancien Méditerranéen, faciès Curacchiaghiu à Levie. *Cahiers Corsica*, 43: 39–48.

Lanfranchi, F. de 1980. L'obsidienne prehistorique corse: Les échanges et les axes de circulation. *Bulletin de la Société Préhistorique Française*, 77 (4): 115–22.

Lanfranchi, F. de 1987a. Le néolithique de Curacchiaghiu. Position chronologique et culture matérielle. Son importance dans l'ensemble corso-sarde. In Guilaine, J., Courtin, J., Roudil, J.-L. & Vernet, J.-L. (eds), *Premières Communautés Paysannes en Méditerranée Occidentale. Actes du Colloque International du C.N.R.S., Montpellier, 26–29 avril 1983*: 433–42. C.N.R.S., Paris.

Lanfranchi, F. de 1987b. Le néolithique de l'extreme sud de la Corse. *Archéologia Corsa*, 10–11 (1985–86): 44–54.

Lanfranchi, F. de 1990. L'alimentation des hommes préhistoriques. Préparation et consommation de quelques espèces végétales. *Archéologia Corsa*, 12–13 (1987–88): 46–53.

Lanfranchi, F. de 1991. Monte Leone (Bonifacio). *Bilan Scientifique du Service Régional de l'Archéologie*: 21–2. Ministère de la Culture et de la Francophonie, Paris.

Lanfranchi, F. de 1992. The megalithic monuments of Corsica and Sardinia: a comparative study. In Tykot, R.H. & Andrews, T.K. (eds), *Sardinia in the Mediterranean: A Footprint in the Sea. Studies in Sardinian Archaeology Presented to Miriam S. Balmuth*: 118–27. Monographs in Mediterranean Archaeology 3. Sheffield Academic Press, Sheffield.

Lanfranchi, F. de 1993. Le Néolithique ancien méditerranéen de la Corse. *Corsica Antica* (juillet 1993): 2–9.

Lanfranchi, F. de 1998. Premier peuplement holocène et néolithique de l'île de Corse. In Balmuth, M.S. & Tykot, R.H. (eds), *Sardinian and Aegean Chronology. Studies in Sardinian Archaeology V*: 53-6. Oxbow Books, Oxford.

Lanfranchi, F. de & Thi Mai, B. 1998. L'oléastre et le lentisque, plantes oléagineuses sauvages dans l'économie néolithique en Corse et en Sardaigne. In Balmuth, M.S. & Tykot, R.H. (eds), *Sardinian and Aegean Chronology. Studies in Sardinian Archaeology V*: 103-10. Oxbow Books, Oxford.

Lanfranchi, F. de & Weiss, M.-C. 1973. *La Civilisation des Corses. Les Origines*. Editions Cyrnos et Méditerranée, Ajaccio.

Lanfranchi, F. de & Weiss, M.-C. 1977. Araguina-Sennola, dix années de fouilles préhistoriques à Bonifacio. *Archeologica Corsa*, 2: 1–167.

Lanfranchi, F. de & Weiss, M.-C. 1994. *Arts et Croyances. Pratiques Funéraires et Symboliques des Populations Préhistoriques Corses*. CRDP de Corse, Ajaccio.

Lanfranchi, F. de, Weiss, M.-C. & Duday, H. 1973. La sépulture prénéolithique de la couche XVIII de l'abri d'Araguina-Sennola. *Bulletin de la Société des Sciences Historiques et Naturelles de la Corse*, 606: 7–26.

Lazrus, P.K. 1992. *Settlement and Land-Use in Two Regions of Sardinia, the Gerrei and the Sinis*. PhD dissertation, Boston University. University Microfilms, Ann Arbor.

Leale Anfossi, M. 1972. Il giacimento dell'Arma dello Stefanin (Val Pennavaira-Albenga). Scavi 1952–1962. *Rivista di Scienze Preistoriche*, 27: 249–322.

Leighton, R. 1992. Stone axes and exchange in south Italian prehistory: new evidence from old collections. *Accordia Research Papers*, 3: 11–40.

Leighton, R., & Dixon, J.E. 1992. Jade and greenstone in the prehistory of Sicily and southern Italy. *Oxford Journal of Archaeology*, 11 (2): 179–200.

Levine, M. 1983. La fauna di Filiestru (Trincea D). In Trump, D.H., *La Grotta di Filiestru a Bonu Ighinu, Mara (SS)*: 109–31. Quaderni 13. Dessì, Sassari.

Lewthwaite, J. 1983.   The Neolithic of Corsica. In Scarre, C. (ed.), *Ancient France. Neolithic Societies and their Landscapes 6000–2000 bc*: 146–83. Edinburgh University Press, Edinburgh.

Lewthwaite, J. 1984a.   The art of Corse herding: Archaeological insights from recent pastoral practices on West Mediterranean islands. In Clutton-Brock, J. & Grigson, C. (eds), *Animals and Archaeology 3: Early Herders and Their Flocks*: 25–37. BAR International Series 202. British Archaeological Reports, Oxford.

Lewthwaite, J. 1984b.   Works and days: archaeological implications of recent settlement and subsistence activities in marginal regions of the western Mediterranean. In Bintliff, J.L. (ed.), *Progress in Mediterranean Studies*. University of Bradford, Bradford.

Lewthwaite, J. 1984c.   Pastore, padrone: the social dimensions of pastoralism in prenuragic Sardegna. In Waldren, W., Chapman, R., Lewthwaite, J. & Kennard, R.-C. (eds), *The Deya Conference of Prehistory. Early Settlement in the Western Mediterranean Islands and their Peripheral Areas*: 251–63. BAR International Series 229. British Archaeological Reports, Oxford.

Lewthwaite, J. 1985.   From precocity to involution: the Neolithic of Corsica in its west Mediterranean and French contexts. *Oxford Journal of Archaeology*, 4 (1): 47–68.

Lewthwaite, J. 1986a.   The transition to food production: a Mediterranean perspective. In Zvelebil, M. (ed.), *Hunters in Transition: Mesolithic Societies of Temperate Eurasia and Their Transition to Farming*: 53–66. Cambridge University Press, Cambridge.

Lewthwaite, J. 1986b.   Nuragic foundations: an alternative model of development in Sardinian prehistory, ca. 2500–1500 BC. In Balmuth, M.S. (ed.), *Studies in Sardinian Archaeology III: Nuragic Sardinia and the Mycenaean World*: 57–74. BAR International Seies 387. British Archaeological Reports, Oxford.

Lewthwaite, J. 1988.   Trial by durée: a review of historical-geographical concepts relevant to the archaeology of settlement on Corsica and Sardinia. In Bintliff, J.L., Davidson, D.A. & Grant, E.G. (eds), *Conceptual Issues in Environmental Archaeology*: 161–86. Edinburgh University Press, Edinburgh.

Lewthwaite, J. 1989.   Isolating the residuals: the Mesolithic basis of man-animal relationships on the Mediterranean islands. In Bonsall, C. (ed.), *The Mesolithic in Europe: Papers Presented at the Third International Symposium, Edinburgh 1985*: 541–55. John Donald, Edinburgh.

Lilliu, G. 1967.   *La Civiltà dei Sardi dal Neolitico all'Età dei Nuraghi*. 2nd edition. ERI, Torino.

Lilliu, G. 1968.   Il dolmen di Motorra (Dorgali-Nuoro). *Studi Sardi*, 20 (1966–67): 74–128.

Lilliu, G. 1988.   *La Civiltà dei Sardi dal Paleolitico all'Età dei Nuraghi*. 3rd edition. Nuova ERI, Torino.

Lilliu, G. 1989.   La Sardegna preistorica e le sue relazioni esterne. *Studi Sardi*, 27 (1988–89): 11–36.

Lo Schiavo, F. 1989.   Le origini della metallurgia ed il problema della metallurgia nella cultura di Ozieri. In Campus, L.D. (a cura di), *La Cultura di Ozieri. Problematiche e nuove acquisizioni. Atti del I convegno di studio (Ozieri, gennaio 1986–aprile 1987)*: 279–92. Il Torchietto, Ozieri.

Loria, D. & Trump, D.H. 1978.   Le scoperte a "Sa 'Ucca de su Tintirriolu" e il neolitico sardo. *Monumenti Antichi dei Lincei*, 49: 117–253.

Magdeleine, J. 1985.   Les premières occupations humaines de l'abri de Strette, Barbaghju. *Archéologia Corsa*, 8–9 (1983–84): 30–50.

Magdeleine, J. 1991.   Une deuxième sépulture pré-néolithique de Corse. *Bulletin de la Société Préhistorique Française*, 88 (3): 80.

Magdeleine, J. & Ottaviani, J.-C. 1986.   L'abri préhistorique de Strette. *Bulletin des Sciences Historiques et Naturelles de la Corse*, 650: 81–90.

Martini, F. 1992.   Early human settlement in Sardinia: the Palaeolithic industries. In Tykot, R.H. & Andrews, T.K. (eds), *Sardinia in the Mediterranean: A Footprint in the Sea. Studies in Sardinian Archaeology Presented to Miriam S. Balmuth*: 40–8. Monographs in Mediterranean Archaeology 3. Sheffield Academic Press, Sheffield.

Meloni, L. 1993.   Le ceramiche Bonu Ighinu e San Ciriaco di Puisteris (Mogoro) nella collezione Puxeddu. *Quaderni della Soprintendenza Archeologica per le Provincie di Cagliari e Oristano*, 10: 5–16.

Michels, J., Atzeni, E., Tsong, I.S.T. & Smith, G.A. 1984.   Obsidian hydration dating in Sardinia. In Balmuth, M.S. & Rowland Jr, R.J. (eds), *Studies in Sardinian Archaeology*: 83–113. University of Michigan Press, Ann Arbor.

Perlès, C. 1987.   *Les Industries Lithiques Taillées de Franchthi (Argolide, Grèce). Tome I: Présentation Générale et Industries Paléolithiques*. Indiana University Press, Bloomington.

Pollmann, H.-O. 1993.   *Obsidian im nordwest-mediterranen Raum. Seine Verbreitung und Nutzung im Neolithikum und Äneolithikum*. BAR International Series 585. Tempus Reparatum, Oxford.

Puglisi, S.M. 1941–42.   Villaggi sotto roccia e sepolcri megalitici nella Gallura. *Bullettino di Paletnologia Italiana*, 5–6: 123–41.

Randle, K., Barfield, L.H. & Bagolini, B. 1993.   Recent Italian obsidian analyses. *Journal of Archaeological Science*, 20: 503–9.

Renfrew, C. 1977.   Alternative models for exchange and spatial distribution. In Earle, T.E. & Ericson, J.E. (eds), *Exchange Systems in Prehistory*: 71–90. Academic Press, New York.

Ricq-de Bouard, M. 1993.   Trade in neolithic jadeite axes from the Alps: new data. In Scarre, C. & Healy, F. (eds), *Trade and Exchange in Prehistoric Europe. Proceedings of a Conference held at the University of Bristol, April 1992*: 61–7. Oxbow Monograph 33. Oxbow Books, Oxford.

Ricq-de Bouard, M. & Fedele, F.G. 1993.   Neolithic rock resources across the western Alps: circulation data and models. *Geoarchaeology: An International Journal*, 8 (1): 1–22.

Robb, J.E. 1994a.   The Neolithic of peninsular Italy: anthropological synthesis and critique. *Bullettino di Paletnologia Italiana*, 85: 189–214.

Robb, J.E. 1994b.   Gender contradictions, moral coalitions, and inequality in prehistoric Italy. *Journal of European Archaeology*, 2.1: 20–49.

Robb, J.E. 1994c.   Burial and social reproduction in the peninsular Italian neolithic. *Journal of Mediterranean Archaeology*, 7 (1): 27–71.

Runnels, C. 1989. Trade models in the study of agricultural origins and dispersals. *Journal of Mediterranean Archaeology*, 2: 149–56.

Runnels, C. & van Andel, T.H. 1988. Trade and the origins of agriculture in the eastern Mediterranean. *Journal of Mediterranean Archaeology*, 1: 83–109.

Sanges, M. 1987. Gli strati del neolitico antico e medio nella Grotta Corbeddu di Oliena (Nuoro). Nota preliminare. *Atti del XXVI Riunione Scientifica, "Il Neolitico in Italia", 7–10 novembre 1985, Firenze*, Volume II: 825–30. Istituto Italiano di Preistoria e Protostoria, Firenze.

Santoni, V. 1989. Cuccuru s'Arriu-Cabras. Il sito di cultura San Michele di Ozieri. Dati preliminari. In Campus, L. (a cura di), *La Cultura di Ozieri. Problematiche e nuove acquisizioni*: 169–200. Il Torchietto, Ozieri.

Santoni, V. 1992. Cuccuru S'Arriu (Cabras). L'orizzonte Eneolitico sub-Ozieri. In Tykot, R.H. & Andrews, T.K. (eds), *Sardinia in the Mediterranean: A Footprint in the Sea. Studies in Sardinian Archaeology Presented to Miriam S. Balmuth*: 157–74. Monographs in Mediterranean Archaeology 3. Sheffield Academic Press, Sheffield.

Sargent, A. 1985. The carbon-14 chronology of the early and middle neolithic of southern Italy. *Proceedings of the Prehistoric Society*, 51: 31–40.

Shackleton, J.C., van Andel, T.H. & Runnels, C.N. 1984. Coastal palaeogeography of the Central and Western Mediterranean during the last 125,000 years and its archaeological implications. *Journal of Field Archaeology*, 11: 307–14.

Sherratt, A. 1981. Plough and pastoralism: aspects of the secondary products revolution. In Hodder, I., Isaac, G. & Hammond, N. (eds), *Pattern of the Past: Studies in Honour of David Clarke*: 261–305. Cambridge University Press, Cambridge.

Sherratt, A. 1982. Mobile resources: settlement and exchange in early agricultural Europe. In Renfrew, C. & Shennan, S.J. (eds), *Ranking, Resource and Exchange: Aspects of the Archaeology of Early European Society*: 13–26. Cambridge University Press, Cambridge

Sherratt, A. 1983. The secondary exploitation of animals in the Old World. *World Archaeology*, 15: 90–104.

Skeates, R. 1992. Thin-section analysis of Italian Neolithic pottery. In Herring, E., Whitehouse, R. & Wilkins, J. (eds), *Papers of the Fourth Conference of Italian Archaeology 3. New Developments in Italian Archaeology Part 1*: 29–34. Accordia Research Centre, London.

Skeates, R. 1994a. A radiocarbon date-list for prehistoric Italy (c. 46,400 BP – 2450 BP/400 cal. BC). In Skeates, R. & Whitehouse, R. (eds), *Radiocarbon Dating and Italian Prehistory*: 147–288. Accordia Specialist Studies on Italy 3, British School at Rome Archaeological Monographs 8. Accordia Research Centre and the British School at Rome, London.

Skeates, R. 1994b. Towards an absolute chronology for the Neolithic in central Italy. In Skeates, R. & Whitehouse, R. (eds), *Radiocarbon Dating and Italian Prehistory*: 61–72. Accordia Specialist Studies on Italy 3, British School at Rome Archaeological Monographs 8. Accordia Research Centre and the British School at Rome, London.

Sondaar, P.Y. 1998. Paleolithic Sardinians: paleontological evidence and methods. In Balmuth, M.S. & Tykot, R.H. (eds), *Sardinian and Aegean Chronology. Studies in Sardinian Archaeology V*: 45-51. Oxbow Books, Oxford.

Sondaar, P.Y., Elburg, R., Klein Hofmeijer, G., Martini, F., Sanges, M., Spaan, A. & de Visser, H. 1995. The human colonization of Sardinia: a Late-Pleistocene human fossil from Corbeddu cave. *Comptes Rendus de l'Académie des Sciences*, 320, série IIa: 145–50.

Spoor, C.F. & Germanà, F. 1987. Proportions of the Neolithic human maxillae from Sardinia. *Bulletins et Memoires de la Société d'Anthropologie de Paris*, 14 (4) 2: 143–50.

Spoor, C.F. & Sondaar, P.Y. 1986. Human fossils from the endemic island fauna of Sardinia. *Journal of Human Evolution*, 15: 399–408.

Tanda, G. 1977. Gli anelloni litici italiani. *Preistoria Alpina*, 13: 111–55.

Tanda, G. 1984. *Arte e Religione della Sardegna Preistoricea nella Necropoli di Sos Furrighesos*. Chiarelli, Sassari.

Tanda, G. 1985. *L'Arte delle Domus de Janas*. Sassari.

Tanda, G. 1989. L'arte dell'Età del Rame in Sardegna. *Rassegna di Archeologia*, 7 (1988): 541–3.

Tanda, G. 1998a. Articolazione e cronologia del Neolitico Antico. In Balmuth, M.S. & Tykot, R.H. (eds), *Sardinian and Aegean Chronology. Studies in Sardinian Archaeology V*. Oxbow Books, Oxford.

Tanda, G. 1998b. Cronologia dell'arte delle *domus de janas*. In Balmuth, M.S. & Tykot, R.H. (eds), *Sardinian and Aegean Chronology. Studies in Sardinian Archaeology V*: 77-92. Oxbow Books, Oxford.

Tangri, D. 1989. On trade and assimilation in European agricultural origins. *Journal of Mediterranean Archaeology*, 2: 139–48.

Tinè, S. 1992. La cronologia assoluta di Monte d'Accoddi. In Tinè, S. & Traverso, A. (a cura di), *Monte d'Accoddi. 10 Anni di Nuovi Scavi. Relazione Preliminare*: 115–17. Istituto Italiano Archeologia Sperimentale, Genova.

Tinè, S. 1998. Unacceptable anomalies or incorrect use of radiocarbon dating in Sardinia? In Balmuth, M.S. & Tykot, R.H. (eds), *Sardinian and Aegean Chronology. Studies in Sardinian Archaeology V*: 25-7. Oxbow Books, Oxford.

Tinè, S., Bafico, S., Rossi, G. & Mannoni, T. 1989. Monte d'Accoddi e la cultura di Ozieri. In Campus, L.D. (ed.), *La cultura di Ozieri. Problematiche e nuove acquisizioni*. Atti del I convegno di studio, Ozieri, gennaio 1986-aprile 1987: 19-36. Il Torchietto, Ozieri.

Tinè, S. & Traverso, A. (a cura di) 1992. *Monte d'Accoddi. 10 Anni di Nuovi Scavi. Relazione Preliminare*. Istituto Italiano Archeologia Sperimentale, Genova.

Tozzi, C. 1977. Le peuplement pléistocène et de l'Holocène ancien de la Sardaigne. In Lanfranchi, F. de & Weiss, M.-C. (eds), *L'aventure humaine préhistorique en Corse*: 72-78. Editions Albiana, Ajaccio.

Trump, D.H. 1983. *La Grotta Filiestru a Bonu Ighinu, Mara (SS)*. Quaderni della Soprintendenza Archeologica per le Provincie di Sassari e Nuoro 13. Dessì, Sassari.

Trump, D.H. 1984a. The Bonu Ighinu Project and the Sardinian Neolithic. In Balmuth, M.S. & Rowland Jr, R.J. (eds), *Studies in Sardinian Archaeology*: 1–22. University of Michigan Press, Ann Arbor.

Trump, D.H. 1984b. The Bonu Ighinu project...results and prospects. In Waldren, W., Chapman, R., Lewthwaite, J. & Kennard, R.-C. (eds), *The Deya Conference of Prehistory. Early Settlement in the Western Mediterranean Islands and their Peripheral Areas*: 511–32. BAR International Series 229 (ii). British Archaeological Reports, Oxford.

Trump, D.H. 1985. Bonu Ighinu – site and setting. In Malone, C. & Stoddart, S. (eds), *Papers in Italian Archaeology IV: The Cambridge Conference*: 185–99. BAR International Series 243. British Archaeological Reports, Oxford.

Trump, D.H. 1986. Beyond stratigraphy – The Bonu Ighinu project. In Balmuth, M.S. (ed.), *Studies in Sardinian Archaeology, Volume II: Sardinia in the Mediterranean*: 8–17. University of Michigan Press, Ann Arbor.

Tykot, R.H. 1994. Radiocarbon dating and absolute chronology in Sardinia and Corsica. In Skeates, R. & Whitehouse, R. (eds), *Radiocarbon Dating and Italian Prehistory*: 115–45. Accordia Specialist Studies on Italy 3, British School at Rome Archaeological Monographs 8. Accordia Research Centre and the British School at Rome, London.

Tykot, R.H. 1995. *Prehistoric Trade in the Western Mediterranean: The Sources and Distribution of Sardinian Obsidian*. Ph.D. thesis, Harvard University. University Microfilms, Ann Arbor.

Tykot, R.H. 1996. Obsidian procurement and distribution in the central and western Mediterranean. *Journal of Mediterranean Archaeology*, 9: 39–82.

Tykot, R.H. 1997. Characterization of the Monte Arci (Sardinia) obsidian sources. *Journal of Archaeological Science*, 24: 467–79.

Ugas, G. 1990. *La Tomba dei Guerrieri di Decimoputzu*. Norax 1. Cagliari.

Vigne, J.-D. 1984. Premières données sur les débuts de l'élevage du Mouton, de la Chèvre et du Porc dans la sud de la Corse (France). In Clutton-Brock, J. & Grigson, C. (eds), *Animals and Archaeology 3. Early Herders and their Flocks*: 47–65. BAR International Series 202 British Archaeological Reports, Oxford.

Vigne, J.-D. 1987. L'exploitation des resources alimentaires carnées en Corse, du VIIe au IVe millénaire. In Guilaine, J., Courtin, J., Roudil, J.-L. & Vernet, J.-L. (eds), *Premières Communautés Paysannes en Méditerranée Occidentale. Actes du Colloque International du C.N.R.S., Montpellier, 26–29 avril 1983*: 193–9. C.N.R.S., Paris.

Vigne, J.-D. 1988. *Les Mammifères Post-Glaciares de Corse, Étude Archéozoologique*. Gallia Préhistoire Supplement 26. C.N.R.S., Paris.

Vigne, J.-D. 1992a. Rapport annuel de fouille sur le site de Monte Leone, campagne de 1992 (Monte Leone, Bonifacio, Corse). *Bilan Scientifique du Service Régional de l'Archéologie*. Ministère de la Culture et de la Francophonie, Paris.

Vigne, J.-D. 1992b. The meat and offal weight (MOW) method and the relative proportion of ovicaprines in some ancient meat diets of the north-western Mediterranean. In Maggi, R., Nisbet, R. & Barker, G. (eds), *Atti della Tavola Rotonda Internazionale, Archeologia della Pastorizia nell'Europa Meridionale, Chiavari, 22–24 settembre 1989*: 21–47. *Rivista di Studi Liguri*, 57 (1991). Istituto Internazionale di Studi Liguri, Bordighera.

Vigne, J.-D. 1998. Preliminary results on the exploitation of animal resources in Corsica during the preneolithic. In Balmuth, M.S. & Tykot, R.H. (eds), *Sardinian and Aegean Chronology. Studies in Sardinian Archaeology V*: 57-62. Oxbow Books, Oxford.

Webster, G.S. 1990. Labor control and emergent stratification in prehistoric Europe. *Current Anthropology*, 31.4: 337–66.

Webster, G.S. 1996. *A Prehistory of Sardinia 2300–500 BC*. Monographs in Mediterranean Archaeology 5. Sheffield Academic Press, Sheffield.

Whitehouse, R. 1981. Megaliths of the central Mediterranean. In Evans, J.D., Cunliffe, B. & Renfrew, C. (eds), *Antiquity and Man: Essays in Honour of Glyn Daniel*: 106–27. Thames and Hudson, London.

Whitehouse, R. 1987. The first farmers in the Adriatic and their position in the neolithic of the Mediterranean. In Guilaine, J., Courtin, J., Roudil, J.-L. & Vernet, J.-L. (eds), *Premières Communautés Paysannes en Méditerranée Occidentale. Actes du Colloque International du C.N.R.S., Montpellier, 26–29 avril 1983*: 357–66. C.N.R.S., Paris.

Williams-Thorpe, O., Warren, S.E. & Barfield, L.H. 1979. The distribution and sources of archaeological obsidian from Northern Italy. *Preistoria Alpina*, 15: 73–92.

Williams-Thorpe, O., Warren, S.E. & Courtin, J. 1984. Sources of archaeological obsidian from Southern France. *Journal of Archaeological Science*, 11 (2): 135–46.

Zilhão, J. 1993. The spread of agro-pastoral economies across Mediterranean Europe: a view from the far west. *Journal of Mediterranean Archaeology*, 6 (1): 5–63.

A 'Social' Structure and 'Social Structure'

Recent Architectural Finds from the Middle Neolithic Site at Capo Alfiere, Calabria

Jonathan Morter

This paper considers the implications of some recent architectural finds from excavations at a Middle Neolithic site on the eastern coast of Calabria. Work at the site of Capo Alfiere has revealed a Neolithic level with two stretches of large stone walling, apparently part of some sort of enclosure, around a hut structure. Dated by radiocarbon to the later fifth millennium cal.BC, this complex seems to be similar to several features found quite recently in Sicily. Taken together these structures suggest an emerging pattern of similar sites. This paper attempts to place them within a broader context, with the intent of beginning an exploration of the purpose of such buildings within the Neolithic society of the area.

THE SITUATION OF THE SITE OF CAPO ALFIERE

The subject of this paper, Capo Alfiere, is a site on the eastern coast of Calabria just south of the present town of Crotone (fig. 1). At present, Capo Alfiere has a cliff-top situation overlooking the Ionian Sea. The Neolithic ceramics from the University of Texas excavations there are of a type known as Stentinello. This name is derived from a site on Sicily where the style was first distinguished by Paolo Orsi (1890) at the close of the last century. The pottery is distinguished by finewares with elaborate impressed decoration. Stentinello style ceramics are found on Sicily, the Aeolian Islands, Malta and across the southern half of Calabria. As such, they represent a regional stylistic variation from that of the southeastern part of the Italian peninsula where painted finewares are considered diagnostic in the Middle Neolithic. Their date range is very broadly within the fifth millennium BC. Within Calabria, the majority of previous work on this period has been done by Albert Ammerman and his team (i.e. Ammerman 1985; Ammerman et al. 1988), over the last fifteen years or so. This has included both widespread reconnaissance surveys plus intensive survey and excavation in the area of Acconia, which is on the west coast facing the Aeolian group and the nearest obsidian sources on Lipari.

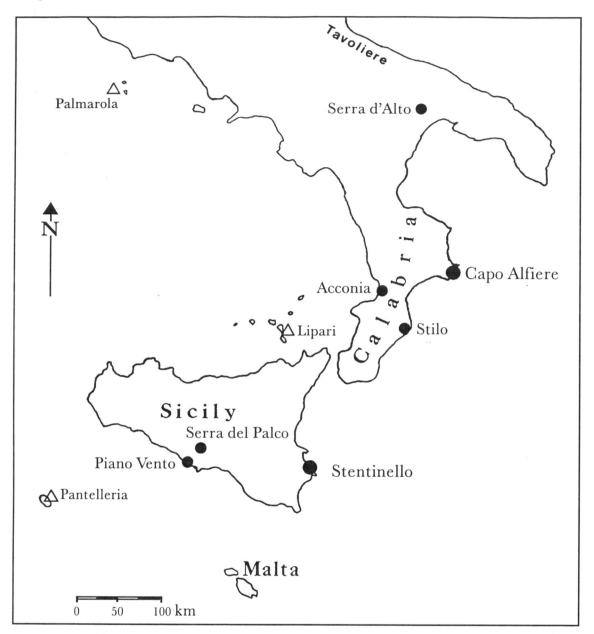

Fig. 1 Map of southern Italy showing main locations mentioned in the text

The scenic cliff-top position of Capo Alfiere has meant that it has been subject to erosion by the sea, in addition to heavy damage by recent agriculture. This location is similar to that of the type site of Stentinello, near Syracuse, which was a settlement, with a circumference ditch, on the Sicilian coast. However, there is accumulating evidence to suggest that, along this stretch of Calabrian coastline, the level of the sea has risen dramatically since Neolithic times, probably by at least 10 metres, and possibly considerably more. This means that at the time of its occupation this site was not immediately on the coast.[1] Despite our best efforts, we have as yet been unable to find any trace of a circuit ditch around the Neolithic site at Capo Alfiere, so in that regard this site seems more similar to the Stentinello settlements in western Calabria traced by Ammerman, who has argued there for a shifting occupation of small clusters of houses (Ammerman 1985: 97). Two seasons of excavations at Capo Alfiere have shown that the site has at least two main strata producing Stentinello style material. I wish to concentrate on the later of these two. The extent of the lower stratum exposed was quite limited, and we do not have sufficient material to make a significant contribution to the present arguments. The surviving portions of the upper stratum represent the majority of the structural elements recovered and these will be the focus here.

THE ARCHITECTURAL ELEMENTS AT CAPO ALFIERE

Two types of structural features have been found in the higher stratum. First, there were two lengths of stone walling, each about one metre thick, running approximately perpendicular to each other, which seem to form part of an enclosure within the broader area of the site. Within the 'L' delineated by the surviving portions of the big walling was an area of cobble paving. This pavement did not abut the large walls at any point, but terminated with a distinct edge. These features appear to have been related stratigraphically, and for present purposes will be considered contemporaneous (fig. 2).

The pavement edge clearly outlines the shape of a structure. The eastern portion of the building is now gone. It was cut through by a recent ditch and all traces further to the east have been removed by ploughing and the erosion of the edge of the cliff at that point. Estimates of the original size and shape of the building must be made on the basis of the surviving part. Perhaps half remains.

The edges of the cobbling survive with sufficient clarity to indicate the wall lines (but not the walls themselves) around the three remaining sides of the building. Remaining cobbling was sparser in the centre. One complete side of the structure is clear. This is the western side, and it was 4.8 metres long. For the other dimension, just over 3 metres survives on the north side, before it was truncated by post-Neolithic activity. Interestingly, the corners of the pavement were rounded, rather than forming a sharp angle.

Although the flooring was stone, it appears that the walls were probably wattle and daub. Along the west side, the cobbles against the wall line tipped upwards at the very edge. This can be seen as indicating their having been placed immediately against a wall. Despite careful examination, no trace of posts or a sleeper beam trough was seen along the wall line. One definite post socket was discovered, with wedging rocks, just inside the cobble paving (rather than on the wall line) near the northwest corner. A corresponding gap in the pavement at the southwest corner, might be interpreted as a pad for another upright there. As no stone wall socle was found, it must be assumed that the sides of the building were entirely wattle and daub. The curved corners support this idea, for, as Shaffer (1983: 416) notes, to prevent cracking daub plastering at corners is better curved rather than squared. However, the rubble that covered the flooring did not contain much obvious intact daub-like material. Sintered daub is a diagnostic characteristic of buildings from Middle Neolithic sites at Acconia on the west coast (Shaffer 1983), and occurs at this site too. However, it is absent in any concentration in the rubble overlying this pavement. This presumably means one of three things:

    1) that the construction was not wattle and daub;

    2) that the daub used here was not fired and dissolved after its collapse

    3) that a reed thatch or some such construction was employed.

Given the sharp and distinctly tipped edge to the cobbled floor indicating that a wall was present, one of the two latter possibilities seems plausible.

Other facets of this building survive, allowing description beyond shape. Set into the floor of the structure was a hearth, and, to the north of that, a basin quern. The hearth was set in a slight basin-shaped depression and had a slab floor. A thick lens of ash was preserved on it because the area had been sealed by later modifications to the floor. As it was damaged on all sides except the north, it was difficult to judge the original size of the hearth, but it appeared to have been about one metre across. It was just under two metres from the north edge of the paving (where the relation is clear) and approximately two metres from the western and southern edges. The intention of the builders may have been to place the hearth in the centre of the structure. If so, then one can suggest that the structure itself was built to be approximately square. This would make it about 4.8 metres to a side.

The quern was inset into the floor immediately beside the hearth, and to the north. At the northern end, extending the work surface, was a very carefully prepared, flat plaster

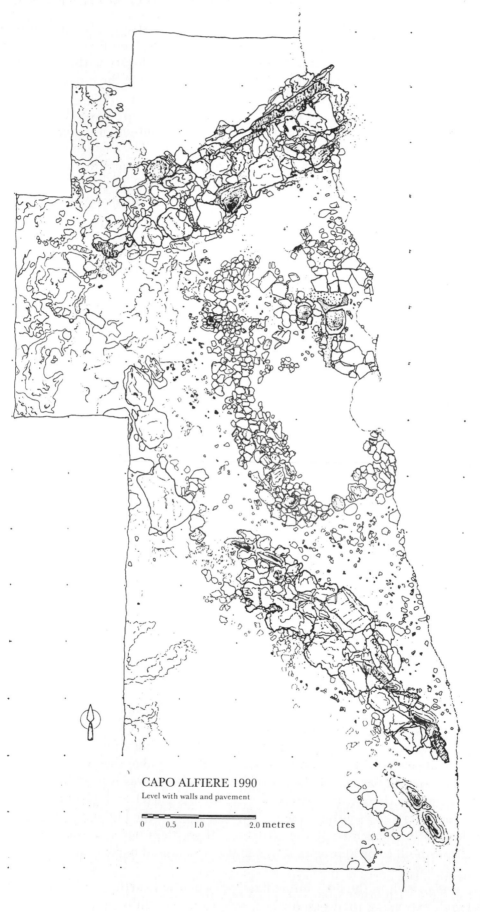

CAPO ALFIERE 1990
Level with walls and pavement

0   0.5   1.0   2.0 metres

Fig. 2   Plan showing location of features in the higher Neolithic stratum at Capo Alfiere

pavement, possibly incorporating some lime to give a caliche effect. Beyond that, a group of noticeably larger calcareous slabs indicated a distinct area within the paved flooring of the hut. The *in situ* fragments of a small vase with anthropomorphic features (nose and eyes) were found scattered on this portion of the pavement.

The hearth area, quern, and vase fragments had been sealed by a subsequent baked mud floor at this point. We obtained two radiocarbon dates from this spot. One from the hearth ash (5650 ± 70 BP [TX-7043] yielding a calibrated date of between 4681 and 4358 cal.BC), and one from the burnt floor make-up above it (5450 ± 60 BP [TX-7042], giving a calibrated date of between 4459 and 4222 cal.BC). These dates, along with that from a nearby pit obtained earlier (5410 ± 80 BP [TX-5785], which calibrates to between 4369 and 4040 cal.BC), cluster in the second quarter of the fourth millennium BC (uncalibrated), or in the second half of the fifth millennium BC when calibrated.

The two big walls are very interesting and elaborate constructions. They appear to be contemporary with the structure indicated by the pavement beside them and so would also date to the second half of the fifth millennium BC (calibrated). There are two stretches of this walling, forming two sides of what appears to be some form of enclosure. The northern wall, running approximately east-north-east to west-south-west, was the first feature noticed in 1987 when cleaning off a section along the modern ditch through the site. The ditch cut the wall, removing any traces of the feature in the direction of the cliff edge. West of the ditch, 5.3 metres of this walling were traced before rising bedrock met the bottom of the plough zone and all Neolithic deposits lost. The western wall is best preserved five metres to the south of the northern. There, a five metre length is oriented northwest to southeast, passing within half a metre of the southwestern corner of the cobble pavement. Decapitated slabs and rock impressions show that the wall continued to the modern ditch line, although ploughing has now removed all traces of it there. Following this wall line northwest towards the north wall, it is difficult to be sure if the western wall originally curved slightly to parallel the western side of the cobble pavement before meeting the north wall, or if it continued in a more closely northwestern direction for the remaining two and a half metres to a junction. Either course has now been lost to the plough. Whatever its position, it seems certain that the two walls met, and can be presumed to form the corner of an enclosure, within which was the cobble pavement and structure that it represents.

As has been remarked, the size of these walls is impressive, but the construction technique is also intriguingly idiosyncratic. Very large boulders of the local calcareous bedrock, up to a metre in any one direction, were used in these walls. Frequently these were slab-like in shape, making construction quite easy even when none of the rocks seem deliberately dressed. Both walls have a central core of drystone construction, built in courses. There was clear evidence of the use of a foundation trench for both walls. Three courses are standing in the section of the best preserved part of the north wall, although this does not amount to much of the probable original standing height. On one or both sides of the core of both walls is a further line of large slabs, untrimmed but up to a metre in length and up to 20 centimetres thick, set on edge against the wall face. Where these remain vertical they have been broken off (by ploughing) at the level of the surviving wall top, so it is impossible to say how tall they originally were.

The presence of these vertical slabs is odd, but so is their manner of installation. Examination of the mutilated ends of both of the walls (where cut by ploughing or the modern ditch) showed that the vertical slabs on the inside of the enclosure, that is facing towards the cobble pavement, had been planted prior to the construction of the core of the wall. In both cases, small wedging rocks were present beside the verticals. The horizontal courses, central to the wall, were then laid over the small wedges. On the 'outer' face, the only evidence is from the north wall where the vertical slabs were propped against the wall core and then wedged with other stones dropped into the foundation trench (this is shown schematically in fig. 3). Along both wall lines, several vertical slabs had been 'popped' out

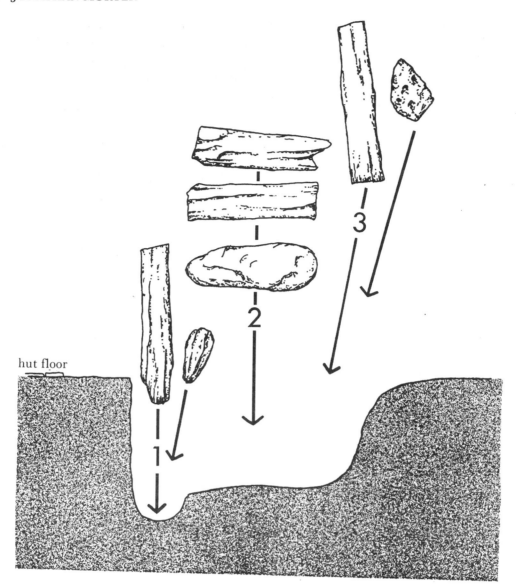

hut floor

Fig. 3   Schematised diagram of the proposed sequence of construction of the major walls at Capo Alfiere. Interior to the enclosure to the left

by ploughing, but the impression left by the rock was evident by its colour and softer fill. Thus, some traces of 'missing' stretches of the walls were recoverable.

The sequence of construction of the walls can now be proposed. First, a line of large slabs was erected, probably in a narrow trench, on one side and at the base of a shallow foundation trench. These uprights were wedged with small rocks and probably dirt. Second, a multi-course drystone wall, incorporating some very large boulders, was built, backed against the slabs. Finally, another set of slabs was set upright along the other wall face, and held in place by rocks and earth backfilling any remaining foundation trench.

Crucially, what is unknown is the height of the walls above the first course or so found extant above their original ground surface. Little evidence was available at the site, so much must be inferred from consideration of parallels and possible interpretations. Within the area bounded by the walls was a carpet of stone tumble. This did not seem to extend north of the walls, but an accumulation of sintered daub predominated in the small area protected from ploughing by the 'shadow' of the north wall. To the south, the levels were too disturbed to be reliable, and, for the level in question, largely gone. The rubble carpet was thickest, but also least disturbed, over the area of the hut. It can be assumed that if the wall continued upward incorporating large boulders, these have now been removed by the plough.

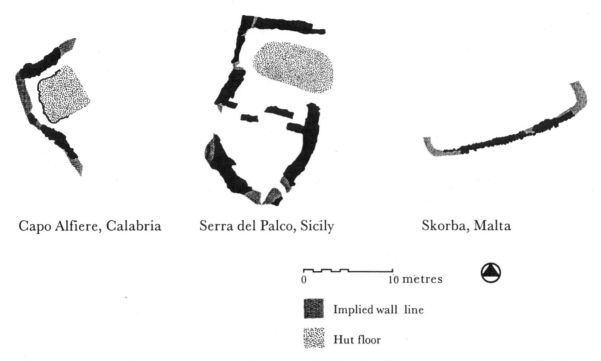

Capo Alfiere, Calabria   Serra del Palco, Sicily   Skorba, Malta

0   10 metres

Implied wall line

Hut floor

Fig. 4   Comparison of plans of three proposed examples of Middle Neolithic enclosures in the Stentinello sphere

EXAMPLES OF SIMILAR CONSTRUCTIONS

To the best of my knowledge, nothing equivalent to the big walls at Capo Alfiere has been found elsewhere in Calabria. The best known area is Acconia, geologically a very different situation. The buildings found there were built on former coastal dunes. Every stone at a site was necessarily a manuport (Shaffer 1983); so, if attempted in similar materials, a construction such as that found at Capo Alfiere, where boulders can be 'quarried' at or near the site, would require much more work.

On Sicily, however, there are at least three sites with potentially similar structures: Serra del Palco, Piano Vento, and Stentinello itself. The net can also be cast a little wider to include Malta. The primary example of a structure that may parallel the walls at Capo Alfiere was discovered at Serra del Palco, in south-central Sicily (La Rosa 1987). Excavations at this site produced an almost complete circuit of what may have been a similar enclosure, and traces of a second wall adjacent to it. The enclosure that is best preserved measured 12 metres east-west and 20 metres north-south (fig. 4). It was apparently built over the remains of a large hut, and was the last phase of a series of Neolithic occupations dating to the Middle Neolithic, including both Stentinello and trichrome painted pottery. The north end of the enclosure was rectilinear in outline, while the south end was apsidal. The longer east and west sides were slightly curved. Construction was of large gypsum blocks with smaller stones as chinking, producing a circuit wall between 1.0 and 1.5 metres wide, and, at its best preserved, 1.6 metres high. Other slabs, set vertically, demarcated a 2.2 by 3.0 metre section in the north east corner. There was some evidence of repair after landslides and modification, possibly for a doorway, at the northeastern corner (La Rosa 1987: 804). To the south of this enclosure was part of a second including the northeast corner with two stretches of walling 10 and 6 metres long remaining. This also succeeded earlier occupations, and included signs of refacing of the eastern wall.

The excavator (La Rosa 1987: 807) proposes that the ceramics from these features are equivalent to those from the well known Stentinello sites around Syracuse (Stentinello, Matrensa, Megara Hyblaea) and to that from Lipari (Castellaro Vecchio). The enclosures he suggests as late in the Middle Neolithic sequence, that is approximately the end of the fifth millennium cal.BC.

The evidence from Piano Vento, in the same region of Sicily as Serra del Palco, was less well preserved. Again, a series of levels of the Middle Neolithic are reported, in the top of which was a line of walling of massive calcareous blocks, associated with a hut and interpreted as part of a 'compound' enclosure (Castellana 1987: 797). The excavator notes the similarity of the remains at this site to those at Serra del Palco.

In reviewing Sicilian evidence, one should also note some walls referred to by Tinè as mentioned by Orsi at Stentinello itself (Tinè 1961). Two stretches are marked as being extant at the beginning of the century. Tinè infers that the traces of walling marked by Orsi on the latter's site map were suspected as Neolithic, but Orsi was not sure that they were part of a hut (Tinè 1961: 116). As these features are now lost, it is impossible to say, but their existence does present the possibility that these were other examples of big walls within a 'Stentinello' site.

Excavations at Skorba on Malta have produced another parallel: a stretch of wall, eleven metres long and 60 to 80 centimetres wide, was found at the earliest level (the Ghar Dalam phase) at that site (Trump 1966). The wall's construction included two faces of stones, "mainly on edge" (Trump 1966: 10), with a rubble fill between. Ghar Dalam is considered equivalent to Stentinello, or even derived therefrom, and dated to the fifth millennium BC. Unfortunately, only one stretch of this wall is known as it ran under a later temple, of the Ggantija phase dating to 3500 BC and later (Trump 1980: 88), and could not be traced further directly. The excavator notes that two soundings were possible further along the assumed line of this feature and both failed to pick it up again although each was only two to three metres from the last visible piece of the wall. He notes the accumulation of debris predominantly along one side, suggesting concentration of occupation to that side (unfortunately, under the later temple). The debris included burnt daub, but it was not possible to tell what derived from the collapse of the wall and hence the nature of its superstructure, or from nearby huts. He could not suggest a firm interpretation "... either as a long rectangular dwelling or as an enclosure wall to a group of more lightly constructed buildings" (Trump 1966: 10).

RECONSTRUCTION OF THE CAPO ALFIERE EXAMPLE

The similarity of the walling at Capo Alfiere to that reported for Sicily and Malta is quite striking. Both the construction materials and techniques, and the overall size seem broadly similar. The dating within a similar cultural context is also comparable. The best preserved examples are those at Serra del Palco, where a complete enclosure was traced.

In the Sicilian parallels, these walls are part of freestanding enclosures, a possibility also put forward for the Maltese example. In all cases, the parallels occur late in the 'Stentinello' phase of the site sequence. This is also true at Capo Alfiere. Thus it seems plausible that the Capo Alfiere example was the corner of a similar enclosure, and this is what is proposed here. Given that assumption, one can also use the likely minimum dimensions of the structure within to suggest the line of the missing parts of the enclosure (fig. 5). The northern side of the cobble paving paralleled the line of the northern stone wall, at a distance of about half a metre, suggesting a conceptually deliberate alignment. If the building represented by the cobbling is assumed generally square (as suggested earlier if the hearth was originally centrally placed) then its northern side would have been about 4.8 metres (although note that this is the missing dimension of the structure, which could have been longer). Given the proposition that the large walls represented an enclosure around the structure represented by the paved floor, an enclosed building at least 4.8 metres along its north side would mean that the large northern stone enclosure wall extended, minimally, one to two metres further to the east than presently survives. This would make the minimum internal length of the north wall at least 6 metres and the external length approximately 8 metres. A returning eastern side would then be assumed approximately matching the surviving western wall. The evidence for the western wall

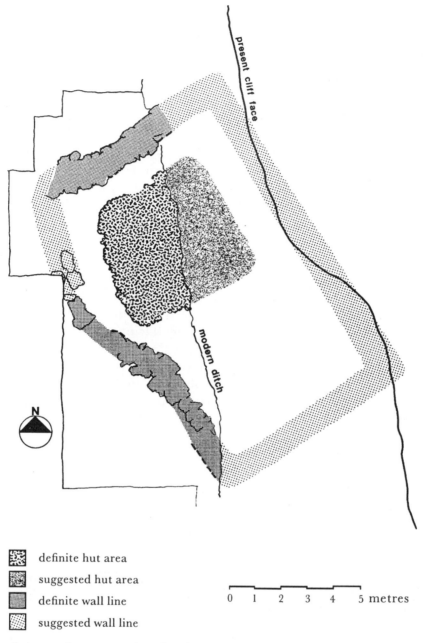

definite hut area

suggested hut area

definite wall line

suggested wall line

0   1   2   3   4   5 metres

Fig. 5   Plan of suggested reconstruction of enclosure at Capo Alfiere, using minimum likely dimensions

suggests that it was at least 11 metres long internally, and probably longer. So the external dimensions of such an enclosure might have been, minimally, 8 by 13 metres. This can be compared with known dimensions of 12 by 20 metres for the better preserved example at Serra del Palco. If the assumption of similarity of shape is correct, these measurements suggest a broadly comparable conception. The Capo Alfiere dimensions might actually have been as large or larger.

An assessment of the original height, or nature, of the construction of the enclosure walls at Capo Alfiere is problematic. Nonetheless, certain points can be made. The largest concentration of sintered daub was against the north face (here presumed to be the outside) of the northern enclosure wall. Within the enclosure, the majority of debris, presumed to be from building, was rocky tumble that did not include serious boulders (in the metre-long range found in the walls). The extent to which the top of the Neolithic deposit at the site has been decapitated by later activity is difficult to assess. Especially in the case of big stones, both the recent presence nearby of a drystone structure and ploughing probably mean that long term quarrying and agricultural clearance have removed the evidence. Having said that, the materials used in the surviving walls, and the sheer size of them (a metre or more wide) strongly suggest that a substantial structure should be anticipated. Again, the Serra del Palco example with a surviving wall height of 1.6 metres and its construction of big boulders seems to bear a close affinity to what might be anticipated at Capo Alfiere. This line of reasoning suggests that the carpet of smaller stones within the enclosure was the result of the collapse of the hut structure and/or the initial decay of the walls, and that major boulders higher in the walling that might have fallen over the tumble have been lost.

It is difficult to assess the purpose of the slab facings to the enclosure walls. Indeed, the sequence of construction found argues against their being structurally significant. A similar technique setting slabs on edge was reported at both Serra del Palco and Piano Vento, and at Skorba, although only on Malta is specific mention made of the wall facings being so constructed (Trump 1966). That the vertical pieces on the inside were installed first strongly suggests that they did have intrinsic significance. Their positioning prior to the construction of the body of the wall, and on the inside, facing the hut wall, seems to argue against anything as prosaic as, for example, protecting the base of a plastered wall against damage from livestock. The excavators at both Serra del Palco (La Rosa 1987) and Piano Vento (Castellana 1987) have both tentatively suggested that these enclosures were defensive. Again, the peculiar placement of the facing slabs, and the sequence of construction, would seem to argue against this at Capo Alfiere. Placing interior vertical facing stones first would not appear to be a requirement if defence was the primary consideration, although it might have been a subsidiary rationale.

To summarise, the reconstruction suggested is a hut structure within a large enclosure wall. The hut was approximately rectangular, probably even roughly square. Its construction was presumably of wattle and daub, with rounded corners, a central hearth, and cobble flooring. This building was set at the back of, or possibly in one corner of, an enclosure wall, which may have been as much as 2 metres high, and was certainly a metre thick. The interior face of at least the lower part of the wall was faced with undressed slabs, set vertically. Open space within the enclosure would have been in the southern portion, and, depending on the precise position of the eastern wall, possibly on the eastern side too. It is not clear whether this was the only complex of its type in the settlement. At Serra del Palco, two such are adjacent and assigned to the same stratum, although one cannot be certain of their exact contemporaneity. No similar features were noted in any excavations or standing sections elsewhere at Capo Alfiere, but the rest of the site has been severely damaged, so this must remain inconclusive.

Regardless of whether the walling forms an enclosure, as suggested here based on the Sicilian and Maltese examples, one should note the similarities of all the reported parallels. They date from late in each 'Stentinello' occupation. The sites have roughly equivalent geologic conditions (easy supply of building stone). Given the varying degree of survival, the scale of the constructions seems broadly similar. And, construction using slabs set on edge is recorded in several instances as well. The Capo Alfiere example appears to be the first known Calabrian example of something occurring across the 'Stentinello' sphere in the late Middle Neolithic.

THE 'HISTORICAL CONTEXT'

To place the arguments that come next in some sort of context, the difficulties of the southern Italian cultural sequence must be considered. Relative dating is achieved from the succession of ceramic types that were produced. A sequence is often based on a happy coincidence of fieldwork and suitable deposits, and then extrapolated to areas where less is known, such as eastern Calabria. In theory, the use of Stentinello finewares should be followed in the later Middle Neolithic by recognisable polychrome painted finewares. These come in several varieties, of which one of the most recognisable is called the Serra d'Alto style named after a type site near Matera in southeastern Italy. The Late Neolithic then sees the replacement of painted styles with a monochrome finish, frequently burnished, known in this area as Diana after a site on Lipari.

Diana is a distinctive horizon throughout southern Italy, Sicily, and adjacent islands. As such, it appears that the area of south central Calabria, Sicily, and islands, previously covered by the Stentinello sphere is no longer using its own distinct pottery. Ammerman (1979) has proposed that Diana is a period of major exploitation of the Lipari obsidian sources, with a widespread distribution network.

In Calabria, two further points are of particular interest. First, data from the surveys at both Acconia (i.e., Ammerman 1985) and Stilo (Hodder & Malone 1984) indicate that the settlement pattern may have shifted from smaller, less aggregated villages or hamlets in the Stentinello phase to apparently much more extensive and/or aggregated settlement by the Diana phase. Survey and other data that I have access to from the Crotone area tend to support this finding. Second, in all three areas there is minimal recognisable late Middle Neolithic material, that is Serra d'Alto style pottery or an equivalent. It does exist here, but the quantities, compared with that assignable to earlier and later periods, are very small. This lacuna has been noted before in southern Calabria (i.e. Ammerman 1985) and the suggestion made for either an occupational hiatus, or that this painted fineware pottery was not being widely used in south central Calabria, and so is not a reliable horizon marker.

The evidence from Capo Alfiere clearly relates to these questions, particularly in considering the interpretation of the structures at the site. The radiocarbon dates from the enclosure level are late for the Stentinello portion of the sequence. This concurs with its stratigraphic position, but the dates are later than expected. The finer pottery from this level is both Stentinello and also a fine slipped and burnished type without other decoration. Occasional examples, such as the anthropomorphic vase recovered from the pavement surface, seem to be a mix of the two ideas with a changed surface treatment and colour but retaining impressed decoration and Stentinello motifs. Additionally, the chipped stone assemblage from this level was approximately 70% obsidian as opposed to about 30% other, mostly cherts. This contrasts with that securely attributable to the lower stratum, where around 20% was obsidian. While I hesitate to suggest that this material may be signalling a direct transition between Stentinello and Diana, it does seem a logical possibility; one that will need further investigation. Occasional Diana diagnostics have come from the surface at Capo Alfiere, but none occurred in this stratum. Personally, I see no reason to automatically assume a general hiatus in occupation. This site might indicate that, for south and central Calabria at least, we should be looking for something transitional between the impressed decorative tradition of Stentinello and the burnished finewares of Diana.

DISCUSSION

What was this stone enclosure's function, and what was it doing here? To review the main points:

- The enclosure at Capo Alfiere appears to be similar to several others found in Stentinello or related contexts.
- The walls are big, but probably not defensive; in fact, the very idiosyncratic construction at Capo Alfiere argues for a non-defensive interpretation.
- This structure does not appear to have been the only edifice at the site. Although we cannot be sure how much has been lost over the cliff, the site stretches 50 metres or more along the cliff edge, as far as can be gauged from the artefact scatter.
- The stone enclosure at Capo Alfiere has late radiocarbon dates for a Stentinello occupation, and is at the top of the stratigraphic sequence at this site. It fits at the point where Stentinello pottery ends and something else begins.

– The examples of similar structures are also late in the Stentinello sequence at their particular sites. As such, we seem to be dealing with a phenomenon happening rather late in the sequence at several points in the 'Stentinello area'.

An enclosure implies a demarcation of space within the settlement. An enclosure can be both inclusive and exclusive. In this case, the substantial nature of the construction of the walling would be more than was necessary for simple exclusionary purposes (a wattle fence could serve as adequately for many purposes). It makes a statement through the investment of effort in its construction, both in the elaboration and the massiveness of the end result. Conversely, the care taken with the interior facade of the walling – in the placement of the facing slabs – implies an inward rather than outward focus to the architecture enclosed. That is, the purpose was not only exclusionary, but also served to embellish the interior space thus distinguished.

Whether or not the final product could have been described as monumental, the investment of effort in the elaboration and massiveness of the construction is intriguing. Trigger (1990: 125) has referred to the expenditure of effort on architecture for non-utilitarian (from our perspective) purposes as a demonstration of "political power in the ability to control energy". This might represent an effort either at personal enhancement, such as a prestige marker of an individual dwelling, or, and much more likely in this case, a communal focus such as a shrine. Interpretation as a shrine would suggest communal activity in delineation, and then embellishment, of a sacred space within the settlement. In this regard it is interesting that, as noted above, the possible Maltese example of such a Neolithic enclosure, at Skorba, is directly underneath a later megalithic temple.

For enclosures within a settlement, another southern Italian comparison is the horseshoe-shaped 'compounds' known within the larger ditched settlements on the Tavoliere (for example, see Jones 1987; Tinè 1983). These enclosures within enclosures were marked out by ditches, as was the site perimeter around them. They have been interpreted as delineating compounds for sub-units within the settlements, such as family groups. Brown (1991: 22) has suggested that they indicate much continuing autonomy within the larger, ditched settlements dating to the Middle Neolithic on the Tavoliere; settlements that may have been conglomerations of the much smaller 'homesteads' seen for the Early Neolithic. Here all the evidence to date – which is limited – indicates that a major function of the subordinate ditches was space demarcation within the overall community. The large number of these subordinate enclosure ditches at the Tavoliere sites does not suggest either a communal, or ideological, purpose there.

All of the examples of walled enclosures from Stentinello contexts noted (Capo Alfiere, Serra del Palco, Piano Vento, Skorba) occurred relatively late in their local Stentinello sequence. Capo Alfiere, where three tightly-grouped radiocarbon dates place Stratum II in the later fifth millennium cal.BC – the point in time that is now considered the beginning of the Late Neolithic (Brown 1991; Whitehouse 1986) in southern Italy – is perhaps the clearest demonstration of this. The limited evidence available indicates that a shift in settlement pattern also occurred at about this time, with sites becoming somewhat fewer but also larger in the Late Neolithic.

It is difficult to tell if the enclosures such as the one at Capo Alfiere are related more to the agglomeration process apparently underway, or to the preceding settlement system. It is not yet clear whether sites with circumference ditches (*villaggi trincerati* in the Italian nomenclature, known both from Sicily and on the Italian mainland north of Calabria) existed in Calabria during either the Middle or Late Neolithic. It is also difficult to say at present, whether the settlement pattern discerned, particularly that for the sites with Stentinello material, represents a fairly dense coverage of small, but stable settlements, or if this is a palimpsest of shifting occupation sites.

One should note, however, that in several other parts of Europe megalithic or earthwork constructions have been taken to indicate the need for communal focus or territorial identity among early Neolithic groups, particularly where a shifting or ephemeral settlement system is associated. That is, in some areas shrines or burial monuments occur before substantial settlement sites, and can be interpreted as providing social cohesion to an otherwise dispersed farming occupation (Sherratt 1990: 149).

It is difficult to say whether the entity at Capo Alfiere might have had a similar role as a community or multi-community focus within a dispersed settlement pattern. At present, as far as one can tell, none of these walled enclosures in the Stentinello sphere appears to have derived from a conceptually similar earlier entity, functional or architectural. As an architectural phenomenon they all seem to appear in the late Middle Neolithic in their respective local sequences. The near contemporaneity of the construction of similar, but geographically separated, features, argues for a uniform activity or phenomenon across the Stentinello sphere at that time.

The question, then, is whether these structures were themselves a response to a general uniform cultural and environmental situation, or to a variety of different situations confronting people of a relatively uniform cultural background; or were they an autochthonous development from a relatively uniform cultural identity in this corner of the Italian peninsula and nearby islands?

If the structure were seen as a shrine within a site area, the most direct explanation might be to postulate this as part of a response to social cohesion problems caused by increasing site size and population agglomeration then presumably underway as part of the transition to the Late Neolithic. Recent evidence suggests a suite of changes that coincide with the transition to the Late Neolithic, reflected in the recovered material culture components. New evidence is coming to light on some aspects of cult practice (Whitehouse 1990). The appearance of intra-site shrines, if that was what these walled enclosures were, might then have coincided with these developments.

The data from southern Italy in general is not replete with examples of Neolithic communal or ceremonial structures, and this is germane in pursuing the idea of the Capo Alfiere structure as a shrine. This may be a result of the considerable destruction of all but the largest features at open settlement sites, introducing a recovery bias. A number of cave deposits, contextually a radically different situation, do seem to have had a ritual character. Some evidence is now emerging for an increase in such activity in the Middle to Late Neolithic. On the basis of some cave paintings, Whitehouse (1990: 21) has argued for the general development of a cave cult across southern Italy and Sicily in the later phases of the Neolithic, with a particular focus on 'secret' sites of difficult access, probably for some form of male initiation rite, given the contents of the drawings on the walls. However, this form of activity would seem quite distinct from conspicuous communal constructions, such as has been suggested here for the find at Capo Alfiere.

Obviously, the arguments presented here remain somewhat tenuous given the present state of knowledge of this stage of Calabrian prehistory. Understanding of the increasing amount of information on the 'Stentinello' phenomenon is also hampered by a lack of work on the subsequent Late Neolithic occupation in this corner of Italy. The preceding attempts to interpret a surprise finding at Capo Alfiere, the large stone structures. Hopefully, it will also serve to illustrate some of the continuing lacunae in our database, and provoke further discussion on our understanding of the workings of Neolithic society in this part of the world.

NOTES

1   Evidence includes submerged quarrying and structural features of the Classical and later periods reported by Gino Cantafera (personal communication 1990), a talented amateur underwater archaeologist, and Dott. Domenico Marino (personal communication 1990), a prehistorian from Crotone, and corroborative geomorphological evidence from the Crotone area, noted by James Abbott (personal communication 1990; see also Abbott & Valastro 1992), project geomorphologist.
2   This includes preliminary examinations of the data from the University of Texas survey south of Crotone. This project is still in progress (for preliminary findings see D'Annibale 1990). Other recent work includes that of Marino (1983; 1989) and Nicoletti (1989).

BIBLIOGRAPHY

Abbott, J.T., & Valastro, S. 1992.   The Holocene alluvial records of the Chorai of Metapontum, Basilicata, and Croton, Calabria, Italy. Paper presented for the Symposium Volume 'Mediterranean Quaternary River Environments', Cambridge, United Kingdom, September 28–29, 1992.

Ammerman, A. 1979.   A study of exchange networks in Calabria. *World Archaeology*, 11(1): 95–110.

Ammerman, A. (ed.) 1985.   *The Acconia Survey: Neolithic Settlement and the Obsidian Trade*. Institute of Archaeology Occasional Paper No. 10. London.

Ammerman, A., Shaffer, G.D. & Hartman, N. 1988. A Neolithic household at Piano di Curinga, Italy. *Journal of Field Archaeology*, 15: 121–40.

Brown, K. 1991.   A passion for excavation. Labour requirements and possible functions for the ditches of the '*villaggi trincerati*' of the Tavoliere, Apulia. *Accordia Research Papers*, 2: 7–30.

Castellana, G. 1987.   Il villaggio neolitico di Piano Vento nel territorio di Palma di Montechiaro (Agrigento). In *Atti della XXVI Riunione Scientifica, 'Il Neolitico in Italia,' Firenze, 7–10 novembre 1985*: 793–800. Istituto Italiano di Preistoria e Protostoria, Firenze.

D'Annibale, C. 1990.   Survey in the territory of Croton (with special emphasis on the Greek period) 1983 – present. In Carter, J.C. (ed.), *The Chora of Croton 1983–1989*: 6–13. University Publications, Austin.

Hodder, I. & Malone, C. 1984.   Intensive survey of prehistoric sites in the Stilo region, Calabria. *Proceedings of the Prehistoric Society*, 50: 121–50.

Jones, G.D.B. (ed.) 1987.   *Apulia. Volume I Neolithic Settlement in the Tavoliere*. Reports of the Research Committee of the Society of Antiquaries XLIV. London.

La Rosa, V. 1987.   Un nuovo insediamento neolitico a Serra del Palco di Milena (CL). In *Atti della XXVI Riunione Scientifica, 'Il Neolitico in Italia,' Firenze, 7–10 novembre 1985*: 801–8. Istituto Italiano di Preistoria e Protostoria, Firenze.

Marino, D. 1983.   *Ricerche Preistoriche nel Territorio di Crotone: Tre Stazioni Stentinelliane*. B.A. thesis, Università degli Studi di Bari.

Marino, D. 1989.   Ricerche preistoriche nel territorio di Crotone: il sito neolitico di Capo Alfiere. *Annali della Facoltà di Lettere e Filosofia, Università degli Studi di Bari*: 32: 59–83.

Nicoletti, G. 1989.   *I Siti Contigui di Casa Soverito e Corazzo (Comune di Isola Capo Rizzuto). Distribuzione spazio-temporale delle testimonianze paletnologiche*. B.A. thesis, Università degli Studi di Bari.

Orsi, P. 1890.   Stazione neolitica di Stentinello. *Bullettino di Paletnologia Italiana*, 16: 177–200

Shaffer, G.D. 1983.   *Neolithic Building Technology in Calabria, Italy*. Ph.D. dissertation, State University of New York at Binghamton.

Sherratt, A. 1990.   The genesis of megaliths: monumentality, ethnicity and social complexity in Neolithic north-west Europe. *World Archaeology*, 22(2): 147–67.

Tinè, S. 1961.   Notizie preliminari su recenti scavi nel villaggio neolitico di Stentinello. *Archivio Storico Siracusano*, 7: 113–17.

Tinè, S. (ed.) 1983.   *Passo di Corvo e la Civiltà Neolitica del Tavoliere*. Sagep Editrice, Genova.

Trigger, B. 1990.   Monumental architecture: a thermodynamic explanation of symbolic behaviour. *World Archaeology*, 22(2): 119–32.

Trump, D.H. 1966.   *Skorba. Excavations carried out on behalf of the National Museum of Malta, 1961–1963*. Reports of the Research Committee of the Society of Antiquaries of London XXII. London and Malta.

Trump, D.H. 1980.   *The Prehistory of the Mediterranean*. Yale University Press, New Haven.

Whitehouse, R. 1986.   Siticulosa Apulia revisited. *Antiquity*, 60: 36–44.

Whitehouse, R. 1990.   Caves and cult in southern Italy. *Accordia Research Papers*, 1: 19–38.

An Examination of Architectural Stability and Change

Contributions from Southern Italy

Gary D. Shaffer

One of the largest and potentially most informative artefacts a prehistoric archaeologist can hope to discover is the building. Studies of structures can provide insight into a past group's traditions of architectural design, commitments of constructional labour, patterns of settlement, and ideology (Flannery 1976; Gilman 1987; Milisauskas 1972; Shaffer 1990). Since one of the strengths of archaeology is the ability to examine socio-cultural phenomena over vast spans of time, the discovery of a series of buildings from different time periods in the same region offers many possibilities for the investigation of architectural and architecturally related stability and change. This paper uses a well preserved sample of Italian Neolithic buildings as the starting point for a diachronic analysis of the reasons for general and specific constructional practices in one part of the central Mediterranean. The discussion centres on wattle and daub architecture in which wall frames of lashed or interwoven wooden members (wattles) are thickly plastered with puddled clayey soil (daub; fig. 1). Later, the study considers historically documented buildings in the same region to explore the effects of social, economic, and natural environmental factors on the persistence of architectural tradition.

ARCHAEOLOGICAL BACKGROUND

Surveys in the mid and late 1970s identified a large sample of Neolithic wattle and daub buildings on the western coast of Calabria, the region comprising the 'toe' of southern Italy's 'boot'. The buildings were distributed among several of the 10 Impressed Ware pottery settlements near the present-day village of Acconia. These sites were found approximately 1.5km east of the Tyrrhenian Sea on the Curinga Plain. In addition to architectural materials, the sites yielded elaborately decorated pottery and stone tools predominantly of obsidian. The survey work and the subsequent excavations have been providing significant information on Stentinello period (sixth and fifth millennia BC) building technology and settlement patterns (Ammerman 1985; Ammerman & Bonardi 1981; Ammerman & Shaffer 1981; Ammerman et al. 1988; Shaffer 1983; 1985).

Fig. 1   Corner of a contemporary wattle and daub building located approximately 15km south of the southern Italian village of Acconia

A brief review of some of the data will provide a context for later discussion. The Stentinello structures generally are located towards the edges of large sand dunes, which were formed around the Pleistocene-Holocene transition and are bordered by fluvial terraces (fig. 2). At least 48 buildings, often well-protected by overlying sands, were found in one of the sites alone. Those structures that have been excavated comprise the first good series of Neolithic buildings known for southern Italy, as well as for much of this part of Europe. They are represented, in part, by large quantities of fire-hardened daub; the amount of sintered daub recovered from single structures in these settlements was occasionally over 1000kg (Ammerman & Shaffer 1981; Ammerman *et al.* 1976; 1988).

Experimental, archaeomagnetic, and other original investigations have helped to explain how these small rectangular buildings were constructed and used (Shaffer 1981; 1982; 1983; 1987; 1993). These studies include individually mapping and spatially orienting pieces of wall rubble; developing algorithms for estimating the original layouts of fallen walls; offering means by which one can calculate wall thickness, preserved wall height, and preserved timber length; and devising ways of characterising timber joining practices. Additionally, the study involved experimental archaeology from the start. Full-size wattle and daub buildings were made, allowed to disintegrate, and partially excavated in order to test the analytical procedures of reconstruction and to gain informal insights into building construction and destruction (Shaffer 1982; 1983: 66–137).

Following the detailed analysis of the structural remains, a generalised reconstruction of the wattle and daub building practices at Neolithic Acconia could be offered. The

Fig. 2   View to the south onto the Curinga Plain from Stentinello Site 25 on the northern of three local dunes

reconstruction below is cast in the guise of an ethnographic description, both to provide an image of how the buildings were probably made and to set up a model that can serve an heuristic role in the search for an even better understanding of past architectural practices (Bersu 1940: 84). After the model is presented, an attempt will be made to go beyond the carefully documented description of building dimensions, materials, and joining practices to an examination of certain higher-level questions in architectural archaeology: namely, the nature of stability and change in a constructional method across time and space.

The wattle and daub buildings of the Stentinello groups at Acconia are constructed upon sand dunes. The dunes are utilised, among other reasons, so as to keep buildings out of certain lower lying areas subject to occasional flooding – a potential disaster for mud walls (Baldacci 1958: 39). Builders must therefore haul up clay daubing soil from the fluvial terraces where it is found to construction sites on the sand dunes. Some 5 to 10 tons of soil might be required for making one structure. To help reduce the work of quarrying and transporting this soil, builders attempt to re-use as much of an old structure's daub – already up on the sand dune – as possible. They do this by repuddling the daub from a recently abandoned building or by directly incorporating blocks of hardened daub as filler into a fresh daub wall matrix. If an old building is abandoned, but a new one need not be immediately constructed, the people will set an intense fire to it and thereby harden a good deal of its daub. This fire-hardened daub will then be resistant to the erosive rain that would quickly melt unfired material into the dune. Builders can then use these preserved chunks of sintered daub as wall fill at any future date when new construction is desired. Old daub walls with their re-usable components would act, in a sense, as magnets to attract builders of new structures to adjacent settings.

Besides recycling old daub, the makers of new buildings often collect rocks from old wall footings or hearths to serve similar roles at a new location. Any additional stones will be used as wall fill. Another part of the collection of building materials involves the cutting of willow (*Salix* sp.) or black alder (*Alnus glutinosa*) saplings to serve as members of the wattle framework. Saplings about 6cm in diameter are preferred; however, trees up to over 20cm thick will sometimes be cut and then split longitudinally with wedges. Builders often split the thinner saplings as well – sometimes into quarters – in order both to save themselves from the more arduous task of cutting down the trees and to conserve living trees for other projects.

Once this timber is assembled at the construction site, small pits are dug, into which posts are set for the wall frame. Sand is then placed back in the pits and packed tightly around the posts. The upright saplings form a rectangular outline up to 5.5m long by 4.5m wide, depending on the building's intended function. These posts are not set too closely together. On the other hand, the saplings or wattles attached horizontally to them are quite densely spaced, and sometimes even touch one another. To join the horizontal wattles to the upright saplings, builders use either twined grasses (Gramineae), sedges (Cyperaceae), ferns (*Pteridium aquilinum*, brackens), or supple willow shoots as cordage. Sometimes very little lashing is required, as the slenderer and more flexible wattles may be woven between the posts and stay in position by themselves. Before daub is applied to this supporting timber framework, stones may be set at the bases of the walls as footings, to guard against the erosive effects of moisture. Soil is then puddled with water to a malleable consistency for application as daub. Various grasses, bracken ferns, or sand may be added to the soil to reduce the amount of water needed to puddle it and to diminish the cracking of the daubed walls as they dry.

The walls of the new structure are gradually built up in height with the daub. This daub is usually applied in thicknesses of 12 to 16cm, but these figures can be cut in half when only single sides of a timber frame are heavily plastered. At the top of the walls, roof supports are lashed on to the timber uprights and across the expanse of the building. Slender reeds about 1cm in diameter are set on top of these wooden supports and perpendicular to them. The reeds are furthermore set side by side and extend as eaves over the walls to protect them against the rain. Once reeds are in place to cover the building's interior and all its walls, daub is applied to the reeds as a waterproof coating. Particularly heavy rains will necessitate the occasional patching of the roof and walls with fresh daub.

While certain parts of this model or reconstruction of Neolithic building practices may seem rather static and normative, its main purpose is to provide a rough idea of what manifestations wattle and daub architecture took in the Stentinello settlements near Acconia. The archaeological work behind the model was designed to investigate the variability of constructional practices in space and time, and to explain any observed changes in wattle and daub structures effected by Stentinello builders themselves or by later southern Italians. A comparison of the excavated Neolithic structures has revealed some notable diversity in their architectural details: for example, in the preparation of wattles, use of different types of cordage or lashing, incorporation of different tempers and fillers into daubing soil, and application of varying thicknesses of daub plasters. This study of variability in Stentinello period construction practices is based on the 20 wattle and daub structures excavated in two of the Acconia settlements. Five of these buildings were more or less completely excavated, while the remainder could be only partially examined. The lack of large quantities of daub from these latter structures sometimes precluded their architectural comparison (Shaffer 1983: 413–23).

A few examples will highlight the variability observed among the structures. First, with respect to the preparation of timber for wattlework frames, we note the conspicuously large component of timber imprints with small diameters in the daub from Area J. While the other structures' imprints generally had a large modal diameter just under 7cm, Area J instead had a sizeable mode around 1cm. These small diameters probably represent twigs left attached to the larger saplings. The many leaf impressions found in J's daub also point to this explanation (Shaffer 1983: 432–3). The Area J builders, unlike those of the other structures, did not attempt to strip twigs off from saplings before incorporating the latter into frames as wattles. Another aspect of variability in timber framing concerns the splitting of the wood. The impressions of split timbers were found in most of the excavated buildings. However, Area M stood out with its predominance of split timber lengths over rounded ones. This situation is most consonant with M's builders having consistently split individual timbers a multiple number of times (Shaffer 1983: 361–3). In fact, direct evidence of multiple splitting was seen on one daub fragment with the imprints of two quartered pieces of wood: each timber had a right-angled edge. Furthermore, as Area M represents the youngest structure dated at Acconia (5690 ± 50 BP; P–2948), this great amount of splitting could be the result of a possible depletion of timber resources over time (related to augmented construction demands or uses as fuel?).

One example of diversity in the lashing together of wattle frames is based on a comparison of plant impressions in the daub from structures H, I, J, and M. Buildings H and M yielded the imprints of sedges, possibly used as light cordage (Shaffer 1983: 440–4). On the other hand, sedge impressions were absent in the daub from Areas I and J. As these latter two buildings were set at least 100m farther from the streams and marsh where sedges grow, their builders might well have decided to use other, closer or more available materials as lashing (Shaffer 1983: 469). The presence and absence of Cyperaceae remains in the four structures is also mirrored in the impressions of 'grass-like' bits – possibly the spikelets cut from stems of common reeds (*Phragmites australis*). While these grass-like imprints were common to all the buildings, a relatively much larger quantity of them was found in Areas H and M (Shaffer 1983: appendix 8). The grass-like bits were probably incorporated into moist daub as one type of temper (Shaffer 1983: 447); and those builders closer to the water sources that had the more plentiful stands of these grasses would more likely have used them.

A final example of the variation in Stentinello-age wattle and daub construction concerns the application of daub itself. The thicknesses of daubed walls were quite similar among all structures (Shaffer 1983: 417–18): Settlement i had a mean value of 13.5cm (mode = 15.5cm, s = 3.0cm, n = 7), and Site l's value was 16.5cm (mode = 16.5cm, s = 2.5cm, n = 5). Still, the wall thickness of the Area I building (from Settlement i) was relatively much lower. This structure's wall daub seems to have been just 4.0cm thick; and the wall frame appears to have been plastered heavily only on one side (Shaffer 1983: 236, 418). The builders at Area I, by decreasing wall thicknesses, may well have been trying to cut down their need to carry large amounts of heavy daubing soil up from the fluvial terraces.

DISCUSSION

The several examples of diversity within Stentinello building practices demonstrate that the Neolithic Calabrians were participants in a somewhat dynamic system of architecture. Given their presence for some 1200 years, it would indeed be surprising if they were trapped with immutable skills and traditions on one rung of a prehistoric time ladder. Instead, they were trying out new elements of construction, and probably for several reasons: the desire to test properties of alternative materials, the availability of certain resources, changing ideas of symbolism and prestige, personal style, chance, and so on. While the precise reasons for the architectural diversity at Neolithic Acconia may elude us, it seems that a few, including those regarding daub tempers and cordage, were related to the builders gradually having spread to new construction spots that were more distant from previously used raw materials. Additionally, as with Area I's thinner daub plaster, some builders may have been trying to economise on their labour costs and so experimented with new techniques.

Neolithic dwellers of Acconia had contacts with other early southern Italians through extensive exchange networks for obsidian and probably for other goods (Ammerman 1979; 1985; Ammerman & Andrefsky 1982), and these contacts also may have helped to prompt some of the architectural innovation. New ideas on daub construction could have derived, for example, from direct or indirect contact with residents of the Tavoliere, where daub and plank building techniques were practised at the earlier Neolithic site of Ripa Tetta (Evett 1989; Evett & Tozzi 1989; Tozzi & Tasca 1989). Elsewhere in southern Italy and Sicily, the Stentinello builders of Acconia may have encountered alternative wattle and daub practices at settlements like La Starza (Trump 1957), Favella (Tinè 1962: 39–40; 1964: 280–3), Prestarona (Costabile 1972), Castellaro Vecchio (Bernabò Brea & Cavalier 1980: fig. 34), and Trefontane (Cafici 1915: 487–8).

Building traditions other than wattle and daub could have reached Acconia from several sites as well (Bernabò Brea 1966; Tinè 1961). Builders of massive stone-walled structures (with upper sections perhaps of wattle and daub) at the Stentinello settlement of Capo Alfiere may have exposed Acconia's population to architecture of considerably different materials and proportions. Capo Alfiere has evidenced a structure measuring at least 8 x 9m with rock walls up to 1m thick. This building, which covers almost three times the surface area of the largest excavated structure at Acconia (Area I at 5.5 x 4.5m), has only restricted parallels in scale for the Stentinello age in this part of the Mediterranean (e.g. Serra del Palco on Sicily and Skorba on Malta); its magnitude suggests a building made communally for a purpose other than general habitation (Morter 1990).

Despite the probable exposure of Acconia's Stentinello builders to a range of architectural practices, these people appear to have continued making structures of wattle and daub. One interesting avenue of future research would be the examination of why the Acconia population apparently was not constructing any of the significantly larger buildings like at Capo Alfiere. Perhaps, as is intimated by Morter (1990), certain Neolithic settlements were beginning to distinguish themselves through the development of more visible social hierarchies and political or religious roles.

Unfortunately, the prehistoric sites at Acconia have not yet evidenced recognisable buildings for post-Stentinello periods, including Late Neolithic Diana times which are otherwise well represented by pottery (Ammerman 1985). Structural daub is reported, however, in other parts of southern Italy during the post-Stentinello Neolithic: for example, at Serra d'Alto (Rellini 1925: 259), Monte Acquilone (Manfredini 1968), Contrada Cassone (De Juliis 1975), Casa San Paolo (Vinson 1975), and Passo di Corvo (Bradford 1950: 86–7). At Passo di Corvo on the Tavoliere, Tinè (1983: 50–1, 173) discovered a 40sq.m structure with walls of calcrete blocks; this Middle Neolithic building appeared to be apsidal in form. Elsewhere in the region, Manfredini (1975) found stone walls at the Middle Neolithic site of Monte Acquilone, and Bernabò Brea and Cavalier (1960) reported a rock wall mortared with raw clay from the Late Neolithic at Contrada Diana. From the Early Bronze Age of Sicily there is the additional find at La Muculufa of several circular or ovoid huts with stone socle foundations and wattle and daub walls (McConnell 1992). Other architectural styles from the Bronze and Iron Ages are known from the Aeolian Islands, where sites contain stone-walled hut foundations, the older varieties being oval in shape and the younger examples being rectangular or polygonal and much larger (Bernabò Brea 1957; Bernabò Brea & Cavalier 1956).

The absence of post-Stentinello prehistoric buildings at the Acconia settlements may result from a combination of factors, including the adoption of new land use practices and architectural forms which left more ephemeral archaeological traces. These changes could have arisen from the increasing interaction of peoples with different traditions, as seen, for instance, in the elevated commerce of obsidian and other goods (Bernabò Brea & Cavalier 1980: 677; Shaffer 1983: 18–29). In this regard, it is important to note that wattle and daub buildings may have persisted at the Acconia settlements in later prehistoric times but with one change very critical for archaeological visibility: the termination of intentional burning or firing of daub walls (Shaffer 1983; 1993).

Despite the lack of evidence for post-Stentinello prehistoric structures at the settlements around Acconia, it is interesting that wattle and daub buildings have been made in parts of Calabria up through at least the 1950s. The cultural geographer Baldacci (1949: 97), who studied Calabrian agricultural huts in the mid 20th century, found that the most widespread variety was the rectangular hut. He wrote:

> That which varies [from place to place] is the material for covering the walls and the roof which, according to locality, can be of mud, shrubs, branches, or (fire)wood. The size is generally 3 x 4m .... The hut with walls plastered in mud ... exhibits an internal wooden frame like a grate and, externally, a series of small beams – 'samate' – arranged horizontally at an interval of 50cm.

(Baldacci 1949: 97–8)

Baldacci (1958: 27) added:

> Structures formed of reeds, branches, or small wooden beams and of mud with a little chaff are still common, whether in the town centres or in the rural areas with clayey soils. Such huts are often used as farm buildings, and also as permanent dwellings.

[translations by G. Shaffer]

While one can find striking parallels between these 20th century wattle and daub buildings and those Neolithic ones excavated at Acconia, the similarities are not perfect. Alongside the introduction of more modern building technologies such as cinder block walling, wattle and daub architecture itself has incorporated certain newer elements into its design. My very limited examination of the 20th century structures showed, for example, the substitution of metal nails for vegetal lashing materials and ceramic roofing tiles for reeds. Still, what is more striking than the slight changes in wattle and daub structures are the several strong similarities between the present-day buildings and those made by Stentinello people some 6000 to 7000 years ago.

These architectural traditions include the use of densely-spaced horizontal wattling, the employment of specific plants as framing materials and daub tempers, and the use of rocks as wall fill. While some of these continuities might seem readily explainable, others are more complex and demand greater attention. For example, it would be reasonable to suggest that both Neolithic and contemporary builders chose horizontal wattling rather than vertical wattling, because the former type of framing better provides a key for holding the daubing mud and requires fewer timbers to be in contact with the moist ground and its rotting action (Wauchope 1938: 70–1). Also, we can easily understand how present-day builders, like their precursors, would want to save themselves the trouble of preparing more daub than needed, by incorporating rocks as wall fill.

One of the more complex architectural traditions that also spanned the millennia concerns the addition of blades of bracken ferns to daubing soil as a temper. The impressions of bracken ferns were found on daub fragments in seven of the excavated Neolithic structures from Acconia. As part of the experimental studies of these buildings, brackens were included in the daub of one test structure's walls. This practice was found to reduce the amount of cracking in a daubed wall by helping equalise interior and exterior drying rates, thus potentially increasing a structure's lifespan (Shaffer 1982; 1983: 124–32). Additionally, Shepard (1956: 25) has noted that by including nonplastics (here, the ferns) in a clayey matrix, one can reduce the quantity of water needed to puddle it and render it workable. This factor could have been quite important when either water or moisture-laden soil had to be obtained from a distance.

In this connection, it is most interesting that one of the several common Italian names for *Pteridium aquilinum*, or bracken fern, is *felce capannaia* – fern of the hut (Tozzetti 1858: 181). A local Acconia farmer with personal knowledge of recent wattle and daub construction noted that builders would put the ferns in daub walls so as to reduce the amount of water required to moisten the daubing soil prior to its application; and people were then able to lessen their hauling of water (G. Bova 1982: personal communication). An inquiry over whether the term might also stem from the use of ferns as cordage (Shaffer 1983: 445) met a negative response. This ethno-linguistic evidence is most compelling for arguing that Stentinello builders also added ferns to their daub as temper (cf. Vitruvius, tr. M.H. Morgan 1960: 202).

Several reasons for this seemingly 7000 year old architectural tradition will be discussed after an additional apparent continuity is mentioned. The imprints of willow leaves (*Salix alba*, white willow; *Salix* sp.) were found in six of the excavated Calabrian Neolithic buildings. In some instances it was possible to determine that they were attached to small branches of the original wattle framework. *Salix* was also the tentative identification of small branch impressions in two daub fragments from separate structures (in excavation

Areas J and X). One piece shows two-ply cordage wrapped across the face of a split timber imprint; the two strands of this cord are the potential *Salix* twigs. The other fragment includes the imprint of a lone branch, but this slightly thicker one is also wrapped across a split timber. The nature of their plied and/or flexed positions across large timbers indicates the use of twigs as cordage to bind together members of structural frames.

It is worth mentioning here how the flexible *Salix* branches are widely used in rural areas of Italy today for several purposes, including the tying of grape vines. Rows of pollarded willows, incidentally, are one of the conspicuous springtime sights in the countryside in several Italian regions. In this connection, it is interesting to observe in Italian Renaissance artist Giovanni Bellini's painting *Saint Francis in Ecstasy* (c.1485) a grape arbour lashed together with what appear to be supple twigs; additionally, the same illustration depicts wattlework employed in a garden gate (Hartt 1987: fig. 426). Pollarding, or the harvesting of top branches by cutting them back to the trunk, could conceivably have been practised by the Stentinello builders near Acconia. Some evidence for this possibility is provided by the size of the Neolithic *S. alba* leaves, which are considerably larger than those from unpollarded white willow trees found around the settlements nowadays. The prehistoric leaves, if from pollarded trees, might be larger because such trees do not have as much associated wood for which to provide nutrients; the nutrients present can contribute to the exceptional growth of the lesser amount of branches and leaves (S. Marchiori 1982: personal communication).

The question of why this very plausible Neolithic practice of harvesting willow shoots continued in parts of Italy to the present day deserves careful attention. Our evidence is that these flexible branches served as cordage in Stentinello-age wattle and daub buildings. Such branches are also used as makeshift cordage for several tasks in rural Italy today; and Baldacci (1949: 101) has documented the use of willow twigs by 20th century Calabrian shepherds to lash together the wooden frames of straw or rush covered huts. More research would be required to show that willow shoots were actually employed in the wattlework frames of daubed structures up to recent times (where perhaps nails were unavailable). However, what can now be seen is one aspect of prehistoric, wattle and daub building technology still used in our century in an architectural context.

We might imagine that the Neolithic harvesting of willow shoots for constructional purposes became enmeshed in a regular cycle of agricultural life. While perhaps originally cut infrequently and solely for the joining of timbers in wattlework frames, the willow branches would be recognised for their more general utility in a host of rural chores demanding short lengths of cordage. The early Calabrian farmers could subsequently have added the pollarding of willow trees and use of the shoots to their annual agricultural cycle. A limited constructional practice then could be transformed into a generalised agricultural behaviour and be more likely to continue through time.

Bracken ferns employed prehistorically as temper in daub walls could also have served a number of other uses: for example, as a raw material for bedding, litter, thatch, and rope (Campbell 1831; Tozzetti 1858: 181; Rymer 1976: 166–8; Fletcher & Kirkwood 1979: 597), or as a fuel for fires (Rymer 1976: 165–6; Shaffer 1983: 550–99). Here, as with the willows, Neolithic farmers in Calabria could have been collecting brackens for several uses on an annual basis. While the ferns might have been utilised for tempering daub only once or twice a generation (depending on the life of wattle and daub structures), knowledge of this practice could readily have been passed on and on through connection with the brackens' other, more frequent agricultural uses and possibly through the coining of some precursor to the phrase 'fern of the hut'.

Besides looking at the survivability of constructional details, it is also important to examine the continuation of wattle and daub architecture as a whole. It is obvious that the Stentinello settlers near Acconia found an extremely successful solution to the problem of shelter. The plants, rocks, and soils needed for construction were readily available in this part of sixth and fifth millennium BC Calabria; and they could easily be worked and assembled with Neolithic tools (Shaffer 1983; 1985). The Stentinello builders also esteemed this well-insulated form of architecture (Baldacci 1958: 29–30; Fitch & Branch 1960) so highly that they kept on making it high on the slopes of their preferred settlement locations – sand dunes. This practice, as mentioned earlier, necessarily entailed the hauling of several tons of daubing soil some 100m or more up from fluvial terraces (Shaffer 1983: 528–49).

An examination of the reasons why wattle and daub architecture as a whole lasted until the 20th century in southern Italy is perhaps more difficult. We have seen before how the settlements at Acconia evidenced no post-Stentinello prehistoric buildings. Unfortunately, detailed descriptions of daubed structures from later historic times are also lacking for this area as well as for most of Italy. Architectural historians and others have only recently shown a strong interest in documenting the domestic structures of common people, especially in rural areas such as the far Italian South (Forster 1974; Hooker *et al.* 1925; Lazzaro 1985). Since wattle and daub is a technology associated with vernacular construction, it is not surprising that later Renaissance architects like Serlio and Palladio did not discuss it in their sixteenth century treatises (Palladio 1965; Rosenfeld 1978). Most general works on Italian architecture concern only monumental, civic, and religious buildings rather than small vernacular structures (e.g. Godfrey 1971; Yarwood 1969). More archaeological and historical research is clearly necessary to gather evidence on the continuity of wattle and daub building technology in the years between the end of prehistory and the 20th century.

At present, we are fortunate to have at least a few records of this form of construction for the intervening periods. Vitruvius, for example, mentions wattle and daub in *The Ten Books on Architecture*, written during the time of Augustus; he believed this building form to be a quick and inexpensive way to enclose space, but one that was prone to cracking and very flammable (Vitruvius, tr. M.H. Morgan 1960: 57–8). Also in Roman times, Pliny the Elder (tr. H. Rackham 1952: 385) noted that the construction of wattle and daub party walls was fairly common. Information on the Italian Medieval period indicates that earthen buildings, including those of wattle and daub, became more popular; and existing buildings were often rehabilitated or 'quarried' for building materials (Baldacci 1958: 18–20; Lazzaro 1985: 360–1). This economising in architecture – except for some defensive and religious structures – may have been related to the intrusions of a series of different peoples in southern Italy in the Middle Ages (Baldacci 1958: 18; Hearder & Waley 1966; Schachter 1965: 29–30).

In the absence of detailed documentation on the existence of wattle and daub technology in southern Italy since prehistoric times, we can still offer several explanations for its persistence into the present century. Perhaps the most intuitively acceptable reason is the simplicity with which the construction can take place in areas with suitable clayey soils for daub and a minimal amount of timber for wattles. Baldacci (1958: 29–39) has emphasised this connection between physical environmental factors and the ease of construction for the survival of Italian earthen houses in general.

Elsewhere I have documented the ready availability of raw materials for wattle and daub construction at Acconia; and my experimentation with this form of architecture has demonstrated the short learning curve needed for sufficiency in its basic constructional techniques (Shaffer 1981; 1983; 1985). The scarcity of mature timber resources in Calabria largely prevented the adoption of wooden structures in the region (Delano Smith 1979: 314–17; Schachter 1965: 122–3; Shaffer 1983: 604). Additionally, given the lack of industry and adequate means of transportation in much of Italy until quite recently, especially in the economically depressed South, more modern building supplies could not compete against cheaply or more conveniently obtained, local materials (Baldacci 1958: 40; Schachter 1965: 25). The lack of accessible quarried stone may, in this regard, have prevented the adoption of more stone (or rubble) walled structures by peasant farmers outside of village and town centres.

Unfired mud brick buildings, which historically have been made in several parts of Calabria, may not have enjoyed the same popularity in other zones for several factors. One reason for their scarcity in the Acconia area could be the difficulty of protecting their walls from erosion during the relatively wet winters (Baldacci 1958: 31; Ministero dei Lavori Pubblici 1956: 253–354; Shaffer 1983: 464–6). Wattle and daub structures, whose internal wooden frameworks may be more suitable for the support of rainfall defences like overhanging eaves, skirting stones, and dense latticework of reeds or branches (Baldacci 1958: 31–2), might have predominated here for their closer fit to the natural environment.

Beyond these largely economic and natural environmental factors, Baldacci (1958: 36) noted that the Italian peasant had the propensity to think only of the short term and of the financial benefits that could be accrued immediately from a suggested endeavour. To make a house with modern fired brick or concrete blocks, for instance, would make little sense, because the house itself would not be a money-maker and any savings provided by the brick's longevity would only be evident at some far-off date in an uncertain future (see also Banfield 1958 and Lopreato 1967). Furthermore, Baldacci (1958: 40–1) argued that only when a few builders did realise the convenience provided by the newer materials and their use became a matter of personal prestige did the older earthen structures seriously begin to disappear (see McGuire & Schiffer 1983: 282–3). While these socio-economic and psychological explanations of some of the resistance to architectural change in more recent rural Italy are most intriguing, more research would be necessary to show their value for earlier historic times. With respect to Calabria, it may be fruitful to appraise prehistoric and historical settlements according to relative wealth or command of resources and then to search for architectural developments that might be explicated by past builders wanting to erect prestigious, but perhaps not ostentatious, structures (Wilk 1990: 38–89).

Presently, it is at least possible to characterise more precisely those reasons for the continuity of wattle and daub architecture that relate to the natural environment. Baldacci's (1958: 28–9) argument, for example, that the ease of obtaining raw materials helped the development of strong architectural traditions needs modification, especially for the Acconia area. While Stentinello builders did have abundant sources of clayey soil in fluvial terraces, they chose to go to the considerable trouble of hauling several tons of this material 100m and more up the slopes of adjacent sand dunes to make their habitations. Settlement on the dunes would have offered several benefits: well-drained soils, adequate height above the streams whose occasional floods could quickly destroy mud walls, and perhaps a more centralised location for the conduct of other aspects of Neolithic agricultural and social life (Shaffer 1983: 539; 1985).

An additional reason why Stentinello inhabitants of Acconia built wattle and daub structures over a millennium and why this form of architecture survived in parts of southern Italy through the 20th century relates to anti-seismic properties of the construction. Earthquakes are common in the Italian South and their disastrous effects on people and property are well known (Haas 1911; Riuscetti & Schick 1975; Tobriner 1983). The quake of September 8, 1905, for example, destroyed much of Pizzo, a town located 14km south of Acconia (Haas 1911: 33). As pointed out by Tobriner (1983), a series of strong earthquakes in Calabria in 1783 prompted the ruling Bourbon government to initiate a reconstruction programme that would reduce future seismic damage and save lives.

The new building system was called *la casa baraccata* ('house like a [temporary] hut'), and it centred on adding a special, internal wooden framework of X-shaped braces to rubble walls; these structures would better resist the lateral forces of shock waves. Tobriner (1983: 132) suggested that Bourbon officials devised the *baraccata* system after observing, in earthquake-prone Calabria, the survivability of certain vernacular structures including those of wattle and daub. It would seem that the diagonal bracing created by flexed wattles would help the structures to react to periodic tremors as unitary systems with a better chance of standing. The realisation of Stentinello or later builders that their structures could survive earthquakes better than other known forms of architecture (such as stone and perhaps mud brick or other earthen dwellings: Baldacci 1958: 39–40; Balseiro *et al.* 1981: 28; Cuny & May 1981: appendix B; Spence 1981: 379) may have played a major part in the continuance of wattle and daub construction. In this regard, it is interesting to note that architectural historians have found traces of indigenous earthquake-resistant buildings in the Aegean dating from the Bronze Age (Driessen 1987; Schaar 1974).

CONCLUSIONS

Future studies, including ethnoarchaeological examinations of the final wattle and daub builders in Calabria, should more thoroughly investigate this constructional continuity. Not only would the work provide additional valuable information on architectural practices over a long span of time in one part of the Mediterranean, it would offer clearer insights into the socio-cultural mechanisms which help to perpetuate traditions in general. This paper has presented evidence for the survival of wattle and daub architecture in western Calabria, Italy, from the 6th and 5th millennia BC to the 20th century AD. One can make the very reasonable argument that this building technology as a whole lasted so long primarily because of a closely related set of natural environmental and economic factors. In brief, the building materials were rather inexpensive to obtain and were easy to work; and the completed structures offered comfortable shelter in the given climate and withstood periodic seismic tremors.

Building in wattle and daub persisted, even though other architectural systems like stone and rubble were introduced. These new constructional forms probably appeared in western Calabria as a result of increased interaction between the local inhabitants and outsiders with different kinds of appealing or prestigious architecture. (Still, archaeologists should also look closely at the materials in the spaces between buildings to learn more about the various activity systems which influence the forms a dwelling can take [Rapoport 1990]). While local innovators may have accelerated the acceptance of certain new building forms, it does not appear that they developed essentially new constructional types by themselves. The examination of variability in the Neolithic daubed structures showed how the differences were rather minor, as in the preparation of wattles or in the application of different thicknesses of daub.

Other studies of the southern Italian Neolithic demonstrate increasing social interaction, as, for example, in the exchange of obsidian and other materials. It can be tempting for archaeologists to interpret this interaction as a dynamic social climate in which new ideas could quickly spread and change economic, political, and religious life. Certainly some of these changes occurred. Yet, the present examination of wattle and daub buildings indicates that architecture is not always susceptible to rapid or wholesale alteration. The dynamism of the Neolithic architecture described here is more like that of a covered pot of boiling water. Some steam of constructional innovation escapes from the shaking pot and manifests itself in minor technological or stylistic changes. However, the lid of limiting factors (e.g. natural environmental constraints; existing political, social, and religious values; uneven participation in economic and social exchange) prevents drastic alteration of buildings – the fundamental artefacts of human shelter.

One of the more important observations from the present study of architectural stability and change is that some distinctive individual components of the constructional process (e.g., the uses of bracken ferns for temper and of willow shoots for cordage) apparently became enmeshed in cycles of more generalised agricultural work and continued to the 20th century. The wider application of these architectural elements in rural labour and perhaps in other aspects of life may have helped to reinforce the utility of the constructional system. This phenomenon of the multiple utility of a tradition deserves more attention in the study of socio-cultural stability and change.

ACKNOWLEDGEMENTS

Partial financial support for the research reported upon here was provided by the National Science Foundation under Grant BNS–79–06187 and Doctoral Dissertation Research Grant BNS–8111348. A Dissertation Year Fellowship awarded by SUNY–Binghamton's Department of Anthropology was also of assistance. I originally presented some of the ideas in this paper at the 1984 Built Form and Culture Research Conference, Lawrence, Kansas.

BIBLIOGRAPHY

Ammerman, A.J. 1979. A study of obsidian exchange networks in Calabria. *World Archaeology*, 11: 95–110.

Ammerman, A.J. 1985. *The Acconia Survey: Neolithic Settlement and the Obsidian Trade*. Occasional Publication No. 10. University of London, London.

Ammerman, A.J. & Andrefsky Jr, W.J. 1982. Reduction sequences and the exchange of obsidian in Neolithic Calabria. In Ericson, J. & Earle, T.K. (eds), *Contexts for Prehistoric Exchange*: 149–72. Academic Press, New York.

Ammerman, A.J. & Bonardi, S. 1981. Recent developments in the study of Neolithic settlement in Calabria. In Barker, G. &. Hodges, R. (eds), *Papers in Italian Archaeology II. Archaeology and Italian Society: Prehistoric, Roman and Medieval Studies*: 335–42. BAR International Series 102. British Archaeological Reports, Oxford.

Ammerman, A.J., Bonardi, S. & Carrara, M. 1976. Nota preliminare sugli scavi neolitici a Piana di Curinga (Catanzaro). *Origini*, 10: 109–33.

Ammerman, A.J. & Shaffer, G.D. 1981. Neolithic settlement patterns in Calabria. *Current Anthropology*, 22: 430–2.

Ammerman, A.J., Shaffer, G.D. & Hartmann, N. 1988. A Neolithic household at Piana di Curinga, Italy. *Journal of Field Archaeology*, 15: 121–40.

Baldacci, O. 1949. Capanne agricole e pastorali nella Calabria meridionale. *Rivista di Etnografia*, 3(4): 96–102.

Baldacci, O. 1958. L'ambiente geografico della casa di terra in Italia. In *Studi Geografici Pubblicati in Onore del Prof. Renato Biasutti*. Rivista Geografica Italiana 65 (suppl.): 13–43.

Balseiro, C.N., Cano, J.H. & Giuliani, H. 1981. Behaviour observed in earthen buildings during four destructive earthquakes in Latin American countries. In May, G.W. (ed.), *International Workshop: Earthen Buildings in Seismic Areas, vol. I*: 19–94. University of Mexico, Albuquerque.

Banfield, E.C. 1958. *The Moral Basis of a Backward Society*. Glencoe. The Free Press, Illinois.

Bernabò Brea, L. 1957. *Sicily Before the Greeks*. Thames & Hudson, London.

Bernabò Brea, L. 1966. Abitato neolitico e insediamento Maltese dell'Età del Bronzo nell'Isola di Ognina (Siracusa) e i rapporti fra la Sicilia e Malta dal XVI al XIII sec. a.C. *Kokalos*, 22: 40–69.

Bernabò Brea, L. & Cavalier, M. 1956. Civiltà preistoriche delle Isole Eolie e del territorio di Milazzo. *Bullettino di Paletnologia Italiana*, 65: 7–99.

Bernabò Brea, L. & Cavalier, M. 1960. *Meligunis Lipara I*. Flaccovio, Palermo.

Bernabò Brea, L. & Cavalier, M. 1980. *Meligunis Lipara IV*. Flaccovio, Palermo.

Bersu, G. 1940. Excavations at Little Woodbury, Wiltshire. *Proceedings of the Prehistoric Society*, 6: 30–111.

Bradford, J. 1950. The Apulia expedition: an interim report. *Antiquity*, 24: 84–95.

Cafici, C. 1915. Stazioni preistoriche di Trefontane e Poggio Rosso in territorio di Paternò (Provincia di Catania). *Monumenti Antichi*, 23: 485–540.

Campbell, D. 1831. On thatching with fern. *Prize Essays and Transactions of the Highland Society of Scotland* (N.S.), 2: 184–90.

Costabile, F. 1972. La stazione neolitica di Prestarona in comune di Canolo. *Klearchos*, 14: 5–27.

Cuny, F.C. & May, G.W. (eds) 1981. *International Workshop: Earthen Buildings in Seismic Areas*, vol. III. University of New Mexico, Albuquerque.

De Juliis, E.M. 1975. Gli scavi di Contrada Casone presso San Severo (Foggia). *Atti del Colloquio Internazionale di Preistoria e Protostoria della Daunia*: 122–9. Firenze.

Delano Smith, C. 1979. *Western Mediterranean Europe: A Historical Geography of Italy, Spain and Southern France since the Neolithic*. Academic Press, London.

Driessen, J.M. 1987. Earthquake-resistant construction and the wrath of the "Earth-Shaker". *Journal of the Society of Architectural Historians*, 46: 171–8.

Evett, D. 1989. Ripa Tetta: an early Neolithic site in southeastern Italy. *Old World Archaeology Newsletter*, 13(1): 11–13.

Evett, D. & Tozzi, C. 1989. Il villaggio di Ripa Tetta (Lucera): gli scavi del 1985. *Atti del 7 Convegno sulla Preistoria, Protostoria e Storia della Daunia*, 2: 37–53. San Severo.

Fitch, J.M. & Branch, D.P. 1960. Primitive architecture and climate. *Scientific American*, 203(6): 134–44.

Flannery, K.V. 1976. The early Mesoamerican house. In Flannery, K.V. (ed.), *The Early Mesoamerican Village*: 16–24. Academic Press, New York.

Fletcher, W.W. & Kirkwood, R.C. 1979. The bracken fern (*Pteridium aquilinum* L. [Kuhn]); its biology and control. In Dyer, A.F. (ed.), *The Experimental Biology of Ferns*: 591–636. Academic Press, London.

Forster, K.W. 1974. Back to the farm: vernacular architecture and the development of the Renaissance villa. *Architectura*, 1: 1–12.

Gilman, P.A. 1987. Architecture as artifact: pit structures and pueblos in the American Southwest. *American Antiquity*, 52: 538–64.

Godfrey, F.M. 1971. *Italian Architecture Up to 1750*. Taplinger, New York.

Haas, H. 1911. *Neapel, Seine Umgebung und Sizilien*. Land und Leute, Monographien zur Erdkunde 17. Velhagen & Klasing, Bielefeld.

Hartt, F. 1987. *History of Italian Renaissance Art*. 3rd ed. Harry N. Abrams, New York.

Hearder, H. & Waley, D.P. (eds) 1966. *A Short History of Italy from Classical Times to the Present Day*. Cambridge University Press, Cambridge.

Hooker, M.O., Hooker, K. & Hunt, M. 1925. *Farmhouses and Small Provincial Buildings in Southern Italy*. Architectural Book, New York.

Lazzaro, C. 1985. Rustic country house to refined farmhouse: the evolution and migration of an architectural form. *Journal of the Society of Architectural Historians*, 44: 346–67.

Lopreato, J. 1967. *Peasants No More: Social Class and Social Change in an Underdeveloped Society*. Chandler, San Francisco.

Manfredini, A. 1968. Villaggio trincerato a Monte Aquilone (Manfredonia). *Origini*, 2: 65–101.

Manfredini, A. 1975. Il villaggio di Monte Aquilone (Manfredonia). *Atti del Colloquio Internazionale di Preistoria e Protostoria della Daunia*: 116–21. Firenze.

McConnell, B.E. 1992. The early Bronze Age village of La Muculufa and prehistoric hut architecture in Sicily. *American Journal of Archaeology*, 96: 23–44.

McGuire, R.H. & Schiffer, M.B. 1983. A theory of architectural design. *Journal of Anthropological Archaeology*, 2: 277–303.

Milisauskas, S. 1972. An analysis of linear culture longhouses at Olszanica B1, Poland. *World Archaeology*, 4: 57–74.

Ministero dei Lavori Pubblici 1956. *Precipitazioni Medie Mensili ed Annue e Numero dei Giorni per il Trentennio 1921–1950*. Pubbl. N. 24, Fasc. III. Istituto Polografico dello Stato, Roma.

Morter, J. 1990. The excavations at Capo Alfiere 1987-present. In Carter, J.C. (ed.), *The Chora of Croton 1983–1989*: 14–28. Institute of Classical Archaeology, The University of Texas, Austin.

Palladio, A. 1965. *The Four Books of Architecture*. [Introduction by Adolf K. Placzek. Unabridged and unaltered re-publication of work originally published by Isaac Ware in 1738]. Dover, New York.

Pliny the elder 1952. *Natural History* vol. IX. translator H. Rackham. Harvard University Press, Cambridge.

Rapoport, A. 1990. Systems of activities and systems of settings. In Kent, S. (ed.), *Domestic Architecture and the Use of Space: An Interdisciplinary Cross-Cultural Study*: 9–20. Cambridge University Press, Cambridge.

Rellini, U. 1925. Scavi preistorici a Serra d'Alto. *Notizie degli Scavi*, 1: 257–95.

Riuscetti, M. & Schick, R. 1975. Earthquakes and tectonics in southern Italy. *Bollettino di Geofisica Teorica ed Applicata*, 17(65): 59–78.

Rosenfeld, M.N. (ed.) 1978. *Sebastiano Serlio on Domestic Architecture: Different Dwellings from the Meanest Hovel to the Most Ornate Palace*. The Architectural History Foundation, New York.

Rymer, L. 1976. The history and ethnobotany of bracken. *Botanical Journal of the Linnean Society*, 73: 151–76.

Schaar, K.W. 1974. Traditional earthquake-resistant construction: the Mycenaean aspect. *Journal of the Society of Architectural Historians*, 23: 80–1.

Schachter, G. 1965. *The Italian South: Economic Development in Mediterranean Europe*. Random House, New York.

Shaffer, G.D. 1981. *An Experimental Archaeological Study of Wattle and Daub Structures in Calabria, Italy*. Unpublished Master's Thesis, Department of Anthropology, SUNY-Binghamton.

Shaffer, G.D. 1982. Attempts at maximizing anthropological knowledge of prehistoric buildings. *Antropologia Contemporanea*, 5(1–2): 141–6.

Shaffer, G.D. 1983. *Neolithic Building Technology in Calabria, Italy*. Ph.D. dissertation, Department of Anthropology, SUNY-Binghamton. University Microfilms, Ann Arbor.

Shaffer, G.D. 1985. Architectural resources and their effect on certain Neolithic settlements in southern Italy. In Malone, C. & Stoddart, S. (eds), *Papers in Italian Archaeology IV. Part 2: Prehistory*: 101–17. BAR International Series 244. British Archaeological Reports, Oxford.

Shaffer, G.D. 1987. Experimental archaeology in southern Italy. *Old World Archaeology Newsletter*, 11(1): 12.

Shaffer, G.D. 1990. Housing in less complex societies. In Taylor, L (ed.), *Housing: Symbol, Structure, Site*: 148–9. Cooper-Hewitt Museum, New York.

Shaffer, G.D. 1993. An archaeomagnetic study of a wattle and daub building collapse. *Journal of Field Archaeology*, 20: 59–75.

Shepard, A.O. 1956. *Ceramics for the Archaeologist*. Carnegie Institution of Washington Publication 609. Carnegie Institution, Washington, DC.

Spence, R.J.S. 1981. The vulnerability to earthquakes of low-strength masonry structures. In May, G.W. (ed.), *International Workshop: Earthen Buildings in Seismic Areas*, vol. I: 371–86. University of New Mexico, Albuquerque.

Tinè, S. 1961. Notizie preliminari su recenti scavi nel villaggio neolitico di Stentinello. *Archivio Storico Siracusano*, 7: 113–17.

Tinè, S. 1962. Successione delle culture preistoriche in Calabria alla luce dei recenti scavi in provincia di Cosenza. *Klearchos*, 4: 38–48.

Tinè, S. 1964. Il Neolitico in Calabria alla luce dei recenti scavi. *Atti della VIII e IX Riunione Scientifica*: 277–89. Istituto Italiano di Preistoria e Protostoria, Firenze.

Tinè, S. 1983. *Passo di Corvo e la Civiltà Neolitica del Tavoliere*. Sagep Editrice, Genova.

Tobriner, S. 1983. La Casa Baraccata: earthquake-resistant construction in 18th-century Calabria. *Journal of the Society of Architectural Historians*, 42(2): 131–8.

Tozzetti, O.T. 1858. *Dizionario Botanico Italiano*. 2nd ed. Firenze.

Tozzi, C. & Tasca, G. 1989.   Il villaggio neolitico di Ripa Tetta: i risultati delle ricerche 1988. *Atti del 10º Convegno sulla Preistoria, Protostoria e Storia della Daunia*: 39–58. San Severo.

Trump, D.H. 1957.   The prehistoric settlement at La Starza, Ariano Irpino. *Papers of the British School at Rome*, 25(N.S. vol. 12): 1–15.

Vinson, S.P. 1975.   Excavations at Casa S. Paolo: 1971–1972. *American Journal of Archaeology*, 79: 49–66.

Vitruvius 1960.   *The Ten Books on Architecture*. Translated by Morris H. Morgan (orig. trans. 1914). Dover, New York.

Wauchope, R. 1938.   *Modern Maya Houses: A Study of their Archaeological Significance*. Carnegie Institution of Washington Publication 502. Carnegie Institution, Washington, DC.

Wilk, R.R. 1990.   The built environment and consumer decisions. In Kent, S. (ed.), *Domestic Architecture and the Use of Space: An Interdisciplinary Cross-Cultural Study*: 34–42. Cambridge University Press, Cambridge.

Yarwood, D. 1969.   *The Architecture of Italy*. Harper & Row, New York.

Great Persons and Big Men in the Italian Neolithic

John E. Robb

INTRODUCTION: THE PROBLEM OF THE LATE NEOLITHIC TRANSFORMATION

Middle Neolithic villages across the Italian peninsula were surrounded by ditches several metres deep, often dug into bedrock and sometimes over a kilometre long, which served as both symbolic and actual defensive perimeters. It was an unfriendly world in the fifth millennium, it would appear. Why then do these ditches, and almost all other defensive architecture, vanish in the Late Neolithic, just when, by the evidence of grave goods, material culture and rock art, weapons and warfare became more important than ever? Why do skeletal remains suggest that violence actually declined with the advent of weapon symbolism?

This is only one of a number of Late Neolithic paradoxes in Italy as well as in other parts of Europe. Why did rock art glorify hunting in an overwhelmingly agricultural society? Why does domestic architecture become rare exactly when mortuary architecture begins to flourish? Why does the Late Neolithic, a quantum leap beyond Middle Neolithic villages in long-distance trade, burial elaboration, and economic intensification, appear a devolution if we consider its impoverished range of ceramic decoration, the disappearance of human body imagery, and a far sparser settlement pattern?

Paradoxes such as these reveal the problems with current archaeological social theory. In spite of attempts to find 'classical' chiefdoms in the Italian and European fourth and third millennia, evidence of widespread or substantial inequality is missing, and it is clear that these were thoroughly tribal societies. Typological approaches to tribal society (e.g. Service 1962), however, do not sufficiently describe or explain variety in social organisation. In recent years, the most important theoretical development has been the 'prestige goods economy' model based on structural Marxist concepts (Shennan 1982; 1987). This model, however, remains seriously under-theorised. Archaeologists who have proposed prestige competition as a major force in social evolution – for instance, recent work on factional competition and 'aggrandisers' as social actors – have often implicitly treated prestige as a generalised, culturally neutral quantity. This makes it difficult to explain how prestige relates to other structures, including the semantics of gender, class, and other axes of inequality, and it limits our ability to explain why prestige competition is highly elaborated in some political systems and not in others. Without some specification of the symbolic organisation of prestige, 'prestige' can become so generalised as to become meaningless, with 'prestige good' following 'ritual object' as a coverall archaeological category.

This paper attempts to integrate concepts of prestige, gender and social reproduction in a model of Italian society in the fourth and third millennia BC. The model has two basic theses:

(1) The Late Neolithic-Copper Age represents a shift within the general range of tribal societies from 'Great Man' societies to 'Big Man' societies.

(2) This transition involved a fundamental change in how society was reproduced, particularly in the re-organisation of sources of prestige around a central male gender ideology.

Neither the scope of this article nor the available archaeological evidence allow complete elaboration of these ideas. Nor can I deal adequately with the substantial variation which Italian archaeology shows, even within the peninsular Neolithic alone; both for practical purposes and in the interests of seeing a larger picture I must deal in broad generalities. However, this work is presented as a theoretical model which may help to synthesise existing archaeological data and to provoke theoretical debate and critique.

SOCIAL MODELS FOR THE 4TH–3RD MILLENNIA

From about the mid-fourth millennium, changes swept through Neolithic society which culminated in the Eneolithic and earlier Bronze Age societies of the third millennium (table 1). In settlement patterns, far fewer habitations are known, with only burial and cave sites known in many regions. Defended village sites vanish, re-appearing only in the mid-second millennium. In ceramics, after the fragmented regionalism of Middle Neolithic ceramic styles, widespread ceramic horizons begin to appear, first with elaborate decorated pottery styles such as Serra d'Alto wares, and later, on a wider scale, with dark, highly burnished unpainted wares such as Diana-Bellavista. Chassey wares in Northern Italy and Southern France represent a similar horizon. Increased inter-regional stylistic communication is also suggested by a great surge in long-distance trade in obsidian, flint, fine ceramics and polished stone. Economically, local copper ores were used initially in the Late Neolithic and systematically in the Eneolithic, primarily to make ornaments and soft, probably non-functional daggers and halberds. Direct evidence for the 'secondary products revolution' is slender until the second millennium. However, faunal profiles frequently show increases in caprovines, and the shift to decentralised, insubstantial villages has often been understood as reflecting the needs of a pastoral society. Late Neolithic burial innovations included the common use of burial goods, tomb architecture in defined cemetery areas, communal burials, and secondary burial and skull curation. While regional traditions varied, Eneolithic and Bronze Age burials were placed in trench graves, rock crevices or, especially in the south, in underground communal tombs, and burials included fine vessels, metal objects and flintwork (Barfield 1981; 1986; Barker 1981; Cazzella 1992; Guidi 1992; Malone 1985; Moscoloni 1992; Pellegrini 1992; Robb 1994b; Whitehouse 1984).

It is worth mentioning what did *not* change in this transition. There is little evidence in the Italian fourth and third millennium for any concentration of wealth or power (e.g. mortuary differentiation, architectural differentiation, large-scale storage facilities, complex settlement hierarchies, full time craft specialisation) (cf. Barker 1981). In spite of occasional well-provided burials (e.g. Voza 1975), Eneolithic cemeteries show burial patterns ranging from unexceptional to distinctly uniform and modular. This suggests that political dynamics comprised primarily competition among essentially equal participants rather than the formation of formal social hierarchies.

Table 1   Reconstruction of the Middle-Late Neolithic transition (summary of general trends)

	Middle-Late Neolithic	*Late-Final Neolithic*
Economy	Agricultural, some pastoralism	Agricultural, increasingly pastoral
Settlement	Nucleated, ditched villages	Dispersed sites of variable size undefended
Burial	Primary burial, single inhumations in villages	Varied practices including primary burial, collective tombs in formal cemeteries, skull curation
Exchange	Low-moderate	Intensified
Authority/social regulation	Ritual	Prestige competition
Group membership	Co-residence	Co-history
Prestige sources	Varied	Merged and related via male gender ideology
Gender ideology	Balanced, poorly developed	Integration of male gender ideology into politics

Early Italian farming societies generally conform to the typological model of small-scale tribes (Barker 1981; Cazzella & Moscoloni 1985; Whitehouse 1984). Interpreting the Final Neolithic and Copper Age has been more problematic. Traditional migration models are contradicted by strong evidence of cultural continuity (Barker 1981; Guidi 1992; Pellegrini 1992; Renfrew & Whitehouse 1974). However, the lack of convincing evidence of political centralisation, economic disparities or symbolic hierarchy frustrates attempts to cast Copper Age societies as 'classical' chiefdoms (Peebles & Kus 1977; Service 1962). These dilemmas mirror interpretative problems within the European third millennium: an abortive search for centralised hierarchical chiefdoms on the Polynesian model has culminated in the realisation that, while these societies remained essentially tribal, they nonetheless were organised according to fundamentally different principles than were earlier societies (cf. Shennan 1987).

Recent ethnographic work has revealed great variety in tribal social organisation, reflected not merely in social 'traits' but in the basic principles of social reproduction which allow claims to authority and prestige. Perhaps the best known variety of tribes are 'Big Men' societies. In Sahlins' original picture (Sahlins 1963), entrepreneurial Big Men mobilised economic resources from their kin and supporters and parleyed these into personal status through ceremonial feasts and exchanges, strategically maximising a generic kind of renown. Their leadership only lasted as long as they could attract followers; however, they could provide their kin with some material advantages, sometimes leading to a loose lineal transmission of prominence.

As an alternative model, Godelier (1986; 1991) has proposed the 'Great Man' society (table 2). In Godelier's model, in Great Man societies, only like things can be exchanged. Great Man societies are thus characterised by balanced sister exchange in marriage, limited homicide compensation, and limited ceremonial exchange. Other researchers have focussed on the political structure of Great Man societies. Leadership in Great Man

Table 2 Characteristics of Great Man and Big Man societies (after Knauft 1993: 80)

Great Man Societies	Big Man Societies
Restricted/equivalent exchange	Competitive/non-equivalent exchange
Sister-exchange marriage	Bridewealth marriage
Blood feud	Homicide compensation
Leadership domination through spiritual prerogative or physical coercion	Leadership domination through wealth accumulation
Multiple leadership roles	Coalescence of leadership functions

societies typically is distributed among multiple roles. For instance, Modjeska (1991) lists nine distinct kinds of leader in one transitional Great Man/Big Man society, including 'man with a big name', 'formal instigator of a fight with responsibility for compensation', 'angry man/fierce warrior', sorcerer, orator, wealthy man, 'helping man' (frequent contributor to sacrifices, compensation, etc.), owner of bachelor cult, and cult initiate. Similar statuses in other groups include noted hunters, traders, shamans, spirit mediums and ritual healers. In spite of the 'Great Man' designation, some statuses may be held by women and men or by women alone. In Great Man politics, what is critical is that success or prestige in one realm is not convertible into success or prestige in others; the noted warrior, for instance, cannot manipulate this activity to increase his/her influence in ceremonial exchange. In contrast, at the Big Man end of the spectrum, inter-convertibility among different sources of prestige is the norm. The same activities are distributed over fewer notable statuses, and Big Men typically use generalised 'centrality' and techniques of manipulating obligations to transform the symbolic fruits of one activity into working capital for another.

A third form of authority found in tribes is the chief. Although Service (1962) originally defined chiefdoms as an evolutionary step beyond tribes, hereditary leaders are often found in thoroughly tribal societies (cf. Allen 1984). What is important is not the existence of ranked positions in themselves but rather their incorporation into the central cluster of symbols around which political life revolves. Societies characterised by minimally politicised hierarchies thus form part of the tribal continuum rather than a different category.

Leip (1991) usefully describes the three statuses as idealised extremes at the corners of a triangle of configurational space (fig. 1). As forms of leadership, Great Men, Big Men and other statuses often co-exist within traditional societies (cf. Godelier & Strathern 1991). In one ethnographic case (Tuzin 1991), elder brothers became Great Men while their ambitious younger brothers aspired to become Big Men! Great Man, Big Man and chiefly positions can thus provide alternative strategies to prominence for actors in differing structural positions or with different access to resources. At the same time, one mode may provide a society's dominant social form, opportunities and limitations. Viewing these as continuous possibilities within configurational space emphasises that, while minor changes in emphasis or major transitions may occur, there need not be a single evolutionary pathway. For instance, given the outstanding size and dynamism of many Big Man societies compared with small size, ritual-based character and conservatism of indigenous Melanesian chiefdoms, a rigid evolutionary sequence from Big Men to chiefdoms to states is unlikely (Allen 1984; Leip 1991).

Chiefly societies   Big Man Societies
Centralised leadership   Centralised leadership
Ritually constituted   Secularly constituted
Generalised exchange via wealth   Complex exchange via wealth

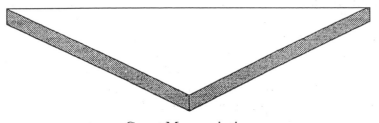

Great Man societies
Decentralised leadership functions
Ritually constituted
Direct exchange

Fig. 1   Patterns of authority and social reproduction in tribal societies (after Liep 1991 with modifications)

Great Man societies furnish a good social model for the Italian Early and Middle Neolithic. While data for this level of interpretation are thin, several points should be noted. Notable statuses are enigmatic and show little clear semantic concentration in the Early-Middle Neolithic, particularly in contrast with later periods. There is no discernable criterion of wealth such as a common scale of grave goods, and idiosyncratically conspicuous grave goods (e.g. Grotta Patrizi, Radmilli 1953) and practices (e.g. Grotta Continenza, Grifoni Cremonesi & Mallegni 1978) probably denote ritual purposes or statuses more than simple consumption or display. Parameters of political life also correspond to the Great Man model. In ethnographically known Great Man societies (e.g. Feil 1987; Godelier & Strathern 1991; Knauft 1993; Kelly 1993), social life is focussed narrowly around a village or small group of villages, often palisaded. Inter-village communication and co-operation is low and typically conducted in an atmosphere of xenophobia and endemic warfare. In Italy, Early and Middle Neolithic settlements were typically small, ditched villages, often with internal segmentation defined by ditched sub-compounds. Burials were scattered about and near settlements and in caves also typically used for habitation. The emphasis placed upon providing a physical boundary for the community, and the placement of burials to identify the history of the group with that of the village, may suggest that the primary means of ascribing group identity and structuring interaction was co-residence, which coincided with a constructed common history centring on the village. That this cognitive definition actually coincided with a rather limited range of communication is suggested by the tendency towards distinct regional pottery styles, and by the low level of inter-regional exchange.

In contrast, Late Neolithic and Eneolithic societies fit the Big Man model much more closely. A key political and economic role of Big Men is as a central 'relationship broker' among kin, fellow villagers, and trading partners, and archaeologically, the primary correlate should be the prominent role of exchange. In the Italian Late Neolithic and Copper Age, obsidian was collected from offshore islands and high-quality flint was mined to provide a prestigious alternative to local stone. Metals likewise may have been developed primarily as an exchangeable, controllable material correlate of value. Both stone and metals were commonly circulated over distances up to 1000km. Broad Late Neolithic ceramic horizons also imply higher interregional communication. While ceramic regionalism reappears in the Eneolithic, high levels of exchange remain, and it is likely that with the spread of metalworking, stylistic links among neighbouring societies were affirmed mainly through metals rather than fine pottery.

Extended exchange was probably supported by intensified agricultural and caprovine pastoralism, possibly involving a re-organisation of labour by age and gender as well as of archaeologically visible settlement patterns (cf. Ehrenberg 1989; Sherratt 1981). Late Neolithic and Copper Age settlement patterns may derive from both to the pragmatic needs of pastoralism and from group definition and relations. The rise of long-term cemeteries distinct from evanescent settlements transferred the architectural definition of the social world from the actual plane of village co-residence to an ideal, constructed plane probably based on genealogy, to judge from the attention paid to ancestral remains in rites of communal burial and skull curation. A shift from co-residence to genealogy as a dominant idiom of social relatedness would have allowed greater flexibility in constructing and manipulating relationships for exchange and alliance.

Why these changes may have occurred is beyond the scope of this article. Great Man societies can move towards Big Man societies as a result of colonial contact (Godelier & Strathern 1991), changes in marriage and exchange patterns (Godelier 1991), warfare (Lemonnier 1991) and economic developments (Feil 1987; Modjeska 1991). Perhaps the key point is simply that Great Men and Big Men often co-exist as strategic goals within a society; hence, a wide range of relatively slight changes in the conditions of social reproduction could shift the overall balance of choices made by political actors.

GENDER IDEOLOGY AND THE ORGANISATION OF PRESTIGE

Prestige systems mediate between abstract cultural values and actual behaviour. In Great Man and Big Man societies as in most others, gender ideology commonly furnishes the personal symbols upon which political prestige structures are based (Ortner & Whitehead 1981). Great Man and Big Man systems differ in the symbolic organisation of prestige and prestige competition. Within Great Man societies, differences tend to be understood as irreducible. With gender distinctions, for instance, male-female difference is usually considered an uncrossable gulf, hedged with extensive gender hostility, avoidance taboos, and gender-specific initiation systems (Jorgenson 1991). Within genders, Great Men form the "several parts of a collectivity of great men whose specialist and heterogeneous powers cannot be reduced to a single form" (Strathern 1991). In contrast, in Big Man societies, prestige is typically generalised rather than defined by and gained from a single status or situation. The multi-situational aspects of generalised prestige create both a sort of exchangeable symbolic currency such as 'honour' and a group of actors motivated to pursue it. The same logic of interconvertible value underwrites broader strategic manipulations and more strongly elaborated and ideologised redistributive institutions.

Archaeologically, the transition to a generalised form of prestige should leave distinguishable archaeological patterns with two characteristics. Because generalised forms of prestige are grounded in central ideological symbols, prestige goods should be semantically coherent: they will be united by their meaning as well as by costliness, exotic qualities or craftsmanship. Moreover, key symbols should exhibit situational redundancy, turning up in multiple contexts or genres. This is so whether central symbolisms are borne by one or several actual artefacts; an originally functional artefact may give rise to unornamented functional versions, an ornate ritual version, and iconic echoes in other genres and media. In such situations, categorical distinctions will often be expressed through the semantic connotations of the symbol, while quantitative distinctions will be expressed via aesthetic elaborations in its execution. One overall effect of a symbolic transition to generalised prestige may be that an archaeological landscape 'snaps into focus': instead of a dozen 'ritual objects' of unknown meaning, we suddenly have an idea of what a few central symbols were about and how they articulated with political structures.

Between the Late Neolithic and the Copper Age in Italy, multiple sources of prestige may have coalesced into a generalised symbolic currency based upon male gender ideology. Gender ideologies of the Early-Middle Neolithic can be pieced together tentatively, though with little direct evidence specifically for the Late Neolithic. Both males and females occasionally received burial goods and architecture. As in many European Neolithic cultures (Hodder 1990), males were often buried lying on the right side, females and juveniles on the left. In non-burial evidence, rock paintings at Porto Badisco (Graziosi 1980) imply that hunting was a symbolically important male activity. Caves such as Porto Badisco may also have been the loci of male cult activities (Whitehouse 1992). Spatially, the distribution of artefacts and activities may suggest behavioural and cognitive gender associations for concentric zones around the village. Gender associations for villages are not known, although the few figurines known, usually of females, were used and found in villages (Graziosi 1974). Peripheral zones, in contrast, were probably the locus of male activities. Hunting would have taken place in unoccupied areas between villages, and, while the gender associations of exchange are unknown, male-associated cult caves are also usually located in peripheral or marginal locations (Whitehouse 1992). The behavioural genderisation of space is thus at least consistent with Hodder's (1990) *domus-agrios* distinction. The ensemble of data suggests a formal cognitive distinction between males and females and juveniles, systematically applied but without extensive ideological elaboration.

The Eneolithic witnessed major changes with the rise of weapon symbolism (Robb 1994a). Metal daggers and flint and bone skeumorphs were finely made, often of exotic materials, and almost certainly intended for display. Weapons formed a common grave good, and daggers and halberds also occur as images in the Val Camonica rock carvings (Anati 1976) and in other Alpine rock carvings and stelae (Graziosi 1974), as well as in the earliest, contemporary Lunigiana stelae (Ambrosi 1988). Two empirical patterns suggest that weapon symbolism was actually associated with maleness. When representational art depicts the sexual characteristics of individuals using weapons, as at Porto Badisco, they are invariably male (it should be noted that the Porto Badisco images depict people hunting as opposed to using weapons such as daggers which imply inter-personal violence). Secondly, both the Lunigiana stelae and other stelae from Italy and adjacent countries typically either bear weapons or breasts. Roughly equal numbers of the two types are known, and stelae never bear neither or both. If breasts were intended to iconically represent aspects of female gender, it seems safe to read weapons as their counterpart icon for maleness.[1]

As archaeological symbols of a generalised prestige rather than a narrowly defined prowess, weapons possess both symbolic coherence and situational redundancy. As situationally redundant symbols, daggers turn up as actual usable artefacts, as non-functional imitations presumably intended for ritual use, as compressed referents for male gender in depictions of people, presumably funerary monuments, and as isolated, disembodied glyphs presumably of ritual origin. In terms of symbolic coherence, as a 'key symbol' (Ortner 1972) for maleness, their use would have provided a key gesture summarising male *hexis* (Bourdieu 1990) and linking strategic behaviour with gender categories defined by 'inherent' capacities for violence and with cosmological concepts about the nature of males, females and society. Demonstrating that this prestige actually was inter-convertible among different realms of activity is archaeologically difficult, but it is significant that metal weapons particularly were an important end-point for exotic materials, and that being a functional adult male thus required and symbolised integration into exchange networks as well as other types of performance.

We can thus make an incomplete, but coherent and suggestive, account integrating male gender ideology, the control and exchange of prestige symbols, and a shift from Great Man to Big Man societies. This did not involve the invention of a completely new gender ideology; all the relevant symbols were in place in the Middle Neolithic. What changed was the degree to which gender was generalised and used as a central political metaphor for a culturally defined view of power. Gender ideologies may have shifted from a relation of balanced opposition to one of asymmetrical or hierarchical opposition (Dumont 1970).

Accompanying this, certain positions of prestige would have been redefined as 'males only', making it a shift from varied 'Great Persons' to homogenised and restricted 'Big Men'.

This reconstruction bears one major *caveat*. Out of what was certainly a complex and multivocal system, it presents a single gender ideology reconstructed through its 'loudest' symbols and taken at face value. Furthermore, the question of whether males exerted a real gender hegemony (Ortner 1993) is open. The reconstruction above suggests some male control of the production of cosmology. However, there is little evidence for economic or other gender inequality (cf. Barker 1981), and to what degree women were encompassed within the male prestige system or developed alternative ideologies is an open question.

EVOLUTIONARY IMPLICATIONS OF THE GREAT MAN-BIG MAN TRANSITION

The Late Neolithic or Copper Age in Europe is often marked by a succession from large, ritualistic villages to a landscape of decentralised, 'pastoral' societies. Recent interpretations (e.g. Thorpe & Richards 1984) have viewed this as a transition from ritual-regulated to prestige-oriented societies, linking social institutions with individual motivations and extended ideological systems. In this paper I extend this approach to propose that political prestige was redefined in the process, as ritualistic Great Men and Women of narrow competence were transformed into exchange-oriented, generalised Big Men.

As Knauft (1993) argues, relatively minor shifts in cultural emphasis can have major effects for social processes. The ideological re-organisation of prestige would have helped to overcome several structural 'limits to growth' of earlier Neolithic societies. Economically, as Bogucki (1988) notes, probably the most important limiting factor on the Neolithic economy was lack of labour. Tribespeople often produce less than is technologically possible due to social norms governing the disposal of surplus (see originally Sahlins 1972). Within the bounds of a subsistence economy, there was little motivation for overproduction beyond the 'normal surplus' (Halstead 1989) of a safety margin. Tying production to prestige via generalised exchange broke this barrier. Moreover, as long as production was organised around small sub-units of permanent villages, productive expansion was limited by the size of producing groups and the resources locally available. A shift to a much more elastic genealogical framework for group recruitment, coupled with spatial diversification and wider alliances, provided the social framework necessary for economic intensification. Intensification itself would have had decisive unintended consequences, including a new demand for labour, environmental change, population growth, and an increased commitment to once-optional innovations.

The resulting cultural definition of power both contained latent bases for inequality and partially specified the forms inequality would take when it emerged. Its delimitation of male and female spheres of prestige certainly underlay later gender systems. Among political actors, as well, with the activation of kinship to organise socially re-creative activities such as production and exchange, structural differentiation was created. Within categories of actors, individuals were placed in genealogically central and peripheral positions, containing the seeds of a clientage system. As for the nature of inequality, competitive activity within the reciprocal norms of a small-scale society meant that the goal of political activity was primarily the conspicuous consumption and display of prestige goods (Sherratt 1994), rather than the accumulation of wealth as capital. Given this, the rise of enclaves of wealthy Early-Middle Bronze Age elites probably represents not the emergence of fundamentally different societies but rather the local realisation of possibilities latent in a widespread ideological system.

Finally, to return to the paradoxes we began with, re-organising prestige overcame limits of growth imposed by inter-group relations as well. While the imagery of violence is far commoner in the Late Neolithic and afterwards, defensive architecture virtually vanishes at this time. Moreover, preliminary skeletal research suggests that actual rates of

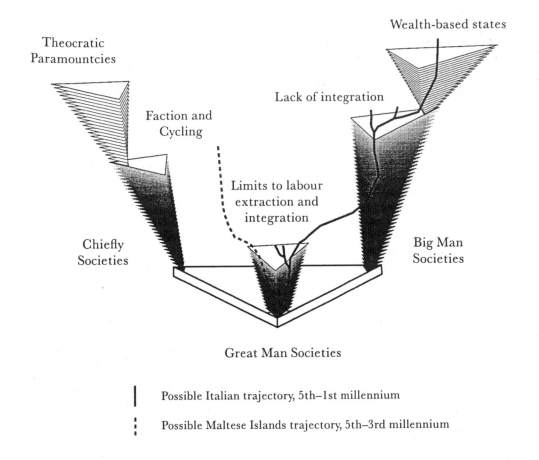

Fig. 2   Some possible evolutionary patterns for the Central Mediterranean

violence-related cranial trauma were far higher in the Neolithic than in the Copper and Bronze Ages (Robb 1997). This apparently paradoxical situation makes sense in light of the comparative ethnography of the Papua New Guinea Highlands. In Great Man societies, endemic warfare proves the limiting factor on settlement. In contrast, Big Man societies with male status hierarchies often glorify violence, but they also tend to have lower rates of homicide and shorter and less drastic conflicts than societies without such hierarchies (Feil 1987; Knauft 1987; 1991). While the symbolism of violence may become much more widespread, actual conflict becomes more limited and more strategically focussed, and alternatives such as peace negotiation and compensation payments become part of the register of politically useful activity.

In evolutionary time, tribal societies appear to have been something of a 'stable attractor', with most extreme developments of one or another variety proving fragile and short-lived. The development of prestige-oriented Big Man societies transcended the limits of scale of Great Man societies, but the resulting groups were still restricted by the limited possibilities of accumulation and coercion in what was still a low-tech, labour-demanding world. There are probably a handful of possible escape trajectories out of tribes (fig. 2). European societies in general never appeared to develop the massively theocratic paramount chiefdoms of the Polynesian variety. Instead, the European social landscape remained essentially segmentary until it was destabilised by the development of wealth as a key to the control of labour in the late second and early first millennium. Under the influence of the Eastern Mediterranean world system, the curiously under-legitimated stratified societies resulting from this rapidly evolved into highly dynamic micro-city-states. The rest is history.

NOTE

1 Burial evidence is somewhat equivocal, however. Individual grave goods associations are known only for Remedello cemeteries, as other Eneolithic cultures practised collective burial. These occasionally contain females buried with daggers and arrow points (e.g. Bagolini 1981). Three inferences are possible: weapons were not associated with maleness in this area; these females were mis-sexed and are actually males (Barfield 1986); or, under some circumstances, it was appropriate to inhume females with male-oriented symbols.

BIBLIOGRAPHY

Allen, M. 1984. Elders, chiefs, and Big Men: authority legitimation and political evolution in Melanesia. *American Ethnologist*, 11: 20–41.

Ambrosi, A. 1988. *Statue-stele lunigianesi.* SAGEP, Genova.

Anati, E. 1976. *Evolution and Style in Camunian Rock Art.* Edizioni del Centro, Capo di Ponte.

Bagolini, B. 1981. *Il neolitico e l'età del rame: ricerca a Spilamberto e S. Cesario, 1977–1980.* Tamari, Bologna.

Barfield, L. 1981. Patterns of North Italian trade, 5000–2000 B.C. In Barker, G. & Hodges, R. (eds), *Archaeology and Italian Society*: 7–51. BAR International Series 102. British Archaeological Reports, Oxford.

Barfield, L. 1986. Chalcolithic burials in Northern Italy: problems of social interpretation. *Dialoghi di Archeologia*, 4: 241–8.

Barker, G. 1981. *Landscape and Society: prehistoric Central Italy.* Academic Press, New York.

Bogucki, P. 1988. *Forest Farmers and Stockherders: early agriculture and its consequences in north-central Europe.* Cambridge University Press, Cambridge.

Bourdieu, P. 1990. *The Logic of Practice.* Stanford University Press, Stanford.

Cazzella, A. 1992. Sviluppi culturali eneolitici nella penisola italiana. In Cazzella, A. & Moscoloni, M. (eds), *Neolitico ed eneolitico*: 351–643. Popoli e civiltà dell'Italia antica, 11. Biblioteca di Storia Patria, Roma.

Cazzella, A. & Moscoloni, M. 1985. Dislevelli culturali nel Mediterraneo centro-orientale fra terzo e secondo millennio a.C. In Liverani, M., Palmieri, A. & Peroni, R. (eds), *Studi di paletnologia in onore di Salvatore M. Puglisi*: 531–47. Università di Roma "La Sapienza", Rome.

Dumont, L. 1970. *Homo hierarchicus: the caste system and its implications.* University of Chicago Press, Chicago.

Ehrenberg, M. 1989. *Women in Prehistory.* University of Oklahoma Press, Norman.

Feil, D. 1987. *The Evolution of Highland Papua New Guinea societies.* Cambridge University Press, Cambridge.

Godelier, M. 1986. *The Making of Great Men: male domination and power among the New Guinea Baruya.* Cambridge University Press, Cambridge.

Godelier, M. 1991. An unfinished attempt at reconstructing the social processes which may have prompted the transformation of great-men societies into big-men societies. In Godelier, M. & Strathern, M. (eds), *Big Men and Great Men: personifications of power in Melanesia*: 275–304. Cambridge University Press, Cambridge.

Godelier, M. & Strathern, A. 1991. *Big Men and Great Men: personifications of power in Melanesia.* Cambridge University Press, Cambridge.

Graziosi, P. 1974. *L'arte preistorica in Italia.* Sansoni, Firenze.

Graziosi, P. 1980. *Le pitture preistoriche di Porto Badisco.* Martelli, Firenze.

Grifoni Cremonesi, R. & Mallegni, F. 1978. Testimonianze di un culto ad incinerazione nel livello a ceramica impressa della Grotta Riparo Continenza di Trasacco (l'Aquila) e studi dei resti umani cremati. Atti, *Società Italiana di Scienze Naturali*, 85: 253–79.

Guidi, A. 1992. Le età dei metalli nell'Italia centrale e in Sardegna. In Guidi, A. & Piperno, M. (eds), *Italia Preistorica*: 420–70. Laterza, Rome.

Halstead, P. 1989. The economy has a normal surplus: economic stability and social change among early farming communities of Thessaly, Greece. In Halstead, P. & O'Shea, J. (eds), *Bad Year Economics*: 68–80. Cambridge University Press, Cambridge.

Hodder, I. 1990. *The Domestication of Europe.* Basil Blackwell, London.

Jorgenson, D. 1991. Big men, great men and women: alternative logics of difference. In Godelier, M. & Strathern, M. (eds), *Big Men and Great Men: personifications of power in Melanesia*: 256–72. Cambridge University Press, Cambridge.

Kelly, R. 1993. *Constructing Inequality: the fabrication of a hierarchy of virtue among the Etoro.* University of Michigan Press, Ann Arbor.

Knauft, B. 1987. Reconsidering violence in simple human societies: homicide among the Gebusi of New Guinea. *Current Anthropology*, 28: 457–99.

Knauft, B. 1991. Violence and sociality in human evolution. *Current Anthropology*, 32: 391–428.

Knauft, B. 1993. *South Coast New Guinea Cultures: history, comparison, dialectic.* Cambridge University Press, New York.

Lemonnier, P. 1991. From great men to big men: peace, substitution and competition in the Highlands of New Guinea. In Godelier, M. & Strathern, M. (eds), *Big Men and Great Men: personifications of power in Melanesia*: 7–27. Cambridge University Press, Cambridge.

Liep, J. 1991. Great man, big man, chief: a triangulation of the Massim. In Godelier, M. & Strathern, M. (eds), *Big Men and Great Men: personifications of power in Melanesia*: 28–47. Cambridge University Press, Cambridge.

Malone, C. 1985. Pots, prestige and ritual in Neolithic Southern Italy. In Malone, C. & Stoddart, S. (eds), *Papers in Italian Archaeology IV: the Cambridge conference*: 118–51. BAR International Series 245 (ii). British Archaeological Reports, Oxford.

Modjeska, N. 1991. Post-Ipomoean modernism: the Duna example. In Godelier, M. & Strathern, M. (eds), *Big Men and Great Men: personifications of power in Melanesia*: 234–55. Cambridge University Press, Cambridge.

Moscoloni, M. 1992. Sviluppi culturali neolitici nella penisola italiana. In Cazzella, A. & Moscoloni, M. (eds), *Neolitico ed eneolitico*: 11–349. Popoli e civiltà dell'Italia antica, 11. Biblioteca di Storia Patria, Roma.

Ortner, S. 1972. On key symbols. *American Anthropologist*, 75: 1338–46.

Ortner, S. 1993. On gender hegemony. *Critique of Anthropology*.

Ortner, S. & Whitehead, H. 1981. Introduction: accounting for sexual meanings. In Ortner, S. & Whitehead, H. (eds), *Sexual Meanings*: 1–28. Cambridge University Press, New York.

Peebles, C. & Kus, S. 1977. Archeological correlates of ranked society. *American Antiquity*, 42: 471–84.

Pellegrini, E. 1992. Le età dei metalli nell'Italia meridionale e in Sicilia. In Guidi, A. & Piperno, M. (eds), *Italia Preistorica*: 471–516. Laterza, Rome.

Radmilli, A. 1953. Notizie preliminari sulla grotta sepolcrale "Patrizi" di Sasso Furbara. *Bollettino di Paletnologia Italiana*, 8: 100–4.

Renfrew, C. & Whitehouse, R. 1974. The Copper Age of peninsular Italy. *Papers of the British School at Athens*, 69: 277–84.

Robb, J. 1994a. Gender contradictions, moral coalitions and inequality in prehistoric Italy. *Journal of European Archaeology*, 2: 20–49.

Robb, J. 1994b. Burial and social reproduction in the Peninsular Italian neolithic. *Journal of Mediterranean Archaeology*, 7: 27–71.

Robb, J. 1997. Violence and gender in early Italy. In Frayer, D. & Martin, D. (eds), *Troubled Times: Archaeological and Osteological evidence for Violence and Trauma*: 108–91. Gordon and Breach, New York.

Sahlins, M. 1963. Poor man, rich man, big man, chief: political types in Melanesia and Polynesia. *Comparative Studies in Society and History*, 5: 285–303.

Sahlins, M. 1972. *Stone Age Economics*. Aldine, Chicago.

Service, E. 1962. *Primitive Social Organization*. Random House, New York.

Shennan, S. 1982. Ideology, change and the European Bronze Age. In Hodder, I. (ed.), *Symbolic and Structural Archaeology*: 155–61. Cambridge University Press, Cambridge.

Shennan, S. 1987. Trends in the study of later European prehistory. *Annual Review of Anthropology*, 16: 365–82.

Sherratt, A. 1981. Plough and pastoralism: aspects of the secondary products revolution. In Hodder, I., Isaac, G. & Hammond, N. (eds), *Pattern of the Past: studies in honor of David Clarke*: 261–305. Cambridge University Press, New York.

Sherratt, A. 1994. The emergence of elites: earlier Bronze Age Europe, 2500–1300 BC. In Cunliffe, B. (ed.), *The Oxford Illustrated Prehistory of Europe*: 244–77. Oxford University Press, Oxford.

Strathern, M. 1991. One man and many men. In Godelier, M. & Strathern, M. (eds), *Big Men and Great Men: personifications of power in Melanesia*: 197–214. Cambridge University Press, Cambridge.

Thorpe, I. & Richards, C. 1984. The decline of ritual authority and the introduction of beakers into Britain. In Bradley, R. & Gardiner, J. (eds), *Neolithic Studies*: 67–78. BAR British Series 133. British Archeological Reports, Oxford.

Tuzin, D. 1991. The cryptic brotherhood of big men and great men in Ilahita. In Godelier, M. & Strathern, M. (eds), *Big Men and Great Men: personifications of power in Melanesia*: 115–29. Cambridge University Press, Cambridge.

Voza, G. 1975. Considerazioni sul Neolitico e sull'Eneolitico in Campania. *Atti della XVII Riunione Scientifica dell'Istituto Italiano di Preistoria e Protostoria*: 51–84. Firenze.

Whitehouse, R. 1984. Social organisation in the neolithic of southeastern Italy. In Waldren, W., Chapman, R., Lewthwaite, J. & Kennard, R.-C. (eds), *The Deya Conference of Prehistory. Early Settlement in the Western Mediterranean Islands and their Peripheral Areas*: 1109–33. BAR International Series 229 (iv). British Archaeological Reports, Oxford.

Whitehouse, R. 1992. *Underground Religion: cult and culture in prehistoric Italy*. Accordia Research Centre, London.

Farmers or Pastoralists in Sardinian Prehistory?

Settlement and Environment

Paula Kay Lazrus

One of the recurrent themes in the literature dedicated to the prehistory of Sardinia is the dichotomy between Pre-Nuragic agriculturalists and Nuragic pastoralists (Tanda & Depalmas 1991; Lilliu 1988; Foschi Nieddu 1988; Fadda 1985). Whether implicit or explicit, this theory assumes that there was a major economic and social transformation between the Neolithic and Bronze Ages. In part, the foundation for such an assumption may be found in the contemporary social, political and historical dynamics of the island (Lewthwaite 1984b: 252–3); the archaeological basis is open to debate. One of the consequences of the application of these contemporary analogies is the depiction of Neolithic farmers as peaceful and egalitarian people with a predominantly agricultural economy, while the Bronze Age inhabitants are described as 'warrior-pastoralists' living in a stratified society and increasingly dependent on specialised pastoralism.

In recent years the existence of intensive specialised pastoralism in different areas of the Mediterranean has been questioned in light of new theoretical research paving the way for re-evaluations of the archaeological data. The findings from such research are applicable to Sardinia (Jongman 1988; Garnsey 1988; Barker 1989; Halstead 1990). Settlement studies focussing on the interaction between the inhabitants and their environment have altered the way in which we evaluate ancient economies; this has affected theories addressing issues such as the shift from spring-fed to dry agriculture (Sherratt 1980; van Andel & Runnels 1987), intensive or extensive farming (Halstead 1987a; 1987b), and the development of pastoralism as a specialised economy (Halstead 1990; Cherry 1988; Whittaker 1988; Barker 1989). Several recent studies of Sardinian archaeology have begun to question the validity of the currently accepted model of social and economic development in the Neolithic and Bronze Ages, requiring us to re-examine the data and our understanding of these crucial periods in Sardinia's prehistory (Lo Schiavo 1981; Castaldi 1984a; 1984b; Lewthwaite 1984a; 1984b; Rowland 1991; Webster 1991; Lazrus 1992). It is my opinion that there is very little evidence to support the notion of a major economic transition between the Pre-Nuragic and Nuragic period. In fact, I would contend that there is no economic change of import during the Neolithic and Bronze Ages. The question of whether there was a major alteration in the economic strategies and social structure of the Pre-Nuragic and Nuragic inhabitants of Sardinia is vitally important for our understanding of the island's prehistory and deserves an in-depth re-appraisal.

```
                                                                    ───── AD 800
                        ROMAN
                                                                    ───── 238 BC
                        PUNIC
                                                                    ───── 550 BC
I
R   A           LATE NURAGIC - PHOENICIAN
O   G
N   E
                                                                    ───── 1115 BC
B
R   A
O   G           NURAGIC
N   E
Z
E
                                                                    ───── 1500 BC
                              - - - - - - - -     Early        1515
                                         Sa
C                                                 Nuragic      1690
H                              Turricula          - - - - - -  1732
A                 Noeddos
L                    II        - - - - - -        - - - - - -  1888
C                                                              1890
O                    - - - - - -                  Monte        1966
L     - - - - - -                                 Claro        2049
I                 Noeddos
T   Bonnanaro        I                            - - - - - -  2274
H
I                    - - - - - -                               2854
C                 - - - - - -                                  2890
              Abealzu-Filigosa                                 3360 BC
N   IV.
E               OZIERI
O
L
                                                                    ───── 4300 BC
N   III.
E               BONU IGHINU
O
L
                                                                    ───── 4600 BC
N   II.
E               FILIESTRU
O
L
                                                                    ───── 5250 BC
N   I.
E               CARDIAL
O
L
```

Fig. 1 Proposed alternative to the standard Sardinian chronology (cal.BC, two sigma)

THE NEOLITHIC

Archaeological evidence for Early Neolithic settlement in Sardinia is composed of cave and open-air sites distributed throughout the island. Examples include the Grotta Corbeddu (NU), Su Carroppu (CA), and the Grotta Verde, Grotta Filiestru and Grotta del'Inferno all from the province of Sassari. The majority of the remains assigned to this period come from sites disturbed prior to archaeological investigation (Trump 1983: 3). The Grotta Corbeddu and the Grotta Filiestru provide the best documented evidence for Early Neolithic farmers. Artefactual evidence includes cardial ceramics, obsidian, querns, evidence for pigments, domesticated plants and the bones of domesticated animals (Cherry 1990: 176; Trump 1983). While our understanding of the economic and social aspects of Sardinia's Early Neolithic society is still being defined, Trump has suggested that the cave of Filiestru was inhabited by a small group of people (10–15) representing perhaps 2–3 families, many less than generally attributed to open-air sites. On the basis of the archaeological remains, he hypothesises that the people living in the caves practised mixed agriculture, growing emmer and einkorn wheats and raising sheep, pigs and cows (Trump 1983: 89; 1984: 514). A more recent assessment by Foschi Nieddu (1991: 25) appears to support this theory. Given the locations of the caves and the greater abundance of vegetation present on the island in antiquity, the inhabitants undoubtedly supplemented their diet of domesticates by collecting wild foods and hunting game. Atzeni (1985: 31) reports finds of wild boar, deer and hare (*Prolagus sardus*) and a variety of sea shells in some Early Neolithic assemblages, which would support such a hypothesis.

The Middle Neolithic is associated with the appearance of the Bonu Ighinu pottery type, found in open village and cave sites. Stratigraphic data are available from the caves of Su Tintirriolu (SS) and Filiestru. Bonu Ighinu pottery has also been found at open-air sites such as Cuccuru s'Arriu, Conc'Ailloni and Puisteris (all in the province of Oristano). Small limestone female figurines, lithic artefacts including arrowheads and knives in obsidian and chert, grinding stones and spherical hammer stones/pestles in basalt and sandstone are also common (Atzeni 1985: 27; Santoni 1987b; Foschi Nieddu 1991: 25). Rock-cut tombs are characterised by single primary inhumations, secondary deposits and multiple burials (Santoni 1987b: 452). In evaluating the Filiestru data, Trump has noted that occupation was less intense than in the Early Neolithic and that the number of wheat grains, pigments, querns and awls recovered was reduced. In addition to the aforementioned finds, a small number of prime joints of domestic animals made up the faunal assemblage, leading him to propose that at this time the main settlement was elsewhere (presumably an open-air settlement). He concludes that the cave was utilised by shepherds and their flocks on a sporadic basis at this time (Trump 1984: 514), although the visits could have been relatively frequent and the period of usage prolonged. Other known cave sites may have been utilised in a similar fashion, but because of their disturbed nature or lack of survey data for the surrounding region, they may have been incorrectly classified as primary pastoral settlements. The mis-classification of temporary cave sites as primary settlements would skew our interpretations of these sites by placing greater emphasis on the pastoral aspects of subsistence when in reality pastoral activities formed an integral part of an integrated mixed farming economy.

The Late Neolithic (Final/Recent) period in Sardinia is associated with a very distinctive decorated pottery first identified at the cave site of San Michele di Ozieri (SS), thus giving the name San Michele or Ozieri to the cultural complex associated with this time period.[1] Archaeologically, the period between the Late Neolithic through the Middle Bronze Age is fraught with chronological problems. Some authors would identify Ozieri as belonging strictly to the Late Neolithic (Contu 1988; Lilliu 1988; Trump 1983; 1990; Lo Schiavo 1984; Ugas et al. 1989) while others would extend it from the Neolithic into the Chalcolithic, sometimes identifying a 'sub-Ozieri' phase (Atzeni 1985; 1987; Santoni 1982; Ugas 1993; Tykot 1994). Part of the inconsistency stems from the habit of identifying ceramic styles with anthropological cultures. Once classified these styles/cultures are then arranged in a linear evolutionary scheme, often distorting what may indeed be co-existent regional or sub regional variations. Typological studies have concentrated primarily on decorated wares, creating false relationships between items that may be contemporary but belong to different functional spheres. Only nine radiocarbon dates from three sites are available; although inadequate, they appear to sustain the hypothesis that Ozieri ended with the Neolithic.

Archaeologically, the Ozieri period represents the earliest island-wide association of a group of cultural features. Identifiable material remains include settlements, tombs and architectural structures for presumably communal activities. The ceramics are often decorated with incised lines filled with white paste or red ochre. There exists a wide repertory of decorations and forms found both at settlements and in tombs. The numerous open-air sites are distinguished by the dense presence of organic remains mixed with lithics and ceramic wares (both decorated and undecorated). The few sites that have been excavated reveal huts that are primarily circular or elliptical in shape. A recent survey in the Sarrabus region resulted in the identification of three Late Neolithic settlements in the Flumendosa valley; two of these are in the vicinity of *stagni* (brackish lagoonal features typical of the coastal regions of Sardinia), while the third is located along a seasonal stream that parallels the Flumendosa (Usai 1990). Similar settlements have been found in the vicinity of the *stagni* of Santa Giusta (OR), Santa Gilla (CA) and Cabras (OR) (Locci 1989; Depalmas 1989; Lazrus 1992). Other open-air sites are located in and around the Campidano plain. Not far from the *stagno* of Monlentargius at the site of Su Coddu (CA), excavations have uncovered huts, wells, storage silos and hearths. The shallow structures were found both as single cells and complex agglomerations constructed in cane covered with mud; some retained traces of mud plaster (Ugas *et al.* 1989: 9–10). Several of the settlement sites are quite large extending over several acres such as San Gemiliano and Monte Olladiri in the province of Cagliari. Puisteris, Cuccuru s'Arriu and perhaps Conc'Ailloni are also several acres in size.

In addition to the settlements which are rich in ceramic, lithic and organic remains, there are a variety of funerary structures constructed during the Late Neolithic. There are rock cut tombs known as *domus de janas*, dolmens and menhirs. The *domus de janas* range from simple single chamber tombs to fairly complex structures with multiple chambers. Menhirs are found individually or in pairs. The majority of the tombs were used as collective burials; most of the sites were disturbed prior to archaeological investigation. The menhirs of this period are usually undecorated.

Domus de janas tombs, monumental cist graves and menhirs are usually located in the upland or mountainous regions of moderate-difficult accessibility. The upland areas would have been covered in heavy vegetation, an environment that may have been perceived as inhospitable for settlement. While labour-intensive land clearance would have been necessary for settlements, the existing conditions would have provided a resource-rich habitat ideal for other activities. The relative inaccessibility may also have resulted in the perception that this zone provided a special environment for collective activities including burial.

Economic Data for the Neolithic and Social Reconstruction

Floral and faunal data that would aid in understanding the economic strategies of the Late Neolithic inhabitants are rare although the situation is slowly improving. The presence of sea shells mixed with bones and other organic materials is often utilised as the identifying surface feature of Late Neolithic sites, yet this association has rarely been tested in a systematic fashion. In the Late Neolithic levels from Filiestru, Trump (1983: 79) found an increase in the number of pig bones attributable to this period and overall a decrease in the usage of the cave site at this time. Botanical remains recovered from Late Neolithic sites include: *Triticum aestivum/durum, T. monoccum, T. dicoccum, Hordendum hexasticum, H. vulgare nudum, Lens esculenta, Vica faba* and *Pisum sativum*. The remains point to an agricultural regime characterised by crop rotation (Piga & Porcu 1990: 572).

A number of small samples of organic material from surface deposits belonging to Pre-Nuragic scatters located near the southwest portion of the *stagno* of Cabras have been collected. While there are obvious problems with floating samples of this type due to contamination, several samples were examined (Lazrus 1992). Samples taken from five Pre-nuragic scatters provided a limited amount of information concerning plant use including a single wheat seed and two culm fragments (Lazrus 1992: 415–16). The molluscan remains represented edible species and were present in seven Pre-Nuragic findspots and six transect areas. The bivalves *Mytilus*, *Ostrea*, *Cerastoderma* and *Venerupis* were the most numerous (Lazrus 1992: 400–8). They are commonly found on rocky submerged areas along the coastline or on sandy/muddy bottoms in marine-brackish waters (D'Angelo & Gargiullo 1978). The molluscan remains are not concentrated in a single portion of any of the individual Sinis findspots, and this seems typical of the other open-air sites in Sardinia. Pig and cattle bones predominated in the limited assemblage composed of bones from the flotation samples and collected during field walking. Today sheep represent the most common animal kept in the Sinis, which is utilised primarily for agriculture (barley, wheat, artichokes and beets). Because of the small sample size it was not possible to provide conclusions regarding the age at death of the animals nor to calculate minimum numbers of individuals (Lazrus 1992: 425–7). Despite the limited data provided by this experiment the results can be utilised together with the existing evidence to provide a baseline for further investigations of the plants and animals utilised in the Pre-Nuragic economy.

Observing the evidence for social organisation and economy of the Late Neolithic inhabitants, the most striking aspect is the relatively uniform distribution of material goods and open-air sites together with a range of funerary forms and other monuments. The settlements are located on arable soil utilising either dry or spring-fed agricultural techniques. The *stagni*, for example, are brackish and there are not always springs or ephemeral streams in the vicinity of the settlements along their shores. Querns, grinding stones and spherical pestles or hammers are common on these sites. Occasionally spindle whorls, loom weights or net weights are found. Storage pits, a feature expected of an agricultural community, were excavated at Su Coddu, but this is the only site where they have been explicitly identified (Ugas *et al.* 1989: 9).

Given the available data, a mixed farming economy supplemented by fishing, shellfish collecting, hunting and presumably the collection of wild plants, represents a plausible interpretation of the Late Neolithic economy. The social organisation of the Late Neolithic population is generally presumed to be egalitarian. While it is probable that the inhabitants were living in loosely aggregated settlement areas, few villages have been extensively excavated to provide data about the internal structure of the sites themselves. We are not able to discern at present whether the hearths are generally located in communal areas, which might indicate the sharing of foodstuffs throughout the community and a pooling of resources, or whether cooking was done within restricted family units, extended or not. These questions are important if we are to understand the mechanisms for risk management, the control of access to resources and the emergence of an elite within the community. It is also necessary if we are to understand how these mechanisms of control are integrated within the social structure of the society (Halstead 1989). The small numbers of farm animals and shellfish may represent strategies of diversification functioning to offset the risks in crop yield. What we do not know is whether plants and animals represent equally important portions of the economy or whether these resources were the property of the community or of individuals. It is also unclear whether the decorated wares represent status items, social tokens or special purpose articles. The funerary monuments are of interest because not all of the burials are communal, yet there seems to be no specific differentiation in the quality of grave goods associated with the tombs. Perhaps social differentiation was expressed through the elaborateness of the funerary structure itself, and not the individual grave goods. If this is true, then we need to have greater chronological resolution on the tombs to pinpoint those in use contemporaneously, and we must attempt to understand which village(s) are associated with which tomb(s). It is probable that future investigations will support the hypothesis that the Late Neolithic inhabitants did not have an egalitarian social organisation, but lived in an increasingly ranked society. Such a multi-community society integrated through kinship and shared cultural activities is supported by the island-wide presence of the large cist graves, the menhirs, and dolmens. These features indicate that there is a social organisation shared by many communities on the island. The monuments in the upland regions would have functioned as the focal point for multiple groups to congregate for specific events and would have served to bind the society together beyond the local scale. Such a community may have officials or other leaders (more or less permanent) without having a distinctive elite class.

THE CHALCOLITHIC

The Chalcolithic period is particularly ill defined. I have suggested elsewhere (Lazrus 1992: 28–41; 1995) that a re-evaluation of the radiocarbon dates, the context(s) of the material(s) dated and the myriad of 'cultures' assigned to this time period can improve our ability to understand the social, political and economic dynamics of the Chalcolithic. The many ceramic styles that characterise this period are each identified with a different culture including Filigosa, Abealzu, Monte Claro, Beaker, Bonnanaro, Noeddos and Sa Turricula. A restructuring of the data requires us to acknowledge the contemporaneity of several of the existing 'cultures' by placing them together within the time period c.3360 and 1500 cal.BC.[2] The primary motivation for classifying all of these different ceramic cultures as a group is that the same criteria utilised to describe Ozieri sites are often applied to these later formations (cf. Santoni 1985; Usai 1989). Although it is not common to include the Bonnanaro, Noeddos and Sa Turricula 'cultures' in the Chalcolithic rather than the Bronze Age, I feel that they are more clearly understood in this context. In addition, undecorated ceramics have not received much attention, although they are abundant during and after the Ozieri period. *Domus de janas* and dolmens continued to be the funerary forms; menhirs were still in use. Occasionally they are decorated with schematic representations of daggers and/or figures. Towards the end of the period the first galley graves may have been constructed. Some tombs were utilised continually from one period to the next, others were newly constructed and continued in use into the Bronze Age. In addition to these features, there are two special-purpose sites that appear at the beginning of this period. The more renowned is located at Monte d'Accoddi (SS). This structure consists of a large (37.5m x 30.5m and 9m high) artificial platform reached by a ramp on which was a rectangular structure for ritual practices (Tinè *et al.* 1989; 1992). An equally imposing structure (57m x 51m and preserved to 6m) is located at Biriai (Castaldi 1992: 77). The platform at Monte Accoddi and many of the menhirs continued to be utilised at least until the beginning of the traditional Bronze Age (c.800 BC). The menhirs with representations of daggers are generally assigned to the Chalcolithic rather than the Late Neolithic (Castaldi 1984a: 575). The attributes assigned to the 'ages,' stone, copper, bronze or iron, usually characterise the period when this particular material came into widespread use together with other social, economic and political changes. As there is no appreciable increase in the usage of copper or its alloys at the beginning of Sardinia's traditional Bronze Age, nor major changes in social and economic organisation, there seems no reason to consider the materials from this time period as belonging to the Early or Middle Bronze Ages. An all-encompassing period titled Chalcolithic or Proto-Nuragic is more appropriate.

Biriai (NU) is one of the few Chalcolithic sites to have been excavated. The excavations have revealed houses, part of a sanctuary and Monte Claro pottery. Other open-air sites such as San Gemiliano, Monte Olladiri, Cuccuru s'Arriu and those around the area of Conc'Ailloni all continue to be inhabited at this time and produce Filigosa, Monte Claro and other ceramic wares. Castaldi has concluded that the people living at Biriai had an agro-pastoral economy and that they were involved in an increasingly complex exchange network (Castaldi 1984a; 1984b). Finds from around the *Stagno* of Cabras appear to support this interpretation (Santoni 1989; Depalmas 1989; Locci 1989; Lugliè 1989; Lazrus 1992). The earliest corridor or protonuraghi now appear, sometimes in association with one of the groups of ceramic wares assigned to this time period, although Sa Turricula and Noeddos wares have not been found in association with early nuragic structures. Beaker ceramics, which are known primarily from funerary contexts, may represent exchanges of prestige goods destined for this specific context.

There appears to be no distinctive break in land-use, settlement or other cultural customs from the Neolithic to Chalcolithic or between the Chalcolithic and the traditional Early/Middle Bronze Ages. The overlaps in radiocarbon dates noticeable in Figure 1 only reinforce the interpretation that these ceramic types represent a series of contemporary and regional styles. Economically, there is no indication of any substantial change with regard to the preceding period. Based on the currently available published data, it can be stated that the mixed agro-pastoral economy established in the Late Neolithic represents a successful adaptation that remained stable well into the succeeding periods.

THE BRONZE AGE

It is during the Bronze Age (here defined as the period between c.1500–1115 cal.BC) that the first simple single-tower *nuraghi* appear. These tronco-conic towers with corbelled vaults have from one to three stories reached by an internal spiral stairway. The simple *nuraghi* are eventually joined by complex multi-towered structures used and re-used into the Roman period. The towers, ubiquitous structures on the Sardinian landscape, have formed the focus for many studies of Sardinian archaeology. Our knowledge of the function(s) of these towers is still extremely limited, but they remain the defining feature of the Bronze Age Nuragic culture.

Culture however, is rarely delineated by a single attribute and the Nuragic culture is no exception to the rule; it is composed of a rich complex of monuments and material goods. By concentrating so heavily on the *nuraghi*, scholars have neglected complementary studies that undoubtedly hold the key to our understanding of Nuragic society and the enigmatic towers. Aside from the *nuraghi*, there are ritual monuments such as the *tempio a pozzo* (temple well), quarries, a variety of funerary monuments including *allée couvertes* (gallery graves), cave tombs known as *tafoni* and large free-standing tombs known as the *tombe di giganti*. As with the *domus de janas*, the tombs are generally utilised for communal burials with a variety of grave goods. Some of the tombs are utilised into the Iron Age. There are numerous village settlements situated in a wide range of landscapes, sometimes in association with simple or complex towers.

The ceramics associated with the Nuragic period include combed ware and a light grey ware. Lithic tools include sickle blades, grinding stones, spherical pestles/hammers, as well as the *testa di mazza*, a doughnut-shaped stone presumed to have served as a hammer or weapon. Bronze becomes increasingly important towards 1200 BC and thereafter. The majority of bronze artefacts have been retrieved from hoards, wells, or undetermined locations and several of the complex *nuraghi* have provided evidence for smelting and smithing activities (Balmuth 1992: 681; Gallin & Tykot 1993). The wide variety of bronze items of local and external manufacture include tools such as pickaxes, chisels, tongs, as well as copper ingots and other necessities of the smith. Swords, daggers and spearheads are also among the bronze artefacts. Numerous diminutive bronze statues appear towards the very end of the Bronze Age. These portray boats, carts, animals and people engaged in a variety of daily and ritualised activities.

An examination of the location of both simple and complex towers reveals that they are distributed throughout the island, at an array of elevations and topographic locations from the coast to the mountains. Few of the estimated 7000[3] *nuraghi* have actually been excavated due to the technical difficulties and great expense involved.[4] Although the simple towers were in use before the construction of the complex towers, some simple *nuraghi* date no earlier than the Iron Age (Michels & Webster 1987); all of the towers are constructed without the use of mortar. The *nuraghi* may appear in a solitary context or in conjunction with villages, terraces, internal wells, and/or *enceinte* walls.

The problem for understanding the land-use, economy and social organisation of the people who constructed the *nuraghi* revolves around the issue of contemporaneity. While information is available on the general distribution of the *nuraghi* from surveys, aerial photographs, and topographic maps, these sources do not usually distinguish between simple and complex towers, defining all as belonging generically to the Nuragic Period. It is highly unlikely that all of these towers were in use simultaneously. Until it is possible to distinguish those towers that are contemporary (at least within a given area), researchers will be hard pressed to understand the relationship between the *nuraghi*, land-use practices and the structure of Nuragic society as a whole.

In my analysis of a group of towers from the Sinis and the Gerrei regions, I attempted to address some of these issues. Part of the study focussed on the differences between the distribution of all Nuragic structures in the two areas and the location of all the *nuraghi*. An attempt was made to account for the diverse locations of simple and complex towers, although the inability to pinpoint which elements were contemporary was a grave handicap (Lazrus 1992: 182–204). The image that emerges from the Sinis/Gerrei study is of a society that is making full and varied use of the landscape. The island-wide distribution of Nuragic features indicates, at a minimum, an increase in settlement throughout the island with respect to the preceding periods. Villages in the Nuorese, Gerrei, Sinis, northern Arborese and Sassarese regions, for example, exist both as individual agglomerations of huts and in conjunction with *nuraghi* (Fadda 1985; Galli 1983; Dyson & Rowland 1988; 1989; Rowland & Dyson 1991; Gallin 1991; Lazrus 1992). Not surprisingly, many Nuragic villages (particularly those without towers) have relatively easy access to the *tempi a pozzo*, and both villages and towers have access to the tombs which may be located in areas accessible to more than one settlement. Whether in the mountains, hills, or lowlands both villages and towers are often situated where there is good arable land and other abundant resources ranging from marine or fresh water, to forests and minerals. In the Sinis, Gerrei and Northern Arborese, for example, the majority of simple towers are situated above good fertile land. This would be a logical choice if one were trying to conserve valuable arable land for agricultural purposes. The complex towers, on the other hand, are often located in areas where transit and access took strategic precedence over the necessities of cultivation. Nothing in the placement of these structures would lead one to believe that agriculture had been abandoned in favor of specialised pastoralism. In fact, specialised pastoralism would not have been as productive in antiquity as it might be today because much of island was still covered in thick Mediterranean forest or lush high macchia. Even much of the lowland terrain would have been more or less densely wooded (Piga & Porcu 1990; Brigaglia 1982). The limited environmental evidence from archaeological contexts combine with textual evidence from the Roman period onwards to confirm that Sardinia was once an extremely lush island covered in pine, juniper, laurustinus, broom, hawthorn, cedar, oak, lentisk, strawberry tree, myrtle, and artemisia (XXI Communità Montana 1989: 21; Piga & Porcu 1990: 571). To have concentrated on specialised pastoralism would have required the clearance of even more substantial tracts of land than that required for agriculture in order to provide sufficiently large grazing areas to support a large herd. In addition, specialised pastoralism would have been a far riskier investment of resources than mixed farming as it increased reliance on a single source of food/wealth for trade surpluses necessary to obtain staples (Halstead 1990: 69).

Aside from the rich and varied resources available to the inhabitants of lowland and upland alike, there is no indication from the archaeological record (e.g. a substantial increase in specialised dairy or textile equipment, or specialised structures for animals, stalls or milking pens), to support a shift in economic strategy between the Late Neolithic and the Bronze Age. Archaeological excavations of Bronze Age sites continue to report an abundance of basalt and sandstone grinding stones, modest numbers of spindle whorls, loom and net weights, as well as fine and common ceramic wares including those for storage and cooking. The analysis of faunal remains from a variety of sites includes cattle, sheep, goat and pig in addition to deer and boar (Rowland 1987; Piga & Porcu 1990; Gallin & Fonzo 1992: 287–95). These analyses indicate that raising animals was an integral part of the economy, but the small number of animals and the age at death data do not support the notion of a specialised economic sector. While the grinding stones may have been used for wild and domesticated plants or pigments, and the spindle whorls for spinning flax, or other plant fibres in addition to sheep or goat hair, none of the evidence indicates that the Nuragic inhabitants altered their economy in a dramatic manner from mixed agriculture to specialised pastoralism.

From the social perspective we have further confirmation of continuity in social structure rather than change at least in the early part of the period. There do not seem to be any major changes in social structure until the very late Bronze Age or Iron Age. Burial customs continue to be shared among the island's inhabitants, although there are some regional variations. Communal burial customs continue and there is little evidence for differential status in burial (Moravetti 1985; cf. also Bonzani 1992: 214). The re-utilisation of a Neolithic tomb at Sant'Iroxi (CA) at the end of the 17th/early 16th centuries BC for a collective burial that included grave goods of high quality including 13 swords and 6 daggers in arsenical copper (Ugas 1992: 223) illustrate aspects of continuity with the preceding period as well as signs of change. It is still a communal burial but the richness of the grave goods may have taken the place of constructing a new and more elaborate monument.

The increasing complexity of the *nuraghi*, which are a continuing expression of the monumental architecture that first emerged in the Late Neolithic, indicates the mobilisation of labour on a larger scale and/or the presence of emerging elites within the society. The question of how much labour or political power would have been necessary to build a *nuraghe* is still under investigation, although Webster and Trump have recently suggested that it was less than we expect (Webster 1991; Trump 1992). The small bronze statues which appear late in the Bronze Age portray figures with shields, swords, bows and arrows, people carrying and working with animals, making bread and carrying grain. They are a clear illustration of the range of activities and roles of different individuals. Both men and women are portrayed, and both appear in attitudes of daily activity as well as those which may be construed as ceremonial in nature. This variety of activities, offerings and roles indicates that both men and women are engaged in activities considered vital to the society as a whole. While some of the male figures are dressed in relatively elaborate gear it is not clear if the paraphernalia is attributable to their particular role and/or status within society or whether it represents some idealised member of society.

The first markedly different burials are found at Is Arrutas and Monte Prama in the Sinis. The Is Arrutas tombs are dated no earlier than the fourth century BC, those at Monte Prama to the 8th–6th centuries BC (Moravetti 1985: 151; Tronchetti 1978: 589–90; 1981: 525–7). The Monte Prama tombs are designated Nuragic, but are dated to the Phoenician period. The 30 tombs of Monte Prama represent individual burials in well-like tombs covered by sandstone slabs, above which was a rubbish pile formed of fragments of nearly life-sized male figures as well as models of *nuraghi*. The statues are carved in limestone and they have been dated by the excavator to the fourth-third centuries BC. Although this is considered a Nuragic burial site, the local population was already in full contact with the Phoenicians, and by the period in which the statues were built, with the Punic colonisers. Rowland (1992) has recently investigated the duration of the Nuragic period, suggesting that it continued well into the Roman period, and Webster and Webster

(1998) have pushed this idea even further. I am more inclined to question whether the mixed population that was emerging is better described as Punic-Sardo or Palaeosardo (cf. Tronchetti 1991: 207). The tombs of Monte Prama reflect the contact between the local inhabitants and the colonisers and echo Nuragic, Phoenician and Punic artistic and funerary endeavours. By the time the latest burials were interred and the statues carved, the population of the Sinis was already very much Sardo-Punic rather than strictly Nuragic. It is only toward the end of the Late Bronze and Iron Ages with the emergence of the highly fortified complex *nuraghi*, and specialised bronze production, that we can begin to see the emergence of a society that may be classified as increasingly stratified. Burials on the other hand continue to be communal in nature without a major disparity in grave goods. There is no evidence until well into the Iron Age and beyond for the development of cities and they are founded by foreigners. During the whole of the Nuragic we still lack substantial data for centralisation of control or regionalised power structures, not to mention any form of redistribution or highly differentiated craft specialisation with the exception of bronze metallurgy, a later development (cf. Yoffee 1993 for further discussion of the problems in identifying chiefdoms).

At no point in either the Neolithic or Bronze Ages does there seem to be any evidence for the emergence of a new economic strategy. The question thus still remains as to why many authors portray the Nuragic population as one of elite warrior-pastoralists. The current hypothesis of a population of professional sheep herders continually raiding one another does not stand firm against the evidence. Rowland (1991: 92) has suggested that they be referred to as "warrior-farmers". The warrior-pastoralist image is based partially on a transference of modern images and politics back into the past, which seeks selective confirmation from the Late Bronze Age *bronzetti* portraying men with swords and shields or wrestling. This ignores all of the figures of people offering bread-like cakes, of cattle, boars, deer, or baskets of food. There are very few statues representing sheep; most (> 100) represent oxen and there are also deer (Lo Schiavo 1981; Brigaglia 1982). Oxen would have been a highly prized animal for ploughing, not to mention expensive to maintain, thus it is not surprising to find frequent portrayals. Some of the men with bows and arrows (those without shields for example), could be celebrating a mythical or ideal personage or more likely the hunter rather than the warrior, given the full repertoire of figures. As for the bronze implements themselves, as stated earlier, the number of tools is certainly equal to that of weapons, alleviating the necessity to rely heavily on the warrior hypothesis.

CONCLUSIONS

After evaluating the current data, there seems to be no firm basis for asserting that there was any major transformation in economic strategy during the Neolithic and Bronze Ages on Sardinia. In fact, I would suggest that there is no clear-cut evidence that there was a major transformation in the mixed farming economy until at least the late 1800s when external market and political pressures left the inhabitants no other viable form of economy (Day 1982: 27–32; Brigaglia 1982: 186–92; Lazrus 1992: 281–92). The notion of a warrior-pastoralist society is one that has been projected upon the ancient inhabitants, perhaps as a way of reinforcing the antiquity of current economic and social behaviours on the island. The extant archaeological data support the hypothesis that Sardinia was inhabited by a vital, thriving and stable community with a limited to moderate degree of social stratification. The inhabitants practised farming and small scale animal husbandry supplemented by hunting, fishing and gathering, trade and mining during the Neolithic and Bronze Ages. It can be observed that from the Late Neolithic onward, a steadily increasing number of diverse environments and landscapes are exploited and there is certainly room to entertain the possibility of local variations in economic strategy. In general, however, economic diversification, not specialisation, appears to characterise the Pre-Nuragic and Nuragic cultures of Sardinia. A strategy of diversification would have increased the possibilities and complexities of inter- and extra-island exchange, and augmented the social mechanisms involved in hedging against the risks of crop failure and in confronting incursions from foreigners wishing to settle the island. A broad based economy which exploited a variety of ecosystems and utilised all of the food and material resources available, including stones and metals, would have made the Late Neolithic and Bronze Age societies extremely stable. The gradual increase in the complexity of monuments that are distributed in the landscape indicates the richness and sophistication of religious and daily activities, most of which appear to be communal rather than individual in nature. With further study directed at establishing which monuments and artefacts are in fact contemporary we should be able to move closer to understanding the social and economic dynamics of prehistoric Sardinia.

ACKNOWLEDGEMENTS

I am appreciative of the comments offered by Robert J. Rowland, Jr on an earlier draft of this paper, and to the editors of this volume. I offer a warm thank you to Vito and Franca Gentile for hospitality and the use of their computer. Thank you also to Marco for infinite patience and understanding.

NOTES

1 In this paper the term Ozieri is used.
2 The term Chalcolithic is fairly neutral and useful in that sense; however, a more culturally specific term such as Proto-Nuragic could be utilised to signify change with respect to the Prenuragic while accounting for the earliest Nuragic features that emerge during this period.
3 Trump has recently suggested that 7000 may be a low estimate, since survey projects regularly produce evidence for unrecorded towers (Trump 1992: 199).
4 Seven excavation seasons of one or two months at the Nuraghe Arrubiu (NU) has cost the Soprintendenza di Sassari 900 million Italian lira or c.$640,000.00 US dollars (Lo Schiavo 1992: 682).

BIBLIOGRAPHY

Atzeni, E. 1962. I villaggi preistorici di San Gemiliano di Sestu e di Monte Olladir di Monastir presso Cagliari e le ceramiche della "facies" di Monte Claro. *Studi Sardi*, 17: 3–216.

Atzeni, E. 1985. Tombe Eneolitiche nel Calgiaritano. In Sotgiu, G. (ed.), *Studi in Onore di Giovanni Lilliu per il Suo Settantesimo Compleano*: 11–50. Istituto di Antichità Archaeologica e Arte, Facoltà di Lettere, Cagliari.

Atzeni, E. 1987. Il Neolitico della Sardegna. *Atti della XXVI Riunione Scientifica dell'Istituto Italiano di Preistoria e Protostoria, "Il Neolitico in Italia"*, vol. 1: 381–400. Istituto Italiano di Preistoria e Protostoria, Firenze.

Balmuth, M.S. 1992. Archaeology in Sardinia. *American Journal of Archaeology*, 96(4): 663–97.

Barker, G. 1989. The archaeology of the Italian shepherd. *Proceedings of the Cambridge Philological Society*, 215: 1–19.

Bonzani, R. 1992. Territorial boundaries, buffer zones and sociopolitical complexity: a case study of the nuraghi on Sardinia. In Tykot, R.H. & Andrews, T.K. (eds), *Sardinia in the Mediterranean: A Footprint in the Sea. Studies in Sardinian Archaeology Presented to Miriam S. Balmuth*: 210–20. Monographs in Mediterranean Archaeology 3. Sheffield Academic Press, Sheffield.

Brigaglia, M. 1982. Il paesaggio agrario. In Manconi, F. & Angioni, G. (eds), *Le Opere e i Giorni: Contadini e Pastori nella Sardegna Tradizionale*: 186–95. Silvana Editoriale, Milano.

Castaldi, E. 1984a. La cultura calcolitica di Monte Claro nel sito di Biriai. In Waldren, W., Chapman, R., Lewthwaite, J. & Kennard, R.-C. (eds), *The Deya Conference of Prehistory. Early Settlement in the Western Mediterranean Islands and their Peripheral Areas*: 567–84. BAR International Series 229. British Archaeological Reports, Oxford.

Castaldi, E. 1984b. L'architettura di Biriai. *Rivista di Scienze Preistoriche*, 34: 119–54.

Castaldi, E. 1992. Il santuario di Biriai. In *Monte d'Accoddi. 10 Anni di Nuovi Scavi*: 77–81. Istituto di Archeolgoia Sperimentale e la Soprintendenza Archeologica di Sassari e Nuoro, Genova.

Cherry, J.F. 1988. Pastoralism and the role of animals in the pre- and protohistoric economies of the Aegean. In Whittaker, C.R. (ed.), *Pastoral Economies in Classical Antiquity*: 6–34. The Cambridge Philological Society, Supplementary volume 14. Cambridge.

Cherry, J.F. 1990. The first colonization of the Mediterranean islands: a review of recent research. *Journal of Mediterranean Archaeology*, 3: 145–221.

Contu, E. 1974. La Sardegna dell'Età Nuragica. In Tusa, V., Contu, E. & Mansuelli, G., *Popoli e Civiltà dell'Italia Antica*, volume 3: 145–203. Biblioteca di Storia Patria, Roma.

Contu, E. 1985. Il Nuraghe. In *Civiltà Nuragica*: 45–110. Electa, Milano.

Contu, E. 1988. Problematica ed inquadramento culturale. In Atzeni, E., Contu, E. & Ferrarese Ceruti, M.L., L'età del rame nell'Italia insulare: La Sardegna. *Rassegna di Archeologia*, 7: 441–8.

D'Angelo, G. & Gargiullo, S. 1978. *Guida alle Conchiglie Mediterranee*. Fabbri, Milano.

Day, J. 1982. Alle origini della povertà rurale. In Manconi, F. & Angioni, G. (eds), *Le Opere e i Giorni: Contadini e Pastori nella Sardegna Tradizionale*: 13–33. Silvana Editoriale, Milano.

Depalmas, A. 1989. Il materiale preistorico di Isca Maiori nella collezione Falchi di Oristano. *Studi Sardi*, 28: 37–59.

Dyson, S. & Rowland, Jr, R.J. 1988. Survey archaeology in the territory of Bauladu. Preliminary Notice. *Quaderni della Soprintendenza Archeologica di Cagliari e Oristano*, 5: 129–40.

Dyson, S. & Rowland, Jr, R.J. 1989. The University of Maryland Wesleyan University Survey in Sardinia – 1988. *Quaderni della Soprintendenza Archeologica di Cagliari e Oristano*, 6: 157–85.

Fadda, M.A. 1985. Il villaggio. In *Civiltà Nuragica*: 111–31. Electa, Milano.

Foschi Nieddu, A. 1988. La cultura di Abealzu-Filigosa: La Tomba I di Filigosa (Macomer, Nuoro). *Rassegna di Archeologia*, 7: 5–21.

Foschi Nieddu, A. 1991. Il Neolitico Antico e Medio. In *Sardegna Archeologica*: 22–6. Ministero dei Beni Culturali, Roma.

Galli, F. 1983. *Archeologia del Territorio: Il Comune di Ittireddu (SS)*. Quaderni della Soprintendenza di Sassari e Nuoro 14. Dessì, Sassari.

Gallin, L.J. 1991. Architectural evidence for the defensibility of the territory of Sediolo (Oristano). In Santillo Frizell, B. (ed.), *Arte Militare e Architettura Nuragica*: 65–71. Skrifter utgivna av Svenska Institutet i Rom. Stockholm.

Gallin, L.J. & Fonzo, O. 1992. Vertebrate faunal remains at the Nuragic village of Santa Barbara, Bauladu (OR). In Tykot, R.H. & Andrews, T.K. (eds), *Sardinia in the Mediterranean: A Footprint in the Sea. Studies in Sardinian Archaeology Presented to Miriam S. Balmuth*: 287–93. Monographs in Mediterranean Archaeology 3. Sheffield Academic Press, Sheffield.

Gallin, L.J. & Tykot, R.H. 1993. Metallurgy at Nuraghe Santa Barbara (Bauladu), Sardinia. *Journal of Field Archaeology*, 20(3): 335–45.

Garnsey, P. 1988. Mountain economies in southern Europe. Thoughts on the early history, continuity and individuality of Mediterranean upland pastoralism. In Whittaker, C.R. (ed.), *Pastoral Economies in Classical Antiquity*: 196–209. The Cambridge Philological Society, Supplementary volume 14. Cambridge.

Halstead, P.L. 1987a. Man and other animals in later Greek prehistory. *Annual of the British School at Athens*, 82: 71–83.

Halstead, P.L. 1987b. Traditional and ancient rural economy in Mediterranean Europe: plus ça change? *Journal of Hellenic Studies*, 107: 77–87.

Halstead, P.L. 1989. The economy has a normal surplus: economic stability and social change among early farming communitites of Thessaly, Greece. In Halstead, P. & O'Shea, J. (eds), *Bad Year Economics*: 68–80. Cambridge University Press, Cambridge.

Halstead, P.L. 1990. Present to past in the Pirdhos: diversification and specialization in mountain economies. *Rivista di Studi Liguri*, 56(1–4): 61–80.

Halstead, P.L. 1992. Agriculture in the Bronze Age economy: towards a model of Bronze Age palatial economy. In Wells, B. & Skydgaard, J.E. (eds), *Agriculture in Ancient Greece*: 105–17. Skrifter utgivna av Svenska Institutet i Athens 4. Stockholm.

Jongman, W. 1988. Adding it up. In Whittaker, C.R. (ed.), *Pastoral Economies in Classical Antiquity*: 210–12. The Cambridge Philological Society, Supplementary volume 14. Cambridge.

Lazrus, P.K. 1992. *Settlement and Land-Use in Two Regions of Sardinia, the Gerrei and the Sinis*. Ph.D. dissertation, Boston University. University Microfilms, Ann Arbor.

Lazrus, P.K. 1995. A re-examination of Sardinian chronology. Poster presented at the international colloquium on Sardinian Stratigraphy and Mediterranean Chronology, Tufts University.

Lewthwaite, J. 1984a. The art of corse herding: archaeological insights from recent pastoral practices on west Mediterranean Islands. In Clutton-Brock, J. & Grigson, C. (eds), *Animals and Archaeology 3. Early Herders and their Flocks*: 25–37. BAR International Series 202. British Archaeological Reports, Oxford.

Lewthwaite, J. 1984b. Pastore, Padrone: The social dimensions of pastoralism in prenuragic Sardinia. In Waldren, W., Chapman, R., Lewthwaite, J. & Kennard, R.-C. (eds), *The Deya Conference of Prehistory. Early Settlement in the Western Mediterranean Islands and their Peripheral Areas*: 251–68. BAR International Series 229. British Archaeological Reports, Oxford.

Lilliu, G. 1988. *La Civiltà dei Sardi dal Paleolitico all'Età dei Nuraghi*. 3rd edition. Nuova ERI, Torino.

Locci, C. 1989. Ceramiche di cultura Monte Claro nell'insediamento preistorico di Conca Illonis-Cabras. *Studi Sardi*, 28: 61–72.

Lo Schiavo, F. 1981. Economia e società nell'età dei nuraghi. In *Ichnussa: La Sardegna dalle Origini all'Età Classica*: 255–347. Libri Scheiwiller, Milano.

Lo Schiavo, F. 1984. Appunti sull'evoluzione culturale della Sardegna nell'età dei metalli. *Nuovo Bullettino Archeologico Sardo*, 1: 21–40.

Lo Schiavo, F. 1992. Nuraghe Arrubiu. *American Journal of Archaeology*, 96(4): 682–4.

Lugliè, C. 1989. Ceramiche eneolitiche dall'insediamento di Fenosu-Palmas Arborea (Oristano). *Studi Sardi*, 28: 74–100.

Michels, J.W. & Webster, G.S. (eds) 1987. *Studies in Nuragic Archaeology*. BAR International Series 373. British Archaeological Reports, Oxford.

Moravetti, A. 1985. Le tombe e l'ideologia funeraria. In *Civiltà Nuragica*: 132–80. Electa, Milano.

Piga, A. & Porcu, M.A. 1990. Flora e fauna della Sardegna Antica. *L'Africa Romana*, 7: 569–97.

Rowland Jr, R.J. 1987. Faunal remains of prehistoric Sardinia: the current state of the evidence. In Michels, J. & Webster, G. (eds), *Studies in Nuragic Archaeology*: 147–61. BAR International Series 373. British Archaeological Reports, Oxford.

Rowland Jr, R.J. 1991. Contadini-guerrieri: an alternative hypothesis of Sardinian cultural evolution in the Nuragic Period. In Santillo Frizell, B. (ed.), *Arte Militare e Architettura Nuragica*: 87–117. Skrifter utgivna av Svenska Institutet i Rom, Stockholm.

Rowland Jr, R.J. 1992. When did the Nuragic period in Sardinia end? In *Sardinia Antiqua. Studi in onore di Piero Meloni in occasione del suo settantesimo compleanno*: 165–75. Edizioni della Torre, Cagliari.

Rowland Jr, R.J. & Dyson, S. 1991. Survey archaeology in Sardinia. In Barker, G. & Lloyd, J. (eds), *Roman Landscapes. Archaeological Survey in the Mediterranean Region*: 54–61. Archaeological Monographs of the British School at Rome 2. British School at Rome, London.

Santoni, V. 1982. Cabras-Cuccuru S'Arriu – nota preliminare di scavo 1978, 1979, 1980. *Rivista di Studi Fenici*, 10: 103–10.

Santoni, V. 1985. Tharros – il villaggio nuragico di Su Muro Mannu. *Rivista di Studi Fenici*, 13: 33–143.

Santoni, V. 1987a. Le stazioni nuragiche all'aperto nell'entroterra del Golfo di Cagliari. In *Cultura di Paesaggio e Metodi del Territorio*: 63–88. Cagliari.

Santoni, V. 1987b. Cabras (Oristano). Necropolo neolitica sull'isolotto di Cuccuru S'Arriu. In Perego, F. (ed.), *Memorabilia: Il Futuro della Memoria 3*: 451–5. Laterza, Roma.

Santoni, V. 1989. Cuccuru S'Arriu – Cabras. Il sito di cultura San Michele di Ozieri. Dati preliminari. In Campus, L. (ed.), *La Cultura di Ozieri*: 169–200. Edizioni il Torchietto, Ozieri.

Sherratt, A. 1980. Water, soil and seasonality in early cereal cultivation. *World Archaeology*, 11(3): 313–30.

Tanda, G., & Depalmas, A. 1991. Saggio di analisi del territorio nella Sardegna centrale. In Santillo Frizell, B. (ed.), *Arte Militare e Architettura Nuragica*: 143–62. Skrifter utgivna av Svenska Institutet i Rom, Stockholm.

Tinè, S, Bafico, S., Rossi, G. & Mannoni, T. 1989. Monte d'Accoddi e la Cultura di Ozieri. In Campus, L. (ed.), *La Cultura di Ozieri. Problematiche e nuove acquisizioni*. Atti del I convegno di studio, Ozieri, gennaio 1986-aprile 1987: 19–36. Edizioni il Torchietto, Ozieri.

Tronchetti, C. 1978. Monte Prama. *Studi Etruschi*, 46: 589–90.

Tronchetti, C. 1981. Monte Prama. *Studi Etruschi*, 49: 525–7.

Tronchetti, C. 1991. L'iconografia del potere nella Sardegna arcaica. In Herring, E. Whitehouse, R. & Wilkins, J. (eds), *Papers of the Fourth Conference of Italian Archaeology 1. The Archaeology of Power. Part 1*: 207–20. Accordia Research Centre, London.

Trump, D.H. 1983. *La Grotta di Filiestru a Mara (SS)*. Quaderni 13 della Soprintendenza di Sassari e Nuoro. Dessì, Sassari.

Trump, D.H. 1984. The Bonu Ighinu project... results and prospects. In Waldren, W., Chapman, R., Lewthwaite, J. & Kennard, R.-C. (eds), *The Deya Conference of Prehistory. Early Settlement in the Western Mediterranean Islands and their Peripheral Areas*: 511–32. BAR International Series 229. British Archaeological Reports, Oxford.

Trump, D.H. 1990. *Nuraghe Noeddos and the Bonu Ighinu Valley*. Oxbow Books, Oxford.

Trump, D.H. 1992. Militarism in Nuragic Sardinia. In Tykot, R.H. & Andrews, T.K. (eds), *Sardinia in the Mediterranean: A Footprint in the Sea. Studies in Sardinian Archaeology Presented to Miriam S. Balmuth*: 198–203. Monographs in Mediterranean Archaeology 3. Sheffield Academic Press., Sheffield.

Tykot, R.H. 1994. Radiocarbon dating and absolute chronology in Sardinia and Corsica. In Skeates, R. & Whitehouse, R. (eds), *Radiocarbon Dating and Italian Prehistory*: 115–45. Accordia Research Centre, & British School at Rome, London.

Ugas, G. 1992. Considerazioni sullo sviluppo dell'architettura e della società nuragica. In Tykot, R.H. & Andrews, T.K. (eds), *Sardinia in the Mediterranean: A Footprint in the Sea. Studies in Sardinian Archaeology Presented to Miriam S. Balmuth*: 221–34. Monographs in Mediterranean Archaeology 3. Sheffield Academic Press, Sheffield.

Ugas, G. 1993. *San Sperate dalle Origini ai Baroni*. Norax 2. Edizioni della Torre, Cagliari.

Ugas, G., Usai, L., Nuvoli, M.P., Lai L. & Marras, M.G. 1989. Nuovi dati sull'insediamento di Su Coddu-Selargius. In Campus, L. (ed.), *La Cultura di Ozieri*: 239–78. Edizioni il Torchietto, Ozieri.

Usai, E. 1989. La Cultura Ozieri a Pimentel e a Siddi. In Campus, L. (ed.), *La Cultura di Ozieri*: 217–30. Edizioni il Torchietto, Ozieri.

Usai, D. 1990. Modelli di insediamento nel Sarrabus dal Neolithico all'Età del Bronzo. *Quaderni della Soprintendenza Archeologica di Cagliari e Oristano*, 7: 117–34.

van Andel, T.H., & Runnels, C. 1987. *Beyond the Acropolis: A Rural Greek Past*. Stanford University Press, Stanford.

Webster, G.S. 1991. Monuments, mobilization and Nuragic organization. *Antiquity*, 65: 840–56.

Webster, G.S. & Webster, M. 1998. The chronological and cultural definition of Nuragic VII, AD 456–1015. In Balmuth, M.S. & Tykot, R.H. (eds), *Sardinian and Aegean Chronology. Studies in Sardinian Archaeology V*: 383–95. Oxbow Books, Oxford.

Whittaker, C.R. 1988. Introduction. In Whittaker, C.R. (ed.), *Pastoral Economies in Classical Antiquity*: 1-5. The Cambridge Philological Society, Supplementary volume 14. Cambridge.

XXI Communità Montana del Sarrabus-Gerrei-Villasalto 1989. *Piano degli Interventi per la Sistemazione Idrogeologica e Idraulica del Territorio della XXI Communità Montana del Sarrabus-Gerrei. Premessa, Territorio, Clima, Idrologia e Vegetazione*.

Yoffee, N. 1993. Too many chiefs? In Yoffee, N. & Sherratt, A. (eds), *Archaeological Theory: Who Sets the Agenda?*: 60–78. Cambridge University Press, Cambridge.

Long-term Dynamics of an Island Community

Malta 5500 BC – 2000 AD

Simon Stoddart

Malta, a large island with a safe harbour which opens to the east. Malta has a city. It abounds in pasture, flocks, fruit and, above all, honey.

(Idrisi)

There is a small rock situated at the southern extremity of Italy, which possessing both advantages (that is, geographical position and a good harbour), appears to me to be eminently calculated for commanding the Mediterranean.

(Mark Wood. Letter to William Pitt and Henry Dundas on 14 November 1796)

Only the things of fantasy are beautiful. And memory too is fantasy . . . Malta is nothing but a poor, harsh island and the people are as barbarous as when St. Paul was shipwrecked there. Only, being in the sea, it allows imagination to venture into a fable of the Moslem and Christian world, as I have done, as I have been able to do.... Others would say history, but I say fable.

(Leonardo Sciascia. *The Council of Egypt*)

INTRODUCTION

Small islands exhibit highly distinctive trajectories of social and political development and cyclic interaction with their neighbours. They also produce very varied reactions to outsiders, both in fact and fiction. There is always controversy about the nature of that extra-insular interaction (Bradley 1984), but, outside archaeology, this is normally perceived on a very short time scale. Whereas studies of the *longue durée* have received great emphasis by archaeologists in recent years (Barker 1991; Knapp 1992), the convenient units formed by islands have been rarely addressed, and, indeed, Braudel (1972) himself writes relatively little about Malta. This paper addresses these issues of long term political development and external interaction for the island of Malta, linking sources and periods which are rarely combined in one account since disciplinary borders have to be crossed (Blouet 1984).

Information on the island of Malta increasingly provides a rare combination of archaeological and anthropological information for a well defined unit of modest size (310 square kilometres). It has been suggested that the seemingly diverse strands of this island history provided by prehistorians, classical archaeologists, historians, historical geographers and cultural anthropologists can be drawn together into a coherent account (Stoddart 1992). This paper represents a first outline attempt to do precisely that, by employing material culture in its broadest sense (including settlement and monument organisation) to reconstruct the social dynamics of this island society. This will be explored in terms of the spatial dynamics of the island society and its relations with the outside Mediterranean world.

THE CONTEXT OF THE SOUTHERN CENTRAL MEDITERRANEAN

As discussed elsewhere (Stoddart in press), Malta is the second largest island group of the southern central Mediterranean after Sicily. It is an island group that offers the potential for self-sustained agricultural development, provided population levels are not too high. It is unique in the southern central Mediterranean in providing a capacity for self-sustenance in an isolated location. The island group is closer to Sicily and thus to the northern rim of the Mediterranean, but the mediating islands of Lampedusa and Linosa could have offered an alternative linkage to the southern rim of the Mediterranean. The strategic position of Malta astride the eastern approaches to the western Mediterranean offered a third choice, linkage to the eastern Mediterranean. At different times of occupation by human populations, different selections have been made with radically different consequences on its social and political development.

THE IMPORTANCE OF CHRONOLOGY

The Maltese islands have an unusually sensitive chronological sequence in prehistory for a small island group. This was initially based on ceramic sequences elaborated by Evans (1953; 1971) and Trump (1966) and then given depth by radiocarbon chronology and its calibration. This relative chronological accuracy allows a broad sweep of processual analysis. It is at the level of this broad sweep that the later historic periods will be documented. The end date of 2000 AD is partly rhetorical and indeed documentary historians should not expect the level of detail of documentary periods, but a broad perspective perceived from prehistory.

The relative chronological precision allows a perception of pace and rates of change. The length of the early Neolithic stylistic phase is potentially quite long (up to 1000 years); whereas the length of the middle and later Neolithic stylistic phases are relatively short (100 and 300 years). The formative phases of the temple constructing period are also equally short followed by longer phases in main and final temple building periods. The phase immediately following the abandonment of temple construction is once again a long (up to 1000 year) phase. These cycles of stylistic representation appear to reflect the dynamism of social and political change.

One element that remains uncertain is the degree of discontinuity, and potential abandonment, between stages of political development in the Maltese islands. Anati (1988) has suggested that there may be significant phases of abandonment of the Maltese islands in prehistory and this may also have occurred in historical periods. It seems probable that this was a rare occurrence given the sufficient size of the Maltese islands to sustain self-sufficient agricultural production. The relative size of the islands should also rule out migration and invasion as powerful political forces for social and political change at the level that has frequently been suggested. In this sense, one can contrast the size of the Lipari islands which were much more vulnerable to political intervention (Stoddart in press).

COLONISATION (GHAR DALAM)

The Maltese islands were first colonised by relatively permanent human populations at c.5500 BC. The prerequisite was agriculture. The surface area and biomass of the islands were simply too small (Malone in press) to allow for hunting and gathering populations to maintain a stable presence on the islands and their relative isolation made more occasional visits an improbability. The long period (up to 1000 years) of early agriculture in the islands was a phase of inter-connected intermittent agriculture in many of the smaller islands of the southern central Mediterranean (Stoddart in press). Stylistic inter-connections were maintained with considerable similarities in pottery; the only major distinctions rest on the modern political context of their findspot (Italy – Stentinello; Malta – Ghar Dalam).

CONSOLIDATION (GREY AND RED SKORBA)

The prerequisite for permanent occupation was probably a form of more intensive agriculture. This would have involved extensive clearance of any climax vegetation and the available scanty records of the palaeoenvironment reinforce this impression. Provided water and uneroded sediment were supplied, the islands could have provided an extremely effective agricultural base which in turn could lead potentially to fairly rapid social and political change. The phases of consolidation of permanent occupation were relatively short lived and suggest a much more rapid pace of change. In spite of this, considerable stylistic contacts were maintained with the rest of the Mediterranean world, with a strong similarity of appearance and decorative elements particularly between Diana (Italy) and Red Skorba (Malta).

One interesting development in this phase was the construction of a building in the Red Skorba phase at Skorba which has been interpreted as a shrine (Trump 1966: 11–14). This oval building, 8.40 by 5.40m in size, with an adjoining D-shaped structure, 5.60 x 3.20m in size, surrounded by courtyards, contained five figurines, an unusual amount of pottery and animal bone (including about six reworked goat crania). If this interpretation is correct, ritual activity was still very strongly embedded in domestic activity, in contrast to later developments in the Maltese islands.

RITUALISATION (ZEBBUG)

Divergence of the Maltese islands from their neighbours first became apparent in the subsequent phase of the fourth millennium BC. The style of Zebbug pottery resembles San Cono – Piano Notaro styles in many but not all respects (Evans 1953: 78) and the linkage has often been stressed in terms of exchange processes such as for ochre (Maniscalco 1989), greenstone axes (Malone et al. 1995a) and other products. However, the prominence of collective burial ahead of patterns in Sicily and peninsular Italy suggests a precocious social and political process in Malta.

Settlement evidence is unfortunately lacking to give a balanced picture of social change. However the available funerary evidence suggests major changes. It is suggested that competitive exchange processes in Malta were providing an opportunity for consolidation of political organisation around kin groups, whose increasing focus was displayed in collective family burials joined with the products of their successful exchange. The Zebbug phase probably represents the first steps towards a separation of the ritual and domestic spheres of activity which was to see its climax with the construction of temples in the next phases.

RITUAL DIVERGENCE (GGANTIJA, TARXIEN)

By the Ggantija phase in the later fourth millennium BC, the distinctive cultural and political development of Malta had become fully apparent. The island enters a period of longer stylistic phases, suggesting that this highly ritualised landscape had a strong element of stability. Indeed the overall length of the temple construction and use is more than one thousand years.

The landscape of the Maltese islands became highly structured into three well defined focal zones (Bonanno *et al.* 1990): temples, funerary hypogea and settlement sites. The clusters of temples were highly visible points within the landscape which provided material for internal competition within the individual Maltese communities, employing mechanisms not unlike those that can be seen in the smaller Maltese villages today (Boissevain 1969). The impressive temple structures had formal facades sheltering the complexly articulated internal space of central corridors which led to symmetrically arranged apses and altars, embellished with vegetal, animal and anthropomorphic sculptures. The communal focus of the community appears to have been provided by the main burial hypogeum, whereas the factions within the community played out their rivalry in the construction and embellishment of temples.

The burial dimension is currently being investigated by new fieldwork. The most famous burial hypogeum, Hal Saflieni, was unfortunately cleared of its skeletal contents and associated symbolic artefacts at the turn of the century without effective records. Fortunately, a comparable site, the Brochtorff Circle, serving the Gozo prehistoric community, is currently being excavated by an Anglo-Maltese project. These excavations, in the course of completion at the time of writing (1994), display numerous signs of communal ideology, even if these may potentially mask incipient divisions within the community. The buried community represents all ages and sexes in roughly natural proportions (allowing for taphonomy) and there are no symbolic indications that this buried community is merely one elite segment.

The human bones show considerable reworking through their post-life history. Full articulation is rare and significant in its placing within the site. The bones were most probably incorporated in repetitive multi-stage rituals that constantly emphasised the apparent unity of the community in death, although showing selective differentiation along lines of gender and age. For example, one most significant articulated body was a male placed in a pit immediately in front of the main megalithic threshold to the site. His articulated body had then been covered with the partial remains of other individuals (of both sexes), surmounted by a display of predominantly male skulls and finally sealed by a layer of cobbles. All participants in the death rituals at the Brochtorff Circle had to pass over this ancestor when gaining access to the deeper recesses of the monument, either to visit or add to their ancestors.

The final component of the structured landscape is the least understood: the settlements. Only two instances of published domestic structures contemporary with the building of temples were known as of 1994. The first underlies the temple at Skorba (Trump 1966). The second was partly preserved under a field wall in Gozo (Malone *et al.* 1988). However, if these structures are representative, it is clear that much less time and labour was invested in these structures and that they did not contain the art or reworked exotic materials found in the temples and burial places.

The construction of the temples coincides with a cycle of cultural, and possibly also physical, isolation of the Maltese islands. The complex symbolic patterning of the Maltese landscape is quite different from the rest of the central Mediterranean (Malone *et al.* 1995b). This isolation was characterised by an increasing investment of time and labour in local products. The limestone geology provided ready building stone for the temples, including both rubble infill (coralline limestone) and carved facing (globigerina limestone). In addition, the globigerina limestone provided a fine medium for small, refined sculptures. Other sculptures were fashioned out of local clays. Exotic materials, such as greenstones, appear to have been less readily available from outside the islands, and consequently treated as more precious than locally available products. Greenstones in particular were sacralised by perforation and transformation into pendants which were sometimes cached in temples (and perhaps the burial hypogeum of Hal Saflieni, although the context is lost) (Skeates 1995; Malone et al. 1995b).

At the end of the long period of temple building and use, opportunities for the mechanism of promotion appeared (Flannery 1972). Ritual specialists operating under the ethos of communal responsibility, that was retained in the outward presentation of the burial hypogea, appear to have begun to subvert the rituals of the temples to their own political advantage. The ready and shallow access to the Maltese temples began to be restricted by blocking off entrances and constricting lines of vision to their inner areas. It is highly probable that the majority of the population was kept in the forecourt areas with only fleeting glimpses of the increasingly complex rituals taking place within (Bonanno et al. 1990; Stoddart et al. 1993). These changes in the late Tarxien period, however, contained the elements of the destruction of what had been a very stable society. Without the institutions of state organised societies and the ultimate sanction of coercion, the opportunistic ritual specialists were unable to maintain control of society for the same long periods. Environmental deterioration may also have contributed to the eventual termination of the active use of this highly ritualised landscape (Malone et al. 1993).

RE-INCORPORATION WITHIN THE MEDITERRANEAN (TARXIEN CEMETERY)

An area of major debate remains the nature of the transition between the political organisation of the Tarxien phase and that of Tarxien Cemetery (c.2500 BC). It is clear that the complex tripartite elements of the landscape in the Tarxien phase were replaced by only one archaeologically visible element: cremation burial and possibly associated dolmen burials. No well defined settlements have been discovered, unless the newly discovered occupation at the Brochtorff Circle counts as such.

Until recently most interpretations have envisaged a complete collapse of the preceding political organisation and its wholesale replacement by a new population (Evans 1971: 224). A number of factors suggest that the changes may have been more ideological and political rather than cataclysmic and genetic. The temples and the Brochtorff Circle hypogeum underwent a radical change of use rather than a simple abandonment. Part of the Tarxien temple was employed as a burial ground, although a stratigraphic discontinuity is generally suggested between these two phases. The Brochtorff Circle was selectively covered with domestic deposits and distinctive ceramic vessels were placed at the limits of the cave burial complex. Some material from both the temples of Borg in Nadur and Skorba shows continued occupation after the disuse of the temples. Furthermore Evans (1984) has suggested that the break in material culture may not be as severe as originally suggested and some elements of the material culture from the Brochtorff Circle appear to support this (Trump pers. comm.).

There is, therefore, some tentative evidence that the new cultural organisation of Tarxien Cemetery recognised and respected or reacted against the preceding Tarxien monuments. The respect is suggested by the choice of temples and burial places for continued occupation of a different nature: most particularly the Cemetery at Tarxien, the offering vessels at Brochtorff Circle and the reorganisation of altars at Tas-Silg (Brusasco 1993: 14). Other evidence suggests some slighting of the Brochtorff monument: a broken stone statuette and shrine. Further work is needed to establish the relationship.

Whatever the nature of the political transition, at this same point, Malta was re-incorporated back into the Mediterranean system. The styles of pottery, the cremation rites, the first clear presence of copper alloys, as well as the abandonment of the preceding distinctive Maltese temple rituals, all point to completely re-assessed cultural attitude to the Mediterranean.

Once again the contacts were towards Sicily, as particularly indicated by the finds of Tarxien Cemetery material on the island of Ognina off Sicily, in association with but outnumbering finds of the contemporary Castelluccio style of Sicily (Bernabò Brea 1966; 1976–77). Bernabò Brea also suggests that the stylistic connections reach as far as Capo Graziano in the Lipari islands.

DEFENSIVE SETTLEMENTS (BORG IN NADUR/BAHRIJA)

In the succeeding Borg in Nadur and Bahrija phases, the evidence becomes once more reassuringly domestic in character. The inhabitants retired to defensive sites, often naturally defended on the tops of plateaux. The duration of these ceramic styles is also long and seemingly stable in spite of the instability of the contemporary Mediterranean that is suggested by the choice of settlement location. These sites took the character of farming villages with the types of material culture to be expected in mature, stable, farming communities.

Mediterranean links are detectable both through shared stylistic networks and the discovery of some Maltese material culture in Sicily and some exotic material culture in Malta. At Ognina, occupation by a seemingly Maltese community continues through this period (Bernabò Brea 1966). One fragment of Mycenaean pottery has been found at Borg in Nadur (Vagnetti 1982) and possibly another at Tas-Silg (Cagiano De Azevado et al. 1964–73).

INCORPORATION BY EXTERNAL STATES

The incorporation of Malta into the Phoenician orbit is currently the subject of some debate (Brusasco 1993). The re-analysis of Tas-Silg suggests a relative break between the indigenous Bronze Age populations and the incoming Phoenician groups. In my opinion, whatever the stratigraphic evidence from the ritual site of Tas-Silg, it would be more informative to look at a domestic context, when available, to establish the relationship. Certainly, the political take-over by the Phoenicians of the full archipelago suggests a relatively small indigenous population and/or a very effective political strategy of control and domination of the original inhabitants.

The timing of the Phoenician take-over of Malta appears to be early compared to other areas, provided one discounts the textual accounts of Phoenician colonies in the western Mediterranean from the late second millennium BC (Moscati 1993). Malta provided a rare natural harbour of the condition of Tyre or Arvad in the western Mediterranean, a position shared only by Gadir and Motya (Aubet 1993). Occupation appears to have taken place in the second half of the eighth century BC. In the initial phase of Phoenician colonisation, Malta had a centrality that was only later affected by the rise of Carthage in the Punic period.

Once Phoenician dominance took place it is clear that the small size of the islands provided an unusually favourable context for complete political domination. The islands were so small that a highly centralised urban organisation could be developed, perhaps working through and developing the existing settlement structure and ritual centres (Moscati 1993). The small distances, even with unsophisticated transport, could be easily controlled from two urban centres, Victoria and Rabat, one on each island. In the case of Malta, a second population centre can be detected in the area of modern Valletta from the concentration of tombs and, less securely, a third from the survival of an ashlar masonry structure at Zurrieq (Gouder 1979a).

The cultural orientation of the Maltese islands during this period was strongly eastern. Phoenician artefacts show vigorous connections with Egypt via the Levant. This pattern has been strengthened by the recent study of museums collections and material found in the excavations at the temple of Tas-Silg (Hölbl 1989; Gouder 1979a; 1979b; Frendo 1993). The latter finds include an ornamental ivory fragment in the form of a stylised palmette and small palmiform limestone pillars. In the later Punic phase the islands became more marginal and were curiously marked by a lack of direct contact with the Sicilian colonies (Moscati 1993).

Malta had some strategic importance at the end of the Carthaginian occupation. This was sufficient for the islands, on the border between Roman and Carthaginian political spheres, to be devastated by a Roman raid in the First Punic War (c.255 BC). The Carthaginian military presence in the island was consequently strengthened in response to this threat. However, as the conflict between the power blocs of the Mediterranean intensified, Malta was absorbed into the Roman orbit as the Carthaginian empire was defeated.

INCORPORATION BY EXTERNAL EMPIRE

In 218 BC, Malta was incorporated into the Roman Empire (Bonanno 1992) and became an administrative unit of Sicily. However, the effects of political incorporation took a long time to implement. Malta remained culturally Punic. The first Latin inscription is dated to some two centuries after occupation. The settlement pattern retained the highly centralised form of the Punic period. Most of the population was concentrated into the two towns, one on each island. The main town of Malta was under modern Mdina and, although only the subject of limited investigation, does show some signs of wealth and links to imperial iconography in a *domus* excavated in the early part of the century.

Dispersed settlement has been uncovered in the countryside of Roman Malta, but this does not appear to have been as dense as many other classical landscapes. Some thirty villas have been located in Malta. Several have revealed agricultural fittings, but the majority appear to be more retreats from town life. It can be tentatively suggested that a considerable degree of agricultural activity would have been based in the nucleated communities which would have been in easy communication with considerable portions of the agricultural landscape within a one hour travel time. The presence of a number of defensive towers suggests the relative insecurity of rural life even during the Roman empire (Trump 1972: 89), perhaps reinforcing the tendency towards nucleation rather than dispersed settlement.

Gozo presents a very similar pattern of life in the Roman period, although on a smaller scale. The centre of modern Rabat was the location of the main Roman settlement. This nucleated centre has also provided evidence of imperial iconography, modified to reflect the changing political climate of Rome. The famous Ramla villa was a country retreat with heated baths on a sandy beach. The Xewkija villa, located at the extreme range of easy access from Rabat, was set up for agricultural purposes.

The most informative element from the documentary evidence is its silence. The incorporation of Malta within a much broader political entity cancelled the importance of the island on a wider scale. Malta was not involved in the military activities which attract documentary accounts since she was now a small island in the centre of the empire. Equally Malta was of no administrative or political importance, incidental to the economic and political processes of the empire.

ARAB AND MEDIEVAL PERIOD

The immediately post-Roman period has been little researched and documentary records contain little information. The islands were peripheral to the main political developments of the central Mediterranean and contained low levels of population. The islands had no strategic role and once the compass was invented could be as easily avoided as encountered (Luttrell 1975: 18).

The islands were taken over by Arab rulers in c.870 AD. At this stage an increase in documentary coverage allows an impression of low population and non-intensive land use to be more firmly established, although allowance must be made for the greater aridity of the lands from which the Arab chroniclers came (Blouet 1984: 36). One chronicler, Al-Himyari, appears to describe a quite heavily vegetated island during the eleventh century with sufficient timber for shipbuilding (Fiorini 1993a: 176). This might be interpreted as the product of a major cycle of regeneration of the forests under low population conditions at the end of the Roman Empire. The roughly contemporary twelfth century account of Idrisi, emphasising pasture, flocks, fruit and honey, may be more realistic (Luttrell 1975: 32). Population levels were most probably below 10,000 throughout this time (Blouet 1984: 38; Wettinger 1969). Alternatively, clearance in the prehistoric period may have been exaggerated. Certainly by the fifteenth century, the deforestation of the islands had been completed once more at a time when population levels reached about 20,000 (Blouet 1984: 39).

A liminal period followed the Arab after about 1090 AD when the Normans intermittently took an interest in the islands, but the cultural and spatial geography of the islands were very little affected (Blouet 1984: 36–7). The re-organisation of Malta as part of the Sicilian kingdom of Frederick II after about 1220 led to more profound changes (Blouet 1984: 37) which eventually switched the external cultural relations of the islands from the south and east to the north. In this context, Italian and Spanish names became dominant amongst the ruling class. The degree of political intervention by the Sicilian rulers fluctuated over time and its organisation was generally archaic (Luttrell 1975: 14–15).

The settlement organisation up to about 1400 seems to have been largely dispersed. The three nucleated centres were Mdina and its suburb (Rabat) at the centre of the island and a coastal castle (castrum maris) and its suburb (Birgu) (Fiorini 1993a: 121). It was only the economic competition provided by the introduction of cotton production and the increased insecurity of the fifteenth century that led to nucleation of population in fewer centres (Blouet 1984). The more vulnerable Gozo appears to be an exception to this rule, since almost all population was always concentrated in the area around the citadel in the centre (Fiorini 1993a: 120–1), although Blouet (1984: 82) appears to consider the pattern to have been similar to Malta with dispersed settlement pattern as a starting point and the later creation of villages.

KNIGHTS

The arrival of the Knights in 1530 drew Malta firmly back into the international arena. The islands were no longer dependent on their own resources. The economic catchment of the Order of St John drew in revenue that could be invested in the island (Hoppen 1973). Building (with trade and privateering) was one of the few areas where investment could be made (pre-shadowing some very modern developments). One immediate effect was a steady rise in population from about 17,000 in 1524 to 43,000 in 1617 (Mallia-Milanes 1992: 4–5). This trend was only interrupted by minor deviations on an archaeological time scale such as famine and plague and the Great Siege which caused a slight drop in population and was the proximate cause of a major investment in defensive infrastructure.

Another major impact was that of urbanisation (Fiorini 1993b). It appears that the urban population changed from 5% before the arrival of the Knights to 54% in the 1760s (Mallia-Millanes 1993: 15). The patterns of urbanisation were also different. Whereas previous urban populations had been concentrated at Mdina in the centre of the island since the Bronze Age, the new nucleation was in coastal Valletta, the new centre of power.

Fortification was another long-term trend that was closely linked to this new centre of power (Hoppen 1979). The siege, a major part of the mythology of event conscious historians, "only helped to delay, not inspire, the realization of the new fortress city" of Valletta (Mallia-Millanes 1993: 10). The long term strategic role of Malta in the new political context required powerful naval and military defences; the timing was incidental to the long term political process. Coastal areas were also fortified and given watch towers which converted attitudes towards the sea. An inward looking society was once more transformed into an outward looking society.

MODERN

The modern period adds further elements to the cycle of relationships to the outside world. The British period placed the island once more within a wider imperial network, serving broader strategic interests. Population levels and corresponding demographic densities continued to increase from the 100,000 inhabitants in 1800 to over double one hundred years later, making the islands one of the most densely occupied areas of the world.

Migration out of the islands also gathered pace, at first in the Mediterranean and then particularly following the Second World War towards the New World and Australasia. Independence has brought increasing prosperity through tourism, and the fruits of an independent international role in trade, commerce and income from an exported labour force. The British geographers commissioned to predict areas of future economic development failed to see the potential of independence (Bowen-Jones et al. 1962) since their perspective only perceived Malta as a fragment of empire. None of the novel economic areas are topics covered by the Durham geographers who perceived the islands principally in terms of an agriculture which historically has never had the potential to bring expansive prosperity. Independence has also brought both a southern directionality towards the Arab world and, more recently a revived linkage to the northern rim of the Mediterranean.

CONCLUSION

The Maltese islands illustrate very well the fluctuating patterns of internal political development and external relationships. Insularity played a prominent role in some of these cycles of development. The most notable was in prehistory during the building of the temples, but there were notable time-lags derived from previous phases which reinforce the insularity of the islands (Luttrell 1975: 14–15). Punic traditions continued into the Roman period. Arab culture continued under the Normans.

Some other broad trends can be detected through this global approach to the island's development. Malta was a politically independent entity for the first four millennia of its development, but state formation, or rather state take-over from the east, brought more or less complete dependency for almost three millennia until recent independence. The predominant cultural orientation has been towards the northern shores of the Mediterranean with notable phases of insularity (fourth to third millennium BC), orientation to the east (early first millennium) and to the south (immediately post-Classical). After the slow growth of the early agricultural societies, settlement nucleation appears to have been the predominant trend. This probably occurred in fourth and third millennia BC (although difficult to detect) and was certainly a strong trend throughout the first millennia BC and AD. The incorporation within the geo-political frameworks of the Knights and then the British, led to a shift in nucleation from the ancient centres of the islands to the fortified coastal ports serving needs far from the shores of Malta. This shift in nucleation was accompanied by a demographic explosion above the level sustainable from local agricultural resources, the situation which had dominated all previous development.

In summary, these small islands show an intriguing complexity of development which can potentially be explored with a detail difficult to undertake in larger landmasses. That detail forms part of a future project.

ACKNOWLEDGEMENT

I would like to thank Richard Bradley whose closing remarks at a conference in Bristol (1993) first suggested this theme.

BIBLIOGRAPHY

Anati, E. 1988. Considerazioni sulla preistoria di Malta. Nota preliminare. In Fradkin, A. & Anati, E. (eds), *Missione a Malta. Ricerche e studi sulla preistoria dell'arcipelago maltese nel contesto mediterraneo*: 1–49. Jaca Book, Milano.

Aubet, M.E. 1993. *The Phoenicians and the West. Politics, Colonies and Trade*. Cambridge University Press, Cambridge.

Barker, G. 1991. Two valleys, one valley: an Annaliste perspective. In Bintliff, J. (ed.), *The Annales School and Archaeology*: 34–56. Leicester University Press, Leicester.

Bernabò Brea, L. 1966. Abitato neolitico e insediamento maltese dell'età del bronzo nell'isola di Ognina (Siracusa) e i rapporti fra la Sicilia e Malta dal XVI al XIII a.C. *Kokalos*, 12: 40–69.

Bernabò Brea, L. 1976–77. Eolie, Sicilia e Malta nell'età del bronzo. *Kokalos*, 22–23: 33–111.

Blouet, B. 1984. *The Story of Malta*. Progress Press, Valletta.

Boissevain, J. 1969. *Saints and Fireworks. Religion and Politics in Rural Malta*. Athlone Press, London.

Bonanno, A. 1986. A socioeconomic approach to Maltese prehistory. The temple builders. *Malta. Studies of its Heritage and History*: 17–46. Mid-Med Bank Limited Interprint Ltd., Malta.

Bonanno, A. 1992. *Roman Malta. The Archaeological Heritage of the Maltese Islands*. World confederation of Salesian past pupils of Don Bosco, Lugano.

Bonanno, A., Gouder, T., Malone, C. & Stoddart, S. 1990. Monuments in an island society: the Maltese context. *World Archaeology*, 22(2): 190–205.

Borg, V. 1986. Malta and its palaeochristian heritage: a new approach. *Studies of its Heritage and History*: 47–86. Mid-Med Bank Limited Interprint Ltd., Malta.

Bowen-Jones, H., Dewdney, J.C. & Fisher, W.B. 1962. *Malta. Background for Development*. Department of Geography, University of Durham, Durham.

Bradley, R. 1984. *The Social Foundations of Prehistoric Britain. Themes and Variations in the Archaeology of Power*. Longmans, London.

Braudel, F. 1972. *The Mediterranean and the Mediterranean World in the Age of Philip II*. Collins, London.

Brusasco, P. 1993. Dal Levante al Mediterraneo centrale: la prima fase fenicia a Tas-Silg, Malta. *Journal of Mediterranean Studies*, 3(1): 1–29.

Cagiano De Azevado, M., Caprino, C., Ciasca, A., Coleiro, E., Davico, A., Garbini, G. & Saverio Mallia, F. 1964–73. *Missione Archeologica Italiana a Malta. Rapporti Preliminari delle Campagne 1963–1970*. Istituto di Studi del Vicino Oriente, Università di Roma, Roma.

Cutajar, D. & Cassar, C. 1986. Malta's role in Mediterranean affairs: 1530–1699. *Studies of its Heritage and History*: 105–49. Mid-Med Bank Limited Interprint Ltd., Malta.

Evans, J.D. 1953. The prehistoric culture sequence of the Maltese archipelago. *Proceedings of the Prehistoric Society*, 19: 41–94.

Evans, J.D. 1971. *The Prehistoric Antiquities of the Maltese Islands: A Survey*. Athlone Press, London.

Evans, J.D. 1984. Maltese archaeology – a reappraisal. In Waldren, W., Chapman, R., Lewthwaite, J. & Kennard, R.-C. (eds), *The Deya Conference of Prehistory. Early Settlement in the Western Mediterranean Islands and their Peripheral Areas*: 489–97. BAR International Series 229. British Archaeological Reports, Oxford.

Fiorini, S. 1993a. Malta in 1530. In Mallia-Milanes, V. (ed.), *Hospitaller Malta. Studies on Early Modern Malta and the Order of St. John of Jerusalem*: 111–98. Mireva Publications, Msida.

Fiorini, S. 1993b. Demographic growth and urbanisation of the Maltese countryside to 1798. In Mallia-Milanes, V. (ed.), *Hospitaller Malta. Studies on Early Modern Malta and the Order of St. John of Jerusalem*: 296–310. Mireva Publications, Msida.

Flannery, K.V. 1972. The cultural evolution of civilisations. *Annual Review of Ecology and Systematics*, 3: 399–426.

Frendo, A. 1993. Some observations on the investigation of the Phoenicians/Canaanites in the Ancient Mediterranean World. *Journal of Mediterranean Studies*, 3(2): 169–74.

Gouder, T. 1979a. Phoenician Malta. *Heritage*, 1: 173–86.

Gouder, T. 1979b. Some amulets from Phoenician Malta. *Heritage*, 1: 311–5.

Graburn, N.H. (ed.) 1976. *Ethnic and Tourist Arts*. University of California Press, Berkeley.

Hölbl, G. 1989. *Ägyptisches Kulturgut auf den Inseln Malta und Gozo in Phönikischer und Punischer Zeit. Die Objekte im Archäologischen Museum von Valletta*. Verlag der Österreichischen Akademie der Wissenshaften, Wien.

Hoppen, A. 1973. The finances of the order of St. John of Jerusalem in the sixteenth and seventeenth centuries. *Europe Studies Review*, 3(2): 103–19.

Hoppen, A. 1979. *The Fortification of Malta by the Order of St. John. 1530–1798*. Scottish Academic Press, Edinburgh.

Knapp, A.B. (ed.) 1992. *Archaeology, Annales and Ethnohistory*. Cambridge University Press, Cambridge.

Luttrell, A. 1975. Approaches to medieval Malta. In Luttrell, A. (ed.), *Medieval Malta. Studies on Malta before the Knights*: 1–70. British School at Rome, London.

Macarthur, R.H. & Wilson, E.O. 1967. *The Theory of Island Biogeography*. Princeton University Press, Princeton.

Mallia-Milanes, V. 1992. *Venice and Hospitaller Malta. 1530–1798. Aspects of a Relationship*. Publishers Enterprises Group Ltd., Marsa.

Mallia-Milanes, V. 1993. Introduction to Hospitaller Malta. *Hospitaller Malta. 1530–1798. Studies on Early Modern Malta and the Order of St. John of Jerusalem*: 1–42. Mireva publications, Msida.

Malone, C. in press. Processes of colonisation in the central Mediterranean. *Accordia Research Papers*.

Malone, C., Bonanno, A., Gouder, T., Stoddart, S. & Trump, D. 1993. The death cults of prehistoric Malta. *Scientific American*, 269(6): 110-7.

Malone, C., Stoddart, S., & Trump, D. 1988. A house for the temple builders. Recent investigations on Gozo, Malta. *Antiquity*, 62: 297-301.

Malone, C., Stoddart, S., Bonanno, A., Gouder, T. & Trump, D. (eds) 1995a. Mortuary ritual of fourth millennium BC Malta: the Zebbug period chambered tomb from the Brochtorff Circle (Gozo). *Proceedings of the Prehistoric Society*, 61: 303-45.

Malone, C., Stoddart, S. & Townsend, A. 1995b. The landscape of the island goddess? A Maltese perspective of the central Mediterranean. *Caeculus*, 2: 1-15.

Maniscalco, L. 1989. Ochre containers and trade in the Central Mediterranean Copper Age. *American Journal of Archaeology*, 93(4): 537-41.

Miller, D. 1980. Settlement and diversity in the Solomon Islands. *Man*, 15: 451-66.

Moscati, S. 1993. Some reflections on Malta in the Phoenician World. *Journal of Mediterranean Studies*, 3(2): 286-90.

Sciascia, L. 1993. *The Council of Egypt*. (translated from the Italian by Adrienne Foulkes). Harper Collins, London.

Skeates, R. 1995. Animate objects: a biography of prehistoric "axe amulets" in the central Mediterranean region. *Proceedings of the Prehistoric Society*, 61: 279-301.

Stoddart, S. 1992. Towards a historical ethnology of the Mediterranean. *Current Anthropology*, 33(5): 599-60.

Stoddart, S. in press. Contrasting political strategies in the islands of the southern central Mediterranean. *Accordia Research Papers*.

Stoddart, S., Bonanno, A., Gouder, T., Malone, C. & Trump, D. 1993. Cult in an island society: prehistoric Malta in the Tarxien period. *Cambridge Journal of Archaeology*, 3(1): 3-19.

Trump, D.H. 1966. *Skorba*. Research Reports of the Society of Antiquaries of London 22. London.

Trump, D.H. 1972. *Malta. An Archaeological Guide*. Faber, London.

Vagnetti, L. (ed.) 1982. *Magna Grecia e Mondo Miceneo. Nuovi documenti. XXII Convegno di Studi sulla Magna Grecia, Taranto, 7–11, ottobre 1982*. Istituto per la Storia e l'archeologia della Magna Grecia, Taranto.

Wettinger, G. 1969. The militia list of 1419-20: a new starting point for the study of Malta's population. *Melita Historica*, 2: 80-106.

Wettinger, G. 1986. The Arabs in Malta. *Studies of its Heritage and History*: 87-104. Mid-Med Bank Limited Interprint Ltd., Malta.

Short-term Cultural Dynamics within the Mediterranean Cultural Landscape[1]

Sebastiano Tusa

In order to understand the cultural dynamics of Sicily between the end of the third and the second millennium BC, and their relations with events elsewhere in the Mediterranean, I have separated out different cultural phenomena and treated them individually. However, this is only for reasons of clarity. I also continually cross-refer between phenomena and trace their inter-connected dynamics, which is the only way that permits one, in my opinion, to identify the actual evolutionary mechanisms (fig. 1).

THE BELL BEAKER PHENOMENON IN SICILY

In Sicily, Bell Beakers (*bicchieri campaniformi*) are concentrated largely in the western parts of the island in two areas: one northern and one southern (fig. 2). In the northwestern area there are many Beakers, and decoration using the *pointillé* technique is typical. In the southwestern area, the Beaker presence is more marked and is characterised by a high level of integration with the local Malpasso and Naro-Partanna cultural groups. Beyond these areas, the rest of the island is only marginally affected by Beaker elements (Tusa 1987; 1993b).

The zones of particular interest for the Bell Beaker phenomenon are the Oreto Valley in the north, and the Modione and Belice Valleys to the south, suggesting an overall north-south axis of penetration. In these areas, Beaker elements are sufficiently dense that one should not speak of intrusive elements but rather of a true, chronologically and geographically definable, cultural entity. The main material typological characteristics of this culture[2] show chronological and geographical dynamics on the territorial scale (Pacci 1987b). The two areas adopt and adapt differing aspects of the Beaker decorative repertoire[3], signalling differing ethnic or chronological dynamics with varying levels of cultural integration within local traditions.

The Northwest

Chronologically, it seems that the evidence for Beakers in the northwestern zone precedes that of the southwest. The initial Bell Beaker elements lack influences from indigenous cultures, and there are several indications of connections between this part of the island

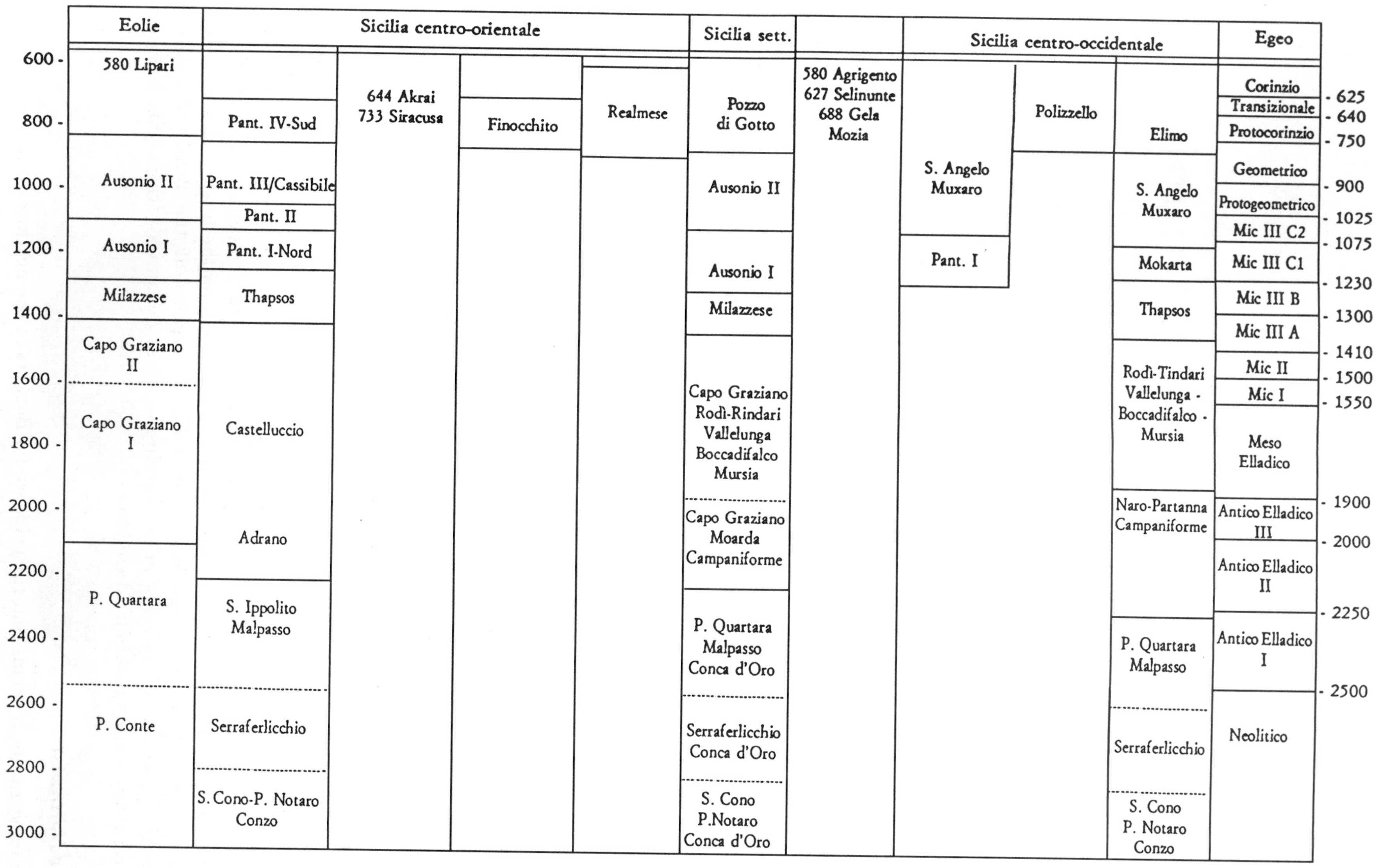

Eolie	Sicilia centro-orientale	Sicilia sett.	Sicilia centro-occidentale		Egeo	
580 Lipari	644 Akrai / 733 Siracusa	580 Agrigento / 627 Selinunte / 688 Gela Mozia		Polizzello	Corinzio	625
	Pant. IV-Sud		Elimo		Transizionale	640
					Protocorinzio	750
Ausonio II	Pant. III/Cassibile	Pozzo di Gotto		S. Angelo Muxaro	Geometrico	900
	Pant. II	Ausonio II	S. Angelo Muxaro		Protogeometrico	1025
Ausonio I	Pant. I-Nord			Pant. I	Mic III C2	1075
		Ausonio I	Mokarta		Mic III C1	
Milazzese	Thapsos	Milazzese			Mic III B	1230
			Thapsos		Mic III A	1300
Capo Graziano II		Capo Graziano Rodi-Rindari Vallelunga Boccadifalco Mursia	Rodi-Tindari Vallelunga - Boccadifalco Mursia		Mic II	1410
	Castelluccio					1500
Capo Graziano I					Mic I	1550
					Meso Elladico	
	Adrano	Capo Graziano Moarda Campaniforme	Naro-Partanna Campaniforme		Antico Elladico III	1900
P. Quartara	S. Ippolito Malpasso	P. Quartara Malpasso Conca d'Oro	P. Quartara Malpasso		Antico Elladico II	2000
					Antico Elladico I	2250
P. Conte	Serraferlicchio	Serraferlicchio Conca d'Oro	Serraferlicchio		Neolitico	2500
	S. Cono-P. Notaro Conzo	S. Cono P. Notaro Conca d'Oro	S. Cono P. Notaro Conzo			

(Left date scale: 600, 800, 1000, 1200, 1400, 1600, 1800, 2000, 2200, 2400, 2600, 2800, 3000)

Fig. 1 Sicilian relative chronologies between the Copper Age and Greek Colonisation

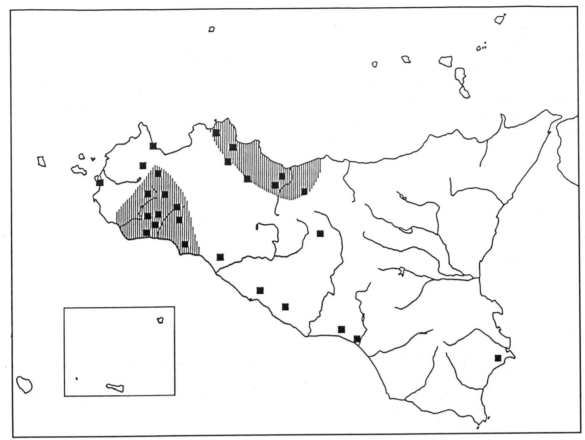

Fig. 2   Distribution of Bell Beakers in Sicily

and wider Bell Beaker circles from the formative phase onwards (Bosch Gimpera 1967; Clarke 1970). Examples include the V-perforated button from tomb II at Uditore, near Palermo, datable to around the middle of the 3rd millennium BC (Cassano *et al.* 1975[4]), as well as burials in hypogea and the Carini beaker, also in the Palermo area, from the beginning of the Eneolithic, elements that appear connected to the genesis of Bell Beaker culture (Bovio Marconi 1945) (fig. 3).

Thus, formative Bell Beaker elements appear precociously in the northwest, while in the southwest their arrival dates to a mature phase of the phenomenon. If one hypothesises that the start of the contacts between the formative Bell Beaker culture and northwestern Sicily began as early as the third millennium, we may place the arrival of the mature Beaker elements at the end of that millennium. At this time, in combination with the development of the Malpasso facies, a true Bell Beaker cultural horizon invades the southwest of the island, and occasionally sends its products further south and east.

Fig. 3   Conca d'Oro Culture (Copper Age): grave goods from Partanna (Palermo). In the centre, the so-called Carini Beaker

In the northwestern area the Bell Beaker culture acquired new forms as it evolved, although this zone never used painted decoration, which occurred widely elsewhere in the island. The so-called Moarda style represents the acquisition of the idea of *chiaroscurale chroma* by Bell Beaker potters. Here two ceramic traditions, the Bell Beaker and the Capo Graziano, both based on the use of incised and impressed decoration, came into contact. This is illustrated by the finds from Villafrati (Von Andrian 1878) and Moarda (Bovio Marconi 1945), where there are both ceramics of Capo Graziano style, possibly imported directly from the Aeolian Islands, and pieces of Cypriot affinity probably mediated through the Aeolian Islands (fig. 4).

Fig. 4 Ceramics from Villafrati (Palermo) (top) with vase with Cypriot affinity to left and Bell Beaker in centre; ceramics from Moarda (Palermo) (middle and bottom) with the jug at bottom showing the incised decoration of the Capo Graziano type

Fig. 5   Ceramics of the Bell Beaker facies from southwestern Sicily (from Segesta, Marcita, Naro and Marcita respectively)

The Southwest

In the southwestern zone, the concentration of sites of the Bell Beaker culture appears heavier than in the northwest, especially in the territories of Castelvetrano, Partanna, Salemi and Sciacca (i.e. the lower valleys of the Belice and Modione) (Tusa 1987; 1990a; 1993b). The arrival of the Bell Beaker in the southwestern area is belated. Proof of this comes from Roccazzo in the hinterland of Mazara del Vallo, which has no Beaker elements in burial assemblages characterised by ceramics of the Piano Notaro – Conca d'Oro type (Tusa 1990a). However, the nearby site of Marcita shows the association of Beakers with Malpasso elements at a time when the Naro-Partanna proto-Castelluccio style was already fully developed. The direct cultural and technological connections between the Bell Beaker tradition and that of the Castelluccio facies of Naro-Partanna suggests a process of cultural syncretism in which both traditions gave and received ceramic elements (Pacci 1982; Pacci & Tusa 1990) (fig. 5). Thus the Beaker and its decoration acquired a bichrome finish, while painted pedestal cups acquired simple or hatched horizontal linear decoration. The Beaker was integrated into the local assemblage, displaying a notable adaptability. The typical *pointillé* decoration is present, but beakers were also sometimes painted in bands of alternating black and red. This is part of the creation of a painted and impressed ceramic style; besides the beaker, this style includes a wide range of hemispherical bowls on a high foot (similar to the Castelluccio form) finely decorated with patterns of alternating chequers, chevrons, zig-zags and triangles, expertly applied in black and red (Tusa 1987; 1990a; 1993b) (fig. 6).

 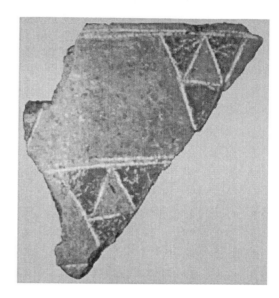

Fig. 6   Ceramics of the Bell Beaker facies from southwestern Sicily from Marcita: right, fragment decorated *a pointillée* with white paste in the grooves and black paint on a red ground

There was a parallel adoption of Beaker elements into local proto-Castelluccio production. In both shape and decoration, the vases of the Naro-Partanna style acquired Beaker elements. On the typical tronco-conical bowls with high pedestals, parallel lines of linear elements with gridding and hatching appear, that imitate *pointillé* decoration but are executed in paint (fig. 7). The Bell Beaker form itself has its upper part stretched to form one-handled bottle with painted Beaker motifs (Pacci & Tusa 1990).

Thus the Beaker culture and the indigenous proto-Castelluccio fused; while each maintained its own heritage intact, experimentation produced typologically mixed forms. In this part of Sicily the Bell Beaker society, integrated like this into the Malpasso and proto-Castelluccio traditions, lasted until the expansion of the Thapsos-Milazzese culture into this area at the beginning of the Middle Bronze Age.

Beakers elsewhere in Sicily

Elsewhere on the island Beaker elements are clearly intrusive, if the eastern limit of the Beaker cultural area is extended to include the Platini basin (and perhaps beyond) taking account of the evidence of Ribera, San Bartolo and Naro (De Miro 1968a). Outside this area, it is clear that the Beaker-like finds from Manfria (Orlandini 1962) and Grotta Palombara (Tinè 1960–61), near Gela and Syracuse respectively, are intrusive elements in other, Malpasso and Castelluccio cultural facies.

Origins of Sicilian Beakers

A Sardinian origin for Sicilian Beakers now seems plausible for both geographical and typological reasons. There are very strong typological similarities with the Iglesiente-Sulcis and Cagliari regions, where we find not only identical beakers, but also similar decoration with circles found on polypod vessels, and a wide range of the decorative repertoire. There are also credible analogies in other classes of material such as the miniature axe pendants

Fig. 7   Ceramics of the Naro-Partanna facies from Naro (Agrigento), Partanna and Marcita (Trapani)

Fig. 8 Trepanned skull from a tomb with Bell Beaker and
ceramics of the Naro-Partanna facies from Partanna (Trapani)

and in the use of dentalium shells and boar tusks for ornaments (Atzeni 1980; Ferrarese
Ceruti 1981). Another parallel occurs in the medico-ritual sphere, since there is evidence
of cranial trepanation (which was often survived), found in tomb XVI of Su Crucifissu
Mannu (Ferrarese Ceruti 1972–74) and at Sisaia (Ferrarese Ceruti & Germanà 1978) in
Sardinia, and in Sicily at Partanna (fig. 8).

On the other hand, I do not see any connections with Bell Beakers in the Italian
peninsula (Barfield 1976). The similarity with polypod vessels of Grotta del Fontino
(Grosseto) must clearly have been mediated via Sardinia (Vigliardi 1979).

DISCUSSION

To summarise, the Beaker Culture arrived first in northwest Sicily, and thereafter pushed
into the southwest, becoming integrated with the local proto-Castelluccio culture. Why did
it stop at the axis from Belice in the south to Imera in the north? This zone, which cuts the
island in two, was always a frontier region between two very different worlds. The area to
the east was always dominated by cultural forces connected with the Aegean. Time and
time again, we see the reflection of Aegean or Anatolian elements in painted (Malpasso,
Castelluccio, and Naro) or incised (Capo Graziano) wares. We find, furthermore, that links
with the nascent Mycenaean world ran along maritime routes connecting the principal
Aegean centres with southeastern Sicily and the Aeolian Islands (Bernabò Brea 1976–77).
This grand Aegean-Mediterranean *koiné* fully included eastern Sicily, but stopped around
the Belice-Imera line. From there westwards, the rest of the island was affected by cultural
phenomena sometimes linked to western Europe (e.g. Bell Beakers) and sometimes to the
eastern Mediterranean (e.g., the phenomenon of Punic colonisation, preceded by Syro-
Cypriot visits[5]) (Tusa 1986).

This unchanging sub-current of Sicilian history was apparent even at this remote period
of prehistory. The two great traditions of European-Mediterranean culture confronted

each other at the time of the diffusion of Bell Beakers and can be seen in the integration of the Beaker style with that of the proto-Castelluccio. This contact, which took place in the southern part of the island, can be linked to the emergence of an east-west axis of communication, as an alternative to that running north to the Aeolian Islands and the Tyrrhenian basin, which would continue to hold a central role in the Mediterranean economy; this was particularly so for relations between the eastern Mediterranean, south-central and western Sicily, Sardinia and the Iberian peninsula (Tusa 1987; 1993b).

But what were the reasons for these ethnic dynamics? What were the stimuli which gave rise to the Bell Beaker culture on the one side, and the Aegean-Anatolian inspired proto-Castelluccio on the other, to reach out towards or against each other? Can one already be dealing with activity around routes for the acquisition of metals? The identification of Beaker workshops for copper working at Son Matge-Valldemosa (Balearics) (Waldren 1979) and at El Ventorro (Madrid) (Harrison *et al.* 1975), and the copper ingots at Ferrandell-Oleza (Balearics) (Waldren 1980; 1984), would support this hypothesis. However, we lack evidence linking Beakers and metallurgy in Sicily itself. Beyond this, it is clear that the Beaker is not an intrusive element in the places where it is in greatest evidence. Its culture is a consistent part of Sicily, deeply rooted and distinct from other contemporary facies.

The problem of ethnicity remains unresolved. Is it correct to speak of a Beaker people as well as a Bell Beaker culture in western Sicily? It is clear that, in the period of expansion of the culture, there were strong social pressures towards a complex restructuring of society. It moved progressively from an egalitarian structure characteristic of Neolithic farming societies to the strongly differentiated, hierarchical model of the developed metal ages. In Sicily, the first elements appear in both the Castelluccio culture and the Capo Graziano culture on the Aeolian Islands, and it develops fully in the Thapsos-Milazzese period. That this social process was related to the advent of metallurgy is certain, even if we cannot nowadays accept Childe's hypothesis in its entirety. Childe (1957) argued that social differentiation resulted from the emergence of craft specialists involved in the world of metallurgy from prospection to manufacture (Childe 1957); but we lack secure data for this, and in Sicily certain essential elements of this process, such as metallurgical prospection, are missing.

As has been noted elsewhere, the Beaker could represent one of the clearer symptoms of the ideological rationalisation of social differentiation, from the beginning of the third millennium BC (Shennan 1982). It may also indicate processes of social or ethnic superimposition, either in process or which had already occurred. In southwestern Sicily, the integration of the Beaker culture with aspects of Naro-Partanna indicates a non-traumatic superimposition and hierarchisation (Pacci & Tusa 1990). It is probable that in northwestern Sicily, such a superimposition was not accompanied by cultural integration and therefore brought about a polarisation of society. This might be explained as the trauma of a dramatic impact caused by the Beaker culture arriving by sea without warning. In contrast, in the southern area there would have been time for gradual penetration. On the other hand, the lack of fortified defensive structures such as occur on the Balearic islands might suggest that there were no severe ethnic confrontations.

The development of increasing social hierarchy in western Sicily between the second half of the third millennium and the middle of the second millennium BC is demonstrated archaeologically by a conspicuous increase in the number of sites, and by their greater concentration around well defined poles. Among the clearest poles are the Conco d'Oro, the area of Salemi, Partanna, the Mazarese hinterland, etc. This settlement organisation serves to indicate the emergence of true chiefdoms that impose themselves on the rest of the territory: a structuring of society based not on differentiation internal to a group, but between different groups. In eastern Sicily, we can observe the same phenomenon among the Castelluccio sites of the Etnean and Hyblaean zones. These linked and confederated settlement structures favoured the transit zones along the great connecting east-west route mentioned earlier that turned to run north-south in its western cusp, running along the valleys of the Imera, Oreto, Belice, Mazaro, Modine and Platani. Current data still do not permit us to delineate precisely the territorial articulation and internal character of these hegemonic centres. Clearly they would not have been isolated sites but rather groups of hegemonic settlements linked together, and hence it would perhaps be better to define them as settlement nodes. It seems likely that they monopolised resources derived from exchange and control of metals (Gilman 1981; Renfrew 1972).

Looking at the Sicilian situation geographically within the wider Mediterranean picture and chronologically within later Sicilian prehistory, an interesting model for understanding the dynamics of the Beakers is that of Braudel. This aims "...to define a hierarchy of forces, of currents, and of particular movements and thence to a reassertion of the complete entity" (Braudel 1973: 69). The incredibly wide diffusion of the Beaker culture can be explained perfectly through a reductive analysis of the phenomenon on a local and synchronic scale. The dynamics of the Beaker phenomenon are incorporated into a model that has multi-regional and diachronic scope. This is what we have sought to do in relating the Beaker presence in Sicily to what was happening elsewhere in the Mediterranean, and especially to the arrival of metallurgy.

THE CASTELLUCCIO CULTURE

Over a large part of Sicily, during the final centuries of the third millennium and the first half of the second millennium BC, we find a ceramic repertoire characterised by unusual vessel forms[6] and by painted decoration in geometric and linear motifs in brown/black on a ground that varies from red and pale yellow to pale rose. This is the complex that Bernabò Brea considers a unitary cultural facies and calls Castelluccio, after its eponymous site in the hinterland of Noto. Castelluccio pottery, although with clear local variants, is found from the extreme west (the territories of Marsala and Mazara) to the whole eastern part of the island (fig. 9). The only zone excluded from this distribution is a northern belt situated between the watersheds of the Madonie, the Nebrodi and the Peloritani and the Tyrrhenian coast, including the Palermo area. However, recent finds in the Grotta di San Teodoro (famous for its Mesolithic burials), on the Messinese Tyrrhenian coast, show that Castelluccio painted pottery did also spread to the north (Spigo 1989). This last discovery challenges the long dominant theory that those zones on the island which did not have Castelluccio material were influenced by the contemporary Rodì-Tindari-Vallelunga (RTV) culture, in the same way that the Aeolian Capo Graziano culture (although geographically limited) and the Mursia culture on Pantelleria did not take up painted decoration and showed marked links with Tyrrhenian peninsular cultures (Tozzi 1968).

The recent excavations at Mezzebbi, near Milena (Caltanissetta), within the main Castelluccio area, also challenge this theory (Privitera 1994). Stratigraphic evidence here shows that there was a slow, but clear and progressive transition between the stratigraphically lower Castelluccio facies and that of Rodì-Tindari-Vallelunga. If this picture is confirmed, the date of the end of the Castelluccio culture, traditionally put a little after the middle of the second millennium BC, would have to be raised by several centuries.

For the origin of the Castelluccio culture, Bernabò Brea has always argued for a direct development from the facies of Sant'Ippolito, referred to as proto-Castelluccio, and the true Castelluccio (Bernabò Brea 1983; 1985; 1988). Such a theory, challenged by Amoroso (1979; 1983; 1984), is based on typological similarities and on shared links with Cyprus (Early Cypriot III: 2300–2100 BC), clearly distinguishable in Sant'Ippolito pottery[7]. Thus, given the connection between Sant'Ippolito and Castelluccio, it is undeniable that there were consistent contacts between eastern and south-central Sicily and the Aegean-Cypriot sphere between the end of the third millennium and the

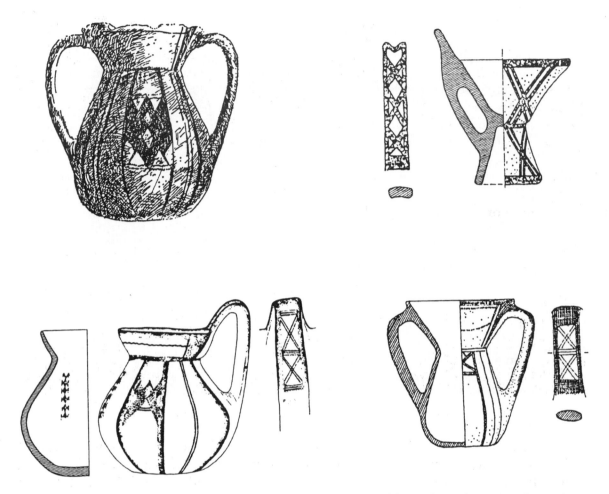

Fig. 9   Ceramics of the Castelluccio facies from Monte Tabuto and Santa Croce Camarina (Ragusa)

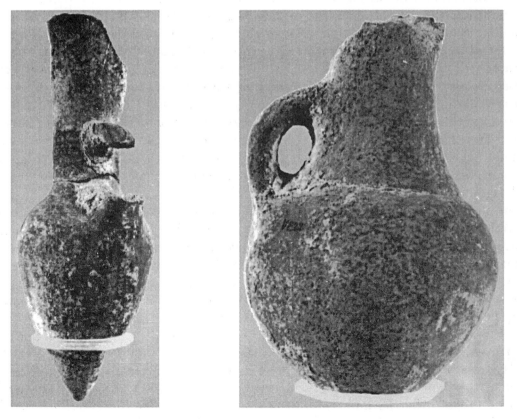

Fig. 10   Ceramics of Cypriot affinity from Durrueli (Agrigento)

Fig. 11   Castelluccio necropolis of Noto Antica (Siracusa) (rock-cut tombs and chambers)

beginning of the second millennium BC (fig. 10). This dating is confirmed by a series of radiocarbon dates on eighteen carbon samples collected at the Castelluccio site of La Muculufa in the hinterland of Licata (average calibrated value 2170 ± 120 BC) (Holloway 1985).

The occurrence of strong Cypriot parallels in the Sant'Ippolito pottery can be understood within the framework of the Aegean-Oriental affinities present in the Castelluccio heritage. In addition, Aegean and Cypriot derived imported ceramics have been found recently at Monte Grande, in the territory of Palma di Montechiaro. The site is characterised by large enclosures and extensive sacred areas (Castellana 1990), and it introduces two new elements in the Sicilian Castelluccio panorama: as well as the imported pottery from Cyprus and the Aegean (along with local imitations) it has a group of buildings that foreshadow the proto-urban planning of the following Thapsos-Milazzese phase. The traditional round or oval huts found here are not isolated, as in all other Castelluccio sites, but are linked organically by enclosures that delimit particular areas, functions, streets and building complexes in a manner that already possesses clear tendencies towards formal planning.

The southeastern area of Sicily, corresponding to the Hyblaean massif dominated by Monte Lauro and including the provinces of Syracuse and Ragusa, was a zone particularly densely populated by the Castelluccians. Numerous groups of rock-cut tombs riddle the evocative *cave*, deep natural gorges produced by fluvial erosion (Orsi 1889; 1892; 1893; 1897). Generally the settlements are located on the limestone plateaux at the edges of the ravines, while their cemeteries were excavated in the rock faces immediately below (fig. 11). The portion of a ravine under the direct control of a Castelluccio settlement constitutes a formidable reservoir of biomass, both in terms of fauna (game and fish) and of optimally available soil for cultivation or pasture. Among the more notable settlement complexes is that of Monte Sallia – Monte Tabuto, in the territory of Comiso. Here high site density can also be explained by the exploitation of local veins of flint, evidence of which is provided by the mines which were excavated by the Castelluccians and later adapted for use as collective tombs (Orsi 1898; Tusa 1990b).

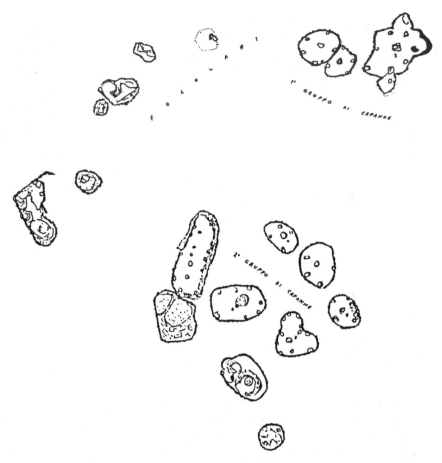

Fig. 12   Plan of the Castelluccio village of Manfria (Gela – Agrigento)

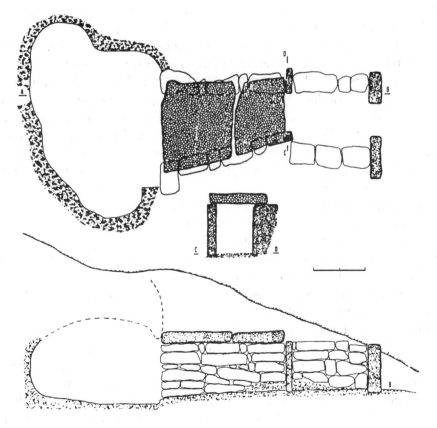

Fig. 13   Chamber tomb and corridor dolmen in contrada Pergola (Salaparuta – Trapani)

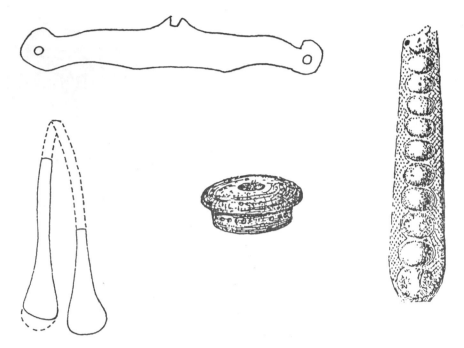

Fig. 14 'Exotic' objects from Castelluccio tomb goods (bronze balance beam and pincers, bone pommel and bossed bone plaque)

The single best known Castelluccio village is that of Manfria, near Gela, outside the Hyblaean area, which was excavated in its entirety (Orlandini 1962). From this site one gains the impression of a society based on small tribal communities, basically egalitarian but united around an entity that might have assumed some hegemonic role. The central structure at Manfria, larger than the others, could have served as a meeting house for the village leaders or as the actual residence of the tribal head (fig. 12). The presence of a well defined area of the village where several small ovens were found might be another indication of the unity and social cohesion of the small village community.

Within the Castelluccio panorama, several 'provinces' can be recognised. The Etna area is distinguished both by its pottery and by its site distribution, which is strongly influenced by its volcanic environment (Cultraro 1989; Orsi 1930–1931). At the opposite end of the island, in the Mazarese and Saccense areas, one can equally clearly distinguish the Naro-Partanna facies (Pacci & Tusa 1990), which is characterised by its clear stylistic and contextual links with the Bell Beakers (fig. 7), as well as its unique architectural tomb forms (chamber tombs with a long corridor *dromos* or dolmens), which must be seen in the context of the so-called reduced megalithism of the Mediterranean (Mannino 1971; Procelli 1981; Tusa 1991a) (fig. 13).

To summarise we might hypothesise the existence of an egalitarian society based on the wide distribution of small tribal settlements across most of the island. As a system of functional relations within each of the districts, we might propose a dichotomy between the majority of each society, with close ties to the Sicilian countryside, and a minority which would have handled relations with the exterior[8].

The funerary evidence also demonstrates a basically egalitarian social organisation, with some burials standing out not for their richness but through their clearly recognisable symbols, probably related to the hegemonic role of the occupant of each tomb. The type of tomb found throughout the island is rock-cut with a simple oval chamber and a flat floor, no longer excavated in the rock from above as in the previous period, but in from a more or less vertical rock-face. The entrance was generally oval or sub-rectangular, closed by a monolithic door or, more rarely, by walling. Occasionally the tomb had a small vestibule or antechamber, accentuated by moulding resembling threshold and door posts between the actual entrance and the burial chamber. In a few cases the tomb was further endowed with

Fig. 15   Tomb door slab from tomb decorated in bas-relief at Castelluccio (left) and views of sculpted tomb facades at Castelluccio and Cava Lazzaro (Siracusa)

external facades with sculpted pilasters to give the impression of a portico framing the entrance to the tomb (Castelluccio, Cava Lazzaro). In three cases, all at Castelluccio, the tombs were closed by sculpted slabs symbolising the sexual act in various different ways; these images, clearly apotropaic in purpose, connected with powers of regeneration and procreation (Tusa 1991b; 1991c) (fig. 15). These figurative pieces, like the sculpted facades, have significant stylistic and cultural affinities to the architectural and sculptural works of the final stage of the great Maltese megalithic culture, characterised by the temples at Tarxien, Mnaidra, etc. The contacts with Malta are also demonstrated by numerous pottery fragments found at Castelluccio and other settlements of the southeastern coast of Sicily (Bernabò Brea 1976–77; 1980; Gnesotto 1982; Guzzardi 1988; Procelli 1981).

Generally grave goods are homogeneous, as is the frequent practice of re-opening the tombs for further burials. This produced an accumulation of enormous quantities of piled-up skeletal remains, but the placement of the skulls along the walls together with vases and other funerary goods, both ornamental and lithic, shows deliberate arrangement.

The substantially egalitarian picture that emerges from the variety of Castelluccio remains is a constant, then, both in the Sicilian interior where this society adapted itself to the barren and monotonous environment of the hills, and on the coast where presumably both fishing and coastal navigation, plus limited forms of exchange, would have had a significant role.

The origins of the Castelluccio culture

The problem that has most engaged students is that of the origins of this culture. On the one hand we have the diffusionist perspective, with Bernabò Brea and Tinè (Tinè 1960–61) as the principal proponents of a migration from the Aegean-Anatolian area. On the other side, I myself believe that, while there are indubitable typological parallels with that area, there is a clear local heritage within the long Sicilian tradition and in particular in the immediately preceding Sant'Ippolito and Malpasso facies. There is also a more extreme, Indo-Europeanist, hypothesis that explains Mediterranean cultural affinities (for example, the diffusion of chamber tombs which will be discussed below) in terms of waves of Kurgan migrations (Zanotti 1986; Zanotti & Rhine 1974). Personally I feel it is better to avoid returning to hypotheses involving major ethnic movements and rather to explain Mediterranean integration in terms of coastal commercial and cultural connections.

In my opinion, we are dealing with a process of cultural integration, both technological and typological, that cannot be explained simplistically in terms of ethnic migrations (Tusa

1991d). Such a process of cultural integration has deep roots and can be traced from the Neolithic Serra d'Alto (or spiral-meander pottery) phase. For the earlier contacts, Bernabò Brea and Cavalier propose clear correlations between the Piano Conte facies and the Poliochni blue phase (EBA in Anatolia), while the Malpasso facies would correlate with the Poliochni red phase (Kalimnos, Chios and Samos) (Bernabò Brea 1976–77; 1985; Cavalier 1960–61). Cazzella also agrees in noting cultural and typological affinities in the pre-Castelluccio period, although with differences. He proposes a correlation between Piano Conte and aspects later than the Early Bronze Age A in Greece and Anatolia, and thus consequently correlates the Malpasso and Piano Quartara facies with Early Helladic II and with middle and late Troy I (2500 BC) (Cazzella 1972). The elements proposed to show such a correlation include burnished pottery, semi-lunate handles, bowls on a perforated conical foot, particularly exaggerated raised handles, and open vessels with horizontal handles.

Such comparisons make clear, however, that we are dealing with the origins of a Mediterranean cultural *koiné* that cannot be explained from the perspective of dynamic source centres from which peoples, cultures and so on were diffused. I disagree, therefore, with the idea of continuous migrations or colonisations, thinking rather of emerging cultural affinities between various coastal peoples who faced each other across a sea that united rather than divided. Moreover, it seems obvious that such contacts would almost always have happened on a wave of economic-commercial relations often undertaken by richer eastern partners but apparently based on equal and non-hierarchical positions. The mechanisms of interrelation between Mediterranean coastal societies during the end of the 3rd and the 2nd millennia BC can be explained well through the 'peer polity interaction' model of Renfrew and Cherry. This model allows one to understand cases of cultural, technological and socio-economic similarity without resorting either to invasion or migration explanations which are not demonstrable archaeologically or to explanations based exclusively on local processes (Cherry 1988; Renfrew 1986).

THE CAPO GRAZIANO CULTURE

With the Capo Graziano Culture, the Aeolian Islands went through a period of great socio-economic revival after the Eneolithic crisis caused by the collapse of demand for obsidian. The basis for the development of this facies is to be found in its distinctive maritime cultural and commercial exchange with the cultures of the surrounding areas[9].

The mid-range maritime traffic (Malta, Sicily and the Italian peninsula) can be fully understood only within the larger context of the contacts between the Aeolian Islands and the Aegean (Tusa 1984; 1985; 1991c). Tangible proof of these contacts are the Mycenaean ceramics datable to the Middle Helladic and Mycenaean I, II and IIIA found almost exclusively in secure Capo Graziano contexts (Vagnetti & Cavalier 1982; Cavalier & Vagnetti 1983; 1984; 1986; Vagnetti 1982). Consequently, the second phase of the Capo Graziano culture (in which, as we shall see, villages began to be established in high zones), should be dated between the mid-16th century and 1400 BC. Thus, presumably, the first phase should be dated to between the 17th and mid-16th centuries BC (Bernabò Brea & Cavalier 1992). Although direct evidence of exchange with the Aegean world is lacking in this first phase, nevertheless, according to the authoritative opinion of Bernabò Brea, strong typological ties exist between Aeolian ceramics and those of the Greek mainland datable to between the proto-Helladic III and the beginning of the Middle Helladic. For Bernabò Brea the Capo Graziano facies is proof of an immigration of peoples from overseas, bringing with them a culture linked to the Early Helladic III and early Middle Helladic of mainland Greece: these would have been the Aeoli mentioned in the Classical sources who, in addition to occupying the plain of Metaponto, would have given the archipelago its name at the conclusion of their Mediterranean peregrinations. The famous find of pottery at Altis at Olympia, which provides the basis for analogies with the Capo

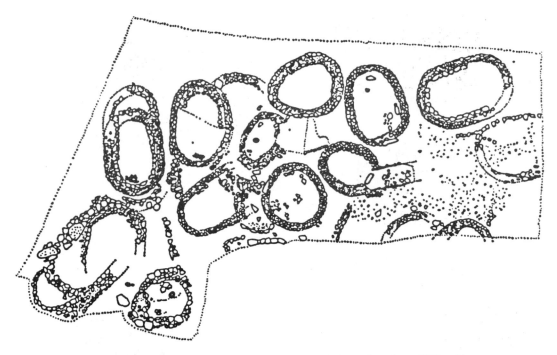

Fig. 16   Plan of the village of Montagnola di Capo Graziano (Filicudi)

Graziano culture, is explained by Bernabò Brea as evidence of "relations, prolonged through the centuries, of these distant western colonies with their original homeland." Thus Bernabò Brea, true to his migrationist hypothesis, must necessarily raise the genesis of the Aeolian culture to the close of the third millennium BC (at the beginning of Early Helladic III) (Bernabò Brea 1985).

However, the limitations of the archaeological data require a certain caution. If we must speak of typological links, before turning to Early Helladic Greece, we should consider the undeniable similarities between the Capo Graziano culture and peninsular and Sicilian cultural entities at the end of the third millennium and the beginning of the second millennium BC (e.g. Cellino San Marco, Conco d'Oro and Bell Beakers) (Tusa 1985). If the Helladic did contribute, it was in the formative stage, and it must have been mediated across a strong local tradition with marked continuity. On the basis of these simple considerations, it seems to me rather hazardous to talk about Early Helladic migrations for the genesis of the Capo Graziano culture, and still more so if one seeks to give an ethnic name to such migrations.

The Capo Graziano culture or facies is found principally in the Aeolian archipelago, but it has very close links with the north coast of Sicily and with the southern shores of the Tyrrhenian side of the peninsula (Bernabò Brea 1989; Damiani et al. 1984; Tusa 1994).

At Filicudi, the site of Capo Graziano itself is concentrated in two distinct nuclei: the more recent is situated on the cliff of the small promontory of Montagnola di Capo Graziano (fig. 16), while the older part is on the saddle that connects this promontory to the rest of the island (Piano del Porto, Filo Braccio and Case Lopez). The more recent site consists of a disorderly agglomeration of more or less circular huts. The building style makes use of the distinctive 'herring-bone' technique, in which superimposed courses of similarly sized stones are arranged in alternating obliquely sloping rows, which has Aegean affinities. Also analogous are the beaten earth pavements covered with pottery fragments, the so-called 'potsherd pavements', constructed at a level slightly lower than the surface outside the buildings (Bernabò Brea & Cavalier 1992). The architecture gives the impression of a largely egalitarian society without rank, wealth or lineage differences. This is supported by the scarcity of evidence of funerary deposits in the Filicudi gorge.

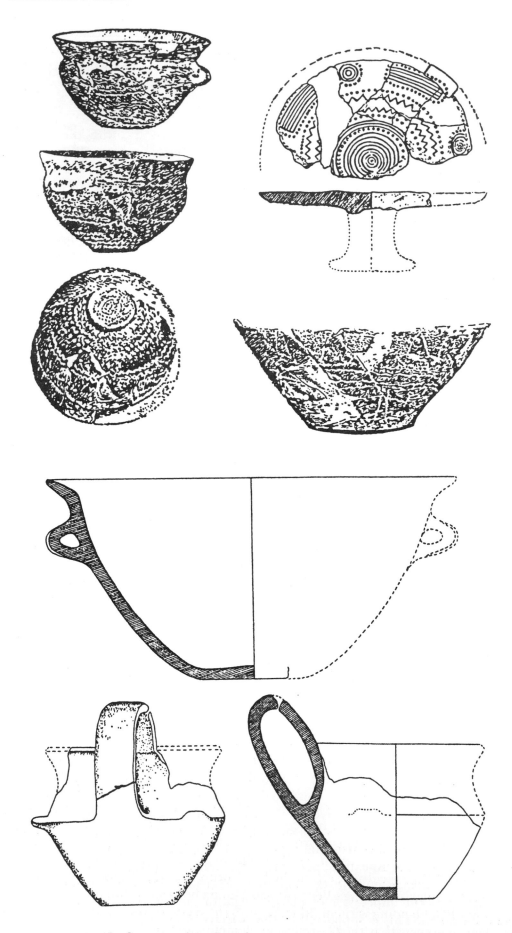

Fig. 17   Ceramics of the Capo Graziano cultural facies from Lipari

In terms of burial evidence we have the cremation cemetery at contrada Diana on Lipari, which is at present the oldest example of this burial custom on the Aeolian Islands and in Sicily (Bernabò Brea & Cavalier 1980; Cavalier 1984–85). Here cinerary urns were arranged horizontally, closed by slabs, sealed with clay at the mouth and protected by a circle of stones. In addition to the ashes of the deceased, the urns contained small vases as offerings; alternatively these were placed externally.

On Lipari the settlement sequence found on Filicudi recurs, with the two sites of contrada Diana (older) and the Acropolis or Castello (more recent) (Bernabò Brea & Cavalier 1980). The Acropolis site could have had a hegemonic function, as is indicated by the presence of a large central hut with an internal partition, and further differentiated by an external rectangular enclosure. Such a structure suggests possible centralised control of the island or the entire archipelago.

This facies is also present on the other islands of the archipelago. There are two sites on Stromboli: Pianicelli, north of Ginostra, and the site near the church of San Vincenzo (Bernabò Brea & Cavalier 1982; Cavalier 1981). The sites on Stromboli explain the links between the Capo Graziano culture and its contemporary on the peninsula, the Proto-Apennine B. The ceramic complexes from Tyrrhenian southern Italy, and in particular those from the sites of Punta di Mezzogiorno on Vivara in the Phlegraean archipelago (Tusa 1994; Damiani et al. 1984), Grotta del Noglio, near Marina di Camerota (Vigliardi 1975), and Grotta Cardini, near Praia a Mare (Bernabò Brea 1989), share typological characteristics constituting a middle to lower Tyrrhenian koiné. These sites also yield some pottery which is very like Capo Graziano types and these are probably objects imported from the Aeolian Islands. The Stromboli sites, thus, make sense only in the context of maritime communication routes between the Aeolian archipelago and the Calabrian-Lucanian-Campanian coasts via the island of Stromboli.

The earliest phase of the Capo Graziano culture is characterised by pottery with thin walls and a shiny black burnished surface. Among the most common forms are small jars (ollette) and carinated bowls (scodelle carenate), cup-dippers (tazze-attingitoio), and globular jugs (orci globulari). The decoration, always incised and not too extensive, consists mostly of isolated linear motifs and impressed cordons in relief. The pottery of the second phase includes more coarse tempered pieces (impasto grossolano) with poorly burnished brown surfaces, as well as a fine impasto with a high burnish. The most typical form is a 'skull cup' with a flat base, with a wide out-turned rim and a small handle below, a form also found outside the Aeolian Islands in the Sicilian Rodì-Tindari-Vallellunga facies and the peninsular Proto-Apennine B. Such cups are often decorated with incised wavy lines or zig-zags, points and isolated metopal spaces on a wavy background; the grooves are often filled with a white substance. Other typical pieces are tronco-conical bowls with an internal handle, decorated both inside and out with rows of dotted triangles, and the so-called a clessidra stands which are also sometimes decorated (fig. 17). The lithic industry is abundant and consists almost entirely of obsidian blades (Bernabò Brea & Cavalier 1980; 1992).

THE RODÌ-TINDARI-VALLELUNGA-BOCCADIFALCO-MURSIA CULTURE

It seems very likely that this horizon, characterised by pottery with grey, carefully smoothed or brown, lightly burnished surfaces, and by carinated bowls sometimes with high raised handles (described as horse-ear type, ad orecchie equine), is in part later then the Castelluccio and Naro-Partanna horizons, though there may have been some overlap. Moreover, there are links between the Rodì-Tindari-Vallelunga facies of this horizon and the succeeding Thapsos culture, e.g. in the bowl forms (fig. 18). Therefore, we may suggest that the Rodì-Tindari-Vallelunga-Boccadifalco-Mursia horizon certainly lasted well into the 16th century BC, blending without difficulty into the nascent Milazzese-Thapsos koiné. It is not so clear, however, that the Castelluccio elements and the painted facies of the Naro-Partanna horizon survived so late.

Recent excavations on the hillside of Serra di Palco, near Milena, greatly strengthen this hypothesis of cultural continuity. The excavated Early Bronze Age levels were identified as rubbish from a nearby settlement. The fine wares appear to consist of two classes: one "in black and occasionally overpainted in white on a red ground", typical of the Castelluccio facies, the other "on a dark ground varying from greys to brown or black, almost always *ripresa alla stecca*", attributed to the Rodì-Tindari facies and similar to that of level D/4 at Chiusazza. The carinated cup-dipper (*tazza-attingitoio*) with a raised handle is the dominant form in the latter class (D'Agata 1987; La Rosa & D'Agata 1988). Such evidence provides stratigraphic support for the sequence derived from typology. In fact, although both classes of pottery are found in association in the lower strata, the painted material progressively decreases in quantity in favour of the unpainted. Thus, we may define an intermediate level between the Castelluccio and Thapsos facies, characterised by the grey-brown pottery of the Rodì-Tindari horizon. This is also reflected in the clear links between several ceramic forms of the Rodì-Tindari and Thapsos horizons; for example the *tazza-attingitoio* that develops in the Thapsos culture into a form with a divided trapezoidal slab handle.

Given this chronological pattern, the nearby settlement of Mezzebbi, where an even older Castelluccio level seems to have been identified, is significant (Privitera 1994). Its antiquity is demonstrated partly by a more complex decorative synthesis rooted in the Serraferlicchio horizon (Arias 1937) where one finds frequent overpainted white decoration, and also, most significantly, by the presence of associated Beaker pottery (Bovio Marconi 1963).

This evidence would seem to confirm the extension of the cultural dynamics identified in the Belice valley to the Platani valley also, i.e. an archaic Castelluccio facies associated with Bell Beakers, traditionally labelled Naro-Partanna, followed by a brief period of diffusion of Castelluccio pottery, during which the Beaker elements diminish to nothing, finally developing into the true Rodì-Tindari facies. Obviously on the Platani the presence of Bell Beakers is much more fleeting, indicating that, as noted above, the existence of true ethno-cultural Beaker entities was limited to the lower and middle Belice (Tusa 1987; 1990a; 1993b).

Such a pattern involves only one part of the island, excluding both the Syracuse-Ragusa area, traditionally Castelluccio, and the northern zones, traditionally within the Rodì-Tindari facies.

Demonstrating its strong links to the Tyrrhenian tradition, the Rodì-Tindari facies shows typical 'mixing' of funerary practices, which also occurs in the contemporary Capo Graziano facies, where rock-cut tombs and cremation burials co-exist. In the recently discovered necropolis at Torrente Boccetta, near Messina, the rite of *enchytrismos* burial[10] occurs, as in other cemeteries in the area (Scibona 1984–85; Villari 1981a; 1981b; 1981c; Voza 1982). The presence of this type of burial emphasises the Tyrrhenian affinity of this cultural facies, and also allows us to suppose that the Rodì-Tindari-Vallelunga facies was involved in the genesis of the Thapsos culture, since the rite of *enchytrismos* burial is also partially present there also.

The cultural context of the 16th and 15th centuries BC in the lower Tyrrhenian area

In order to understand the Capo Graziano culture better, particularly in its earlier phase, it is useful to trace its effects on the coastal zones of the lower Tyrrhenian. The Phlegraean islands offer an excellent point of reference, particularly Vivara with its rich and full archaeological record (Cazzella *et al.* 1991). Moreover, the Vivaran Proto-Apennine settlements, datable to the 16th and 15th centuries BC, with their notable quantities of Aegean pottery (mostly from one phase of their occupation), would have had a significant role in Tyrrhenian and Mediterranean relations and would have maintained close links with the Aeolian peoples. These centuries were crucial for the Italian peninsula in the development of both internal and external relations: relations within the sphere of the

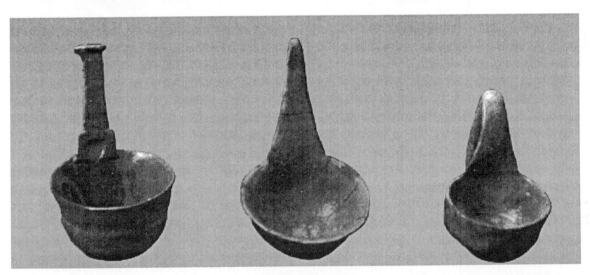

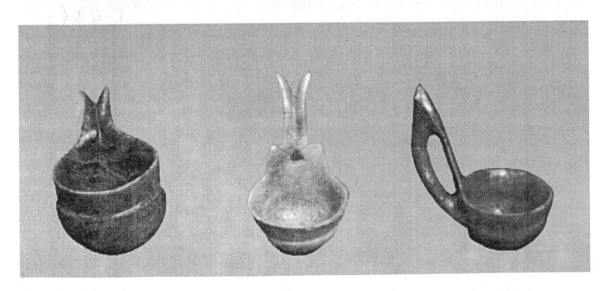

Fig. 18   Ceramics of the Rodì-Tindari-Vallelunga facies from Ciavolaro (Ribera-Agrigento)

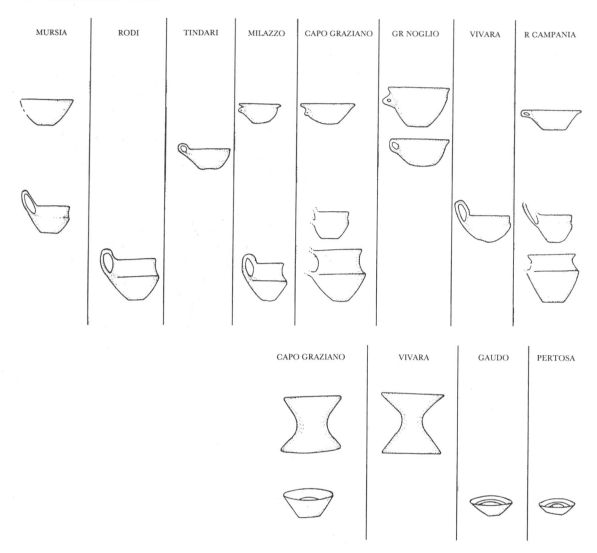

Fig. 19 Diagram of ceramic forms comparing the facies of Rodì-Tindari-Vallelunga, Capo Graziano and Proto-Apennine B

Proto-Apennine B inter-connected the various regions of the peninsula, the Aeolian Islands and Sicily; while relations with the Aegean are shown by the presence of Late Helladic I – IIA – IIB – IIIA1 wares (Bernabò Brea 1985). The two areas of relations were clearly interrelated, both within each region and between the southern peninsula, the Aeolian Islands and Sicily.

In an early phase, corresponding to the facies of Punta di Mezzogiorno on Vivara, contacts with the Aegean must have been sporadic or indirect, given the rarity of imported pottery. We may note in this connection that the most southern part of Calabria, south of the Gulf of Sant'Eufemia, has yielded no Proto-Apennine material. This zone clearly gravitated towards Sicily and the Aeolian Islands, within the spheres of cultural influence of the Capo Graziano and Rodì-Tindari-Vallelunga facies. This is the case, for example, for the sites of Capo Piccolo (Crotone) and S. Domenica di Ricadi (Tropea), which can be taken as typical of a south-central Calabrian facies, differing from the Proto-Apennine B but connected to it through links to sites in the Upper Ionian area and in south-central Puglia and which is very similar to the contemporary Aeolian and Sicilian cultures. At Capo Piccolo the ceramic complex shows marked similarities to the Rodì-Tindari-Vallelunga facies and has also produced a fragment of Mycenaean pottery attributable to between Late Helladic I and II (Lattanzi *et al.* 1987). At S. Domenica di Ricadi, in spite of the wide chronological range of the grave goods (from Early to Late Bronze Age), the presence of Capo Graziano type material is nonetheless attestable, and even imported

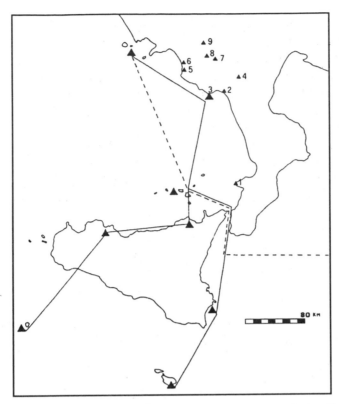

Fig. 20   Diagram of central Mediterranean relations in the first half of the 2nd millennium BC (solid lines indicate the relations betweeen the Proto-Apennine B, Rodì-Tindari-Vallelunga and the Tarxien cemetery facies; the dotted line indicates the connecting route between the Mycenaean centres and the Tyrrhenian). 1. S. Domenica di Ricadi; 2. Praia; 3. Grotta del Noglio; 4. Latronico; 5. Paestum; 6. Gaudo; 7. Polla; 8. Pertosa; 9. Buccino

Mycenaean elements are found, such as the ornamental seed pearls set in a vitreous paste (Ardovino 1977; Pacci 1987a).

The Aeolian culture was strong enough to reach up the Tyrrhenian as far as Vivara. It is actually in the Punta di Mezzogiorno facies that we see a true diffusion of Capo Graziano styles and decorative elements. The close typological links between Punto di Mezzogiorno and the southern Tyrrhenian, particularly with the Aeolian Capo Graziano II facies and the Sicilian Rodì-Tindari-Vallelunga-Mursia facies, are shown by very precise similarities in the pottery[11] (Tusa 1985) (fig. 19). Thus groups of Capo Graziano type projected strongly towards the southern Tyrrhenian coast, especially the north and east. As well as the Sicilian-Aeolian connections at Vivara and in Calabria, just described, there are also similarities in the Grotta Cardini at Praia a Mare (lower stratum) (Bernabò Brea 1989) and Noglio (Vigliardi 1975). There are, in fact, diffuse typological similarities even in coastal Puglia (Cavallino – cap. I, S. Vito dei Normanni, Grotta del Fico di Santa Maria al Bagno di Nardo and the Salentine caves) and in the interior Apulian-Lucanian-Campanian zones (Tufariello, Polla 5, San Marco di Metaponto, San Candida, San Martino di Matera, Porto Perone I G/5K, Scoglio di Tonno, Torre de Passeri, Heraclea di Policoro, Sorgenti del Serino, Pertosa) (Damiani *et al.* 1984; Peroni 1989).

What happened towards the north also occurred in the south with the projection of Capo Graziano elements to Sicily (Tusa 1985). Moreover, the Capo Graziano/Rodì-Tindari-Vallelunga-Mursia *koiné* had a greater diffusion than we had realised until very recently. It penetrated into zones that had previously been considered the exclusive area of the Castelluccio culture, like Valsavoja (Spigo 1984–85) at the southern margins of the Catania plain; Milena, in the Platani Valley (La Rosa & D'Agata 1988; La Rosa 1994); and Serralonga in the lower Belice valley (Marazzi & Tusa 1987; Tusa 1990a). Thus, at a certain point, a centripetal movement seemed to carry a new cultural facies from the northern and eastern coasts towards the centre of the island, supplanting the Castelluccio culture there. Thus over most of the island, there was a topographic superimposition of the new Rodì-Tindari-Vallelunga facies over the Castelluccio culture.

During this period, relations between the Aeolian Islands, Sicily, and Malta were characterised by an expansion from north to south, with the emergence of a common cultural *koiné* presumably based on shared sources. A clear maritime line of connection united the Aeolian Islands with several sites in southeastern Sicily (Ognina, Vendicari, Castelluccio), as far as Malta where the Tarxien Cemetery facies shows very close typological analogies with the Aeolian facies (Bernabò Brea 1976–77; Tusa 1985) (fig. 20). Clearly, therefore, around the middle of the 16th century BC the coastal societies of the Aeolian Islands and north-central Sicily succeeded in influencing distant areas with their products and culture: their influence can be traced from the south-central peninsula as far as Latium and Tuscany (e.g. Pantani di Sabaudia and Tre Erici) in the north, to Malta in the south (Tusa 1985).

In this first phase of the Proto-Apennine B (the mid-16th century BC and the following decades), this strong Aeolian expansion to the north and south corresponds to a major concentration in the Aeolian Islands of almost all the Aegean imports attributable to Late Helladic I in the lower Tyrrhenian area. Thus it follows that the Aeolian Islands were not simply active in exchange with the Aegean, but they may have had a monopoly control over it, attracting to the islands the flow of traffic that issued through the Straits of Messina (Marazzi 1988).

VIVARA

During this first phase of the Proto-Apennine B, Vivara occupied a subordinate position in the Campanian area, as the nearby site of Palma Campania on the edge of Vesuvius shows (Alborie Livadie & D'Amore 1980). Relationships within the Tyrrhenian area were dominated by the Capo Graziano societies of the Aeolian Islands, both economically, in trade with the Aegean, and in craftsmanship, in terms of their influence on peninsular ceramics in the first phase of Proto-Apennine B (Tusa 1994).

In the second half of the 16th century BC, during the second settlement phase at Punta Mezzogiorno on Vivara, the first Late Helladic I ceramics appear. At this time Vivara's relations with mainland sites intensify at the expense of links with the Aeolian Islands. The appearance of imported ceramics, the presence of metal and the reduced contacts with the Aeolian Islands together indicate the establishment of direct links with the Aegean, replacing the cumbersome intermediation of Capo Graziano (Tusa 1994).

However, the situation really changed radically with the second phase of the Proto-Apennine B at Vivara, exemplified by the site at Punta d'Alaca. The consolidation of relations with the peninsula coincided with the firm establishment of the east-west axis which supplanted the north-south one (Vivara-Aeolian Islands) which had characterised exchanges with the eastern Mediterranean in the preceding period. In consequence, pottery of the Late Helladic IIA, IIB, and IIIA1 appeared in abundance. The settlement itself was transferred from the coast to the higher part of the island, suggesting concern with control of the sea, rather than direct contact with it. The acquisition of an autonomous role in the maritime trade, no longer subordinate to the Aeolian islanders, would inevitably have generated conflicts of interest that would have made the Vivarese more cautious and attentive to dangers coming from the sea, even if it did not degenerate into violent conflict. The topographic dominance of the site is reflected in its internal structures. There was one large rectangular building, with two small attached semi-subterranean, circular silos, while the other huts had oval plans and were smaller in size (Tusa 1991d). Similar structures are found on the peninsula: Palma Campania (Alborie Livadie & D'Amore 1980), Tufariello di Buccino (Holloway 1975) and Punta Manaccora-Castello (Rellini 1934). A similar larger structure is also found on Lipari, at Contrada

Diana in the village of the earlier phase of the Capo Graziano culture (Bernabò Brea & Cavalier 1960).

The existence of structures of varied sizes, functions or shape in the same cultural facies (remembering that on Vivara, in the older Proto-Apennine B site of Punto Mezzogiorno, the huts were exclusively large and circular) is a phenomenon encountered elsewhere, but especially in those sites where Aegean influence is most notable (Tusa 1994). This is true of the Aeolian Islands, especially in the Capo Graziano culture: here we find rectangular (Diana), apsidal (Castello: g11) and circular huts (Bernabò Brea & Cavalier 1980).

However, at a certain point Vivaran society underwent a further profound change. Both the location of sites and other cultural features changed markedly. The final Proto-Apennine B settlement at Punta d'Alaca was abandoned and left to decay slowly. The isthmus zone, Punta Capitello, was settled again with a village, now almost entirely eroded, which must have occupied the crags overlooking the sea in the zone connecting Vivara with Procida – Santa Margherita. This last prehistoric settlement on Vivara is of typical Apennine culture, with pottery forms dominated by incised and excised spiral and meander decoration (Barker 1991–92; Pacciarelli 1991–92; Puglisi 1959). Imported Aegean pottery disappears almost completely, except for two fragments. The disappearance of Aegean connections and the integration of Vivara into the sphere of the Apennine culture indicates the end of the previously dominant role of the island in trade with the Aegean. It probably fell again into the commercial orbit of other entities in the zone.

This is the time during which the Thapsos culture emerged in Sicily and attracted the bulk of the Aegean and Aegean-Oriental traffic towards the west. With this strong presence in the lower Tyrrhenian and an obstructionist partner in the Ionian, the role of Vivara and the coastal centres on the peninsula as a bridgehead for Aegean traffic declined. In this changed situation the renewed power of the Aeolian, and above all Sicilian, partnership was decisive. The Thapsos culture arose in southeastern Sicily, with its visibly acculturated coastal centres which assumed in a dominant way the role of exchange foci in the trade with the Mycenaean citadels. Thus, the centre of gravity of maritime trade, at the Mediterranean level, shifted once more to the south, in the Tyrrhenian and Ionian sphere; and to the east in the Ionian-Adriatic sphere, towards Puglia, the other strong pole of acculturation and exchange at this time.

Fig. 21   Ceramics of the Thapsos-Milazzese facies

Fig. 22 Imported ceramics (1–5: Mycenaean; 6–7: Cypriot) from contexts of the Thapsos facies, and locally-made bronze sword

THE THAPSOS-MILAZZESE CULTURE

The ethnic dynamic that affected later Sicilian prehistory took shape most clearly around the middle of the second millennium BC. It was then that Sicily and the Aeolian Islands appeared united, in a way that had never happened before nor would again, in a single culture, that of Thapsos-Milazzese. If we wish to give this culture an ethnic attribution, I think we can accept the hypothesis of La Rosa (1989), suggesting that the Thapsos culture represents the emergence of a unitary Sican culture (fig. 21)[12].

There is an abundance of imported Mycenaean and Cypriot pottery (Myc. IIIA–IIIB) in the Thapsos sites of southeastern Sicily (fig. 22). To this we must now add the evidence from the Milena area in the Platani valley, where Mycenaean IIIA ceramics have been found. Together with the well-known vase of 'Marina di Girgenti' found and published earlier by Orsi, this is the earliest evidence of an Aegean presence in this area (La Rosa 1979; 1986).

This takes us back to the recognition of an earlier phase of the Thapsos culture, at least in southwestern Sicily, characterised by precocious contact with the Aegean world; this earlier phase would have occupied most of the 14th and 13th centuries BC, judging by the Mycenaean imports. The first phase of the Thapsos culture, that of Serra di Palco, is characterised by the predominance of open forms and by the clear retention of typological aspects from the preceding Rodì-Tindari facies. This confirms Bernabò Brea's hypothesis that the Thapsos culture probably developed out of the Rodì-Tindari facies (D'Agata 1987; La Rosa & D'Agata 1988).

The floruit of the Thapsos culture is represented by the development of the typical brownish grey pottery, which first appeared in Castelluccio contexts and increased during the Rodì-Tindari facies. In the Thapsos period we find standardised production of this

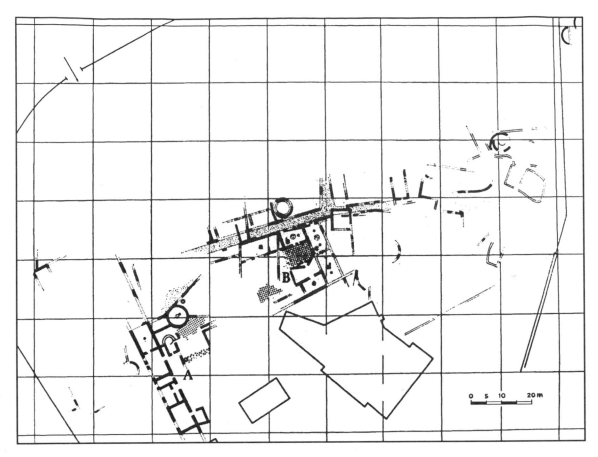

Fig. 23   Plan of the proto-urban centre of Thapsos

pottery, at least of the tablewares. This strengthens the hypothesis of the initial emergence of craft specialisation as early as the mid-second millennium BC and of a long developmental process for it (D'Agata 1987; La Rosa & D'Agata 1988).

This first phase of the Thapsos culture, datable to the 14th century BC, is followed by the Platani phase, known for the *tholoi* of Monte Campanella and the tombs of Caldare, which can be dated to the 13th century (De Miro 1968b; La Rosa 1980–81; 1986).

The presence of imported Mycenaean materials in this period suggest that the increasingly visible indications of acculturation (e.g. the emergence of funerary rituals attributable to 'Aegeanised' personages of rank such as those Monte Campanella and Caldare), do not emerge from nothing but from a substratum of contacts with the Aegean which had existed for a century already. Moreover, the recent discoveries at a Castelluccio site – Monte Grande – with an abundance of foreign material of Aegean and Cypriot provenance confirm the formation of a precocious enclave of contact with the eastern Mediterranean in the Nisseno-Agrigento territory.

Returning to southeastern Sicily, the rich topographic data, especially in the Ragusa area (Guzzardi 1985–86), allow us a better understanding of settlement dynamics, and thus of the historical logic behind the ecosystemic relations of the various cultures in question. In particular, in the transition from the Castelluccio to the Thapsos phase, there was a marked contraction in the numbers of settlements. This can be explained both by an increase in the size of settlements and by the emergence of hierarchised forms of population distribution.

In eastern Sicily the Thapsos culture shows true signs of acculturation, especially on the type site. It seems clear that by this time a true elite emerged in society, which fashioned its behaviour and character along the lines of Aegean models that reached Sicily with the increasingly frequent commercial contacts. This is concretely visible in the acquisition of architectural models of Aegean inspiration that have their most complete expression in

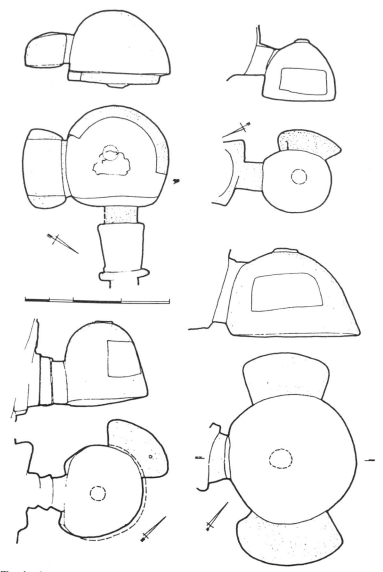

Fig. 24 Tomb plans and sections of the Thapsos facies in southern and southeastern Sicily

the building with a central courtyard. Such a structural model, composed of adjacent rectangular rooms opening onto a central courtyard, clearly suggests the existence of some degree of planning, even embryonic forms of urbanism. At Thapsos even in the first phase (15th–14th centuries BC) one sees an 'urban' distribution of buildings preceding the establishment of the central courtyard structures. Circular huts of the traditional type are still present, but are distributed in 'lots' defined by perimeter walls enclosing well defined spaces and set into a network of streets that, although by no means as regular as the later one, nevertheless divided up the area of the settlement (Voza 1984–85) (fig. 23).

The introduction of Aegean models of behaviour is visible in the 'fashion' of embellishing tombs with architectural details of Aegean inspiration like vaulted roofs, benches and lateral niches (Tomasello 1986) (fig. 24) and in grave goods with imported Helladic and Aegean-Eastern materials. However, the processes behind this concrete example of cultural change did not take root at random but in places where phenomena of cultural diversification were already happening.

Thus, although there were undoubted Mycenaean influences, the Thapsos settlement system was also governed by a local evolutionary process which was already tending towards a degree of 'urban' planning. This process cannot have been limited to the site of Thapsos, but would also have applied to the other centres of the east coast, such as Cozzo del Pantano and Ortygia. Recent evidence from Syracuse serves to demonstrate even more

Fig. 25   Ivory comb (centre top) from Marcita (Trapani). Bronzework (left) from Caldare (Agrigento): sword and two vessels (above), basin from Enkomi (Cyprus) (below). Syro-Palestinian statuette depicting Reshef found in the sea off Selinunte (right)

clearly the Thapsos culture's external relations. A tomb (D/1970) was found in the vicinity of the altar of Heiron II with local, Mycenaean and Cypriot ('White Shaved' and 'Base Ring') pottery together with a steatite seal. This find contributes to the identification, among the many traces of pre-Greek settlement on Ortygia, of a stratum that is perhaps earlier than any known so far and which appears to contain material of a "clear Thapsos aspect" associated with a rectilinear hut wall (Voza 1984–85).

Moving to western Sicily, important new data have improved our understanding of the known territorial distribution of the Milazzese-Thapsos facies at this end of the island. Excavation of a settlement in contrada Marcita, near Castelvetrano, revealed strips of flooring and the remains of perimeter walls of a hut (Valente 1986). The chronological position of the settlement is provided by the presence of *lebetiforme* basins on a high foot, decorated with applied cordons or incised festoons, sometimes supplied with high forked flat handles, and carinated bowls with pointed handles and wide pans with internal partitions. Close to the settlement, a chamber tomb was excavated containing around 100 individual burials. From among the piles of bones in the chamber came an ivory comb, which has precise parallels in form and decoration (incised circles) in the eastern Mediterranean, especially at Hama, Megiddo and Beitsan (Tusa 1986). Such evidence fits perfectly with the recovery several decades ago of the well-known bronze statuette portraying a Syro-Palestinian divinity (Reshef) from the sea off Selinunte, a short distance from Marcita (V. Tusa 1971).

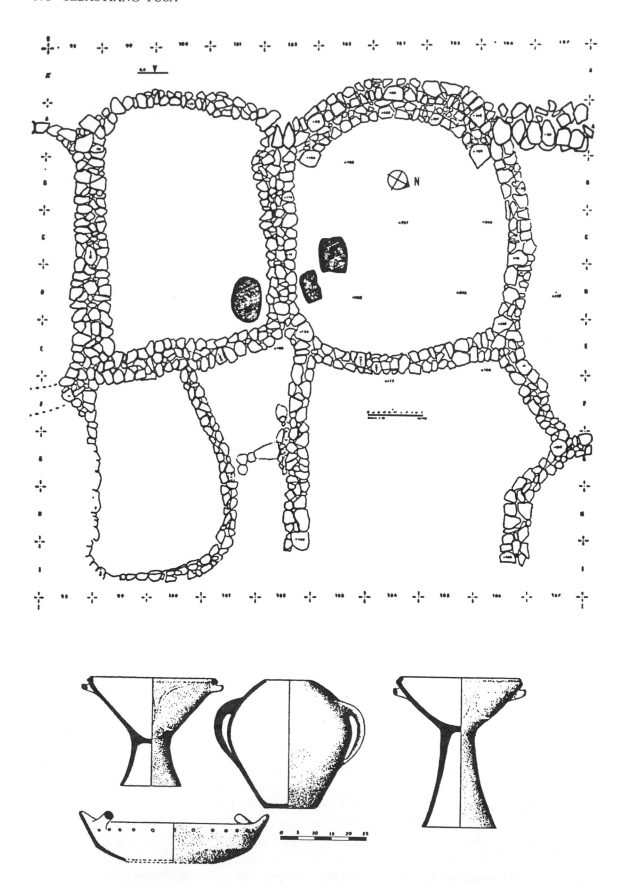

Fig. 26 Top: partial plan of the village of Faraglioni di Ustica. Bottom: ceramics of the Milazzese facies from the middle village

This evidence (fig. 25), together with the presence of Cypriot elements in the Agrigentino (e.g. the basins from Caldare, Cannatello (Mosso 1907; 1908; Vagnetti 1968) and Milena (La Rosa 1979; 1980–81; 1986)), suggests a sort of division of the Thapsos coastal groups' commercial contacts between two sets of partners: Mycenaean in eastern Sicily and Syro-Palestinian and Cypriot further west (De Miro 1968b).

USTICA

One cannot conclude this review of the Thapsos culture presence in western Sicily without mentioning the very interesting settlement of Faraglioni on the island of Ustica (Holloway 1991; Holloway & Lukesh 1991; Mannino 1979; 1982). At Le Faraglioni, a large inhabited area at the edge of a plateau overlooking the sea was enclosed by a massive wall. Inside parts of habitation structures have been excavated, characterised by a high level of planning. Here the traditional hut form was regularised and adapted to create true multi-roomed structures, which nonetheless clearly reveal their modular origin in many characteristic architectural features such as the curved walls and the links between them. This proto-planned layout could not have been executed without an overall scheme for dividing up the settlement area. Such a scheme has been revealed through research on the symmetrical planning of the individual elements and the organisation of the streets and paved courtyards between them.

If there were any doubts about the maritime orientation of this settlement in the light of its topographic position and its island location, they would be immediately dispelled by the artefacts from the site. Containers clearly destined for maritime transport are in the great majority. There are numerous jugs and wide pans characterised by rims pierced with many adjacent holes; their lids have similar perforations (fig. 26). In addition, as well as ceramics of local origin, there is Mycenaean IIIB pottery, probable Apennine fragments, and necklace beads in a vitreous paste similar to Mycenaean ones (Holloway & Lukesh 1991; Valente 1986). The overall scarcity of Mycenaean material would reinforce the hypothesis that, in this period, Sicily was divided into two spheres of influence: an eastern one pervaded by elements of Mycenaean origin, and a western one perhaps linked commercially to the Mediterranean Levant.

Having said that, the role of the Mycenaeans within the ambit of Tyrrhenian trade was decisive, even if it is clear that they inserted themselves into pre-existing routes and that, even in situations of clear acculturation like Thapsos, which absorbed cultural and craft influences, the coastal cultures remained anchored to their own particular traditions. Consequently, we cannot talk of a phenomenon of 'colonisation', as some have done. Even if the Mycenaean and Aegean-Oriental merchants played an important role in the development of proto-urbanism in coastal Sicily, it is clear that this stimulus acted on populations already inclined to change. Thus the concept of colonisation or even of cultural integration, is not only incompatible with the socio-economic level of the coastal societies of Sicily, but has never been supported by any archaeological evidence. Indeed, the very success of Mycenaean trade would have necessarily been based on the exploitation of existing lines of communication and, therefore, on the consolidated knowledge of maritime routes held by indigenous coastal societies which were already trading their own products (Bietti Sestieri 1985; 1988; Holloway 1981; Marazzi 1988; Tusa 1985).

NOTES

1   This article was translated from Italian by Jon Morter, with some further adjustments by the series editors. Bibliographic note: Two reference works were referred to so frequently while writing this article that citing them continuously would have become too cumbersome: Bernabò Brea (1958) and Tusa (1993a).

2   Pointillé decoration, bichrome pointillé decoration, incised decoration, red slipped Beaker ceramics, polypodal vases, and V-perforated buttons.

3 The simple *pointillé* decoration is nearly uniformly present both in the northwest and the southwest. All examples of painted *pointillé* decoration, both all red and red and black bichrome, are from the southern area.

4 There is an analogous situation on nearby Malta, at Ta Trapna, where a V-perforated button was found in a context from the first half of the third millennium BC (Evans 1971).

5 As demonstrated by the presence of the statuette of Reshef found in the sea off Selinunte and by the Marcita comb, probably a product of Syro-Palestinian artisans (see below).

6 E.g. cups on a high foot (or a *'clessidra'*) and amphorae with upraised handles.

7 E.g. bottles with high neck and sloping rim, and ovoid bowls with vertical handle connecting rim and base.

8 Indicated by the presence of imported materials, such as the pottery at Monte Grande and 'exotic' objects like the famous bossed bone plaques (Adamo 1989), the bone sword pommel from Monte Sallia (Orsi 1923) and the little bronze balance beams (Orsi 1892) (fig. 14), and also by specific and differing funerary customs, such as that of *enchytrismos* at San Papino and Boccetta in the Messinese (Voza 1982; Scibona 1984–85).

9 In Sicily, Capo Graziano type materials are found in contexts of the Rodì-Tindari-Vallelunga and Castelluccio cultures; there are also typological links with the Tarxien Cemetery culture of Malta which also has the same funerary practice (cremation burial) and finally there are close links with the Proto-Apennine B of the peninsula (Bernabò Brea 1976–77; 1985).

10 Burial in pottery vessels (urns or pithoi).

11 This includes, *inter alia*, decoration with concentric grooves, the *a clessidra* stands, omphalos bowls, bowls *a pseudo-tesa*, bowls of skull-cap form with a ribbon handle rising from the rim, and three vertical applied cordons on the shoulder.

12 The cultural unity of the Sicilian territory is also seen in bronzework. There was in fact a connection between the south-central area of Sicily and the Aeolian Islands in the type of bronze sword with triangular base with three rivets and flat hilt and blade with rhomboidal section and central ribbing. Therefore it seems that there were circles of local craftsmen strongly influenced by the Thapsos culture in the south-central area of the island (D'Agata 1986).

BIBLIOGRAPHY

Adamo, O. 1989. Pendagli e amuleti della facies di Castelluccio in Sicilia. *Archivio Storico per la Sicilia Orientale*, 85: 7–68.

Albore Livadie, C. & D'Amore, L. 1980. Palma Campania (Napoli). Resti di abitato dell'età del bronzo antico. *Notizie degli Scavi* (serie 8), 34: 59–101.

Amoroso, D. 1979. Insediamenti castellucciani nel territorio di Caltagirone. *Kokalos*, 25: 25–53.

Amoroso, D. 1983. Un corredo tombale del museo della ceramica di Caltagirone e la fase di Thapsos nel territorio calatino. *Archivio Storico per la Sicilia Orientale*, 79(3): 259–77.

Amoroso, D. 1984. *Recenti Ricerche sui Rapporti tra la Sicilia e il Vicino Oriente ed il Problema della Genesi delle Culture di S. Ippolito e Castelluccio*. Catania.

Ardovino, A.M. 1977. Tombe a grotticella a Santa Domenica di Ricadi. *Klearchos*, 73–76: 5–17.

Arias, P.E. 1937. La stazione preistorica a Serraferlicchio presso Agrigento. *Monumenti Antichi dei Lincei*, 36: 693–842.

Atzeni, E. 1980. Vornuraghenzeit. In Thimme, J. (ed.), *Kunst und Kultur Sardiniens*: 15–44. Karlsruhe.

Barfield, L.H. 1976. The cultural affinities of Bell-Beakers in Italy and Sicily. In Lanting, J.N. & van der Waals, J.D. (eds), *Glockenbecher symposion Oberreid 1974*: 307–22. Fibula-Van Dishoek, Haarlem-Bussum.

Barker, G. 1991–92. Modelli di sussistenza nell'età del bronzo dell'Italia centro-meridionale. *Rassegna di Archeologia*, 10: 189–95.

Bernabò Brea, L. 1958. *La Sicilia Prima dei Greci*. Il Saggiatore, Milano.

Bernabò Brea, L. 1976–77. Eolie, Sicilia, e Malta nell'età del bronzo. *Kokalos*, 32–33: 33–110.

Bernabò Brea, L. 1980. Beziehungen zu Malta, Sizilien und zu den Äolischen Insel. In Thimme, J. (ed.), *Kunst und Kultur Sardiniens*: 192–9. Müller, Karlsruhe.

Bernabò Brea, L. 1983. La prima e la media età del bronzo nell'Italia meridionale. *Magna Grecia*, 1–2: 1–3.

Bernabò Brea, L. 1985. *Gli Eoli e l'Inizio dell'Età del Bronzo nelle Isole Eolie e nell'Italia Meridionale*. Napoli.

Bernabò Brea, L. 1988. L'età del rame nell'Italia insulare: la Sicilia e le isole Eolie. *Rassegna di Archeologia*, 7: 496–506.

Bernabò Brea, L. 1989. La grotta Cardini nel quadro dell'età del bronzo dell'Italia meridionale. *Memorie dell'Istituto Italiano di Paleontologia Umana*, 4: 187–211.

Bernabò Brea, L. & Cavalier, M. 1960. *Meligunis Lipara* I. Flaccovio, Palermo.

Bernabò Brea, L. & Cavalier, M. 1980. *Meligunis Lipara* IV. Flaccovio, Palermo.

Bernabò Brea, L. & Cavalier, M. 1982. Scavi e rinvenimenti archeologici nelle isole Eolie: 1977–1982. *Beni Culturali Ambientali*, 3: 145–8.

Bernabò Brea, L. & Cavalier, M. 1992. *Meligunis Lipara* VI. Flaccovio, Palermo.

Bietti Sestieri, A.M. 1985. Contact, exchange and conflict in the Italian Bronze Age: the Mycenaeans on the Tyrrhenian coasts and islands. In Malone, C. & Stoddart, S. (eds), *Papers in Italian Archaeology IV*: 305–37. BAR International Series 245. British Archaeological Reports, Oxford.

Bietti Sestieri, A.M. 1988. The "Mycenaean connection" and its impact on the central Mediterranean societies. *Dialoghi di Archeologia* (3 ser.), 6(1): 23–51.

Bosch Gimpera, P. 1967. Relaciones prehistoricas mediterraneas. *Annales de Anthropologia*, 4.

Bovio Marconi, J. 1945. La cultura tipo Conca d'Oro della Sicilia occidentale. *Monumenti Antichi dei Lincei*, 40: 1–176.

Bovio Marconi, J. 1963. Sulla diffusione del Bicchiere *campaniforme* in Sicilia. *Kokalos*, 9: 93–128.

Braudel, F. 1973. *Scritti sulla Storia* (Italian trans.). Einaudi. Milano.

Cassano, S.M., Manfredini, A. & Quojani, F. 1975. Recenti ricerche nelle necropoli eneolitiche della Conca d'Oro. *Origini*, 9: 153–271.

Castellana, G. 1990. *Un Decennio di Ricerche Preistoriche e Protostoriche nel Territorio Agrigentino.* Palermo.

Cavalier, M. 1960–61. Les cultures préhistoriques des iles éoliennes et leurs rapports avec le monde égéen. *Bulletin de Correspondance Hellenique*, 84: 319–46.

Cavalier, M. 1981. Villaggio preistorico di S. Vincenzo. *Sicilia Archeologica*, 46–47: 27–54.

Cavalier, M. 1984–85. Attività archeologica nelle isole Eolie. *Kokalos*, 30–31: 698.

Cavalier, M. & Vagnetti, L. 1983. Frammenti di ceramica "matt painted" policroma da Filicudi (isole Eolie). *Mélanges de l'Ecole Française de Rome, Antiquité*, 95(1): 335–44.

Cavalier, M. & Vagnetti, L. 1984. Materiali micenei vecchi e nuovi dall'Acropoli di Lipari. *Studi Micenei ed Egeo-Anatolici*, 25: 143–54.

Cavalier, M. & Vagnetti, L. 1986. Arcipelago eoliano. In Marazzi, M., Tusa, S. & Vagnetti, L. (eds), *Traffici Micenei nel Mediterraneo: Problemi Storici e Documentazione Archeologica*: 141–6. Istituto per la storia e l'archeologia della Magna Grecia, Taranto.

Cazzella, A. 1972. Considerazione su alcuni aspetti eneolitici dell'Italia e della Sicilia. *Origini*, 6: 171–299.

Cazzella, A., Damiani, I., di Gennaro, F., Marazzi, M., Moscoloni, M., Pacciarelli, M., Rosi, M., Sbrana, A., Tusa, S. & Vezzoli, L. 1991. *Vivara – Centro Commerciale dell'Età del Bronzo – Gli Scavi dal 1976 al 1982*, vol. I. Bagatto Libri, Roma.

Cherry, J.F. 1988. Pastoralism and the role of animals in the pre- and protohistoric economies of the Aegean. In Whittaker, C.R. (ed.), *Pastoral Economies in Classical Antiquity*: 6–34. Cambridge University Press, Cambridge.

Childe, V.G. 1957. *The Dawn of European civilization.* Routledge & Kegan Paul, London.

Clarke, D.L. 1970. *Beaker Pottery of Great Britain and Ireland.* Cambridge University Press, Cambridge.

Cultraro, M. 1989. Il castellucciano etneo nel quadro dei rapporti tra Sicilia, Penisola Italiana ed Egeo nei secc. XVI e XV a.C. *Il Sileno*, 15(1–2): 259–86.

D'Agata, A.L. 1986. Considerazioni su alcune spade siciliane della media e tarda età del bronzo. In Marazzi, M., Tusa, S. & Vagnetti, L. (eds), *Traffici Micenei nel Mediterraneo: Problemi Storici e Documentazione Archeologica*: 105–11. Istituto per la storia e l archeologia della Magna Grecia, Taranto.

D'Agata, A.L. 1987. Un tipo vascolare della cultura di Thapsos: il bacino con ansa a piastra bifida. *Studi Micenei ed Egeo-Anatolici*, 26: 187–98.

Damiani, I., Pacciarelli, M. & Saltini, A.C. 1984. Le facies archeologiche dell'isola di Vivara e alcuni problemi relativi al Protoappenninico B. *Annali Istituto Universitario Orientale Napoli*, 6: 1–38.

De Miro, E. 1968a. Preistoria dell'Agrigentino. Recenti ricerche e acquisizioni. In *Atti della XI e XII Riunione Scientifica, Firenze, 11–12 febbraio 1967; Sicilia, 22–26 ottobre 1967*: 117–27. Istituto Italiano di Preistoria e Protostoria, Firenze.

De Miro, E. 1968b. Il Miceneo nel territorio di Agrigento. *Atti e Memorie del I° Congresso Internazionale di Micenologia*, 1: 73–80.

Evans, J.D. 1971. *The Prehistoric Antiquities of the Maltese Islands.* Athlone Press, University of London.

Ferrarese Ceruti, M.L. 1972–74. La tomba XVI di Su Crucifissu Mannu e la cultura di Bonnannaro. *Bullettino di Paletnologia Italiana*, 81: 113–218.

Ferrarese Ceruti, M.L. 1981. La cultura del vaso campaniforme. Il primo bronzo. In *Ichnussa*: 55–66. Libri Scheiwiller, Milano.

Ferrarese Ceruti, M.L., & Germanà, F. 1978. *Sisaia.* Quaderni 6 della Soprintendenza ai Beni Archeologici per le Provincie di Sassari e Nuoro. Dessì, Sassari.

Gilman, A. 1981. The development of social stratification in Bronze Age Europe. *Current Anthropology*, 22(1): 1–23.

Gnesotto, F. 1982. Il sito preistorico di Casalicchio-Agnone in territorio di Licata (Agrigento). In *Studi in Onore di Ferrante Rittatore Vonwiller*, I: 195–220. Società Archeologica Comense, Como.

Guzzardi, L. 1985–86. Nuovi dati sulla cultura di Thapsos nel Ragusano. *Archivio Storico per la Sicilia Orientale*, 82(1–2): 219–40.

Guzzardi, L. 1988. Scavi e ricerche preistoriche a sud di Siracusa. In *Atti del VI Convegno Nazionale di Preistoria e Protostoria*. Pescia.

Harrison, R.J., Quero, S. & Priego, C.M. 1975. Beaker metallurgy in Spain. *Antiquity*, 44: 273–80.

Holloway, R.R. 1975. Buccino: The Early Bronze Age village of Tufariello. *Journal of Field Archaeology*, 2: 11–81.

Holloway, R.R. 1981. *Italy and the Aegean 3000–700 B.C.* Louvain-la-Neuve.

Holloway, R.R. 1985. Scavi archeologici alla Muculufa e premesse per lo studio della cultura castellucciana. In *Atti della Seconda Giornata di Studi sull'Archeologia Licatese e della Zona della Bassa Valle dell'Himera, Licata – 19 Gennaio 1985*: 69–90.

Holloway, R.R. 1991. Ustica, località Faraglioni. Rinvenimento di una scultura della media età del bronzo. *Sicilia Archeologica*, 77: 81–6.

Holloway, R.R. & Lukesh, S.S. 1991. Ustica. Report on the excavations of the Bronze Age site of Faraglioni 1990. *Archäologischer Anzeiger*, 1990: 359–65.

La Rosa, V. 1979. Sopralluoghi e ricerche attorno a Milena nella media valle del Platani. *Cronache di Archeologia*, 18: 1–27.

La Rosa, V. 1980–81. La media e tarda età del bronzo nel territorio di Milena. Rapporto preliminare sulle ricerche degli anni 1978–1979. *Kokalos*, 26–27: 642.

La Rosa, V. 1986. Nuovi ritrovamenti e sopravvivenze egee nella Sicilia meridionale. In Marazzi, M., Tusa, S. & Vagnetti, L. (eds), *Traffici Micenei nel Mediterraneo: Problemi Storici e Documentazione Archeologica*: 79–92. Istituto per la storia e l'archeologia della Magna Grecia, Taranto.

La Rosa, V. 1989. Le popolazioni della Sicilia: Sicani, Siculi, Elimi. In *Italia*: 5–13. Libri Scheiwiller, Milano.

La Rosa, V. 1994. Le nuove indagini nella media valle del Platani. In Tusa, S. (ed.), *La Preistoria del Basso Belice e della Sicilia Meridionale nel Quadro della Preistoria Siciliana e Mediterranea*: 287–304. Palermo.

La Rosa, V. & D'Agata, A.L. 1988. Uno scarico dell'età del bronzo sulla Serra del Palco di Milena. *Quaderni dell'Istituto di Archeologia della Facoltà di Lettere e Filosofia della Università di Messina*, 3: 5–15.

Lattanzi, E., Marino, D.A., Vagnetti, L. & Jones, R.E. 1987. Nota preliminare sul sito preistorico di Capo Piccolo presso Crotone. *Klearchos*, 113-6: 25-44.

Mannino, G. 1971. La tomba di contrada Pergola. *Sicilia Archeologica*, 15: 52–6.

Mannino, V. 1979. Ustica. *Sicilia Archeologica*, 41: 7–40.

Mannino, V. 1982. Il villaggio dei Faraglioni di Ustica. Notizie preliminari. In *Studi in Onore di Ferrante Rittatore Vonwiller*, I: 279–97. Società Archeologica Comense, Como.

Marazzi, M. 1988. La più antica marineria micenea in occidente. *Dialoghi di Archeologia* (3 ser.), 6(1): 5–22.

Marazzi, M. & Tusa, S. 1987. Selinunte e il suo territorio – analisi storica e progetto di ricognizione. *I Quaderni di Sicilia Archeologica*, 1: 39–109.

Mosso, A. 1907. Villaggi preistorici di Caldare e Cannatello. *Monumenti Antichi dei Lincei*, 18: 572–683.

Mosso, A. 1908. Le armi più antiche di rame e di bronzo. *Memorie dell'Accademia Nazionale dei Lincei*, 12.

Orlandini, P. 1962. *Il Villaggio Preistorico di Manfria, presso Gela*. Palermo.

Orsi, P. 1889. Appunti per la paletnologia di Siracusa e del suo territorio. *Bullettino di Paletnologia Italiana*, 15: 48–58.

Orsi, P. 1892. La necropoli sicula di Castelluccio (Siracusa). *Bullettino di Paletnologia Italiana*, 18: 1–94.

Orsi, P. 1893. Scarichi del villaggio di Castelluccio (Sicilia). *Bullettino di Paletnologia Italiana*, 19: 30–51.

Orsi, P. 1897. L'età della necropoli di Castelluccio in provincia di Siracusa. *Bullettino di Paletnologia Italiana*, 23: 104–5.

Orsi, P. 1898. Miniere di selce e sepolcri eneolitici a Monte Tabuto e Monte Racello presso Comiso (Siracusa). *Bullettino di Paletnologia Italiana*, 24: 165–206.

Orsi, P. 1923. Villaggio, officina litica e necropoli del I periodo siculo a monte Sallia, presso Canicarao (Siracusa). *Bullettino di Paletnologia Italiana*, 43: 3–25.

Orsi, P. 1930–31. Abitazioni e sepolcri siculi di Biancavilla. *Bullettino di Paletnologia Italiana*, 50–51: 134–47.

Pacci, M. 1982. Lo stile "protocastelluzziano" di Naro. *Rivista di Scienze Preistoriche*, 37: 187–216.

Pacci, M. 1987a. Revisione e nuove proposte d'interpretazione per i materiali delle tombe di Santa Domenica di Ricadi. *Sicilia Archeologica*, 64: 35–52.

Pacci, M. 1987b. Regional aspects of Bell Beaker culture: western Sicily, Italy. In Waldren, W.H. & Kennard, R.C. (eds), *Bell Beakers of the Western Mediterranean*: 565–90. BAR International Series 331. British Archaeological Reports, Oxford.

Pacci, M., & Tusa, S. 1990. *La Collezione dei Vasi Preistorici di Partanna e Naro*. Sellerio, Palermo.

Pacciarelli, M. 1991–92. Considerazioni sulla struttura delle comunità del bronzo medio dell'Italia centro-meridionale. *Rassegna di Archeologia*, 10: 265–80.

Peroni, R. 1989. Protostoria dell'Italia continentale – La penisola italiana nelle età del bronzo e del ferro. *Biblioteca di Storia Antica*, 9. Editori Riuniti, Roma.

Privitera, F. 1994. La stazione di Mezzebbi nel contesto del bronzo antico del territorio di Milena. In Tusa, S. (ed.), *La Preistoria del Basso Belice e della Sicilia Meridionale nel Quadro della Preistoria Siciliana e Mediterranea*: 339–56. Palermo.

Procelli, E. 1981. Il complesso tombale di contrada Paolina ed il problema dei rapporti tra Sicilia e Malta nella prima età del bronzo. *Bollettino d'Arte*, 9: 83–110.

Puglisi, S.M. 1959. *La Civiltà Apenninica*. Olschki, Firenze.

Rellini, U. 1934. Secondo rapporto preliminare sulle ricerche preistoriche condotte sul promontorio del Gargano. Ricerche degli anni 1932–33. (Appendice di Baumgärtel, E. Stratigrafia del "Grottone di Manaccore" – scavi dell'anno 1932: 20–58). *Bullettino di Paletnologia Italiana*, 54: 1–64.

Renfrew, C. 1967. Colonialism and megalithismus. *Antiquity*, 41: 276–88.

Renfrew, C. 1972. *The emergence of civilization: the Cyclades and the Aegean in the third millennium B.C.* Methuen, London.

Renfrew, C. 1986. Introduction: peer polity interaction and socio-political change. In Renfrew, C. & Cherry, J.F. (eds), *Peer Polity Interaction and Socio-political Change*: 1–18. Cambridge University Press, Cambridge.

Scibona, G. 1984–85. Messina: notizia preliminare sulla necropoli romana e sul giacimento preistorico del torrente Boccetta. *Kokalos*, 30–31: 855–62.

Shennan, S. 1982. Ideology, change and the European Bronze Age. In Hodder, I. (ed.), *Symbolic and Structural Archaeology*: 155–61. Cambridge University Press, Cambridge.

Spigo, U. 1984–85. Ricerche e rinvenimenti a Brucoli (c.da Gisira), Valsavoia (Lentini), nel territorio di Caltagirone, Adrano e Francavilla di Sicilia. *Kokalos*, 30–31: 866–75.

Spigo, U. 1989. Archeologia. In *Ippopotami di Sicilia*: 107–15. Messina.

Tinè, S. 1960–61. Giacimenti dell'età del rame in Sicilia e la "cultura tipo Conca d'Oro". *Bullettino di Paletnologia Italiana*, 13: 113–51.

Tomasello, F. 1986. L'architettura funeraria in Sicilia tra le media e tarda età del bronzo: le tombe a camera del tipo a tholos. In Marazzi, M., Tusa, S. & Vagnetti, L. (eds), *Traffici Micenei nel Mediterraneo: Problemi Storici e Documentazione Archeologica*: 93–104. Istituto per la storia e l'archeologia della Magna Grecia, Taranto.

Tozzi, C. 1968.   Relazione sulla I e II campagna di scavi effettuati a Pantelleria. *Rivista di Scienze Preistoriche*, 23: 315–88.

Tusa, S. 1984.   Sicilia e relazioni tirreniche nell'Antica Età del Bronzo. *Libera Università Trapani*, 3(8): 99–106.

Tusa, S. 1985.   Tyrrhenian relations and Mycenaean exchange in the Early Bronze Age. In Malone, C. & Stoddart, S. (eds), *Papers in Italian Archaeology IV. Part iii*: 339–53. BAR International Series 245. British Archaeological Reports, Oxford.

Tusa, S. 1986.   Dinamiche storiche nel territorio selinuntino nel II millennio alla luce delle recenti ricerche in contrada Marcita (Castelvetrano). In Marazzi, M., Tusa, S. & Vagnetti, L. (eds), *Traffici Micenei nel Mediterraneo*: 133–40. Istituto per la storia e l'archeologia della Magna Grecia, Taranto.

Tusa, S. 1987.   The Bell Beaker in Sicily. In Waldren, W.H. & Kennard, R.C. (eds), *Bell Beakers of the Western Mediterranean*: 523–50. BAR International Series 331. British Archaeological Reports, Oxford.

Tusa, S. 1990a.   *La Preistoria nel Territorio di Trapani*. Ediprint, Siracusa

Tusa, S. 1990b.   La collezione di vasi castellucciani da Monte Tabuto (Ragusa) presso il Museo Preistorico Etnografico "L. Pigorini". *Sicilia Archeologica*, 73: 65–76.

Tusa, S. 1991a.   The megalith builders and Sicily. *Journal of Mediterranean Studies*, 1(2): 267–85.

Tusa, S. 1991b.   Considerazioni sulla religiosità delle popolazioni pre-elleniche siciliane tra il paleolitico superiore e l'età del bronzo. *MUQOS*, 3: 167–88.

Tusa, S. 1991c.   South-Western Sicily during the Early Bronze Age and its correlation with the eastern Mediterranean. In *Proceedings of the 6th International Colloquium on Aegean Prehistory*: 64–9. Athens.

Tusa, S. 1991d.   Scavi alla Punta d'Alaca. In *Vivara – Centro Commerciale dell'Età del Bronzo – Gli scavi dal 1976 al 1982*, vol. I: 75–93. Bagatto Libri, Roma.

Tusa, S. 1993a.   *La Sicilia nella Preistoria* (II edizione). Sellerio, Palermo.

Tusa, S. 1993b.   Il bicchiere campaniforme in Sicilia: evento, congiuntura o dinamica strutturale. In *Studi in Onore di V. Tusa*: 203–14. Padova.

Tusa, S. 1994.   La dinamica insediamentale nel quadro dei rapporti tra le culture del XVI e XV secolo a.C. nel basso Tirreno. In *Vivara – Centro Commerciale dell'Età del Bronzo*, vol. II. Bagatto Libri, Roma.

Tusa, V. 1971.   Sicilia. In *L'Espansione Fenicia nel Mediterraneo*: 175–91. CNR, Roma.

Vagnetti, L. 1968.   I bacili di Caldare sono ciprioti? *Studi Micenei ed Egeo-Anatolici*, 7: 129–38.

Vagnetti, L. 1982.   Lipari. In Vagnetti, L. (ed.), *Magna Grecia e Mondo Miceneo. Nuovi documenti. XXII Convegno di Studi sulla Magna Grecia, Taranto, 7–11, ottobre 1982*: 132–5. Istituto per la storia e l'archeologia della Magna Grecia, Taranto.

Vagnetti, L. & Cavalier, M. 1982.   Filicudi. In Vagnetti, L. (ed.), *Magna Grecia e Mondo Miceneo. Nuovi documenti. XXII Convegno di Studi sulla Magna Grecia, Taranto, 7–11, ottobre 1982*: 136–8. Istituto per la storia e l'archeologia della Magna Grecia, Taranto.

Valente, I. 1986.   Indizi di presenza micenea nella Sicilia occidentale durante la media età del bronzo. In Marazzi, M., Tusa, S. & Vagnetti, L. (eds), *Traffici Micenei nel Mediterraneo*: 123–31. Istituto per la storia e l'archeologia della Magna Grecia, Taranto.

Vigliardi, A. 1975.   Il Bronzo "apenninico" della Grotta del Noglio (Marina di Camerota, Salerno. *Rivista di Scienze Preistoriche*, 30: 279–346.

Vigliardi, A. 1979.   Rapporti tra Sardegna e Toscana nell'eneolitico finale-primo bronzo: la Grotta del Fontino nel Grossetano. In *Atti della XXII Riunione Scientifica*: 247–88. Istituto Italiano di Preistoria e Protostoria, Firenze.

Villari, P. 1981a.   I giacimenti preistorici del Monte Belvedere e della Pianura Chiusa di Fiumedinisi (Messina) e la successione delle culture nella Sicilia Nord-orientale. *Sicilia Archeologica*, 46–7: 111–21.

Villari, P. 1981b.   Considerazioni sulla presenza di alcuni bronzi in una capanna del periodo di transizione tardo eneolitico – prima età del bronzo del monte Belvedere di Fiumedinisi (Messina). *Atti della Società Toscana di Scienze Naturali*, Memorie, serie A, 87: 465–74.

Villari, P. 1981c.   *Monte di Giove e Fiumedinisi*. Messina.

Von Andrian, F.F. 1878.   *Prähistorische Studien aus Sizilien*. Berlin.

Voza, G. 1982.   L'attività della Soprintendenza ai Beni Archeologici della Sicilia Orientale dal 1976 al 1982. *Beni Culturali Ambientali*, 3: 93–137.

Voza, G. 1984–85.   Attività nel territorio della Soprintendenza alle Antichità di Siracusa nel quadriennio 1980–1984. *Kokalos*, 30–31: 666–8.

Waldren, W.H. 1979.   A beaker workshop area in the rock shelter of Son Matge, Valldemosa. *World Archaeology*, 11(1): 43–67.

Waldren, W.H. 1980.   The settlement complex of Ferrandell-Oleza. A beaker settlement from the Balearic Island of Mallorca. *Donald Baden Powell Quaternary Research Centre DAMARC Series 8*. Oxford and Deya de Mallorca.

Waldren, W.H. 1984.   Chalcolithic settlement and beaker connections in the Balearic Islands. In Waldren, W., Chapman, R., Lewthwaite, J. & Kennard, R.-C. (eds), *The Deya Conference of Prehistory. Early Settlement in the Western Mediterranean Islands and their Peripheral Areas*: 911–65. BAR International Series 229. British Archaeological Reports, Oxford.

Zanotti, D.G. 1986.   The evidence of Kurgan Wave Three (c.3000–2800) in the western Mediterranen. Part one: Malta. *Journal of Indo-European Studies*, 14(1–2): 1–25.

Zanotti, D.G. & Rhine, B.A. 1974.   The catacomb variant of south Russia and its extension within the Mediterranean. *Journal of Indo-European Studies*, 2(4): 333–59.

The Sicilian Bronze Age Pottery Service

Laura Maniscalco

From the Early Bronze Age to the Early Iron Age, for a period of more than one thousand years, the same basic pottery service can be identified both in huts and in tombs of Sicily. This service is constituted by two elements which are always present – a vase on a pedestal and a dipper – as well as by other elements such as *amphorae*, *paterae*, and *pithoi*. A short survey of the different chronological facies in which this service is attested will show how this service remained essentially the same even though the style of the wares changed.

DEVELOPMENT OF CERAMIC ASSEMBLAGES

During the Early Bronze Age Castelluccian culture (2000–1400 BC) the basic domestic assemblage consisted of a chalice vase with a deep bowl on a pedestal and a pitcher in the typical black-on-red decoration. The large diameter of the rim of the chalice vase and the raised handle of the pitcher clearly show the function: the chalice vase was used for serving in solid or more likely liquid form, and the pitcher was used for dipping and drinking. The earliest known example of this arrangement (fig. 1) comes from the village of La Muculufa, a site to the east of Agrigento, at the beginning of the Castelluccian culture (c.2200 BC). In Hut 2 these two vessels were associated; other supplementary elements included pithoi with cordon decoration for storing water or food (McConnell 1992). The same set, sometimes with the addition of small amphorae, vessels with an internal bridge (*vasi a ponte*), and braziers (*alari*) come from Villaggio Garofalo, a late Castelluccian site near Adrano on the southern slope of Mount Etna (c.1500 BC) (Cultraro 1988–89). In this case the chalice vase has a high pedestal and the dipping vessel has a cup-like form. Unfortunately, only in a few cases is the description of pottery from other Castelluccian villages excavated in the late 19th century in southeastern Sicily clear and the provenance accurate; nevertheless, we know that the chalice vase was a common element in huts of this culture (Orsi 1930–31: 144).

A different situation appears in Castelluccian necropoleis. From rock-cut Castelluccian tombs there come a great quantity of stone pendants and flint blades, but in respect to the high number of burials per tomb there is a relatively limited amount of pottery. In the few intact tombs found at Castelluccio (Noto) and Melilli (Syracuse) the pottery assemblage usually consists of pithoi, sometimes with animal bones, bowls, and cups (Orsi 1891: tombs 12 and 12 bis; 1892: tomb 32). Orsi (1930–31: 144) noted the difference between the

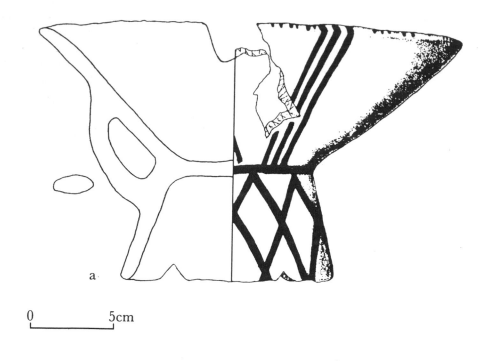

0   5cm

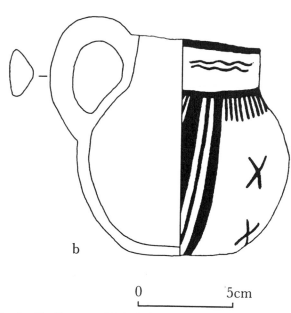

0   5cm

Fig. 1   Chalice vase (a) and pitcher (b) from the village of La Muculufa

abundant, decorated pottery from villages where chalice vases were recovered, and the poor, sometimes undecorated, pottery from tombs. Due to a lack of information, resulting from the fact that most known Castelluccian tombs have been disturbed by clandestine excavators, it is not possible to identify a clear repertoire by type and function, but in any case a distinct pottery funerary assemblage does not yet seem to be well established.

A different combination of vessels may be found in assemblages set in some cases in the court area in front of the tomb chamber. In two burials in the Grotto Pelleriti at Adrano, which belongs to the earlier part of the Castelluccian culture, the external assemblage is constituted by chalice vases and pitchers (sep. 2) and by chalice vases, dipper-cups and *olle*, while the usual ornamental elements and stone tools are signs of personal property (sep. 1) (Cultraro 1988–89). In the late Castelluccian rock-cut Tomb 1S of S. Febronia (Palagonia, Catania) an external assemblage composed of two chalice vases on a high pedestal and a

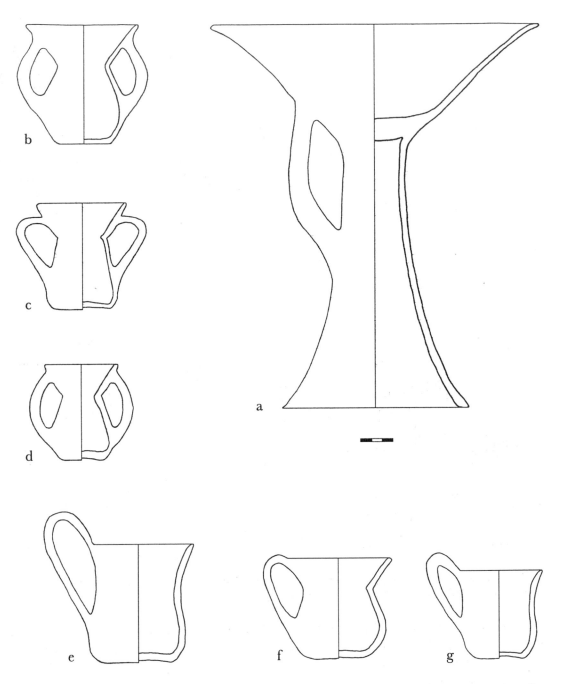

Fig. 2   Chalice vase (a) and dippers (b, c) from the external assemblage of tomb no. 2 at C.da Paolina (from Procelli 1981)

series of at least six dippers (fig. 2) was found in the court before the tomb (Maniscalco 1991). In the necropolis of Melilli in four cases Orsi found an external assemblage, and in three of these there were chalice vases (Orsi 1891: tombs 18, 19, 28, 31). External assemblages, composed of chalice vases, dippers and amphorae, were also found in Tomb 2 in Contrada Paolina, near Comiso (Procelli 1981). An external assemblage was also found in a monumental tomb in C.da Pergola near Salaparuta in western Sicily (Mannino 1971).

During the Early Bronze Age therefore we can see the formation of an arrangement which would become traditional over the following centuries. The origin of the pottery service 'chalice-vase-plus-dipper' seems to lie in the domestic sphere, as one may see in the hut of the early Castelluccian village at La Muculufa. The Castelluccian tombs present an internal assemblage in which a vague typological range of pottery was used to store food for the dead, as shown by the presence of actual animal bones in some of the vessels at

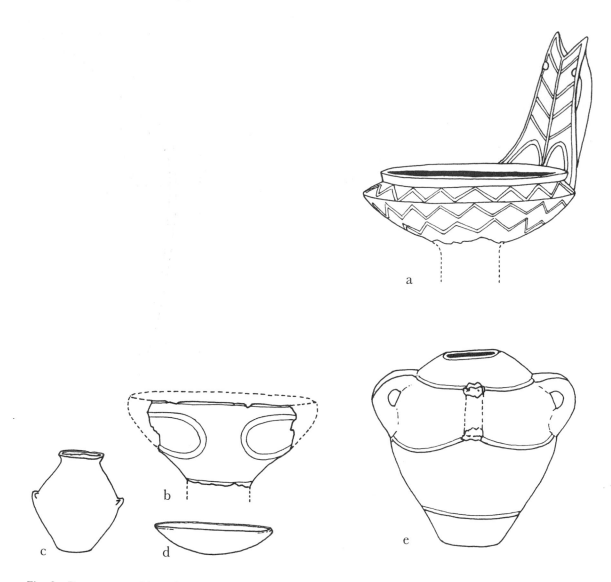

Fig. 3 Pottery assemblage from tomb no. 9 at Cozzo del Pantano (not to scale): pedestalled bowls (a, b), *olletta* (c), patera (d), large cask (e) (from Orsi 1893)

Castelluccio and Melilli. An established set of wares begins to form in Castelluccian tombs only as an external assemblage. Evidently this service was not intended to stand as the deceased's personal belongings in the same way as personal objects such as blades and pendants, but it was an offering from the family to the deceased which reproduced the domestic service.

In the Middle Bronze Age Thapsos culture (1400–1250 BC) huts offer further evidence. The open bowl on a high pedestal in the Castelluccian tradition is also present, but the most important place at the centre of the hut is taken by a basin on a high pedestal with a deep bowl and an inverted rim designed most likely to reduce the spillage of liquid. A large and apparently non-functional bifurcate piaster underscores the ceremonial character of this vessel. Dippers and pithoi in a grey incised ware complete the set in villages such as the eponymous site of Thapsos itself, just north of Syracuse, Madre Chiesa di Gaffe (Licata) and I Faraglioni on the island of Ustica (Voza 1972; 1973; 1976–77; Castellana 1990; Holloway & Lukesh 1991; 1992).

The same assemblage in a somewhat reduced form is also found in Thapsos culture tombs. The rock-cut Tomb 9 of Cozzo del Pantano (Syracuse), a rare undisturbed burial, presents us with the standard funerary assemblage: three skeletons with three basins on pedestals, three small jars (*ollette*), a large cask (*bottino*) and, for the first time, a low dish

Fig. 4   Pantalica necropolis pottery service: (a) chalice vase, (b) pitcher, (c) amphora, (d) patera

(*patera*) (fig. 3) (Orsi 1893; McConnell 1987). As Orsi (1895: 143) summarised it, the large bowl with a bifurcate piaster served for liquid, the cup for dipping, and the plate on a high pedestal for solid food.

A funerary assemblage from Monte Balchino (Caltagirone) (Amoroso 1983) demonstrates how this arrangement became standard. A group of four well-made vessels constitutes a clear pottery service: according to Amoroso, one basin was used for liquid and a dipper for dipping, a basin without a pedestal was used for cooking and a chalice vase for eating (the deep wall and the narrow mouth of this chalice vase recall the Greek cauldron, which was used for boiling meat). All four vessels, which show no signs of use, clearly came from the same pottery workshop: they have the same fabric, the same elegant proportions, and the same kind of non-functional handles. The presence in the same tomb of a sword suggests that it was a prestigious burial.

During the Late Bronze Age Pantalica North culture (1250–1000 BC) most of our evidence comes from tombs rather than from huts (Maniscalco 1985–86). The basic pottery service in the tombs is formed now by either a deep globular vase on a high pedestal or an open bowl on a similar pedestal, a pitcher, an amphora, and a patera in a polished red fabric (fig. 4). Sometimes all the vases are of miniature proportions and in this case the symbolic connotation is even more evident. In fact, in the Pantalica necropolis itself this arrangement is not the most common. From the greater part of the tombs of this period there comes an abbreviation of the traditional set formed only by a pitcher and a bronze instrument (a razor or knife). In this case the depositions are single or at most double, instead of being part of a collective burial. The complete traditional pottery set is usually found at Pantalica, albeit infrequently, in chamber tombs with collective burials, sometimes in monumental rock-cut chamber tombs, in other words in tombs intended from the beginning to be family tombs. In some cases the service is accompanied by gold jewellery. The idea of the ritual banquet clearly is now connected with a distinguished group or family.

Similar traditional arrangements are found in the contemporary necropoleis of Caltagirone and Dessueri (Orsi 1904; 1899; 1913). At Caltagirone the pottery service shows little variation, with a *hydria* and a pitcher; in the Dessueri necropolis there is a greater variety of amphorae, pitchers, and olle. In the Dessueri and Caltagirone necropoleis there

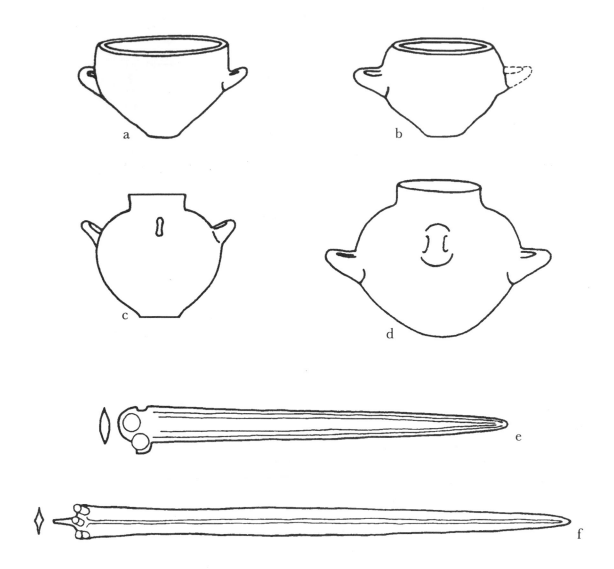

Fig. 5   Burial goods from Caltagirone and Dessueri (from Maniscalco 1985–86)

are sometimes found metal weapons which, together with the basin on a high pedestal, seem to be limited to the tombs of prestigious individuals or warriors (Maniscalco 1985–86) (fig. 5). The presence of an enormous basin on a high pedestal at the so-called *anaktoron* of Pantalica shows the same arrangement in an enlarged version for domestic use in the context of a structure which, because of its monumentality and the presence of an arms foundry, has been interpreted as the seat of a ruler (Orsi 1899; Bernabò Brea 1990: 73). In the more humble domestic context of huts of the village at Sabucina there have been found basins on a high pedestal, amphorae, and *situlae* (Mollo 1987).

During the Final Bronze Age or Cassibile phase (1000–800 BC) the traditional pottery set formed by open bowls on a high pedestal and a pitcher or patera is attested in the chamber tombs of the necropolis at Cassibile (fig. 6). But from the contemporary necropolis at Molino della Badia, where there are pit graves and *enchytrismoi*, we find an abbreviated version: one pitcher and one or more bronze instruments (Maniscalco 1985–86; Orsi 1905; Bernabò Brea *et al.* 1969). It is only with the Iron Age culture of Pantalica South that this millennium-old pottery service gave way to the more simple formula of a pitcher plus bronze objects (a fibula and/or other item), a group related more to the dress of the individuals buried there than to the tomb's funerary assemblage (Bietti Sestieri 1979: 624; Albanese Procelli 1988–89: 265).

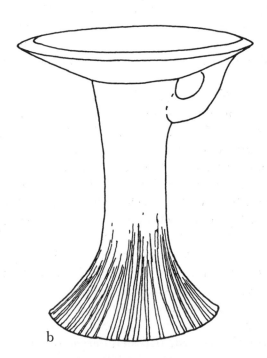

Fig. 6   Pitcher (a) and pedestalled bowls (b, c) from Cassabile necropolis (not to scale) (from Orsi 1899)

DISCUSSION

Through the centuries the standardisation of the set as a service is clearly shown by stylistic change. In the late Castelluccian chalice vase the bowl appears less deep and the pedestal proportionally higher with respect to the early Castelluccian form. The Thapsos 'display' vessels from Monte Balchino were all made by the same workshop, but they were not for daily use; rather they were made especially for funerary deposition, as is clear from the non-functional handles. The symbolic value of food is evident in the miniature version of the pottery set which appears in the Late Bronze Age necropoleis at Pantalica and Dessueri. At the other extreme, the vases on a pedestal from Thapsos and Pantalica, attested sometimes in colossal dimensions of more than one metre, are the monumental finale of this tradition.

The domestic service is probably connected with the development of a typical diet which for several centuries probably experienced little change. We know that in Castelluccian villages goats, sheep and grain were eaten (Orsi 1893), but we know very little about the human diet in other periods. Orsi (1891: 71, 74, 76; 1892: 82) thought that the Castelluccian chalice vase contained water for ritual washing; Holloway and Lukesh (1989) interpret traces of abrasions on the interior of the some bowls as marks made by dippers for drinking wine (Holloway & Lukesh 1989). The evolution of the Castelluccian chalice vase from an early deep bowl, appropriate for liquids, to a late open basin, more likely to contain solid food, can explain the late introduction in the Castelluccian repertory of the amphora as a container for liquid. Also the evolution of the Thapsos bowl on a pedestal (D'Agata 1987: fig. 1) into a deeper vessel can be explained as the fission of a single form into two new versions beginning in the Middle Bronze Age – that is, a deep bowl for liquids and an open bowl for solid food. The overall development of a high pedestal may be due, in fact, to the custom of sitting cross-legged while eating (Holloway & Lukesh 1989). Unfortunately, it is difficult to find more precise explanations for the use through the vessel shape (Smith 1985) when the service is attested most often in the symbolic context of funerary rather than domestic deposits.

Recent studies of the Greek banquet show an evolution from the *phiale*-basin to the cauldron and later to the *krater* which eventually disappeared in the Hellenistic age (Rotroff 1992). These changes parallel the change in Greek society from an aristocracy in the Homeric tradition to a society based on the symposium (Valenza Mele 1982; Schimitt Pantel 1985). It is clear that the persistence in Sicilian prehistory over so long a period of the same elements is related to the existence of a society which for one thousand years had no major changes.

With the beginning of the Bronze Age in Sicily, as in the Italian peninsula, continuity of settlement is very common, sometimes extending into historical times. Attested more often at eastern Sicilian sites such as Pantalica, Cassibile, Ortygia, Paternò, and Dessueri, the continuity of occupation is attested from the Late Bronze Age to the Iron Age and sometimes from even before (Bernabò Brea 1983: 18; see Peroni 1983: 220 for settlement in the Italian peninsula). Together with the topographical rootedness of settlement there developed a more fixed social structure which is reflected clearly in collective burial. The collective tombs were probably family tombs but the size of these burial groups becomes smaller with time. In the Early Bronze Age, the high number of burials per tomb (from tens to in some cases hundreds of individuals) suggests a large group; in the Middle and Late Bronze Ages the burial groups are less numerous (from five to ten individuals per tomb).

If in Early Bronze Age tombs it is possible to distinguish personal tools and ornaments, it is not possible to distinguish a personal pottery service. The service is found on the exterior of the tombs because it is intended to be a gift from the living as a whole to the dead as a whole: the distinction is clear between personal belongings which went into the tombs and the pottery assemblages which were left outside the tombs, supplied to the dead by the survivors as a manifestation of strong social and family continuity. A very similar situation has been observed in settlements and necropoleis of Latium (Rathje 1983; Zevi 1977: 251–5).

In Middle Bronze Age Sicily, on the other hand, the pottery service is brought into the tomb as part of a general reproduction in a funerary context of domestic elements. At times during the Middle Bronze Age, and even more so during the Late Bronze Age, this apparatus becomes the possession of an emergent group, and sometimes it appears in tombs with metal weapons. The differentiation in tombs with emergent 'warrior' tombs has been considered a result of the direct or indirect influence of the Mycenaean presence in Sicily, which is attested in the Middle Bronze Age by the importation of Mycenaean ceramics and metal objects in Thapsos and Milazzese contexts (Vagnetti 1982; Peroni 1983; Bernabò Brea 1989). Aristotle (*Politics*, 7: 5–20) in fact writes that the common meal in Italy is a very old tradition and that it was Italus, king of the Oenotrians, who first introduced common meals. The creation of a standard service both in domestic and in funerary contexts is a sign of the creation of this very sort of ritual, and reflects the religious dimension of eating together, which became a distinct cultural form in the western Mediterranean. The service may even reflect a collective identity and if in its major appearance it is connected with a clan society as in the Early Bronze Age, it disappears with the individual burials of the Late Bronze and Early Iron Ages which may mark the emergence of a new social structure.

BIBLIOGRAPHY

Albanese Procelli, R.M. 1988–89. Calascibetta (Enna) – Le necropoli di Malpasso, Carcarella e Valle Coniglio. *Notizie degli Scavi*, 42–43 (supplemento 1): 161–395.

Amoroso, D. 1983. Un corredo tombale del Museo della Ceramica di Caltagirone e la fase di Thapsos nel territorio calatino. *Archivio Storico per la Sicilia Orientale*, 79: 259–77.

Bernabò Brea, L. 1983. Dall'Egeo al Tirreno all'alba dell'età micenea. Archeologia e leggende. In *Magna Grecia e Mondo Miceneo. Atti del XXII Convegno di Studi sulla Magna Grecia, Taranto, 7–11, ottobre 1982*: 9–42. Istituto per la storia e l'archeologia della Magna Grecia, Taranto.

Bernabò Brea, L. 1989. La Sicilia e le isole Eolie. In *Atti del Congresso L'Età del Bronzo in Italia nei Secoli dal XVI al XIV a.C.*: 105–21.

Bernabò Brea, L. 1990. *Pantalica: ricerche intorno all'anaktoron*. Napoli.

Bernabò Brea, L., La Piana, S. & Militello, E. 1969. Mineo (Catania): la necropoli detta del Molino della Badia: nuove tombe in contrada Madonna del Piano. *Notizie degli Scavi*, series 8, 23: 210–76.

Bietti Sestieri, A.M. 1979. I processi storici nella Sicilia orientale fra la tarda età del bronzo e gli inizi dell'età del ferro sulla base dei dati archeologici. *Atti della XXI Riunione Scientifico: Il Bronzo Finale in Italia*: 599–629. Istituto Italiano di Preistoria e Protostoria, Firenze.

Castellana, G. 1990. Un decennio di ricerche preistoriche e protostoriche nel territorio Agrigentino. *Catalogo della Mostra, Museo Archeologico Regionale, Agrigento*: 39–45.

Cultraro, M. 1988–89. *La cultura di Castelluccio nel territorio di Adrano*. Unpublished dissertation, Facoltà di Lettere e Filosofia, Università di Catania.

D'Agata, A.L. 1987. Un tipo vascolare della cultura di Thapsos: il bacino con ansa a piastra bifida. *Studi Micenei ed Egeo-Anatolici*, 26: 187–98.

Holloway, R.R. & Lukesh, S.S. 1989. Un vase castelluccien au Musée de Princeton. *L'Anthropologie*, 93 (1): 317–20.

Holloway, R.R. & Lukesh, S.S. 1991. Ustica. Report on the excavations of the Bronze Age site of Faraglioni 1990. *Archäologischer Anzeiger*, 1990 (3): 359–65.

Holloway, R.R. & Lukesh, S.S. 1992. Ustica. Report on the excavations of the Bronze Age Site of Faraglioni 1991. *Archäologischer Anzeiger*, 1991 (4): 553–60.

Maniscalco, L. 1985–86. Tipologie funebri nella Sicilia del tardo bronzo: Pantalica, Dessueri, Caltagirone. *Archivio Storico di Sicilia Orientale*, 81–82: 241–65.

Maniscalco, L. 1991. Monumental Early Bronze Age tombs at Palagonia, Sicily. Paper presented at the 93rd Annual Meeting of the Archaeological Institute of America, Chicago, Illinois. Abstract in *American Journal of Archaeology*, 96 (1992): 370–1.

Mannino, G. 1971. La tomba di Contrada Pergola. *Sicilia Archeologica*, 15: 52–6.

McConnell, B.E. 1989. The Castelluccian Village at La Muculufa (Licata, Sicily). *American Journal of Archaeology*, 93: 276–7.

McConnell, B.E. 1987. Architettura domestica e architettura funeraria nel bronzo medio. In *Atti del Convegno Storia e Archeologia della media e bassa Valle dell'Himera*: 73–9.

McConnell, B.E. 1992. The Early Bronze Age village of La Muculufa and prehistoric hut architecture in Sicily. *Americal Journal of Archaeology*, 96: 23–44.

Mollo, R. 1987. Sabucina, recenti scavi nell'area fuori le mura. Risultati e problematiche. In *Atti del Convegno Storia e Archeologia della media e bassa Valle dell'Himera*: 137–81.

Orsi, P. 1891. La necropoli sicula di Melilli (Siracusa). *Bullettino di Paletnologia Italiana*, 17: 53–76.

Orsi, P. 1892. La necropoli sicula di Castelluccio (Siracusa). *Bullettino di Paletnologia Italiana*, 18: 1–34, 67–84.

Orsi, P. 1893. Necropoli sicula presso Siracusa con vasi e bronzi micenei. *Monumenti Antichi dei Lincei*, 2: 5–36.

Orsi, P. 1895. Thapsos. *Monumenti Antichi dei Lincei*, 6: 89–150.

Orsi, P. 1899. Pantalica e Cassibile. *Monumenti Antichi dei Lincei*, 9: 33–146.

Orsi, P. 1904. Siculi e Greci a Caltagirone. *Notizie degli Scavi*: 65–98

Orsi, P. 1905. Necropoli al Molino della Badia presso Grammichele. *Bullettino di Paletnologia Italiana*, 31: 96–133.

Orsi, P. 1913. Necropoli sicule di Pantalica e Monte Dessueri. *Monumenti Antichi dei Lincei*, 21: 301–408.

Orsi, P. 1930–31. Abitazioni e sepolcri siculi di Biancavilla (Catania) entro caverne di lava. *Bullettino di Paletnologia Italiana*, 50–51: 134–47.

Peroni, R. 1983. Presenze micenee e forme socioeconomiche nell'Italia protostorica. In *Magna Grecia e Mondo Miceneo. Atti del XXII Convegno di Studi sulla Magna Grecia, Taranto, 7–11, ottobre 1982*: 211–84. Istituto per la storia e l'archeologia della Magna Grecia, Taranto.

Procelli, E. 1981. Il complesso tombale di contrada Paolina ed il problema dei rapporti tra Sicilia e Malta nella prima età del bronzo. *Bollettino d'Arte*, 9: 83–110.

Rathje, A. 1983. A banquet service from the Latin city of Ficana. *Analecta Romana Instituti Danici*, 12: 7–29.

Rotroff, S. 1992. The missing krater and the Hellenistic symposium. Paper presented at the 94th Annual Meeting of the Archaeological Institute of America, New Orleans, Louisiana. Abstract in *American Journal of Archaeology*, 97 (1993): 340–1.

Schimitt Pantel, P. 1985.   Banquet et cité greque. Quelques questions suscitees par les recherches recentes. *Mélanges de l'École Française de Rome, Antiquité*, 97: 135–58.

Smith, M.F.J. 1985. Toward an economic interpretation of ceramics: relating vessel size and shape to use. In Nelson, B.A. (ed.), *Decoding Prehistoric Ceramics*: 254–309. Southern Illinois University Press, Carbondale.

Vagnetti, L. 1982. Quindici anni di studi e ricerche sulle relazioni tra il mondo egeo e l'Italia protostorica. In Vagnetti, L. (ed.), *Magna Grecia e Mondo Miceneo. Nuovi documenti. XXII Convegno di Studi sulla Magna Grecia, Taranto, 7–11, ottobre 1982*: 9–40. Istituto per la storia e l'archeologia della Magna Grecia, Taranto.

Valenza Mele, N. 1982.   Da Micene ad Omero: dalla phiale al lebete. *Annali dell'Istituto Orientale di Napoli*, 4: 97–133.

Voza, G. 1972.   Thapsos. Primi risultati delle più recenti ricerche. *Atti della XIV Riunione Scientifica in Puglia, 13–16 ottobre 1970*: 175–205. Istituto Italiano di Preistoria e Protostoria, Firenze.

Voza, G. 1973. Thapsos: resoconto sulle campagne di scavo del 1970–71. *Atti della XV Riunione Scientifica, Verona-Trento, 27–29 ottobre 1972*: 133–57. Istituto Italiano di Preistoria e Protostoria, Firenze.

Voza, G. 1976–77.   L'attività della Soprintendenza alle Antichità della Sicilia Orientale, parte II. *Kokalos*, 22–23: 562–8

Zevi, F. 1977.   Alcuni aspetti della necropoli di Castel di Decima. *La Parola del Passato*, 175: 241–73.

Spatial Analysis of a Castelluccian Settlement in Early Bronze Age Sicily[1]

Brian E. McConnell and Bruce W. Bevan

In 1985, R. Ross Holloway presented a general picture of the Castelluccian culture which is found across the eastern two-thirds of Sicily during the Early Bronze Age. He identified a fundamental social difference between a farm (*fattoria*) and a village (*villaggio*) – the farm is a settlement for a single family which works the immediate territory, while a village is a settlement for a number of families each with a distinct identity (Holloway 1985: 73). Holloway, furthermore, described the emergence of the village-centre in Early Bronze Age Sicily as an outgrowth of religious practices rather than as a political or economic phenomenon. Recent fieldwork at La Muculufa now leads us to see the emergence of the village-centre as a matter of defining public and private areas. A more appropriate title for this paper might be: "This land is your land, this land is my land" or "Good fences make good neighbours in Castelluccian Sicily."

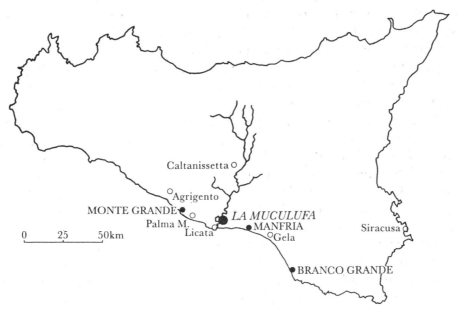

Fig. 1 Sicily

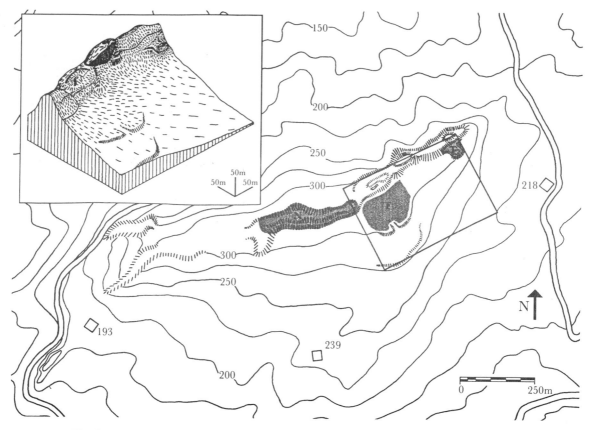

Fig. 2   La Muculufa with excavation-zones F (Field), N (Necropolis) and T (Terrace)

The site of La Muculufa is distributed across a rocky crest located roughly 20km inland along the Salso river valley (fig. 1). It includes a village, a necropolis, and what may be interpreted as an open-air sanctuary (fig. 2). A series of calibrated radiocarbon dates from the open-air sanctuary and from the village date the site to the middle and later third millennium BC (Holloway 1985: 77; McConnell 1992).[2] The architectural remains discovered in the village show that it consisted of round and oblong hut-structures with stone foundations and superstructures in wattle and daub set on a wooden frame. The buildings seem to have been constructed on terraces which were oriented roughly at right-angles to the slope and which utilised natural outcrops in the rock. At least three building-phases can be identified at the site, and the possibility that structures were built and re-built on a seasonal basis should not be ruled out (McConnell 1992).

A major goal of the project is to determine the general layout of the village and how its builders adapted the crest to their specific needs. Exploration of the village has been hampered by the fact that much of it lies beneath 80cm of ploughed soil and further accumulations sometimes totalling over 1.5m in depth. Only in the easternmost sector of the village, where traces of prehistoric dry-wall masonry can be seen, is the ground-surface undisturbed. In order to overcome this situation, a geophysical survey was performed across the central area of the village in June of 1990 (see Bevan [n.d.] for information on methodology and techniques employed in this survey). The geophysical survey used a Geonics Ltd. EM38 electromagnetic induction meter to measure the soil's electrical conductivity and magnetic susceptibility.[3] It was performed over an area measuring 65m east-west by 45m north-south in what appeared to be the centre of the village sector (fig. 3). Surveys were also performed in smaller strips to the east and west of this area. Initial evaluation of the survey data indicated that a distinctive change was to be found within the earth, although in the small rectangular area surveyed at the northeastern corner of the main grid the distinct areas of high and low conductivity did not seem to correlate with an observed pattern of stones which seemed to indicate a hut.

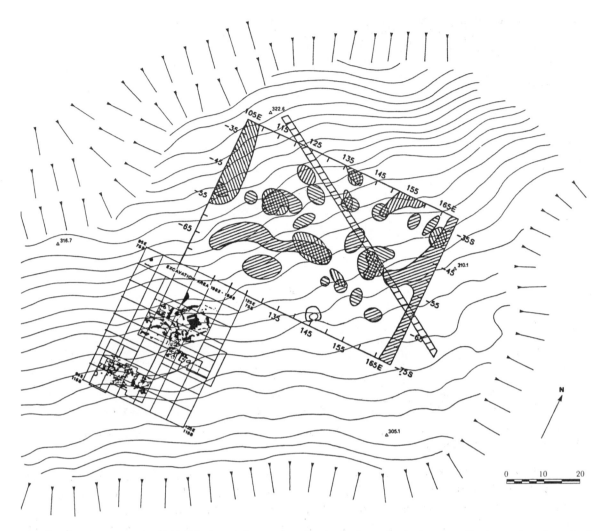

Fig. 3   FIELD zone with 1982–89 excavation area and principal geophysical survey (horizontal and vertical lines indicate high conductivity/susceptibility, diagonal lines indicate low conductivity/susceptibility)

By the end of the 1990 season it was still uncertain what the geophysical pattern of a hut might be. If the hut depression were filled with earth containing few stones, high conductivity and high susceptibility would be expected. Pavements on the hut floors, probably too thin to be detected with a geophysical survey, might nevertheless give an anomaly of high magnetic susceptibility for ceramic fragments and burnt earth likely to be found in association. It was concluded that one or two excavations should be tried on each type of geophysical anomaly and that it might be worthwhile to check one of the areas where only conductivity or only susceptibility indicated an anomaly.

Trenches were opened during a brief excavation campaign the following summer around two anomalies with low susceptibility and conductivity.[4] The area between these anomalies (about 10m or roughly the area equivalent to the width of the terrace of Huts 2 and 3) had indicated an anomaly of high susceptibility/conductivity, and here another excavation area was opened. Further up-slope, in an area of high susceptibility and conductivity another trench was opened. All of the trenches were connected in the course of the excavation and opened to the widest area possible given the available time and manpower (fig. 4).

The prehistoric architectural remains brought to light were of a notable consistency (fig. 5). In the lowermost area of the excavation a wall roughly 6.0m long was found running from southwest to northeast; it separates portions F182 and F183. Constructed in a Castelluccian technique with large stones set vertically in the soil together with smaller stones and traces of gypsum, it seems to have served as a fencing or small terrace wall. At

Fig. 4   View from the crest east across the FIELD excavation zone toward trenches excavated in 1991. 1982–89 excavation area in lower right

the eastern end of the wall there were found several *corni fittili*, a fire-dog and a large quantity of Castelluccian ceramics. The area indicated by an anomaly of high susceptibility/conductivity in portion F190 proved to be the poorly preserved floor of an oval hut defined by bits of terracotta pavement and the rough outline of a stone wall-socle. Very consistent remains of a hut were noted also in portion F181 at a depth of 1.50m beneath the ground-surface out of range of the EM38. In the eastern part of portion F200 a stratigraphic sounding carried to a depth of 1.71m (the 'Test' sondage) revealed four surfaces of beaten earth and gypsum bits. Over the lowermost stratum, there lay a thick stratum of burned soil with many ceramic fragments.

In addition to prehistoric remains, the 1991 campaign found further evidence for occupation of the site in historic times. Sherds of Greek date, including a fragment of Late Corinthian II ware, were found outside of a stratified context. The most surprising discoveries, however, were two skeletons set in pit-graves dug into the prehistoric levels (fig. 6). One of them had been covered with thin gypsum slabs, while the other seemed to lack them (although they may have been removed by ploughing). Both burials were adult inhumations set out straight on their right flank with the face oriented roughly toward the east, and they have been identified as Muslims of medieval date for their lack of grave goods, orientation towards the Mecca and comparison with similar burials elsewhere in Sicily (Castellana & McConnell 1990). Discovery of such burials at La Muculufa forces the excavator to re-evaluate the extent of the medieval settlement discussed in prior communications (McConnell 1990). There may, in fact, have been a greater, more stable settlement at La Muculufa than the fortified outcrop previously posited.

Re-evaluation of the survey data in light of the results of the 1991 excavation produced the following findings. The most distinctive anomaly within the excavation was the area of unusually low magnetic susceptibility and electrical conductivity near 120E 50S. Excavation there in portion F172 revealed a concentration of large boulders and an outcrop of bedrock. The test sondage there suggests that the unexcavated susceptibility

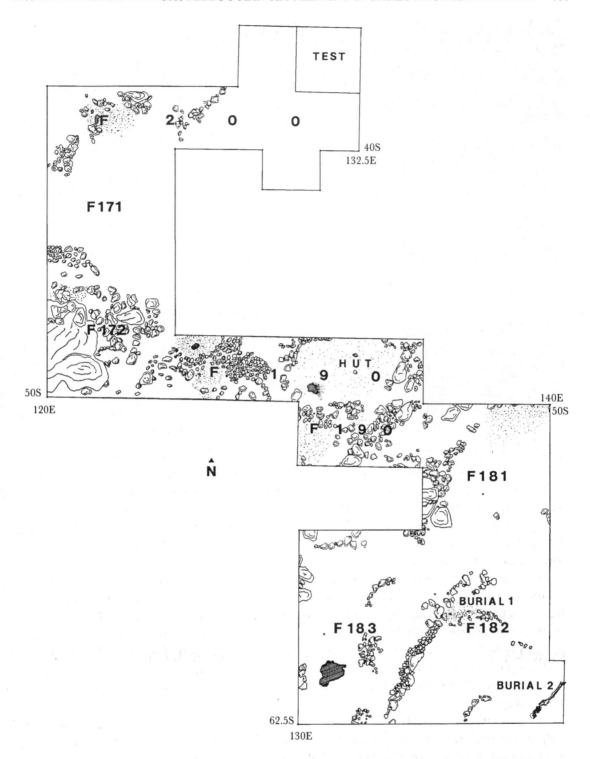

Fig. 5   Plan of trenches excavated in 1991

low which forms a line heading toward the northeast corner of the survey area is likely also to be a dense concentration of stone, probably a terrace wall. The large stones found around 55S 130–135E may possibly be part of a terrace wall as well. The linear susceptibility low indicates the wall is near or slightly downhill from the area of stones, although the geophysical evidence is weak. Despite the distinct northeast trend for the rock alignments and the tendency for some susceptibility anomalies to be aligned in that direction, however, clusters of small rocks would not have been detected by the survey. It is possible that the floor surface with few stones found in F190 correlates with the susceptibility high that is there. On the other hand, the deep deposit found at F181 has no susceptibility anomaly. The feature in area F181 lies in an area of distinctly low

Fig. 6   Portion F182 with medieval Burial 1 along line of Castelluccian wall

conductivity. A test of the back-dirt pile also showed conductivity to be lower there than usual. While it is possible that the archaeological strata can be low in conductivity, they will generally be expected to be high in conductivity because of the greater amount of organic matter they contain. The conductivity is a bit of a puzzle here and the susceptibility data appear to be clearer at this particular site. Neither conductivity nor susceptibility indicate any significant anomaly at the test pit. The medieval inhumation graves were not detected either.

In light of the excavation findings, a new map of the geophysical anomalies was produced indicating a line of at least five structures to the east of excavation portion F200 (fig. 7). This line is roughly parallel to the terraces in portions F80 and F130 found in earlier excavations. While the anomalies themselves are not of the same size, they do not seem to indicate structures of particularly diverse dimensions. It seems likely, given the stratigraphy and sequence in the excavated portions, that there are many more structures than the anomalies indicate and that their disposition is far more complex than it appears on the map.

Analysis of the spatial arrangement of the prehistoric structures at La Muculufa in comparison with that at other Early Bronze Age sites in Sicily is useful in determining the development of prototypes for the kind of structured settlements which appear at coastal trading emporia such as Thapsos and at urban centres of the interior such as Sabucina (Doonan 1993). The alignment of Hut Nos 2 and 3 (lower) and the general arrangement of geophysical anomalies suggests that the village possessed a rational design. Although the location and dimensions of the terraces were determined in part by the disposition of natural rock outcrops, a degree of planning is evident also in their very adaptation to the terrain. This reflects the same approach which adapted the village, the open-air sanctuary and the necropolis to the crest itself. Other evidence of planned organisation in the settlement may be seen in paths which linked its component zones, including evidence for a rising gravel path across the village, three paths to the necropolis with chamber tombs set along them up the southern face of the crest and cuttings in the rock for a major path from the prehistoric necropolis to the open-air sanctuary.[5]

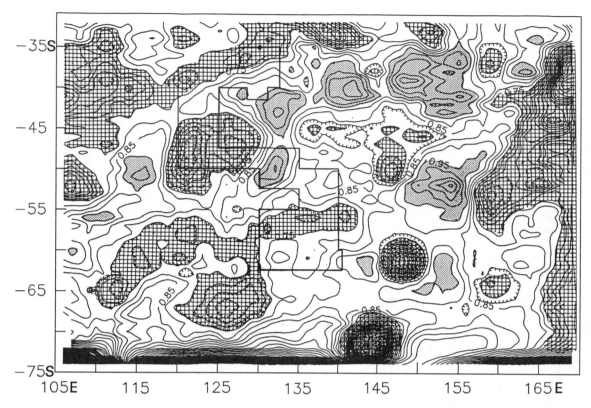

Fig. 7   Interpreted survey-map of smoothed susceptibility anomalies (0.05 ppt contours) with hut-structures (dot-pattern) and rock outcrops and/or terrace walls (hatch-pattern); outline of 1991 excavation area also shown

A rational arrangement of structures has been noted at other Castelluccian settlements. At Branco Grande, a coastal site near the ancient Greek city of Camarina, 17 structures enclosed by a fortification wall within an area measuring 120 x 100m were seen to have been arranged in rows (Orsi 1910: 168; Orsi estimated that originally there had been between 30 and 40 structures here). At Settefarine (Gela), the poorly preserved structures of a Castelluccian settlement seem to have been distributed in groups on hillocks (Orsi 1910: 178). At Manfria (Gela) in an area measuring 60 x 45m nine huts were found in two groups enclosed by a series of hearths in what has been described as a farm compound (Orlandini 1962; cf. Holloway 1985: 73). A series of compounds may be represented by three groups of huts found in contrada Feudo Nobile (Gela) (Adamesteanu 1960).[6]

The structures at La Muculufa themselves are among the larger known in Castelluccian Sicily. A settlement covering an area of about three hectares at S. Croce near Comiso presented at least 11 elliptical huts of which only two were of dimensions similar to those at La Muculufa (Hut 2 measured 7.5 x 7.0m and Hut 3 7.5 x 6.0m; Orsi 1926). At Branco Grande the huts were notably smaller, between 2.0 and 4.2m in maximum dimension, while at neighbouring Poggio Biddini (Acate) the diameters of three Castelluccian structures were between 3.0 and 3.5m (Di Stefano 1976–77; 1984). Hut 9 at Manfria which measured 9.0 x 3.25m seems exceptional but it may find an analogue at La Muculufa in a structure indicated by a large anomaly roughly between 149–157 East and 47–57 South of high magnetic susceptibility and electrical conductivity. Despite the limitations of interpreting the survey data from La Muculufa outlined above, one may see cautiously a general arrangement of small anomalies of high magnetic susceptibility around this larger anomaly. There is, furthermore, a clear trend toward increasing size in structure from the phase of Hut 4 to that of Huts 2 and 3 (lower).

An interesting hypothesis suggested by the data from La Muculufa is that increasing population and settlement density may have led to greater concern for the definition of domestic and personal space both among the living and the dead. The increase in the scale of construction from Hut 4 to Huts 2 and 3 (lower) seems to indicate that the creation of larger buildings forced greater care in the use of space and perhaps greater need for its identification. A series of *corni fittili* were found to have been set around Hut 3 (lower) and perhaps also around Hut 2. They were of different types, and they include one with a greenstone pendant set into the tip and types with arms or wings (*ali*). It is likely that these objects, distinctive already for their form, were also distinguished by colour, inasmuch as traces of red paint were found on the *corno fittile* discovered during the 1991 excavation campaign in area F183. Perhaps they served as markers to indicate the land and buildings of a clan or nuclear family, if not specific individuals, as private property.

Concurrent with this notion of land-use is the tendency in Castelluccian settlements, including La Muculufa, to mark off larger areas by means of stone fences. By no means is this a phenomenon exclusive to the Early Bronze Age. Areas bounded by ditches or fences are known from the Neolithic period on in the Tyrrhenian region both on a large and on a small scale. Best known are the areas enclosed by ditches of the Neolithic period in peninsular Italy on the Tavoliere plain (Tinè 1983). In Sicily, bounded areas of the Neolithic and the Copper Age have been found at Stentinello, Serra del Palco and Piano Vento di Palma di Montechiaro (Castellana 1984–85; La Rosa 1984–85; Tinè 1961). Early Bronze Age settlements with long fences have been found in Castelluccian Sicily at Torricella (Ramacca), Valsavoia (Lentini), Baravitalla (Ragusa) and Monte Grande (Palma di Montechiaro) (Castellana 1990; Di Stefano 1983; Frasca *et al.* 1975; Spigo 1987). E. Procelli (1991) has suggested that these fenced areas may be associated with emergent social groups formed especially through contact with the contemporary megalithic temple culture of the Maltese islands.

A similar argument for the definition of family property may be made for the over 250 tombs which crowd the necropolis above the settlement at La Muculufa (Parker 1985). The original number of tombs is likely to have been higher, but it can no longer be determined because of the continuous collapse of the crest; neither is it possible to determine, for the same reason, the original configuration of the tombs within the necropolis, nor whether divisions among the chamber tombs in the necropolis correspond in some way to divisions within the settlement. It is clear, however, that Castelluccian chamber tombs were used for multiple burials and that the use of crevices as well as chamber tombs for burial at La Muculufa suggests that space in the necropolis was at a premium (McConnell *et al.* 1990).[7]

Economic specialisation may have played a role in the definition of space within Castelluccian communities (Tusa 1983: 307ff., 353). The precise function of any of the hut structures at La Muculufa has yet to be determined; however, an interesting hypothesis has arisen out of the study by Maniscalco of ceramic materials from Hut 2. This structure contained an extraordinary number of ceramics – roughly 150 separate vessels. There is little variation in the vessel shapes (they are restricted to the low pedestal vase (*frutteria*), the dipper (*attingitoio*), and pithoi) and the vessel decoration also appears in a restricted series of variations. Perhaps this hut served as the workshop and/or display area for the products of one or more potters. Already, the hand of a single artist has been identified in connection with ceramics from the sanctuary (Lukesh 1991), and it may be possible to do the same here. Several personal effects were found within the building, including a shell necklace.

The definition of common or non-private space, on the other hand, may lie in Castelluccian religion through the creation of a sanctuary with greater than local significance. Evidence for an open-air sanctuary on a natural terrace at the eastern end of the crest is circumstantial but convincing. It is based upon the discovery of high-quality Castelluccian ceramics together with bones predominantly of sheep or goat and charcoal all tumbled within a deep fill below poorly preserved sections of terrace walling (Cruz-Uribe 1991; Holloway *et al.* 1988).

Although functional aspects of Castelluccian religion are almost as elusive as its spiritual content, the remains at La Muculufa seem to indicate that it involved feasting in a panoramic setting. The view from the sanctuary toward the east focusses upon the distant cone of Mount Etna, and the crest itself is visible to the surrounding region for kilometres. It seems likely that the strangely attractive form of La Muculufa's craggy crest, and the availability of fresh water both from the Salso river and from temporary springs which are known to have flowed out of the crest's crevices drew people to settle there and to focus their religious activities on its eastern terrace. Similarly, the crest could have drawn participants in these activities from surrounding communities on special occasions.[8]

Further research is necessary in order to elucidate these preliminary remarks. It is possible, nevertheless, to state with certainty that the aesthetic aspect of the crest of La Muculufa was paramount to its significance and that the physical form of the crest in part determined the way in which the Castelluccian settlement grew. The geophysical survey in itself provides the direction for future excavation and a limited outline of a possible settlement configuration which includes larger and smaller structures in an apparently organised pattern. By excavating more of these structures we may hope to refine our assessment of the impact of the physical landscape upon human geography in the Castelluccian Early Bronze Age.

NOTES

1   The information presented in this report has been published in an up-dated form in McConnell, B.E., *et al.* 1995. *La Muculufa II, Excavation and Survey 1988–1991, The Castelluccian Village and Other Areas.* Publications d'Histoire de l'Art et d'Archéologie de l'Université Catholique de Louvain, LXXV. Providence, Rhode Island and Louvain-la-Neuve. See also McConnell, B.E. 1993–94. "La Muculufa (Butera, CL). Indagini di scavo e ricerche dal 1988 al 1991." *Kokalos*, 39–40: 771–82; and Holloway, R.R., *et al.* 1996. "La Muculufa: un centro sul fiume Salso e il suo vaggio di contatti." In *L'Antica Età del Bronzo. Atti del Congresso di Viareggio 9–15 gennaio 1995*: 291–303. Firenze.

The present paper was presented as part of the symposium "Social Dynamics of the Prehistoric Central Mediterranean" held at the Fifty-Seventh Annual Meeting of the Society for American Archaeology (Pittsburgh, Pennsylvania, April 8–12, 1992). Research at La Muculufa has been performed as a collaborative project with the Superintendency for Cultural and Environmental Resources of Agrigento and Caltanissetta, Sicily. The authors wish to thank the Superintendent, Dott.ssa G. Fiorentini, and the project director for the Superintendency, Dott.ssa R. Panvini, for their encouragement of this project, as well as the Department of Cultural and Environmental Resources of the Sicilian Regional government for financing the excavation and conservation of excavated materials. Support for the mission to La Muculufa has been provided by the Center for Old World Archaeology and Art, Brown University; special thanks are owed to Prof. R. Ross Holloway and Prof. Rudolf Winkes. Special appreciation is acknowledged to the notaio Dott. G. Navarra for his encouragement, as well as to the Associazione Archeologica Licatese and to its president Arch. P. Meli for help in many aspects of the project. Without the gracious hospitality of the Sig.ra Angela Guido and members of her family, fieldwork would have been impossible. Thanks are owed also to L. Merra and K. Klaiber for their work on the graphic illustrations in this report.

2   Two samples have now been calibrated to the middle of the third millennium BC from Hut 3 (upper) – 3960 ± 70 BP calibrated to 2577–2404 cal.BC (one sigma) – and Hut 3 (lower) – 3990 ± 60 BP calibrated to 2584–2463 cal.BC (one sigma) (A. Long, communication 3 January 1992).

3   Magnetic susceptibility quantifies how well the earth conducts a magnetic field; it is the magnetic analogue of electrical conductivity. In general, rock is rather poor as both an electrical and as a magnetic conductor, while soil is usually a good conductor of both electricity and magnetism. As an additional control an electrical resistivity sounding was performed in one area where there was a high conductivity anomaly. The survey was performed by Dr Bruce Bevan with the assistance of N.E. Peterson and B.E. McConnell. The data were smoothed by least squares calculations and plotted as a contour map by commercially available computer programs.

4   G. Profumo served as excavation assistant and photographer for the Superintendency, and workmen and employees of the impresa V. Ortega (Licata, AG) completed the excavation, cleaning and restoration with enthusiasm and efficiency. Participants in the university mission included Dr B.E. McConnell, Dott.ssa Laura Maniscalco (Soprintendenza ai BB.CC.AA. di Catania), Peter Barrett, Sheila Jay, Owen Doonan (graduate student, Brown University), Pietro Lucchesi (student, University of Palermo), and Dott.ssa Angela Rovida.

5   Similar rock-cut paths are found in association with several Middle Bronze Age tombs near Caltagirone (Amoroso 1987) and at the Early Bronze Age necropolis along the Coste dei Santa Febbronia at Palagonia (Maniscalco 1991).

6   Acknowledgement for this reference is owed to Owen Doonan.

7   It is possible that bones were transferred from the chamber tombs to rock crevice ossuaries such as the one discussed in this publication in order to create space for later burials. Recycling of space in this manner is as much a by-product of crowding as it is a sign of cultural continuity.

8   The landscape at La Muculufa may be compared to locations in North Africa; cf. Louis (1973). Acknowledgement for this reference is owed to James Lewthwaite.

BIBLIOGRAPHY

Adamesteanu, D. 1960.   *Notizie degli Scavi*: 223.

Amoroso, D. 1987.   Una testimonianza di viabilità preistorica: la strada delle tombe nella necropolis della Montagna di Caltagirone. In *Viabilità antica in Sicilia: Atti del Terzo Convegno di Studi, Riposto, Sicilia*: 15–24.

Bevan, B. n.d.   A geophysical survey at La Muculufa. Unpublished report, 17 July 1990.

Castellana, G. 1984–85.   Ricerche nel territorio di Palma di Montechiaro e nel territorio Favara. *Kokalos*, 30–31: 521–7.

Castellana, G. 1987.   Il villaggio neolitico di Piano Vento. *Atti della Riunione Scientifica dell'Istituto Italiano di Pre- e Protostoria*, 26: 793–9.

Castellana, G. 1990.   *Un decennio di ricerche preistoriche e protostoriche nel territorio agrigentino.*

Castellana, G. & McConnell, B.E. 1990.   Work in the countryside of Late Antiquity and Medieval Sicily. *American Journal of Archaeology*, 94: 301.

Cruz-Uribe, L. 1991.   In Holloway, R.R. (ed.), *La Muculufa, the Early Bronze Age Sanctuary: the Early Bronze Age village (excavations of 1982 and 1983)*. Providence.

Di Stefano, G. 1976–77.   Saggi a Poggio Biddini sul Dirillo. *Kokalos*, 22–23: 647–50.

Di Stefano, G. 1983.   *Cava d'Ispica: recenti scavi e scoperte.* Modica.

Di Stefano, G. 1984.   *Piccola guida delle stazioni preistoriche degli Iblei.* Ragusa.

Doonan, O. 1993.   *Domestic Architecture of the Sicilian Bronze Age: a study of social transformation and architectural innovation.* Unpublished Ph.D. dissertation, Brown University.

Frasca, M.F., Messina, F., Palermo, D. & Procelli, E. 1975.   Ramacca (Catania): saggi di scavo nel villaggio preistorico di contrada Torricella. *Notizie di Scavi*: 557–85.

Holloway, R.R. 1985.   Scavi archeologici alla Muculufa e premesse per lo studio della cultura castellucciana. *Atti della seconda giornata di studi sull'archeologia Licatese e della zona della bassavalle dell'Himera, 19 gennaio, 1985*: 69–90.

Holloway, R.R., Joukowsky, M.S. & Lukesh, S.S. 1988.   Mining La Muculufa. *Archaeology*, 41: 40–7.

La Rosa, V. 1984–85.   L'insediamento preistorico di Serra del Palco in territorio di Milena. *Kokalos*, 30–31: 475–82.

La Rosa, V. 1987.   Un nuovo insediamento neolitico a Serra del Palco di Milena (CL). *Atti della Riunione Scientifica dell'Istituto Italiano di Pre- e Protostoria*, 26: 801–8.

Louis, A. 1973.   La vallée du Dra au milieu du XXᵉ siècle (Maroc saharien). In *Maghreb et Sahara: études géographiques offertes à Jean Despois*: 163 ff. Paris.

Lukesh, S.S. 1991.   In Holloway, R.R. (ed.), *La Muculufa, the Early Bronze Age Sanctuary: the Early Bronze Age village (excavations of 1982 and 1983)*. Providence.

Maniscalco, L. 1991.   Monumental Early Bronze Age tombs at Palagonia, Sicily. Paper presented to the 93rd Annual Meeting of the Archaeological Institute of America.

McConnell, B.E. 1990.   L'insediamento medievale alla Muculufa (Butera, CL). *Atti del Convegno "L'Età di Federico II nella Sicilia Centro-meridionale: Città, Monumenti, Reperti", Gela 8–9 dicembre 1990.*

McConnell, B.E. 1992.   The Early Bronze Age village of La Muculufa and prehistoric hut architecture in Sicily. *American Journal of Archaeology*, 96: 23–44.

McConnell, B.E., Morico, G., Corrain, C. & Capitanio, M. 1990.   La Muculufa (Butera, Caltanissetta), stazione siciliana dell'Età del Bronzo Antico. *Archivio per l'Antropologia e la Etnologia*, 120: 115–50.

Orlandini, P. 1962.   *Il villaggio preistorico di Manfria presso Gela.* Palermo.

Orsi, P. 1910.   Due villaggi del primo periodo siculo. *Bullettino di Paletnologia Italiana*, 36: 158–93.

Orsi, P 1926.   Villaggio e sepolcreto sicolo alle Sante Croci presso Comiso (Siracusa). *Bullettino di Paletnologia Italiana*, 46: 5–17.

Parker, G. 1985.   The Early Bronze Age chamber tombs at La Muculufa. *Revue des Archéologues e Historiens d'Arte de Louvain*, 18: 9–33.

Procelli, E. 1991.   Aspetti religiosi e apporti trasmarini nella cultura di Castelluccio. *Journal of Mediterranean Studies*, 2: 252–66.

Spigo, U. 1987.   L'attività della Soprintendenza Archeologica a Lentini negli anni 1977–1985. In *Un trentannio di indagini nel territorio di Lentini antica*: 34. Lentini.

Tinè, S. 1961.   Notizie preliminari su recenti scavi nel villaggio neolitico di Stentinello. *Archivio Storico Siracusano*, 7: 113–18.

Tinè, S. 1983.   *Passo di Corvo e la civiltà neolitica del Tavoliere.* Sagep, Genova.

Tusa, S. 1983.   *La Sicilia nella preistoria.* Sellerio, Palermo.

The Walled Bronze Age Settlement of Coppa Nevigata, Manfredonia and the Development of Craft Specialisation in Southeastern Italy

Alberto Cazzella and Maurizio Moscoloni

At the beginning of the second millennium BC an interesting phenomenon occurs in southeast Italy: the movement of settlements towards the coast. This attraction to the coast is probably connected with the possibility of exchanging goods by sea. That this form of exchange was already practised has been proven by the affinity in the production of some artefacts and by artefacts themselves, and also by the circulation of some insular raw materials such as obsidian. But a specialised interest in the exchange of goods is the principal factor which seems to have determined the existence of these kinds of coastal Bronze Age settlements. Moreover, the presence of such coastal settlements tends to persist over many centuries and influence a process of transformation over time. These phenomena, brought to light some years ago, are difficult to understand fully due to the lack of extensively excavated stratified sites.

EVIDENCE OF CRAFT SPECIALISATION AT COPPA NEVIGATA

The extensive research carried out at Coppa Nevigata (fig. 1) since 1955 (Puglisi 1975; 1982; Cazzella & Moscoloni 1987; 1993) offers us the most information about such settlements. Even here, however, the data directly connected to the earlier moment (Proto-Apennine B) are very scarce due to the limited dimensions of the deep trenches. It is not clear if at this first phase the settlement had been fortified, however, in a hut destroyed by fire there are the initial signs of an activity which will be developed later: the extraction of purple-dye from *Murex*. Evidence of this activity, as in the case of the contemporary Minoan culture (Faure 1991; Reese 1987), consists of heaps of crushed *Murex* shells, a treatment which does not seem to correspond well with an alimentary use. The settlement at Coppa Nevigata was situated near a lagoon but due to its low degree of salinity, as revealed by

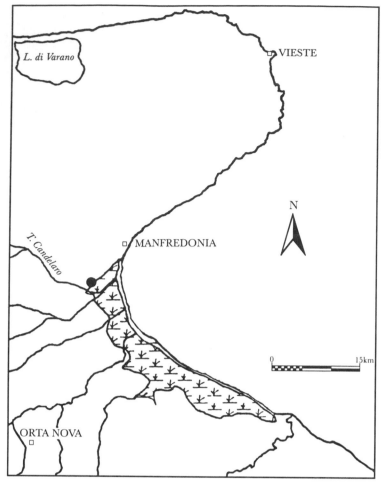

Fig. 1   Coppa Nevigata (circle) and the early lagoon south of the Gargano promontory

Fig. 2   Coppa Nevigata. The first defensive wall (Protoapennine B), with a postern

Fig. 3 Coppa Nevigata. A square 'hearth' close to the Protoapennine defensive wall, fallen into disuse

oxygen isotope analysis (Deith 1987), the *Murex* must have been collected along the sea coast. From the evidence available it is very hard to determine whether this was a specialised activity, but immediately afterwards the settlement was fortified by the construction of a 5m thick wall (fig. 2), a feature indicative of a certain complexity in social structure. In the segment excavated, about 40m long, 3 postern gates and a gate were found. The gate is flanked by two towers, each of them with an internal non-dwelling room and a stairway to reach the top (figs. 5–7). The presence of these non-dwelling rooms near the gate apparently with no external slits does not seem to have been connected with defensive needs but rather served for a routine control on the passage of goods and people to the settlement areas. This hypothesis – difficult to verify – seems to indicate a complex model of social organisation on different levels and with forms of economic and political centralisation. Internal social differences are already evidenced from burial uses in sites near Coppa Nevigata (Cipolloni Sampò 1991–92), but the situation proposed in this case seems to be particularly complex. This construction effort seems to indicate a structured community with a strong interest in defending the chosen site with its commercial qualities. The lagoon itself could have had a defensive function and at the same time provided easy access to the sea.

The pottery production shows some affinity with that of Dalmatia (Early Podusje culture according to Covic (1989) or Dinara I according to Govedarica (1989; Cazzella & Moscoloni 1995)). It is probable that in this phase maritime exchange took place with that area, in addition to the Italian Adriatic coast. Foreign contacts were already established by the period immediately preceding this (the early phase of the Cetina culture and the Early Helladic III: cf. Maran 1987; Rutter 1982). Some of these contacts may also have involved real movements of small groups from the eastern Adriatic or Ionian coast which reached the Aeolian Islands and even Malta (Bernabò Brea 1985).

Like other coastal settlements of southern Italy, Coppa Nevigata could have constituted a diversified centre in relation to the pastoral and agricultural communities of the interior, acting as an intermediary in contacts with the exterior. We do not know if metallurgy was permanently practised in these coastal settlements of southeast Italy, as was the case with those in Calabria (Capo Piccolo: Bianco & Marino 1991–92) and the Aeolian islands (Lipari

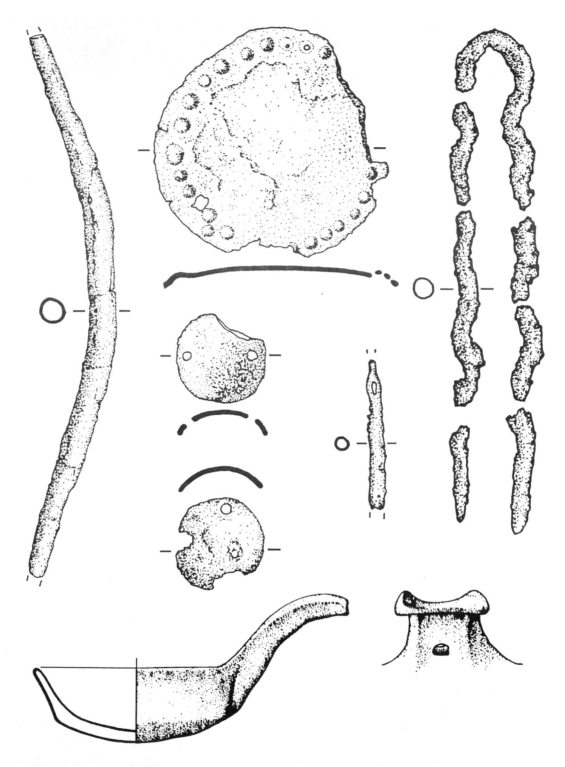

Fig. 4 Coppa Nevigata. Bronze (above) and pottery (below) items from the Early Apennine burial area

acropolis: Bernabò Brea & Cavalier 1980: 244), but a stone mould for an axe as well as 50 axes in bronze found at an interior site, Canne (Nava 1984: 105, n. 40), seem to indicate that the internal communities were able to work the metal, maybe with the presence of itinerant metalworkers, and to accumulate metal artefacts even if copper and tin had to be brought from far away.

The first wall fell into disuse around 1500 BC and a number of ovens or hearths were laid near it (Early Apennine). One of the better preserved examples is, however, different from normal 'bread ovens' due to its quadrangular shape and to the fact that it is delimited

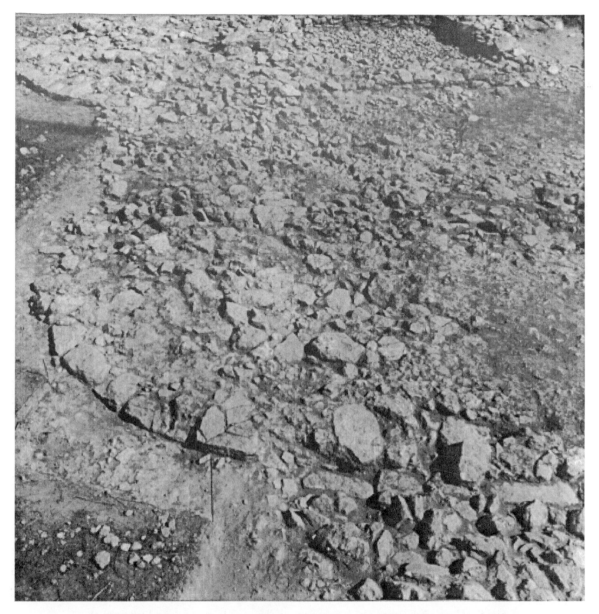

Fig. 5 Coppa Nevigata. The Protoapennine towers, re-used during the Late Apennine, viewed from west

by stones placed edgewise (fig. 3). In addition, it seems that very high temperatures were reached in it with respect to a normal hearth and we can hypothesise that some sort of non-domestic activity, which cannot be defined, took place there.

This space was then utilised as a burial ground (fig. 4). The presence of a burial ground within the living area brings out the differences in burial customs between Coppa Nevigata and adjacent non-coastal sites (with their kin group tombs in hypogea or dolmens). It could somehow indicate, in contrast with the surrounding world, the concept of unity of the community of Coppa Nevigata, without emphasising internal kin groups (Cazzella 1992). Other coastal settlements have highly collective (not necessarily egalitarian) funerary sites too, even if funerary rites differ from Coppa Nevigata (Manaccore natural cave, Trinitapoli 'catacomb': Baumgärtel 1951; Recchia 1993; Tunzi Sisto 1991–92).

In the 14th century BC (Late Apennine), a new boundary wall was built. This new defensive structure is quite complex and the techniques used in its construction were quite elaborate, with the use of selected and semi-processed blocks for the outer face, even though it seems rather improbable that specialists were involved in its planning and construction. They re-used the now blocked towers near the gate (fig. 5).

It seems that after a brief period the defensive wall was no longer utilised, even though we cannot establish, due to erosion of the artificial hill, if another wall had been built. Near

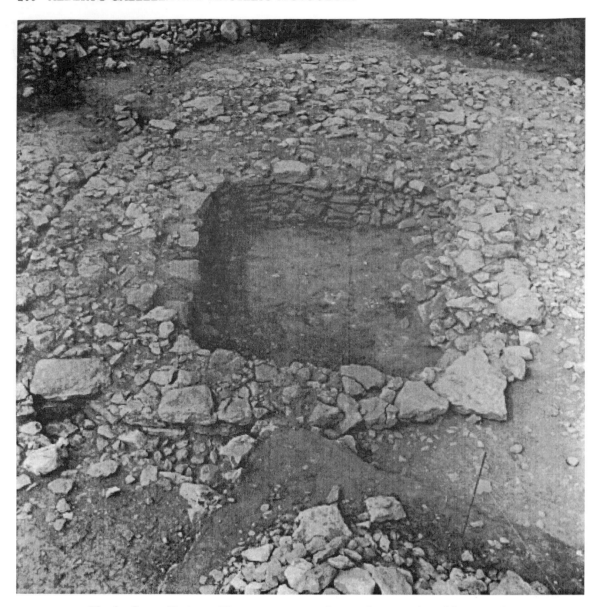

Fig. 6   Coppa Nevigata. The western tower close to the gate, viewed from south

the inner face of the wall on the two sides of the disused gate were built a series of circular non-dwelling structures approximately 2m in diameter (fig. 8). Their function remains problematic, but whether they were used for storage or for some other sort of activity, their concentration presumes some form of accumulation of goods or specialised production. In the area near the gate, signs of an intense and continuous use of fire is evident, in addition to a particular frequency of tools made from bone. In the same area great quantities of *Murex* remains and many turtle skeletons have been found. It is rather difficult to define what kind of activities were carried out here, apart from the probable extraction of purple-dye, but they do not seem to be normal domestic activities. The presence of a space inside the settlement area with specialised characteristics (occupying a larger area than the earlier one with the ovens or hearths: more than 50m along the disused wall) may not have been the result of a spontaneous event but may derive from the choices of the same elite which controlled, or made others control, the access to the settlement area.

The Late Bronze Age (Subapennine) provides us with greater evidence of specialised activities. Copper metallurgy is documented by shapeless lumps of metal, a fragment of ingot and a stone mould; the traces of iron working found during the early 1900s excavations (Mosso 1908: 311–12) could be attributed to the last part of the period under consideration. As far as pottery is concerned there is a major standardisation of the raw

Fig. 7 Coppa Nevigata. Semi-processed blocks of the room inside the western tower

Fig. 8 Coppa Nevigata. Circular structures (left) close to the Apennine wall, fallen into disuse

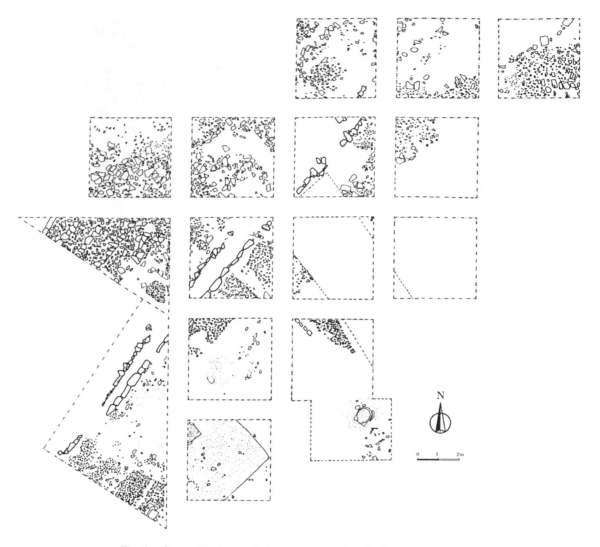

Fig. 9 Coppa Nevigata. Subapennine road and adjacent structures

materials used (Levi *et al.* in press), while the production of painted 'figulina' pottery starts at the end of this period. The production of purple-dye seems to have ceased by this time, maybe due to a major involvement in the Mycenaean network of exchange (shown directly or indirectly by the presence at Coppa Nevigata of painted, wheel-made pottery of Aegean type) which could have made the local production of this colouring agent less appealing. The construction of small straight levelled roads (fig. 9) in the settlement – that gives the impression of a will to regulate the occupation area – and of a two-roomed building (fig. 10) (where a considerable quantity of Mycenaean-type pottery was found) which may somehow be linked to the institutional figure of a chief, date back to this period.

CONCLUDING REMARKS

The overall impression one gets is of a process of transformation of the community that lived at Coppa Nevigata, a process which is common to and part of a more general historical context (southern Italy during the Bronze Age) but which at the same time presents some individual characteristics, the problem being social and not technological (Costin 1991; Dobres & Hoffman 1994).

Like other contemporary coastal settlements at the beginning of the Bronze Age, Coppa Nevigata arose as a stable centre specialising in the exchange of goods and probably in some activity of transformation of products, differentiating itself from a great number of interior settlements for this reason. It is likely that in this phase craftsmanlike activities

Fig. 10   Coppa Nevigata. Two-roomed Subapennine structure, viewed from east

(in this case the extraction of purple-dye) were not carried out by full-time specialists in specially allocated spaces but were more of a semi-domestic nature (a model similar perhaps to the Balkan Chalcolithic: Evans 1978) and utilised local resources. It seems that the same could be said for the production of pottery (which was then exchanged: Bernabò Brea 1978) on the island of Lipari and even the metallurgy carried out there (evidence of pottery production and metallurgy in the hut delta XII of the acropolis village: Bernabò Brea & Cavalier 1980: 244, 518) and on the central coast of Calabria (Bianco & Marino 1991–92), the metal being a 'local' resource (northeast Sicily; internal Calabria). This without excluding the fact that even in some sites in the interior in the vicinity of the mines the extraction of the metal and the manufacturing of some artefacts probably occurred for only a limited period during the year (Sila Mountains, Calabria: Marino, pers. comm., and Tinè 1962–63; Mount Belvedere, Sicily: Villari 1980). On the other hand, the current lack of data seems to indicate that during the first phases of the Bronze Age in southeast Italy, where there was no metal ore, metalworking was not a constant activity in the coastal centres.

At the peak of the Bronze Age, after 1500 BC, there is evidence of the allocation of specific areas at Coppa Nevigata for activities, surely non-domestic (a situation being socially intermediate between a semi-domestic specialised production and a 'manufacturing quarter': cf. Tosi 1984) but not always of identifiable function, and which implied the use of fire. The extraction of purple-dye on a larger scale seems to have had a major significance but maybe salt production was important too: circular structures, similar to Coppa Nevigata and interpreted in relation to salt working, were found in the neighbouring coastal site of Vasche Napoletane (Tunzi Sisto 1993).

Assuming the hypothesis concerning the function of the two rooms in the towers which flanked the gate at Coppa Nevigata to be correct, the relevance of these economic factors can be deduced from the role acquired by the wall; not only as a means of defence but also in the control of the passage of goods. It is probable that during this intermediate phase of the Bronze Age, some modifications in internal social structure took place. The community's sense of unity expressed by burial inside the settlement (assuming this intra-site burial area is not restricted to a single stratum or group), could have had just an ideological meaning,

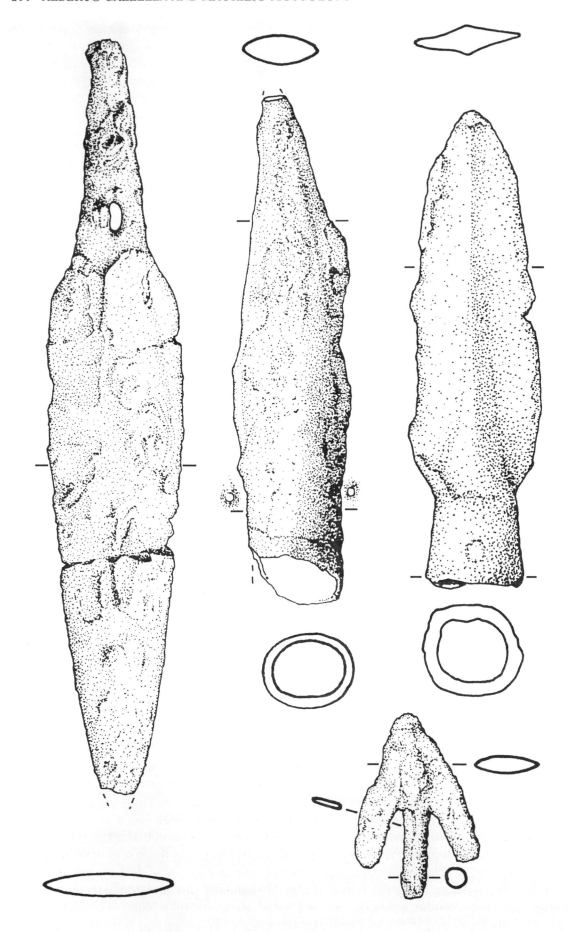

Fig. 11   Coppa Nevigata. Subapennine bronze weapons

surpassed later in this same phase by this activity of control, which in turn suggests the existence of an elite which exercised this control. An increase in the differences within the social structure corresponds in different ways and times, to the general situation in southeast Italy and it is evident that this, in turn, gave rise to an increase in the production and exchange of prestige goods (Cipolloni Sampò 1986: 34).

In the Late Bronze Age, there is more evidence of forms of centralised control at Coppa Nevigata (the laying down of a directional road system inside the living area) and of social structure diversification (cf. the dwelling structure with two rooms and the considerable quantity of Aegean type pottery) together with another change in the role of specialisation. Together with the activation of new non-domestic production using local resources, as pottery making now seems to be, there is the development of bronze metallurgy and ultimately even that of iron, the raw materials being regularly imported from far away. With the introduction from the Aegean world of the donkey (at the moment the earliest Italian evidence is from Coppa Nevigata: Bökönyi & Siracusano 1987: 207) even the overland exchange of goods with the interior could have been more frequent.

There are no traces of fortified walls for this period but the metal weapons found (spearheads, arrowheads, daggers: fig. 11) show that it was far from being a peaceful situation. The weapons (and similarly the ornamental objects in bronze, amber and decorated bone found) were probably not diffused among the whole population but belonged to an elite that cannot be considered as a 'warrior aristocracy,' not sharing, for example, Kristiansen's (1987) criteria set out for northern Europe. Its power in fact derived from its ability to organise the exchange of goods (even if this could easily lead to piracy) and craft production. The military features could have been derived from this particular social position but were not its basis.

The phases succeeding the Late Bronze Age are presently documented only by non-stratified finds; amongst them there is a fragment of an Egyptian stone vase of the early sixth century BC with an inscription of Bokonrinef (Pallottino 1951), a general of pharaoh Psammetic II, suggesting that the site was still included in a network of transmarine contacts.

BIBLIOGRAPHY

Baumgärtel, E. 1951. The cave of Manaccora, Monte Gargano, part I: the site. *Papers of the British School at Rome*, 19: 23–38.

Bernabò Brea, L. 1978. Alcune considerazioni sul carico di ceramiche dell'età del Bronzo di Pignataro di Fuori. *Sicilia Archeologica*, 11: 36–42.

Bernabò Brea, L. 1985. *Gli Eoli e l'inizio dell'età del Bronzo nelle isole Eolie e nell'Italia meridionale.* Quaderni dell'Istituto Universitario Orientale 2, Napoli.

Bernabò Brea, L. & Cavalier, M. 1980. *Meligunis Lipara.* Flaccovio, Palermo.

Bianco, S. & Marino, D.A. 1991–92. L'insediamento di Capo Piccolo di Isola di Capo Rizzuto (Catanzaro). *Rassegna di Archeologia*, 10: 754–5.

Bökönyi, S. & Siracusano, G. 1987. Reperti faunistici dell'età del Bronzo del sito di Coppa Nevigata: un commento preliminare. In Cassano, S.M., Cazzella, A., Manfredini, A. & Moscoloni, M. (eds), *Coppa Nevigata e il Suo Territorio*: 205–10. Quasar, Roma.

Cazzella, A. 1992. Usi funerari nell'Italia meridionale e in Sicilia nel corso dell'età del Bronzo: una riconsiderazione. In Lai, G., Ugas, G. & Lilliu, G. (eds), *La Sardegna nel Mediterraneo tra il Bronzo Medio e il Bronzo Recente (XVI-XIII sec. a.C.)*: 331–41. Edizioni della Torre, Cagliari.

Cazzella, A. & Moscoloni, M. 1987. Età del Bronzo. La ricerca archeologica. In Cassano, S.M., Cazzella, A., Manfredini, A. & Moscoloni, M. (eds), *Coppa Nevigata e il Suo Territorio*: 99–190. Quasar, Roma.

Cazzella, A. & Moscoloni, M. 1993. Nuovi dati sui livelli dell'età del Bronzo di Coppa Nevigata. In *Atti del XIII Convegno Nazionale sulla Preistoria, Protostoria e Storia della Daunia*: 55–65. Archeoclub d'Italia, San Severo.

Cazzella, A. & Moscoloni, M. 1995. Coppa Nevigata nel contesto adriatico dell'età del Bronzo. *Taras*, 16.

Cipolloni Sampò, M. 1986. La tomba tre dell'acropoli di Toppo Daguzzo (Potenza). Elementi per uno studio preliminare. *Annali dell'Istituto Universitario Orientale di Napoli, Archeologia e Storia Antica*, 8: 1–40.

Cipolloni Sampò, M. 1991–92. Le sepolture collettive nel Sud-Est italiano. *Rassegna di Archeologia*, 10: 280–5.

Costin, C.L. 1991. Craft specialization: issues in defining, documenting and explaining the organization of production. In Schiffer, M.B. (ed.), *Archaeological Method and Theory 3*: 1–56. The University of Arizona Press, Tucson.

Covic, B. 1989. Posuska Kultura. *Glasnik Zemaljskog Muzeja Sarajevo*, n.s. A 44: 61–127.

Deith, M.R. 1987. La raccolta di molluschi nel Tavoliere in epoca preistorica. In Cassano, S.M., Cazzella, A., Manfredini, A. & Moscoloni, M. (eds), *Coppa Nevigata e il Suo Territorio:* 101–5. Quasar, Roma.

Dobres, M.A. & Hoffman, C.R. 1994. Social agency and the dynamics of prehistoric technology. *Journal of Archaeological Method and Theory*, 1(3): 211–58.

Evans, R.K. 1978. Early craft specialization: an example from the Balkan Chalcolithic. In Redman, C.L., Berman, M.J., Curtin, E.V., Longhorn, W.T., Versaggi, N.M. & Wanser, J.C. (eds), *Social Archaeology: Beyond Subsistence and Dating:* 113–29. Academic Press, New York.

Faure, P. 1991. La pourpre, invention egéenne. *Aegaeum*, 7: 311–13.

Govedarica, B. 1989. *Rano bronzano doba na producju istocnog Jadrana*. Akademija Nauka i umjetnosti Bosne i Hercegovine, Sarajevo.

Kristiansen, K. 1987. From stone to bronze. The evolution of social complexity in Northern Europe, 2300 – 1200 BC. In Brumfiel, E.M. & Earle, T.K. (eds), *Specialization, Exchange and Complex Societies*: 30–51. Cambridge University Press, Cambridge.

Levi, S.T., Cazzella, A., Moscoloni, M., Fratini, F., Pecchioni, E. & Amadori, L. in press. Analisi archeometrica della ceramica dell'età del Bronzo di Coppa Nevigata: alcune implicazioni archeologiche. *Scienze dell'Antichità*, 7.

Maran, J. 1987. Kulturbeziehungen zwischen dem nordwestlichen Balkan und Südgriechenland am Übergang vom späten Äneolithikum zur frühen Bronzezeit (Reinecke A 1). *Archäologisches Korrespondenzblatt*, 17: 77–85.

Mosso, A. 1908. Stazione preistorica di Coppa Nevigata presso Manfredonia. *Monumenti Antichi dei Lincei*, 19: 305–86.

Nava, M.L. 1984. L'età dei Metalli. In Mazzei, M. (ed.), *Civiltà della Daunia Antica*: 101–36. Electa, Milano.

Pallottino, M. 1951. Vaso egiziano iscritto proveniente dal villaggio preistorico di Coppa Nevigata. *Rendiconti dell'Accademia dei Lincei*, ser. VIII, VI, 11–12: 580–90.

Puglisi, S.M. 1975. L'età del Bronzo nella Daunia. In *Atti del Colloquio Internazionale di Preistoria e Protostoria della Daunia*: 225–34. Istituto Italiano di Preistoria e Protostoria, Firenze.

Puglisi, S.M. 1982. Coppa Nevigata (Manfredonia). In Vagnetti, L. (ed.), *Magna Grecia e Mondo Miceneo. Nuovi Documenti. XXII Convegno di Studi sulla Magna Grecia, Taranto, 7–11, ottobre 1982*: 45–51. Istituto per la Storia e l'Archeologia della Magna Grecia, Taranto.

Recchia, G. 1993. Grotta Manaccora (Peschici), considerazioni sulla grotticella funeraria e sull'area antistante (scavi Rellini – Baumgärtel). *Origini*, 17: 317–401.

Reese, D. 1987. Palaikastro shells and Bronze Age purple-dye production in the Mediterranean Basin. *Annals of the British School at Athens*, 82: 201–6.

Rutter, J.B. 1982. A group of distinctive pattern-decorated Early Helladic III pottery from Lerna and its implications. *Hesperia*, 51: 459–88.

Tinè, S. 1962–63. Ripostiglio di armi da Cotronei (Catanzaro). *Bullettino di Paletnologia Italiana*, 71–72: 227–32.

Tosi, M. 1984. The notion of craft specialization and its representation in the archaeological record of early states in the Turanian Basin. In Spriggs, M. (ed.), *Marxist Perspectives in Archaeology*: 22–52. Cambridge University Press, Cambridge.

Tunzi Sisto, A.M. 1991–92. L'ipogeo di Madonna di Loreto (Trinitapoli, Foggia). *Rassegna di Archeologia*, 10: 545–52.

Tunzi Sisto, A.M. 1993. Aspetti culturali dell'Eneolitico e dell'età del Bronzo nelle saline di Margherita di Savoia. In *Atti del XIII Convegno Nazionale sulla Preistoria, Protostoria e Storia della Daunia*: 39–54. Archeoclub d'Italia, San Severo.

Villari, P. 1980. Considerazioni sulla presenza di alcuni bronzi in una capanna del periodo di transizione Tardo-eneolitico – prima età del Bronzo del Monte Belvedere di Fiumedinisi (Messina). *Atti della Società Toscana di Scienze Naturali*, 87: 465–74.

Human Skeletons from the Greek Emporium of Pithekoussai on Ischia (NA)

Culture Contact and Biological Change in Italy after the 8th Century BC

Marshall Joseph Becker

INTRODUCTION

Prior to 770 BC, decades before any of the Greek city states had attempted to establish colonies in the area of western Italy, merchants from Euboea had established a trading post on an island now known as Ischia, near the southern edge of the Etruscan realm (Buchner 1979). From this easily defended emporium in the Bay of Naples, with its excellent harbour systems for sailing vessels which had limited manoeuvrability, these entrepreneurial Greeks gained access to the market for Etruscan metals and other resources from this rich market (Buchner 1966). In exchange they delivered ceramics and other luxury goods into the local exchange systems. The knowledge which these Greek traders gained about the lands situated between Ischia and their home cities facilitated the development of the first Greek colonies.

Colonists from Euboea settled at the trading station of Pithekoussai, where they were soon joined by merchants from the Phoenician realm. Cumae, nearby on the Italian peninsula, was occupied as a derivative Greek colony after a brief interval, or at the time when the traders at their station on Pithekoussai felt militarily comfortable and could risk exposure to possible attack by the local peoples (cf. Becker 1991). Skeletal remains from Cumae (cf. Buchner 1977) would provide useful data for comparative studies, but the preservation of skeletal materials was not a priority during early excavations at that site.

Local Oscan people also must have lived and married among these Euboeans and Phoenicians, creating a rich cultural cluster and an interesting subject for study. We presume that the impact of this emporium, and its subsequent colony, on the Iron Age people of this part of Italy was far more extensive than just the material results of trade. The biological impact must have been considerable (cf. Bietti Sestieri 1992), and it is this influence which we hope to reveal through these studies.

Although excavations at Pithekoussai began during the nineteenth century, the cemetery area for these ancients was not identified until the excavators found it at the foot of the hill on which the settlement was perched. Detritus from the densely occupied hilltop rapidly covered graves of all periods. The most recent of these graves, dating to the Roman period, lie nearly four metres below the modern surface of the ground. The tombs of these first Greek merchants and early colonists lie another four metres lower, limiting access to these graves.

Modern excavations at the site, beginning in 1952 (see Buchner & Ridgway 1993), found the skeletal material poorly preserved (Becker 1995a). Initial identification of gender was made on the basis of associated artefacts in those few cases where grave offerings were present (see table 1). All of the fibulae found in these graves are of a local variety and usually found as one or more pairs. One subset of these is identified as the 'dragon' type, believed to be the only fibula form associated with males. A bow type, as well as other forms, are believed to be associated only with women. For those graves lacking such diagnostic artefacts, skeletal analysis is critical to the determination of sex. Bone studies are also a means of verifying the initial gender evaluations made by the archaeologists. Also important in this research is the determination of the ages of these people at their deaths. This information provides insights into the structure of the society as it progressed from a trading station to a colony.

All the graves excavated at Pithekoussai appear to be those of common folk, or what Buchner describes as middle class Euboean colonists. However, we have evidence for the presence of Phoenician mortuary customs, as well as some sets of dentition which appear to derive from local peoples (cf. Becker 1986b). Aristocratic graves, such as those found at Velletri and Cumae, have not been discovered at Pithekoussai. Therefore, studies of social class variation which are so important at other sites (d'Agostino 1969; 1977; Becker 1990) are not now a part of this programme. However, the extensive data from this site offer outstanding comparative information for examining the bones of Greek colonists and others throughout this region.

Even more important to the understanding of the general history of this site (Buchner 1971) is the potential for skeletal research to decode information regarding the 'ethnic' origins of these individuals. Although Euboean colonists may be the primary inhabitants of these graves, we can have no doubt that many married Oscan women, both to consolidate trade relationships as well as to forge other alliances. Phoenicians also appear to have been resident at Pithekoussai (cf. Moscati 1986; 1989), giving yet another dimension to this potentially rich study. Considerable archaeological evidence suggests that by 750 BC Phoenicians were being buried in this cemetery, a fact now confirmed from skeletal finds. Phoenicians also may be identifiable using the information from previously studied colonial Carthaginian populations (cf. Becker 1985; 1995b).

Prior to 1992 only one study (Munz 1970) discusses the skeletal material recovered from these important excavations on Ischia, focussing on the dentition from the tombs excavated during the field seasons from 1952 to 1961. This report summarises the interpretations based on evidence from the human skeletal materials from Pithekoussai (Becker & Donadio 1992; Becker 1995a). While cremations are most commonly found in the period from the second half of the 8th century to the early 6th century BC (111 of the 591 tombs known from this period), several examples of cremations also are known to be from later periods. In general, however, cremations appear most characteristic of adult burials of the early period of colonisation. Note should be made that some individuals as young as eight years of age now can be identified among these cremations, but the majority of sub-adults at Pithekoussai were inhumed (table 1). In general the delicate bones of sub-adults are under-represented among the recovered skeletons. The youngest person represented is the inhumation of a child of 2 years (Burial 470). Perinatals and infants may have been buried in the settlement area of the site, following the Greek tradition of *enchytrismos*.

GENERAL GOALS

Three general goals directed the study of the limited skeletal remains recovered from these excavations. The first was to provide basic information of concern to the archaeologists. This included evaluating the age and sex of each individual (see Becker & Donadio 1992), searching for evidence of the possibility that multiple cremations or burials were placed in a single tomb (cf. Becker 1993b), and seeking other data useful in reconstructing culture and culture history.

A second goal was the search for direct biological and other information that might provide clues to the ethnic identification of individuals (Greek, Oscan, Phoenician). Such clues may derive from the skeletal material itself or by aspects of mortuary rituals which may reflect cultural traits. The third goal was to search for evidence that might indicate biological change over time, as a reflection of degree or rate of intermarriage. With the limited evidence available this search focussed on the odontometric data from the inhumations.

MATERIALS

During the 1991 and 1992 study seasons materials from 127 tombs, representing 134 individuals, were available for study (113 from cremations and 21 from inhumations (cf. table 1)). All of the skeletal materials for this study are held in storage at the Villa Arbusto, Lacco Ameno, Ischia. The cremations studied include a number from that portion of the burial area, including the earliest interments at Pithekoussai, dating primarily from the period from 750 to 675 BC. Also included are two later examples (Roman) of the cremations interred over the next five centuries. These data largely relate to those tombs included in the first comprehensive publication of the archaeological data (Buchner & Ridgway 1993). Gender and age evaluations (table 1) are here summarised from the extensive reports deriving from earlier studies (Becker & Donadio 1992; Becker 1993a; 1995a). Fragmentary material from more recently excavated cremations, plus 109 unstudied inhumations from this same burial area, will be the focus of future research. This information should be published with the tomb descriptions in *Pithecusa II*, now in process. Comparative skeletal data from the Greek 'homeland' continues to be sought (Becker 1995a), but at present appropriate skeletal remains from Euboea have yet to be found.[1]

METHODS

Research at Pithekoussai employed several techniques of physical anthropology as a means of solving archaeological problems (cf. Deriu *et al*. 1986; Ubelaker 1989). The analysis of the cremations and inhumations from Pithekoussai employed methods described previously (Becker 1987; Becker & Salvadei 1992), where considerable success was achieved in the identification of age and sex. All of the work was conducted blind (without knowledge of the archaeological evidence for gender) at the Villa Arbusto, which is near the excavation site.

In most cremations the large pieces of bone which normally survive the burning process were crushed to fit them into small containers (cf. Becker 1993a). Remains of individuals placed in larger containers, such as an Attic krater, need not be subjected to comminution. The fire normally causes cracks and fissures to open in the bone, which comminution and/ or the processes of soil compaction in a tomb may cause to open, leaving the burned bones in an even more fragmentary state. Where joins were found between breaks in the bone fragments recovered from these tombs, they were glued using a water soluble polyvinyl acetate solution. The evaluation of age and sex of these cremations, a difficult task, involved visual examination of relative size and contour of each fragment by 2 independent evaluators. Nearly perfect agreement, in all cases but 1, indicated that this method could be replicated. These data were conjoined, and then compared with the gender evaluations provided by the archaeologists. Other materials found with the human bone, including animal bone and ceramic fragments, were separated and repackaged as separate units for future study.

Sex evaluation for the inhumations, where possible, was based primarily on long bone shaft diameters, a technique found extremely effective at Osteria dell'Osa (Becker & Salvadei 1992). Note should be made that the lack of intact crania among the inhumations was not an impediment to this study. Sex evaluation based on cranial morphology and inferred dimorphism, which has been the focus of most earlier studies, provides useful indications of sex in northern European populations. However, Becker and Salvadei (1992) demonstrate that cranial morphology is a poor predictor of sex in central Italy. Therefore, emphasis here was placed on the evaluation of the postcranial skeleton and the dentition. The determination of sex from the teeth, so successfully achieved at Osteria dell'Osa when working with the inhumations (Becker & Salvadei 1992), was reliably evaluated at Pithekoussai for those few inhumations from which dentition was recovered.

This entire population appears relatively slender. Several specific features of the anatomy commonly used to evaluate sex, such as the size of the radius head (see Tomb 167), are not considered to be reliable indicators of sex in this population (cf. Berrizbeitia 1989; Buikstra & Ubelaker 1994). Despite these difficulties, sex was evaluated ('blind') accurately for all of the cremated individuals for whom 200 grams of bone or more were recovered.[2] These findings later were confirmed when artefacts from the same tombs were examined and found to serve as independent means of evaluating gender. The results of this study are summarised below using the categories formulated in the goals stated above.

AGE AND SEX

Sex evaluations based solely on skeletal evaluation were attempted for 120 individuals. At the end of this skeletal study the results were compared with the evaluations of gender based on archaeological evidence (fibula form, etc.) provided by the excavators for those individuals accompanied by 'diagnostic' grave goods. Of 65 individuals with such goods, 64 appear unequivocally identifiable as regards gender based on the associated artefacts. In 50 of the 52 cases (95%) for which more than 200 grams of bone had been recovered we have perfect agreement between the biological sex evaluation and the archaeological evidence for gender. This is about the same level of agreement found in the social assignment of gender as it relates to biological sex in living humans.

Only the remains from Tomb 159 stand out as an example of clear differences between the archaeological and biological conclusions regarding gender and sex. The biological data unequivocally suggest a male, but the archaeological data indicates that a female is present (cf. Markantonatos 1995). This may be a case of confusion in gender assignment at birth, which occurs in all human populations (cf. Meyer-Bahlburg 1994: 22–4). Gender assignment at birth is based on examination of external genitalia and is not necessarily accurate. Alternately, the Tomb 159 situation could be a case of a male playing a female role within this Greek colony (cf. Meindl et al. 1985).

The results of the study may be summarised as follows:

A. The archaeological data suggest that our sex evaluation based on skeletal analysis can be considered to be accurate in almost all cases (98%) where more than 200 grams of bone are present. In many instances an evaluation was attempted when less than 200 grams of bone was recovered, such as Tomb 179 where only fragments of a femur shaft were used to form the sex evaluation. Surprisingly, accuracy in providing sex data was later found to be quite good in the cases where an evaluation was attempted based only on a few fragments of recovered bone. When these evaluations of sex were later compared with gender data from tomb goods even the fragmentary remains from cremations were found to have yielded a high correlation. When using 200 grams as a minimum figure, congruence in these evaluations rose to 95%. However, the 'male' in Tomb 167 was initially identified as a female (F???) based only on the size of a radius head, a trait which was not confirmed as problematical until the end of this research. The male (gender) in Tomb 149 was at first incorrectly identified as female (F???) based only on a piece of right maxilla.

B. The ratio of adult males to females determined through the *archaeological* evidence (associated artefacts, where present) was found to be approximately 40/60. At first this appeared to be independently confirmed through the skeletal analysis, but the combined data-sets significantly reduce the apparent discrepancy. Nevertheless, females continue to outnumber males, but within expected ratios. The total number of identified females (n=68) comprise 51% of the total number of burials available for study (cremations plus inhumations; cf. table 2). The original suggestion that these colonists had a high rate of intermarriage with native women ('local recruitment' of wives), rather than bringing women from their Euboean homeland (Becker 1995a) is no longer clearly indicated.

C. The very preliminary data from the study of only 21 of the inhumations (see table 2) show the ratio of adult males (n=3) to females (n=6) as 33/67, similar to the 40/60 ratio noted by Buchner and Ridgway (1993). However, the eight inhumed children (individuals age 17 and below) for whom we can evaluate gender show a female to male ratio of 37:63, suggesting the possibility that the skewed adult ratio for inhumations must be a function of statistical error and *not* related to an expected higher male infant and child mortality rate.

D. Age evaluations are believed to be more than 95% accurate for adults within the wide range stated in the study (Becker 1995a). Dental eruption sequences were used to evaluate non-adults. Endocranial suture closure, used to evaluate age for the adults, has a ± 10 year possible variation (cf. Meindl & Lovejoy 1985). The skeletal evaluation made of the very fragmentary bones from cremation Tomb 223 indicates that they derive from a female of age 60 years (± 10), and are not the bones of a child as suggested earlier (Buchner & Boardman 1966: 10).

Among the 111 cremated individuals, only three children were identified (ages 8, 10 and 14 years). However, of the 21 inhumations evaluated a total of 12 children were identified (ages 2–11 years). These inhumations may derive from an area in which children predominate, but this also may correlate with a lower status form of burial rite (cf. Bietti Sestieri 1992). Neonates and children dying before reaching two months of age may have been interred within the settlement (see below).

E. Sex could not be determined for any of these cremated children (Tombs 93, 140, 168: ages 10, 8 and 14 respectively). The low incidence of identifiable children among these graves suggests that many of the tombs from which no skeletal remains were recovered may have been those of children. The age of ritual passage into 'personhood', when one was entitled to a burial in the cemetery (cf. Becker 1986a) in this population appears to have been under 8 years, but based on the data available at this time we cannot be more specific. Neonates, foetuses, and children under the age of one year (the largest category of deceased individuals expected in pre-modern populations) may have been buried in very simple fashions within the residential zone. One jar found beneath a floor in the settlement area, in which no trace of bone was detected, may well have been an *enchytrismos*. Several such containers were found in the necropolis and probably represent the burials of infants or young children (cf. Ridgway 1984: fig. 17; Buchner 1982: 277).

F. Among the many questions posed by this study is one concerning possible status variables within the society as revealed by these graves. Although the excavators do not believe that high status graves are apparent, the vast differences in tomb offerings suggest that status differences are considerable. Differences in the age of individuals in cremations as distinct from those in inhumations also suggest status differences. The individual in Tomb 159 was identified as 'male' on the basis of long bone robusticity, but the grave goods indicate that this may be a female. Quite possibly this is an extremely robust female who was a well nourished member of a high status family (cf. Becker 1988).

A number of other questions may be asked regarding differential survival of cremated remains. Quite possibly cremation pyres were of relatively standard size, which would result in smaller individuals (women) being cremated at higher temperatures since their body fluids would not be as highly retardant to the burning process. A pyre which fails to porcelainise the bone of a large male allows that poorly burned material to decay in the ground, resulting in a smaller amount of surviving bone. These factors may result in an apparently larger number of females being represented by surviving bone.

BIOLOGICAL CHANGE THROUGH TIME

Three areas need to be considered in the evaluation of microevolutionary change at this site. First, the absence of intact crania from which metric and non-metric evaluations might have been made forced our attentions to focus on the very limited dental evidence. Although the significance of the incidence of bifurcate roots on maxillary first premolars is not yet clear, note is made of this trait (e.g. Tomb 149) where the actual root is preserved or is suggested by the configuration of the tooth socket. Note should be made that the examination of the tooth socket of the person in Tomb 149 did not easily reveal the bifurcation. Thus, many more examples may exist than are specified in the field record. Bifurcation of the root of maxillary first premolars is a trait commonly found in central Italy, particularly during the period from c.900–600 BC. No evidence of this trait is found among the earliest inhabitants at Pithekoussai, while the later population shows a low incidence, suggesting intermarriage with local Oscan peoples and/or immigration from central Italy (Becker 1995a: 280).

Second, excellent dental health (Becker 1995a: table 2) appears to be the rule at Pithekoussai. In both periods dental attrition rates among cremated individuals appear very low, suggesting dietary and cultural stability through time. These data from the inhumations are too few to be statistically interesting, particularly as 12 of the 21 individuals studied from inhumations are children under 11 years of age. The few adults among these inhumations have very good dentition. When the cremations alone are tabulated by general period, we find that the cremated early colonial population appears to have had an extremely low rate of ante-mortem dental loss (approximately 8%) and that the later people had a similarly low rate. Note should be made that molars as well as anterior teeth are represented in the sample of tooth spaces represented among the cremated remains. However, note also should be made that, in the case of cremations, alveolar survival itself may be a function of dental health. Individuals from whose jaws teeth have been lost by natural processes before death, common in the elderly, generally have alveolar areas which are reduced in size, which renders them more subject to destruction during the cremation process. As of this date the odontometric data from the inhumations of adults (n=9, see table 2) includes insufficient numbers to permit valid statistical comparisons. The available evidence suggests cultural continuities in diet and dental health.

Third, the most evident disease among these people appears in the form of geriatric exostoses. The woman (??) in Tomb 175 has fused cervical vertebrae as well as numerous exostoses on the other surviving vertebrae. The male (???) in Tomb 176 has similar exostoses, as do many other individuals whose remains are found in this sample. Pitting was noted on the interiors of some skull fragments, but all appear to have been non-lethal lesions. No broken bones or malformations were noted among these sparse remains. The individual in Tomb 150 had long bone enlargement (ribs, limbs) that may reflect an anaemic disorder, possibly malaria or thalassaemia but other aetiologies are possible. In general, cremated remains do not provide an ideal situation for the study of palaeopathologies.

ETHNIC IDENTITIES

The most striking evidence of ethnic affiliation derives from the discovery of osteological evidence for behaviours known in the ancient literature. The cremated bones of the child in Tomb 93, dated to the 5th Century BC, include an extremely gracile and unburned ungual (terminal) phalanx believed to derive from an adult female. Since this bone is not part of the child's remains, this phalanx cannot be an *os resectum*, cut from the corpse before cremation. Examples of the *os resectum* have been documented recently from the archaeological record (Bowmer & Molleson 1986; Becker 1988; see also below). This example from Pithekoussai of an unburned adult terminal phalanx with a child's burned bones, found in a red-figure Attic krater of the 5th century which had been placed in a cube of tufa (see Boardman 1980), appears to have been deliberately placed in this krater. This phalanx has been interpreted as a traditional Canaanite finger joint offering (Becker 1995a), a mortuary custom noted in the Old Testament but previously unreported in the archaeological literature of either the Levant or Italy. Such a practice appears to be similar to, but not necessarily related to, the custom of taking an *os resectum* so widely known at this time from sites throughout central Italy. This finding also requires that we rethink the source of the *os resectum* in central Italy. Quite possibly the finger joint removed came from a relative rather than from the corpse. Possible relationships with Levantine documented customs, and alternate interpretations, should be explored.

The discovery among the bones of the cremated female in Tomb 137 of an unburned *os resectum* needs reconsideration in the light of the other findings just noted. Since this terminal phalanx appears likely to have derived from her own hand, her family was utilising mortuary customs best known from central Italy. This suggests that the people involved with Tomb 137 are later Roman occupants of Pithekoussai.

The bones found in Tomb 114 suggest that two cremated individuals were placed in this single tomb, possibly having been burned on separate rather than a single pyre. Although it is possible that the inclusion of the remains of two people (a young female plus a well-represented elderly male) in this context may not have been intentional, the presence of young females in inhumation tombs of old adult males certainly has been noted elsewhere in central Italy (Becker 1990). Joint interments have also been confirmed, albeit infrequently, in cremation burials (Becker 1987; 1988). However, the cremated remains of an older male placed together with bones of a young female have been well documented from several *tombe principesche* of the Orientalising period in Italy (d'Agostino 1969; 1977; Becker 1993b).[3] Burials of secondary individuals together with old males also may be a reflection of status in these communities (cf. Becker 1990).

Some burned remains of mammals (generally sheep or goats) also are found among the cremated bones in several of the Pithekoussai burials (e.g. Tombs 94, 114, 167, 184 and possibly Tomb 200). While some of these animal bones may be accidental inclusions, most appear to be the remains of funerary meals or offerings. The analysis of these bones by a palaeozoologist may shed further light on these mortuary customs and the ethnic identification of the people buried here.

NOTES

1 The author's study of 'Greek colonists' at Metaponto (Becker n.d.) has been replicated recently with satisfyingly similar results as relate to age and sex. However, the interpretations regarding the health of these people based on this second study (Henneberg, Henneberg & Carter 1992) appear drastically different from those of the original study.

2 Sex evaluations were attempted even where as little as two grams of bone were recovered in order to determine the limits to which skeletal analysis can extend. A remarkable degree of agreement was found between the archaeological and skeletal evaluations of sex and gender. In eight of the only nine cases in which there are differences in sex/gender evaluations, the individual is represented by minimal amounts (generally under 120 grams) of bone. If all cases in which under 120 grams of bone were available for evaluation are eliminated from the sample, then we have only four cases of disagreement between archaeological and biological evidence (Tombs 159, 192, 224, 229). Tomb 192 has a possible intrusion and 229 is represented by

only 144 grams of bone. Tomb 224 is an elderly individual and the identification as M?? indicates some tentativeness. Only Tomb 159, for which the biological evidence clearly indicates a male, may be considered as an interesting problem.

3   The single fragment of a bone representing the second woman with the female of Tomb 220 is probably an accidental inclusion, and should not be considered a double burial.

ACKNOWLEDGEMENTS

Sincere thanks are due to Dr Giorgio Buchner for his kind invitation to study these human remains, and for his extensive aid in arranging for this aspect of the research to be completed. Thanks also are due to the Soprintendenza Archeologica for Naples for permission to study these materials, and to Dr Costanza Gialanella (Ispetrice per Pozzuoli e Ischia) for her co-operation in every aspect of this study. Thanks also are due to Prof. Erminio Braidotti (West Chester University) for aid with translations, and to Dott.ssa A. Rè and all the other people on Ischia who assisted this project in so many ways.

Special thanks are due Prof. A. Mennella, *Sindaco* of the Municipio di Lacco Ameno, for his kind permission to use the facilities at the Villa Arbusto to initiate this project (May-June 1991 and 1992), and to Alessia Donadio for assistance in the field. Portions of this paper were presented in the symposium "Social Dynamics of the Prehistoric Central Mediterranean" at the 1992 meetings of the Society for American Archaeology, and at the Fifth Conference of Italian Archaeology (Oxford, Dec. 1992). The comments of colleagues at both meetings were extremely useful in shaping this paper, as were the important suggestions of Dr John Robb and the comments of Dr Robert Tykot, Dina Rudman and 2 anonymous reviewers.

Funding for this project derived from a research award from Daniel and Jacqueline Colyer, supplemented by a small grant for travel from West Chester University of Pennsylvania (CASSDA Grants, Dean J. Skerl, Chair). The aid of Sig. A. Scipione and the owners and staff of the Hotel San Lorenzo at Lacco Ameno is most gratefully acknowledged. Any errors of interpretation or presentation are the responsibility of the author alone.

BIBLIOGRAPHY

Becker, M.J. 1985. Metric and non-metric data from a series of skulls from Mozia, Sicily and a related site. *Antropologia Contemporanea*, 8 (3): 211–28.

Becker, M.J. 1986a. Mandibular symphysis (medial suture) closure in modern *Homo sapiens*: Preliminary evidence from archaeological populations. *American Journal of Physical Anthropology*, 69: 499–501.

Becker, M.J. 1986b. An ethnographical and archaeological survey of unusual mortuary procedures as a reflection of cultural diversity: some suggestions for the interpretation of the human skeletal deposits from excavations at Entella, Sicily, Italy. *La Parola del Passato: Rivista di Studi Antichi*, 226: 31–56.

Becker, M.J. 1987. Appendix 1. Analisi Antropologiche e Paleontologiche: Soprintendenza di Roma. In Bartoloni, G., Buranelli, F., D'Atri, V. & De Santis, A. (eds), *Le Urne a Capanna Rinvenute in Italia*: 235–46. Giorgio Bretschneider, Roma.

Becker, M.J. 1988. The contents of funerary vessels as clues to mortuary customs: identifying the Os Exceptum. In Christiansen, J. & Melander, T. (eds), *Proceedings of the 3rd Symposium on Ancient Greek and Related Pottery [Copenhagen, 1987]*: 25–32. Nationalmuseet, Copenhagen.

Becker, M.J. 1990. Etruscan social classes in the VI century B.C.: evidence from recently excavated cremations and inhumations in the area of Tarquinia. In Heres, H. & Kunze, M. (eds), *Die Welt der Etrusker (International Colloquium, October 1988)*: 23–35. Akademie-Verlag, Berlin.

Becker, M.J. 1991. European trade and colonization in the territory of the Lenape of Pennsylvania during the 17th century: an historical model for Greek colonization in Italy. Paper presented at the International Congress of Americanists, New Orleans, Louisiana, July 1991.

Becker, M.J. 1993a. Human skeletons from Tarquinia: a preliminary analysis of the 1989 Cimitero excavations with implications for the evolution of Etruscan social classes. *Studi Etruschi*, 58 (1992): 211–48.

Becker, M.J. 1993b. Human Sacrifice in Iron Age Italy: evidence from the "Tombe Principesche" numbers 926 and 928 at Pontecagnano (Salerno). *Old World Archaeology Newsletter*, 16 (2): 23–30.

Becker, M.J. 1995a. Human skeletal remains from the pre-colonial Greek emporium of Pithekoussai on Ischia (NA): culture contact in Italy from the early VIII to the II century BC. In Christie, N. (ed.), *Settlement and Economy in Italy 1500 BC to AD 1500: Papers from the Fifth Conference of Italian Archaeology*: 273–81. Oxbow Monograph 41. Oxbow Books, Oxford.

Becker, M.J. 1995b. Human skeletons from recent excavations in various areas of the Lilibeo necropolis at Marsala, Sicily: an analysis of skeletons from excavations at the Via Cattaneo, Corso di Gasperi and Via Berta. *Annali delle Scuola Normale Superiore di Pisa*, 25 (1–2): 118–87.

Becker, M.J. n.d. An analysis of the human skeletal remains recovered by the University of Texas excavations at Metaponto (1979–1989). Report submitted to J.C. Carter.

Becker, M.J. & Donadio, A. 1992. A summary of the analysis of cremated human skeletal remains from the Greek colony of Pithekoussai at Lacco Ameno, Ischia, Italy. *Old World Archaeology Newsletter*, 16 (1): 15–23.

Becker, M.J. & Salvadei, L. 1992. Analysis of the human skeletal remains from the cemetery of Osteria dell'Osa. In Bietti Sestieri, A.M. (ed.), *La Necropoli Laziale di Osteria dell'Osa I*: 53–191. Quasar, Roma.

Berrizbeita, E. 1989. Sex determination using the head of the radius. *Journal of Forensic Sciences*, 29: 1206–13.

Bietti Sestieri, A.M. (ed.) 1992. *La Necropoli Laziale di Osteria dell'Osa*. 3 volumes. Quasar, Roma.

Boardman, J. 1980. *The Greeks Overseas: Their Early Colonies and Trade*. Thames & Hudson, New York.

Bowmer, M. & Molleson, T. 1986. Appendix: Identification of human remains from the hut urns. In Bartoloni, G., "Le urne a capanna: ancora sulle prime scoperte nei Colli Albani." In Swaddling, J. (ed.), *Italian Iron Age Artefacts in the British Museum*: 238–9. British Museum, London.

Buchner, G. 1966. Pithekoussai: oldest Greek colony in the West. *Expedition*, 8 (4): 4–12.

Buchner, G. 1971. Recent work at Pithekoussai (Ischia), 1965–71. *Archaeological Reports for 1970–71*: 63.

Buchner, G. 1977. Cuma nell'VIII secolo a.C., osservata dalla prospettiva di Pithecusa. In *Proceedings of the International Congress "I Campi Flegrei nell'Archeologia e nella Storia" (Roma, 1976)*: 131–48. Atti dei Convegni Lincei. Accademia Nazionale dei Lincei, Roma.

Buchner, G. 1979. Early Orientalizing: aspects of the Euboean connection. In Ridgway, D. & Ridgway, F. (eds), *Italy before the Romans: The Iron Age, Orientalizing and Etruscan Periods*: 129–44. Academic Press, London.

Buchner, G. 1982. Articolazione sociale, differenze di rituale e composizione dei corredi nella Necropoli di Pithecusa. In Gnoli, G. & Vernant, J.-P. (eds), *La Mort, Les Mortes dans les Societes Anciennes*: 275–87. Cambridge University Press, Cambridge.

Buchner, G. & Boardman, J. 1966. Seals from Ischia and The Lyre-Player Group. *Jahrbuch des Deutsches Archäologischen Instituts*, 81: 1–62.

Buchner, G. & Ridgway, D. 1993. *Pithekoussai I. La necropoli: Tombe 1–723 Scavate dal 1952 al 1961*. Giorgio Bretschneider, Roma.

Buikstra, J. & Ubelaker, D. 1994. *Standards for Data Collection from Human Skeletal Remains*. Research Series 44, Arkansas Archaeological Survey. Fayetteville.

d'Agostino, B. 1969. Pontecagnano. Tombe orientalizzante in Contrada S. Antonio. *Notizie degli Scavi*, 1968: 75–196.

d'Agostino, B. 1977. Tombe 'principesche' dell'orientalizzante antico da Pontecagnano. *Monumenti Antichi*, (Serie Miscellanea II, 1) 49: 1–74.

Deriu, A., Buchner, G. & Ridgway, D. 1986. Provenience and firing techniques of Geometric pottery from Pithekoussai: A Mösbauer investigation. *A.I.O.N. Annali del Seminario di Studi del Mondo Classico dell'Istituto Universitario Orientali di Napoli. Archeologia e Storia Antica*, 8: 99–116.

Henneberg, M., Henneberg, R. & Carter, J.C. 1992. Health in Colonial Metaponto. *Research & Exploration*, 8 (4): 446–59.

Markantonatos, M. 1995. Basilicata, South Italy: Elite Iron Age women and the power game. Paper presented at the 60th Annual Meeting of the Society for American Archaeology, Minneapolis.

Meyer-Bahlburg, H.F.L. 1994. Intersexuality and the diagnosis of gender identity disorder. *Archives of Sexual Behavior*, 23 (1): 21–40.

Meindl, R.S. & Lovejoy, C.O. 1985. Ectocranial suture closure: a revised method for the determination of skeletal age at death based on the lateral-anterior sutures. *American Journal of Physical Anthropology*, 68: 57–66.

Meindl, R.S., Lovejoy, C.O., Mensforth, R.P. & Carlos, L.D. 1985. Accuracy and direction of error in the sexing of the skeleton: implications for paleodemography. *American Journal of Physical Anthropology*, 68: 79–85.

Moscati, S. 1986. *Italia Punica* (with S.F. Bondi). Rusconi, Milano.

Moscati, S. 1989. Fenici e Cartaginesi in Italia. *Bolletino di Archeologia*, 1: 38–41.

Munz, F.R. 1970. Die Zahnfunde aus der griechischen Nekropole von Pithekoussai auf Ischia. *Archaeologischer Anzeiger*, 85: 452–75.

Ridgway, D. 1984. *L'Alba della Magna Grecia*. Longanesi & Cie, Milano.

Ubelaker, D.H. 1989. *Human Skeletal Remains: Excavation, Analysis, Interpretation*. Second edition. Taraxacum, Washington, D.C.

Table 1 Age and sex/gender evaluations of the burials

Tomb Number	Age	Skeletal Evaluation of Sex	Archaeological Evaluation of Gender	Cremation (C) or Inhumation (I)
4	5.8	M		I
19	65	F	F	C
21	65	F	–	C
22	3.8	F?		I
23	3.5	M?		I
27	70	F???	–	C
29	6.8	F		I
"	50	F		I
33	45	F?		I
40	65	F?	–	C
42	70	M???	M	C
48	25	F		I
49A	65+	M???		I
49B	45	F???		I
53	45	F??		I
"	4	F???		I
61	55	F	F?	C
62	50	M???	M	C
78	10	M???		I
86	70	M	M	C
87	MA	F	–	C
91	55	M	–	C
93	10	–	–	C
94	70	M	–	C
114	65	M	M	C
"	21	F	/	C
115	OA	M???	F??*	C
117	45	F???	F?	C
118	70	F	–	C
119	65	M	–	C
120	65	F???	F	C
135	65	F?	–	C
136	50	F???	–	C
137	65	F?	–	C
138	65	F??	–	C
139	65	M???	–	C
140	8???	–	–	C
142	23	F	–	C
145	20	F?	F	C
146	60	F???	F?	C
147	A???	F???	–	C
148	A	F???	–	C
149	A??	M???	M	C
150	A	F??	–	C
152	A??	F	F	C
154	50	F?	–	C
155	A	–	–	C

156	60	M	–	C
157	65	F	F	C
158	60	F???	F	C
159	75	M	F**	C
160	60	F	F	C
161	50	M?	–	C
162	YA	M		C
163	MA	F??	–	C
164	MA	–	M/F	C
165	YA???	[F]	F	C
166	20	F	F	C
167	MA?	[M]	M	C
168	14	[M]	M	C
169	65	M??	F*	C
170	MA	–	–	C
172	60	[M]	M	C
173	MA	F	F	C
174	50	F	F	C
175	60	F??	–	C
176	60	M???	–	C
177	A	M?	–	C
178	60	–	–	C
179	YA???	[F]	F	C
180	60	F???	F	C
181	A	F???	F	C
182	MA	F???	F	C
183	70	M???	0	C
184	70	–	0	C
185	A	–	unc.	C
186	A??	–	unc.	C
188	OA	[F]	F	C
189	A	F???	F	C
190	60	M	0	C
191	45	F???	F	C
192	65	F??? (intr.?)	M?*	C
193	40	M???	0	C
194	MA	M???	–	C
195	50	F???	F	C
196	50	F??	F	C
197	70	M??	M???	C
198	45	F	F?	C
199	YA	F	F	C
200	A	F???	–	C
201	70	M???	M??	C
203	60	M	–	C
204	MA	M?	–	C
206	A	F???	M??*	C
208A=209A	50	F?	F	C
209A=208B	65	M??	–	C
210	19	F???	F	C
211	A	M???	–	C

212	55	F??	M?*	C
213	70	M	M	C
215	MA	M?	M	C
216	60	[M]	M?	C
218	50	F	F	C
219	A	M???	–	C
220	A	F	F	C
"	A	F	/	C
221	60	M	M?	C
222	YA	[M???]	M???	C
223	60	F	F	C
224	65+	M??	F*	C
225	YA???	M???	M???	C
226	A	F???	F???	C
227	40	M?	M??	C
229	MA	M???*	M???	C
230	55	F	F	C
231	A	[M???]	M???	C
232	A	F???	F	C
235	50	F???	M??*	C
236	A	F???	–	C
238	A	F???	–	C
239	60	M???	M???	C
240	40	M???	–	C
241	MA	M?	M	C
242	?	?	–	C
243	A	F	F	C
389	7	M???	–	I
390	4	?	–	I
395	A	M??	–	I
"	A	M? [mixed?]	–	I
458	20	F???	–	I
470	2	?	–	I
515	11	?	–	I
519	[5.5]	?	–	I
529	7.5	M	–	I

N=127	134	M=52 (39%)	N=65	N=134
		F=68 (51%)	M=26 (40%)	I=21 (16%)
		?=14 (10%)	F=38 (58%)	C=113 (84%)
			M/F=1 (1%)	

Codes: A = Adult; MA = Mature adult; YA = Young adult; OA = Old adult
M/F = Associated artefacts provide conflicting "gender" data
/ = Second individual, not noted in excavation
0 = No fibula found in grave
Unc. = Noted by excavators as "incerto"

* Archaeological and biological results differ. In the case of T. 149 the biological conclusion has been altered to reflect the archaeological

** The biological evidence clearly indicates a male; the archaeological evidence clearly indicates a female

[ ] Indicates cases where no sex evaluation could be derived from the skeletal evidence, but the archaeological conclusion has been inserted in this column for statistical purposes

Table 2   Age and sex distributions based on combined techniques

	CHILDREN (2–16 years)			ADULTS (17+ years)					
	M	?	F	M	?	F	M	?	F
CREMATIONS N=113	1	2	0	40	9	59	44 (39%)	10 (9%)	59 (52%)
INHUMATIONS N=21	5	4	3	3	0	6	8 (38%)	4 (19%)	9 (43%)
TOTALS N=134	6	6	3	43	9	65	52 (39%)	14 (10%)	68 (51%)

(T. 116, a cremation, is identified archaeologically as Male, but the bones have not been evaluated)

Table 3   Dental attrition from the cremations only, not factored for age (from Becker & Donadio 1992)

TOTALS	No. of Individuals	No. of Tooth Spaces	No. of Teeth Lost	Loss Rate
End 6th century BC – Roman period	9	136	14	10%*
8th–6th centuries BC	26	178	14	8%**

*   Seven of the 14 teeth lost came from the person in Tomb 27. Removing this individual from the sample reduces the loss rate to about 6%

**   Four of the 14 teeth lost came from one person (Tomb 184) age 70 years. Removing this individual from the sample reduces the 'Total' loss rate to under 6%

In both periods dental attrition rates among cremated individuals appear very low, suggesting dietary and cultural stability. These data from the inhumations are too few to be statistically interesting, particularly as 12 of the 21 individuals studied from inhumations are children under 11 years of age. The few adults among these inhumations have very good dentition.

Addresses of Contributors

Albert J. Ammerman
Department of Anthropology
Colgate University
Hamilton NY 13346
USA
aammerman@mail.colgate.edu

Marshall Joseph Becker
Department of Sociology and Anthropology
West Chester University
West Chester PA 19383
USA
mbecker@wcupa.edu

Bruce W. Bevan
Geosight
143 Glen Lake Boulevard
Piyman NJ 08071
USA

Alberto Cazzella
Dipartimento di Scienze dell'Antichità
Università "La Sapienza" di Roma
Via Palestro, 63
00185 Roma
ITALIA

Paula Kay Lazrus
New School for Social Research
175 Water Street
New York NY 10011
USA
pklazrus@erols.com

Roberto Maggi
Museo Archeologico per la Preistoria
e Protostoria del Tigullio
Via Costaguta, 4
16043 Chiavari (GE)
ITALIA

Laura Maniscalco
Soprintendenza ai Beni Culturali ed Ambientali
Via Luigi Sturzo, 62
95100 Catania (CT)
ITALIA
mcconman@ctonline.it

Brian E. McConnell
Soprintendenza ai Beni Culturali ed Ambientali
Via Luigi Sturzo, 62
95100 Catania (CT)
ITALIA
mcconman@ctonline.it

Jonathan Morter[†]
formerly of:
Department of Sociology and Anthropology
College of Charleston
Charleston SC 29424-0001
USA

Maurizio Moscoloni
Dipartimento di Scienze dell'Antichità
Università "La Sapienza" di Roma
Via Palestro, 63
00185 Roma
ITALIA

John E. Robb
Department of Archaeology
University of Southampton
Southampton SO17 1BJ
UK
jer@soton.ac.uk

Gary D. Shaffer
Division of Cultural and Historical Programs
Maryland Department of Housing and
Community Development
100 Community Place
Crownsville MD 21032
USA
shaffer@dhcd.state.md.us

Robin Skeates
School of World Art Studies and Museology
University of East Anglia
Norwich NR 4 7TJ
UK
r.skeates@uea.ac.uk

Simon Stoddart
Dept of Archaeology
University of Cambridge
Downing Street
Cambridge CB2 3DZ
UK
ss16@cus.cam.ac.uk

Sebastiano Tusa
Soprintendenza per i Beni Culturali ed
Ambientali
Sezione Archeologica
Via Ausonia, 122
90100 Palermo
Sicilia
ITALIA

Robert H. Tykot
Department of Anthropology
University of South Florida
4202 East Fowler Avenue, SOC 107
Tampa, Florida 33620-8100
USA
rtykot@chuma1.cas.usf.edu